Adolescent Sexual Behavior in the Digital Age

Adolescent Sexual Behavior in the Digital Age

Considerations for Clinicians,
Legal Professionals, and Educators

EDITED BY

Fabian M. Saleh, MD
Albert J. Grudzinskas, Jr., JD
Abigail M. Judge, PhD

OXFORD

UNIVERSITY PRESS

Oxford University Press is a department of the University of Oxford.
It furthers the University's objective of excellence in research, scholarship,
and education by publishing worldwide.

Oxford   New York
Auckland   Cape Town   Dar es Salaam   Hong Kong   Karachi
Kuala Lumpur   Madrid   Melbourne   Mexico City   Nairobi
New Delhi   Shanghai   Taipei   Toronto

With offices in
Argentina   Austria   Brazil   Chile   Czech Republic   France   Greece
Guatemala   Hungary   Italy   Japan   Poland   Portugal   Singapore
South Korea   Switzerland   Thailand   Turkey   Ukraine   Vietnam

Oxford is a registered trademark of Oxford University Press
in the UK and certain other countries.

Published in the United States of America by
Oxford University Press
198 Madison Avenue, New York, NY 10016

Library of Congress Cataloging-in-Publication Data
Adolescent sexual behavior in the digital age : considerations for clinicians, legal professionals,
and educators / edited by Fabian M. Saleh, Albert Grudzinskas, Jr., Abigail Judge.
    p. ; cm.
Includes bibliographical references.
ISBN 978–0–19–994559–7 (alk. paper)
I. Saleh, Fabian M., 1965– editor of compilation.   II. Grudzinskas, Albert, Jr.,
editor of compilation.   III. Judge, Abigail, editor of compilation.
[DNLM: 1. Adolescent Behavior—United States.   2. Sexual Behavior—United States.
3. Erotica—legislation & jurisprudence—United States.   4. Internet—United States.
5. Sex Offenses—legislation & jurisprudence—United States. WS 462]
RJ503
616.8900835—dc23
2013034258

9 8 7 6 5 4 3 2 1
Printed in the United States of America
on acid-free paper

■ CONTENTS

◾ PREFACE

In the United States, adolescents'[1] use of digital technologies and social media has become a predominant form of communication and socialization. In 2010, U.S. adolescents spent an average of 8.5 hours per day interacting with digital devices, an increase from 6.5 hours in just 2006 (Kaiser Family Foundation, 2010). Mobile phones are the communication centerpiece for contemporary teens, with text messaging via cellphone the most popular form of offline communication among U.S. adolescents today, even above calling (Lenhart, 2009). Although estimates of technology use vary by socioeconomic status, ethnicity, and region, the trend appears to be increased use across the board.

Adolescents' use of mediated technologies and social media is part of what has been termed the digital revolution, or the unprecedented influence of digital technology and social media on the production of knowledge, communication, and creative expression (Giedd, 2012). The term *revolution* importantly suggests upheaval and a reorganization of norms, for it is not merely the emergence of new technology but also the unprecedented pace at which it has been adopted that have caused such widespread change and controversy. The purpose of this book is to examine the contours of this revolution across two complex domains: adolescent sexual behavior and the legal system. We developed an interest in this particular nexus as a result of our respective professional activities in the legal, forensic, and clinical realms where cases involving child and adolescent psychosexual development, digital technology, and some interface with the legal system became increasingly common in our work. During this same period, polarized accounts in the popular media focused on high-profile individual cases that resulted in tragedies (e.g., suicide, electronic harassment, juveniles' felony charges of child pornography), and we became aware of the great need for scholarship that could bring an empirical perspective to bear on these complex, interdisciplinary topics.

It is important to note that the popular discourses of today which alternatively venerate or vilify the effects of digital technology have a long social history. Marvin (1998), for example, showed how debates that followed the introduction of electricity and telecommunications in the late nineteenth and early twentieth centuries on the one hand glorified the potential effects of technology and on the other condemned the same for its disruption of social relationships and hierarchies. We suggest, however, that the effects of the digital revolution may be uniquely polemic and controversial due to the other topics of our analysis: adolescent sexual behavior and the law. A contributor to this collection, Professor Mary Leary, wrote one of the first pieces of legal scholarship on the topic of youth-produced sexual images (i.e., "sexting"; Leary, 2008), and she presciently observed, "Any social problem that exists at the intersection of adolescence, sex, technology, and criminal law compels strong reactions from all sides" (Leary, 2010, p. 2). Leary went on to note that these strong reactions result in "sensationalism and oversimplification of complex and multifaceted issues making it more difficult to discuss the problem rationally and productively" (Leary, 2010, p. 2). Leary's analysis is no less true today, and it remains an important caution as we endeavor to bring an empirical perspective to bear on the current volume's controversial topics.

By way of introducing this collection, we have identified several themes in the chapters that follow, and they also capture important tensions in popular and professional writing about the interface between child and adolescent sexual development, digital technology, and the law. The first theme involves the methodological and conceptual challenges of research on each of the book's major topics. This includes research on childhood and adolescent sexuality, a topic that Drs. Malin and Saleh review in Chapter 3; the methodological dilemmas in research on digital life among adolescents, which Drs. Smahel and Subrahmanyam consider in Chapter 4; and a view from the legal literature on the effects of "new technology" on "old law," which Professor Grudzinskas and colleagues review in Chapter 1.

An additional research challenge is the pace of research and the peer review process relative to rates of digital penetration, or the amount of time it takes for a new technology to be used by 50 million people. As summarized by Giedd (2012, p. 101), the rates of penetration for digital technologies have no historical precedent: "For radio, technological penetration took 38 years; for telephone, 20 years; for television (TV), 13 years; for the World Wide Web, 4 years; for Facebook, 3.6 years; for Twitter, 3 years; for iPads, 2 years; and for Google+, 88 days." This landscape creates an inevitable lag between the day's most popular device or application and professional knowledge about it. Several years ago, for example, a spate of research on the once-popular social networking site MySpace provided an empirical knowledge base of this platform—but by the time this work was published teenagers had largely migrated to Facebook. When we drafted a proposal for the current book, the most popular applications of 2013 (e.g., Twitter, Tumblr, Snapchat, Vine) were not even on our radar. The tensions of "keeping up" are therefore evident in this collection across scientific and legal discourses, with related practical dilemmas for stakeholders such as parents, policymakers, legislators, and attorneys.

The second theme involves the fact that adolescents are often the early adopters and defining users of novel technology. This dynamic, which resembles the prototypical generational gap, has been referred to as the generational digital divide or simply the digital divide (Herring, 2008; Kolodinsky, Cranwell, & Rowe, 2002). This divide has been popularly described by the heuristic of digital natives and digital immigrants, with digital natives defined as those who came of age after 1980, in an era of electronic multitasking, and for whom little distinction is felt between online and offline contexts (Palfrey & Gasser, 2008; Prensky, 2001). It is not merely differences in levels of use or knowledge about technology that defines the digital divide, however, but also the distinct cultural meanings youth make of online spaces. Ethnographic research of adolescents use of social media by Marwick and boyd (2011) exemplifies this point, with adolescent respondents using the term "drama" to describe public gossip and arguments via social media rather than the adult-based language of bullying and victimization. The researchers traced "drama" in this context as a gendered process that helped teens defend against the emotional realities of interpersonal aggression. This work shows the importance of taking an emic approach to research on teens and the digital revolution and how this may help shape more effective social responses.

Generational differences also include the ways in which developmental characteristics of adolescence affect teens' use of digital technology. Such normative features of adolescence include increased sensation seeking or valuing the newness and intensity of experiences (Gardner & Steinberg, 2005), marked psychosexual transition (Diamond & Savin-Williams, 2009), and immature neurodevelopment. Neuroimaging research over the past decade has demonstrated the ways in which adolescent brain development involves a shifting balance between frontal (executive control) and limbic (emotional) systems (Giedd, 2008). Many uses of social media and digital technologies are emotionally driven behaviors for adolescents, thus representing the "perfect storm" (Calvert, 2009, p. 1) for unforeseen intersections with the legal system.

The final theme refers to exactly these clinical, legal, and policy-based challenges that arise from the interface between child and adolescent sexual development and technology. We aim to explore the unforeseen developmental, clinical and legal implications of the digital revolution with respect to adolescents' sexual development and activity within digital networked publics. Although a major part of childhood and adolescent sexual development involves online contexts, there is wide variability in whether an adolescent's use of technology will facilitate or impede the developmental aims of this period. The ways in which communication technologies affect adolescent sexual behavior (and vice versa) therefore remain poorly understood even as these influences affect debates about what constitutes "normal" or atypical adolescent sexual behavior. Further, as many of the chapters will suggest, even if a behavior is deemed prevalent or "common," it is not necessarily either normative or healthy. We have organized the book along these themes in three parts.

Part I includes four introductory chapters on the legal, developmental, and psychological aspects of our book's main topics. Professor Albert J. Grudzinskas, Jr. and colleagues review the legal literature on how novel technologies have challenged existing legal codes in recent case law. Dr. Andrew Harris then presents an overview of the dynamic relationship between youth development, communication technology, norms of social interaction, and popular culture. Drs. Malin and Saleh review the current scientific knowledge about pediatric sexology and summarize the current scientific literature on sexuality, sexual development, and sexual behavior in adolescents. Developmental and social psychologists Drs. Kaveri Subrahmanyam and David Smahel present their co-construction model of adolescent Internet use, which posits the ways in which digital spaces represent an important context for adolescent sexual development. These chapters present the conceptual bedrock of this volume's primary topics: child and adolescent sexual development; how adolescents use technology to navigate developmental demands, notably sexual development; and the unforeseen legal implications that have accompanied the digital revolution.

In Part II, contributors focus on particular devices, applications, and features of digital technologies and applications as well as unforeseen consequences of these interactions. Professor Clay Calvert writes about youth-produced sexual images, or what is colloquially referred to as "sexting," including the history of this controversial topic and its current iterations in psychology and law. Dr. Charles Scott describes the contemporary landscape of social networking, highlighting the increased popularity of microblogging platforms such as Tumblr and Twitter. The difficulty of conducting empirical research on the digital revolution is exemplified by the evolving popularity of social networking sites and social media among adolescents, representing how empirical knowledge about the digital revolution can be a "moving target."

In addition to the potentially adaptive aspects of adolescents' online activities, the digital revolution may also portend new venues for sexual and interpersonal aggression, as well as frank violence and sexual exploitation. Indeed, the popular press has been most likely to focus on this aspect of digital life. Although such perils are real, we aim to emphasize an empirical perspective on these controversial and socially volatile topics in order to place them in context of current scientific knowledge and emergent challenges to existing legal codes. Four chapters take up the issues of sexual violence and interpersonal aggression from the perspective of adolescents as victims and adolescent perpetrators. Dr. Barry Feldman and colleagues critically analyze the literature on cybersexual harassment and suicide in Chapter 7, clarifying the empirical association between cyberharassment and suicidality and reviewing legislative responses to this issue. In Chapter 8, Cyril Boonmann, Professor Grudzinskas, and Dr. Marcel Aebi review what is currently known about the relationship between the Internet and juvenile sexual offending. They highlight how the digital revolution affects the already complex topic of juvenile sex offending and the implications for clinical, forensic, and legal professionals. A similar dynamic is observed in Dr. Abigail Judge and Professor Mary Leary's chapter, which reviews one of the most pernicious crimes against youth: the commercial sexual exploitation of children and adolescents (CSEC) in the United States. The authors review a range of definitions for CSEC and then survey the ways in which technology has transformed the crime's ecosystem, concluding with implications for child victims and future research. Finally, criminologist Lisa Murphy, Rebekah Ranger, and Dr. Paul Fedoroff critically examine how the Internet challenges legal and clinical definitions of child pornography (also referred to as images of child sexual abuse), including the difficulties in creating an international legal definition.

In addition to the implications of the digital revolution for individual adolescents, developmental theory, and the legal system, parallel dilemmas have emerged for the adults responsible for fostering healthy development among teens. This includes mental health professionals, attorneys, policymakers, educators, and parents. Part III of the book describes the implications for these stakeholders, including pragmatic suggestions, potential best practices, and emergent ethical dilemmas. Dr. Andrew Clark describes the implications of the digital revolution on parenting tasks and reviews the available literature on monitoring adolescents' online activities, fostering youth self-disclosure, and risk factors for problematic online activity. Drs. Andrew Harris and Judith Davidson present data from a multistate, mixed-method study that investigated youth and adult perspectives on teen sexting behavior, highlighting important divergences between different stakeholders and suggesting parameters of effective educational responses. In Chapter 13, Drs. Liwei Hua, Scott Yapo's, Amy Yule, and Tristan Gorrindo provide a psychiatric perspective on evaluating technology use among adolescents and offer practical guidance to other mental health professionals. Finally, Drs. Ariel Seroussi, Daniel Bonnicci, Gregory Leong, and Robert Weinstock discuss ethical and legal considerations regarding technology and the Internet as they relate to adolescents and the mental health clinicians charged with their care. The absence of professional consensus about these topics make ethical decision making very complex, and the authors propose a framework for navigating ethical dilemmas in the face of rapid change. Finally, Drs. Christopher Racine and Stephen Bates Billick provide a conclusion that synthesizes the book's themes and suggests practice implications as well as future research directions regarding the study of adolescent sexual behavior in the digital age.

Finally, the Editors would like to thank their loved ones for their patience, support and tolerance of us and this project. Without them, the piles of revisions would long ago have wound up flaming into some late night sky. Specifically, Fabian Saleh thanks his wife, Silvia, and daughter, Olivia. Albert Grudzinskas thanks his wife, Joy, and children Lisa, Jason, daughter in law 'Laine and grandchildren Robert (RJ), Rachel, Rilee, and Daniel. Abigail Judge acknowledges Caedmon Cahill, for stalwart friendship from adolescence to the present, and also her young patients and their families, who teach her about adolescence today.

Fabian M. Saleh
Albert J. Grudzinskas Jr.
Abigail Judge

■ NOTE

1. Although we recognize that adolescence as a developmental phase may continue well beyond age 18, given that neurodevelopment continues into the third decade of life, we have opted to define adolescence in a manner consistent with the age of majority since much of this book focuses on legal matters. We recognize the limits of this definition, however, given the special status and at times contradictory definition of childhood in the U.S. legal system.

■ REFERENCES

Calvert, C. (2009). Sex, cell phones, privacy and the First Amendment: when children become child pornographers and the Lolita effect undermines the law. *CommLaw Conspectus, 18*, 1–71.

Diamond, L. M., & Savin-Williams, R. C. (2009). Adolescent sexuality. In R. M. Lerner & L. Steinberg (Eds.), *Handbook of adolescent psychology: Individual bases of adolescent development* (pp. 479–523). Hoboken, NJ: John Wiley & Sons.

Gardner, M., & Steinberg, L. (2005). Peer influence on risk taking, risk preference, and risky decision making in adolescence and adulthood: An experimental study. *Developmental Psychology, 41*(4), 625–635.

Giedd, J. N. (2008). The teen brain: insights from neuroimaging. *Journal of Adolescent Health, 42*, 335–343.

Giedd, J. N. (2012). The digital revolution and adolescent brain evolution. *Journal of Adolescent Health, 51*, 101–105.

Herring, S. C. (2008). Questioning the generational divide: Technological exoticism and adult constructions of online youth identity. In D. Buckingham (Ed.), *Youth, identity and digital media* (pp. 71–92). Cambridge, MA: MIT Press.

Henry J. Kaiser Family Foundation (2010). *Generation M2: Media in the lives of 8- to 18-year-olds.* Available from http://kff.org/other/event/generation-m2-media-in-the-lives-of/

Kolodinsky, J., Cranwell, M., & Rowe, E. (2002). Bridging the generation gap across the digital divide: Teens teaching Internet skills to senior citizens. *Journal of Extension, 40*(3). Retrieved from http://www.joe.org/joe/2002june/rb2.html

Leary, M. G. (2008). Self-produced child pornography: The appropriate societal response to juvenile self-sexual exploitation. *Virginia Journal of Social Policy and the Law, 15*(1), 1–50.

Leary, M. G. (2010). Sexting or self-produced child pornography? The dialogue continues: structured prosecutorial discretion within a multidisciplinary response. *Virginia Journal of Social Policy and Law, 17*, 1–76.

Lenhart, A. (2009). *Teens and sexting: how and why minor teens are sending sexually suggestive nude or nearly nude images via text messaging.* Pew Research Center.

Marvin, C. 1988). *When old technologies were new: Thinking about electric communication in the late nineteenth century.* New York: Oxford University Press.

Palfrey, K., & Gasser, U. (2008). *Born digital: Understanding the first generation of digital natives.* New York: Perseus Books.

Marwick, A. E., & boyd, d. (2011, Sept. 12). *The drama! Teen conflict, gossip and bullying in networked publics.* A Decade in Internet Time: Symposium on the Dynamics of the Internet and Society. Retrieved from http://ssm.com/abstract=1926349

Prensky, R. (2001). Digital natives, digital immigrants. *On the Horizon, 9*(5), 1–15.

■ CONTRIBUTORS

Marcel Aebi, PhD
University of Zurich
Zurich, Switzerland

Stephen Bates Billick, MD
Clinical Professor of Psychiatry
New York University School of Medicine
New York, New York

Daniel Bonnici, MD, JD
Resident Physician in
PsychiatryDepartment of Psychiatry
and Biobehavioral Sciences
University of California
Los Angeles, California

Cyril Boonmann, MSc
Psychologist Researcher
Department of Child and Adolescent
Psychiatry
VU University Medical Center
Amsterdam
Duivendrecht, The Netherlands

Sara J. Brady, MD
Resident, Harvard Longwood
Psychiatry Training Program
Beth Israel Deaconess Medical Center/
Brigham and Women's Hospital
Boston, Massachusetts

Clay Calvert, JD, PhD
Professor and Brechner Eminent
Scholar in Mass Communication
University of Florida
College of Journalism and
Communications
University of Florida
Gainesville, Florida

Andrew B. Clark, MD
Instructor in Psychiatry, Harvard
Medical School
Massachusetts General Hospital
Cambridge, Massachusetts

Jonathan Clayfield, MA
University of Massachusetts
Medical School
Department of Psychiatry and
Center for Mental Health Services
Research
Worcester, Massachusetts

Richard Cody, JD
Research Coordinator
University of Massachusetts
Medical School
Worcester, Massachusetts

Judith Davidson, PhD
Associate ProfessorGraduate School of
Education
University of Massachusetts Lowell
Lowell, Massachusetts

J. Paul Fedoroff, MD
Director Sexual Behaviours Clinic,
Integrated Forensic Program
Royal Ottawa Mental Health
Centre; Director Forensic
Research Unit
University of Ottawa Institute
of Mental Health Research;
and Head of Forensic Psychiatry
Division
University of Ottawa
Ottawa, Canada

Barry N. Feldman, PhD
Assistant Professor of Psychiatry
Director of Psychiatry Programs in
Public Safety
University of Massachusetts
Medical School
Worcester, Massachusetts

Tristan Gorrindo, MD
Assistant Professor of Psychiatry
Massachusetts General Hospital
Harvard Medical School
Boston, Massachusetts

Albert J. Grudzinskas, Jr., JD
Clinical Associate Professor of
Psychiatry
University of Massachusetts
Medical School
Worcester, Massachusetts

Andrew J. Harris, PhD
Associate Dean of Research and
Graduate Programs
Associate Professor
University of Massachusetts Lowell
College of Fine Arts, Humanities, and
Social Sciences
School of Criminology and Justice
Studies
Lowell, Massachusetts

Liwei L. Hua, MD, PhD
Clinical Assistant Professor
Clinical Director of Child and
Adolescent Psychiatry Ambulatory
Services
University of Michigan
Ann Arbor, Michigan

Abigail M. Judge, PhD
Instructor in Psychology, Department
of Psychiatry
Cambridge Health Alliance
Harvard Medical School
Cambridge, Massachusetts

Mary Graw Leary, JD
Associate Professor of Law
Columbus School of Law
The Catholic University of America
Washington, DC

Gregory B. Leong, MD
Clinical Professor
Department of Psychiatry and
Behavioral Sciences
University of Southern California
Los Angeles, California

H. Martin Malin, PhD, MA, LMFT
Institute for Advanced Study of
Human Sexuality
San Francisco, California

Lisa Murphy, MCA, MCrim, BSS
Sexual Behaviours Clinic, Integrated
Forensic Program
Royal Ottawa Mental Health Centre;
and Forensic Research Unit
University of Ottawa Institute of
Mental Health Research
Ottawa, Canada

Christopher W. Racine, MD, MPH
Forensic Fellow
New York University Department of
Psychiatry
New York, New York

Rebekah Ranger, BSS, BA
Forensic Research Unit
University of Ottawa Institute
of Mental Health Research; and
Sexual Behaviours Clinic, Integrated
Forensic Program
Royal Ottawa Mental Health Centre
Ottawa, Canada

Simha E. Ravven, MD
Law and Psychiatry Division
Yale University School of Medicine
New Haven, Connecticut

Fabian M. Saleh, MD
Assistant Clinical Professor of
Psychiatry
Harvard Medical School
Director, Sexual Violence Prevention
& Risk Management Program (SVP/
RMP)
Forensic Psychiatry Service,
Department of Psychiatry
Beth Israel Deaconess Medical Center
Boston, Massachusetts

Charles L. Scott, MD
Professor of Clinical Psychiatry
Chief, Division of Psychiatry and
the Law
Director, Forensic Psychiatry
Residency Program
Department of Psychiatry and
Behavioral Sciences
University of California-Davis School
of Medicine
Sacramento, California

Ariel Seroussi, MD
Resident Physician in Psychiatry
Department of Psychiatry and
Biobehavioral Sciences
University of California
Los Angeles, California

David Smahel, PhD
Institute for Research on Children,
Youth and Families, Faculty of Social
Studies
Masaryk University, Czech Republic
Brno, Czech Republic

Kaveri Subrahmanyam, PhD
Professor of Psychology, California
State University
Associate Director, Los Angeles and
Children's Digital Media Center
Los Angeles, California

Robert Weinstock, MD
Clinical Professor of Psychiatry
Department of Psychiatry and
Biobehavioral Sciences
University of California
Los Angeles, California

Scott Yapo, MD
Department of Psychiatry
Cambridge Health Alliance
Harvard Medical School
Cambridge, Massachusetts

Amy Yule, MD
Assistant in Psychiatry, Instructor
Massachusetts General Hospital,
Harvard Medical School
Boston, Massachusetts

PART ONE
Introduction

1 New Technology Meets Old Law

■ ALBERT J. GRUDZINSKAS, JR.,
RICHARD CODY, SARA J. BRADY,
FABIAN M. SALEH, AND
JONATHAN CLAYFIELD

■ INTRODUCTION

The law is often slow to respond to scientific and social developments. Responses are often governed not by empirical evidence, developed during systematic study of an issue, but rather by expedient legislative response to the most loudly expressed media coverage of an issue. Examples of such responses have been detailed for a variety of issues relating to human sexuality, including sexual relations between unmarried individuals, sexual relations between members of the same gender, sex offender commitment laws and sex offender registries, pornography in general and child pornography in particular. We will address the broad topics of pornography and child pornography and efforts by prosecutors, legislatures, and courts to respond to the explosion of technology and its impact on the dissemination of this material through these avenues. The chapter will consider in particular how child pornography laws have been used by prosecutors in situations such as "sexting" (electronic dissemination of self-created images) by adolescents, without regard to the evidence regarding risk and potential for harm, considered by legislators at the time the statutes were created or by the court when relevant decisions were rendered and without regard to consequences and impact. We will review the arguments for and against harsh punishment for child pornography offenders and consider the same in light of the concept of sentencing proportionality and the original intent of the statutes—protection of children. The efficacy of negative sanctions in reducing recidivism will also be considered. The chapter will conclude with a discussion of attempts by various jurisdictions to develop laws that address these issues. This chapter will provide background to guide the discussion of legal developments in topics such as sexting, cyber-bullying, and the use of the Internet to sexually exploit children, adolescents, and young adults addressed later in this volume.

■ THE PROBLEM

In May 2008, a 17-year-old Wisconsin teen was charged with criminal libel and defamation, sexual exploitation of a child (by a person under 18 years of age), possession of child pornography by a person under 18 years of age, and causing mental harm to a child for posting nude photos of his ex-girlfriend on his MySpace page. The photos were sent to him by his ex-girlfriend, but the accused disseminated them on social media as "revenge" when they broke up (*Wisconsin v. Phillips*, 2008). The Court accepted his plea of guilty to causing mental harm to a child, as part of a plea bargain, and the remaining charges were dismissed. He was, however, sentenced to 100 hours of community service and three years' probation. During probation, he was ordered not to "own, operate, or possess a computer, software modem, cell phone or any gaming system that has Internet access capabilities including Facebook and MySpace" (*Wisconsin v. Phillips*, 2008).

In December 2008, a 15-year-old Ohio girl was arrested and charged in juvenile court for "possessing criminal tools and the illegal use of a minor in nudity-oriented material." The girl, who faced felony charges and possible registration as a sex offender, allegedly took nude photos of herself and sent them to other minors in her high school. If convicted, the girl could have faced a sentence of anywhere from probation to several years in a juvenile detention center, as well as being ordered to register as a sex offender under Ohio law (Michaels, 2008).

In 2009, a number of Greenburg, Pennsylvania, high-school students faced child pornography charges after three teenage girls allegedly took nude or semi-nude photos of themselves and shared them with male classmates via their cellphones. The female students, all 14 or 15 years old, faced charges of manufacturing, disseminating, or possessing child pornography, while the boys, who were 16 and 17, faced charges of possession of child pornography. The photos were discovered after school officials seized a cellphone from a male student who was using it in violation of school rules and found a nude photo of a classmate on the phone. Police were called in and their investigation led them to other phones containing more photos (Pilkington, 2009).

In 2010, at Susquenita High School, near Harrisburg, Pennsylvania, eight students, ranging in age from 13 to 17, were accused of using their cellphones to take, send, or receive nude photos of each other and in one case a short video alleged to be depicting oral sex. The investigation resulted in a felony pornography charge for each minor. Ultimately, the students agreed to take a class on victimization and perform community service. After completing the so-called "diversionary program" and a period of probation, the juvenile conviction records would be expunged for five students without juvenile records, and one-year probation for the youth with a prior record (Elias & Victor, 2010).

In another school in the same county, 20 students at Tunkhannock High School were threatened with felony child pornography charges unless they agreed to a five-week, 10-hour educational course designed by the prosecutor in conjunction with two social service agencies. The underlying incident involved pictures of two young teenage girls from the waist up, one dressed in an opaque white bra, the other in a bathing suit, and a picture of one older teen who took a seminude picture of herself exposing her breasts but covering the rest of her body with a towel, and saved the picture to her phone. A teacher confiscated her phone one morning before class (the school bans student cellphone use on school grounds). When the photos were found, the students and others in possession of the photos were also charged with possessing child pornography by the Wyoming County (PA) District Attorney. To avoid the charges, the students were offered a plea, which included submitting to a five-week course on violence and victimization, meeting twice a week. However, the three young women (initially, but only one continued to press for appellate review) sued the school, seeking damages for invasion of privacy and accusing the school of violating their First Amendment right to free speech and Fourth Amendment protection from illegal searches and seizure. The appellants also claimed a violation of the Fourteenth Amendment substantive due process right "to raise their children without undue state interference" (*Miller v. Mitchell*, 2010). The expressed sentiment among law enforcement and district attorney was that of "example setting"; while the charges and the punishments seem harsh, local officials sought to set a precedent for indecent behavior that may or may not be directly addressed under current child pornography statutes (*Teen sues Pennsylvania school district in sexting case, claiming principal looked at her nude photos*, 2010). A U.S. District Court judge eventually enjoined the district attorney's office from initiating criminal charges against the three plaintiffs (*Miller v. Mitchell*, 2010).

On January 14, 2010, Phoebe Prince, a 15-year-old "new girl" recently emigrated from Ireland, committed suicide after a prolonged and systematic period of bullying and harassment that included the use of Twitter, Craigslist, Facebook, and Formspring at her new school in South Hadley, Massachusetts. Eight Massachusetts teens were eventually indicted for their actions in the case, charged with violating Ms. Prince's civil rights, criminal harassment, and in two cases with statutory rape (ultimately dismissed at the request of the victim's family) (Khadaroo, 2011; Masslive, 2013). The case eventually led to Massachusetts adopting a comprehensive antibullying law that requires all school districts to submit a plan for approval by the Department of Education (Massachusetts General Laws, 2013).

All of the above incidents indicate areas of social interaction where society may have an interest in regulating conduct. Yet each example was regulated by laws in existence at the time that were not designed to address the specific issues presented. Additionally, none of the existing laws considered the special developmental concerns that adolescent participation in these activities may bring to bear on the issues. As noted above, the idea that an issue grabs the public's attention (and, more often today, is driven by media focus on a topic) and creates a clamor for legislatures to address the perceived shortcomings of the law is not new. The pattern of societal behavior that leads to legislative response, identified by Sutherland (1950) to demonstrate the development of sex offender commitment laws, is strikingly similar to the pattern in effect in recent years with respect to the development of sexting and cyber-bullying laws in the United States. A state's fears are first aroused by media attention to conduct involving sexual expression (or, in the sex offender commitment example, by a heinous crime), frequently involving a child victim. A protracted public debate adds to the fear. The fear is seldom related to the statistical evidence supporting risk of harm or even of further offenses. This leads to the next step in the process, the agitation of community activity and the call for protective legislation. The next step often involves the appointment of a study group or task force to draft such legislation. The final step is the presentation of the law as the most scientific and enlightened method of protecting society from dangerous conduct and to "save the children" (Grudzinskas, Brodsky, Federoff, et al., 2009; Sutherland, 1950).

■ NORMATIVE BEHAVIOR

The question of what is "normal" behavior in a sexual context is difficult to answer. It becomes more difficult when we add in consideration of adolescent behavior. Despite research clearly demonstrating that even young children engage in a broad range of sexual behaviors without any evidence of a history of abuse (Friedrich, 2003), beliefs persist that such conduct is not "normal" (Jackson, 1990). Normative behavior is the result of an evolutionary process. Consensus is difficult to reach when the institutions that help define the consensus are themselves evolving under pressure to change (Fagan, 2009). For example, one can consider the evolution of issues related to consensual sexual contact between members of the same gender. At Common Law, this was a capital offense. During the trial of Oscar Wilde for "gross indecency" for engaging in consensual sex with another adult male, Justice Wills, who had for many years presided over countless rape and murder trials, declared Wilde's case to be "the worst" he had ever tried and that the defendant was deserving of the "severest" punishment. Justice Wills stated, "In my judgment it [the sentence of two years in jail] is totally inadequate for a case such as this." (Hyde, 1948, pp. 59–60, 63). The U.S. Supreme Court, in the case of *Lawrence v. Texas*, held that the Texas statute making it a crime for two persons of the same sex to consensually engage in certain intimate sexual conduct violates the Due Process Clause. The Court noted that there had been no showing of a government interest that overrode the right to privacy. The Court opined, "Our obligation is to define the liberty of all, not to mandate our own moral code" (*Lawrence v. Texas*, 2003). Recent legal developments with respect to gay marriage demonstrate that issues other than morality—contractual issues, issues of support, and public health issues (*Goodridge v. Dept. of Public Health,* 2003) and estate tax issues (*U.S. v. Windsor,* 2013)—may well influence the development of the definition of "normality." When one adds the complexity of adolescent development, the endeavor becomes particularly difficult. Issues relating to sexual development and behavior in children and adolescents are addressed in

Chapters 3 and 4 and should be considered in conjunction with the materials presented below.

▪ OBSCENITY LAWS AND THE DEVELOPMENT OF CHILD PORNOGRAPHY JURISPRUDENCE

As we have already noted, the legal response to issues regarding adolescents and their use of evolving media for sexual expression has often used the law developed with respect to pornography and child pornography. To understand how, if, and why this approach may have validity, it is important to understand how this area of the law developed, and the issues sought to be addressed by obscenity laws and child pornography laws in particular. Two presidential commissions considered recommendations on a national response to pornography. In 1970, the Lockhart Commission recommended eliminating all criminal penalties for pornography except for pornographic depictions of minors or sale of pornography to minors. The Meese Commission in 1985 recommended continued enforcement of all laws regulating hard-core pornography, including adult-only versions. To consider whether such use is appropriate, it is important to understand the evolution of obscenity laws in the United States, the rationale for legislative responses, and the response of the Supreme Court to challenges to these laws. The issue of what is obscenity and what to do about it has been argued about for decades. From the consideration of whether James Joyce's *Ulysses* tended to "stir the sex impulses or to lead to sexually impure and lustful thoughts" (*United States v. One Book Entitled* Ulysses *by James Joyce*, 1934) through Justice Stewart's "I know it when I see it" pronouncement (*Jacobellis v. Ohio*, 1964), a definition remained hard to express.

In its decision in *Miller v. California* (1973) the U.S. Supreme Court defined the standards that were to be used to identify obscene material that a state might regulate without infringing on the First Amendment (made applicable to the states through the Fourteenth Amendment). The question before the court was whether the sale and distribution of obscene material was protected under the First Amendment. The Court ruled that it was not; it indicated that obscene material is not protected by the First Amendment. However, the Court acknowledged the inherent dangers of any undertaking to regulate any form of expression and said that state statutes designed to regulate obscene materials must be carefully limited. The Court, while finding that it was unreasonable for the Court to articulate a single formulation for all 50 states, held that obscene materials would be defined as those that the average person, applying contemporary community standards, find, taken as a whole, appeal to the prurient interest; that depict or describe, in a patently offensive way, sexual conduct specifically defined by applicable state law; and that, taken as a whole, lack serious literary, artistic, political, or scientific value (*Miller v. California*, pp. 30–35).

In its decision in *New York v. Ferber* (1982) the U.S. Supreme Court upheld a New York statute prohibiting persons from knowingly promoting sexual performances by children under 16 by distributing material that depicts such performance. The Court found that the legislative judgment that child pornography is harmful to the physiological, emotional, and mental health of children passes First Amendment scrutiny. The Court held that the State's interest in protecting children allows laws prohibiting distribution of images of sexual performances by minors even where the content does not meet tests of obscenity. The Court further found that child pornography may be banned without first being deemed obscene under *Miller* for five reasons:

1. The government has a very compelling interest in preventing the sexual exploitation of children.
2. Distribution of visual depictions of children engaged in sexual activity is intrinsically related to the sexual abuse of children. The images serve as a permanent reminder of the abuse, and it is necessary for government to regulate the channels of distributing such images if it is to be able to eliminate the production of child pornography.
3. Advertising and selling child pornography provides an economic motive for producing child pornography.
4. Visual depictions of children engaged in sexual activity have negligible artistic value.
5. Thus, holding that child pornography is outside the protection of the First Amendment is consistent with the Court's prior decisions limiting the banning of materials deemed "obscene" as the Court had previously defined it. For this reason, child pornography need not be legally obscene before being outlawed (*New York v. Ferber*, pp. 756–765).

In *Miller v. California*, the Court held that the First Amendment allowed the government to restrict obscenity. In *New York v. Ferber*, the Court held that the government could restrict the distribution of child pornography to protect children from the harm inherent in making it. Before 1996, Congress defined child pornography with reference to the *Ferber* standard. In passing the Child Pornography Prevention Act of 1996 (CPPA), Congress added the two categories of speech in this case to its definition of child pornography that were subsequently challenged (*Ashcroft v. Free Speech Coalition*, 2002). This case addresses a number of issues raised for consideration by this book.

The CPPA first prohibited "any visual depiction, including any photograph, film, video, picture, or computer or computer-generated image or picture" that "is, or appears to be, of a minor engaging in sexually explicit conduct." This provision was ostensibly designed to capture a range of depictions, sometimes called "virtual child pornography," which include computer-generated images, as well as images produced by more traditional means such as using youthful-looking actors. A second CPPA provision prohibited "any sexually explicit image that was advertised, promoted, presented, described, or distributed in such a manner that conveys the impression it depicts a minor engaging in sexually explicit conduct."

The Free Speech Coalition[1], fearing that Congress's expanded definition of child pornography would endanger their legitimate activities, filed a lawsuit seeking to enjoin enforcement of the CPPA in the U.S. District Court for the Northern District of California. They alleged that the first provision, prohibiting images that "appear to be" children engaged in sexual activity, and the second, prohibiting speech that "conveys the impression" that the images depict minors engaged in sexual activity, were overbroad and vague and had a chilling effect on their legitimate work. The District Court disagreed, adding that the overbreadth claim was specious as it was "highly unlikely" that any "adaptations of sexual works like *Romeo and Juliet...* will be treated as 'criminal contraband.'" (*Ashcroft* p. 243)

The Ninth Circuit reversed, reasoning that the government could not prohibit speech merely because of its tendency to persuade its viewers to engage in illegal activity. It ruled that the CPPA was substantially overbroad because it prohibited material that was neither obscene nor produced by exploiting real children, as *Ferber* prohibited. The court declined to reconsider the case *en banc*. The government asked the Supreme Court to review the case, and it agreed, noting that the Ninth Circuit's decision conflicted with the decisions of four other circuit courts of appeals. Ultimately, the Supreme Court agreed with the Ninth Circuit. The Court held that the two provisions of the CPPA were unconstitutional because they abridged "the freedom to engage in a substantial amount of lawful speech." The Court found that "While the Government asserts that the images can lead to actual instances of child abuse, the causal link is contingent and indirect. The harm does not necessarily follow from the speech, but depends upon some unquantified potential for subsequent criminal acts" (*Ashcroft*, p. 250) As we have seen in the cases noted above, assertions of harm are an important consideration in the application of obscenity laws and particularly child pornography laws by prosecutors to engagement in technology-based sexual expression by adolescents.

After the Court's decision in *Free Speech Coalition*, Congress produced legislation known as the Prosecutorial Remedies and Other Tools to End the Exploitation of Children Today Act of 2003. Taking its lead from the Free Speech opinion, Congress outlawed solicitation and pandering.[2] On April 26, 2004, as part of an undercover operation aimed at combating child exploitation on the Internet, Special Agent Timothy Devine of the U.S. Secret Service, Miami Field Office, entered an Internet chat room using the screen name "Lisa n Miami." Devine observed a public message posted by a user employing a sexually graphic screen name, which was later traced to the defendant Williams. After a series of online exchanges, Williams posted a hyperlink that Devine accessed. The computer hyperlink contained, among other things, seven images of minors engaging in sexually explicit conduct. The nude children in the photos were approximately five to 15 years old, displaying their genitals and/or engaged in sexual activity. Secret Service agents executed a search warrant of Williams' home. Two computer hard drives seized during the search held at least 22 images of minors engaged in sexually explicit conduct or lascivious display of genitalia. Most of the images depicted prepubescent children and also depicted sadomasochistic conduct or other depictions of pain. Williams was charged with one count of promoting, or "pandering," material "in a manner that reflects the belief, or that is intended to cause another to believe," that the material contains illegal child pornography, which carries a 60-month mandatory minimum sentence. Williams was also charged with one count of possession of child pornography under 18 U.S.C. § 2252A(a)(5)(B). Williams filed a motion to dismiss the pandering charge on the grounds that 18 U.S.C. § 2252A(a)(3)(B) is unconstitutionally overbroad and vague. While the motion was pending before the trial court, the parties reached a plea agreement by which Williams would plead guilty to both counts but reserve his right to challenge the constitutionality of the pandering provision on appeal. The court sentenced Williams to 60 months.

On review, the U.S. Supreme Court held (*United States v. Williams*, 2008) that the federal statute prohibiting the "pandering" of child pornography (offering or requesting to transfer, sell, deliver, or trade the items) did not violate the First Amendment, even if a person charged under the code did not in fact possess child pornography with which to trade. The decision overturned the 11th Circuit ruling that the statute was facially void for overbreadth and vagueness. The Supreme Court reasoned that there is no First Amendment protection for offers to engage in illegal transactions and that banning "the collateral speech that introduces such material into the child-pornography distribution network" does not in fact criminalize a "substantial amount of protected speech" (*Williams*, p. 297).

The Court further opined that the statute would not be construed to punish the solicitation or offering of "virtual" pornography. The Court stated that "an offer to provide or request to receive virtual child pornography is not prohibited by the statute." A crime is committed only when the speaker believes or intends the listener to believe that the subject of the proposed transaction depicts real children rather than computer-generated/animated child pornography and thus the statute comports with *Ashcroft*.

■ DISPROPORTIONATE SENTENCING

It is important to understand why the use of existing laws cannot address issues created by adolescent sexting. The laws as developed were designed to protect children. The concept of proportionality in sentencing was abandoned for ideological reasons having little to do with empirically developed evidence of dangerousness and risk for reoffending. To apply these laws to teens who possess an image of themselves or of one intimate partner, without the revictimization profit motive most often cited to support strict sentencing, begins a spiral that has repeatedly failed in U.S. corrections policy. The debate over what empirical evidence of dangerousness exists in the adult child-pornographer world has not been resolved. To apply these laws to the examples listed at the beginning of this chapter is unconscionable. The competing arguments regarding child pornography harm may be best summed up by recent testimony before the U.S. Sentencing Commission.

The Commission hearings brought into focus the divisive nature of the topic of child pornography. Since the focus of the guidelines is to proportionately punish offenders, the issues of the risk of offenders to reoffend were a primary focus. The following will present a representative view of the positions taken by the opposing sides. On one side, Susan Howley, Chair of the Victims Advisory Group, in written testimony asserted that:

> The proliferation of child abuse images increases the risk of future victimization and harms the victims who are the subject of those images. It increases the risk of victimization because repeated exposure to those images normalizes the sexual assault of children, promoting cognitive distortions. A meta-analysis of published research on the effects of pornography found that: "the results are clear and consistent; exposure to pornographic materials puts one at increased risk for developing sexually deviant tendencies, committing sexual offenses, experiencing difficulties in one's intimate relationships, and accepting the rape myth." (Howley, 2012, p. 10)

In concluding, Howley stated, "The seriousness of crimes involving child sexual abuse images warrants a strong response to offenders. As one victim has stated, 'Unlike other forms of exploitation, this one is never ending. Every day people are trading and sharing videos of me as a little girl being raped in the most sadistic ways'" (Howley, 2012, p. 11).

In response, Michael C. Seto, PhD, CPsych, of the Royal Ottawa Health Care Group, in written testimony asserted that:

> Seto et al. (2011) identified 21 studies, representing a total of 4,464 online offenders, that reported on contact sexual offending history. Approximately 1 in 8 (12 percent) of the online offenders (mostly in trouble for child pornography offenses) had an official record for sexual offending, but approximately 1 in 2 (55 percent) admitted having committed a contact sexual offense in the subset of six studies that had self-report data (totaling 523 online offenders). The self-report is more tentative because of the smaller number of studies and the smaller sample size, but it does contradict the idea that most online offenders have already committed contact sexual offenses, even if some of those who denied any prior sexual contacts were lying. (Seto, 2012, p. 23)

Seto also explained that not all persons who view or collect child pornography meet diagnostic criteria for pedophilia. He concluded by noting, "Follow-up research suggests there are meaningful distinctions to make among child pornography offenders. In particular, child pornography possession-only offenders appear to be [at] very low risk of sexual recidivism, in contrast to those with any prior or concurring criminal convictions or those who engage in other sexual offending (e.g., attempted or actual contacts with a child, production of child pornography)" (Seto, 2012).

The situations discussed above, as we have seen, simply do not apply to the teen sexting world. The concept of proportionality in sentencing traces its Common Law roots to the Magna Carta's prohibition in 1215 that "amercements" (fines) may not be "excessive." When imprisonment became a common-law sanction, courts extended the principle to prison terms. The English Bill of Rights in 1689 repeated the principle of proportionality—that punishment should not by reason of its excessive length or severity be greatly disproportionate to the offense charged (*Solem v. Helm*, 1983). This principle later appeared in the Eighth Amendment's declaration that "Excessive bail shall not be required, nor excessive fines imposed, nor cruel and unusual punishment inflicted."

For years, a debate about sentencing reform and the need for sentencing uniformity was waged in Congress and in the political arena. The end result was the Sentencing Reform Act (Reform Act) of 1984 (Comprehensive Crime Control Act of 1984, Title II). The U.S. Sentencing Commission is an independent agency in the judicial branch established by the Reform Act. The principal purpose of the Reform Act is to "establish sentencing policies and practices for the federal criminal justice system that will assure the ends of justice by promulgating detailed guidelines prescribing the appropriate sentences for offenders convicted of federal crimes" (*U.S. Sentencing Guidelines Manual*, 2011). The Reform Act provides for the development of guidelines that will "further the basic purposes of criminal punishment: deterrence, incapacitation, just punishment, and rehabilitation" (*U.S. Sentencing Guidelines Manual*, 2011, p. 1). The Reform Act provides detailed instructions to the Commission to create categories of offense behavior and offender characteristics. These factors are then entered on a sentencing grid that provides judges with the range of sentences to impose.

The basic objective of the Reform Act was to enhance the ability of the criminal justice system to combat crime through an effective, fair sentencing system. Congress sought to accomplish this by seeking honesty in sentencing (which included the elimination of parole), seeking reasonable uniformity in sentencing for similar criminal offenses, and seeking a system of proportionality that imposes appropriately different sentences for criminal conduct of differing severity. The Commission sought to solve both the practical and philosophical problems of developing a coherent sentencing system by taking an empirical approach. It began with pre-guidelines sentencing practices (based on the U.S. Parole Commission's guidelines and statistics), a 10,000-person presentencing investigation dataset, and the substantive elements of the various federal crimes. The result was a sentencing matrix supported by empirical data whenever possible.

Ignoring the principle of separation of powers, Congress has on numerous occasions "intervened" in the Commission's mandate. In 2003, as part of the Prosecutorial Remedies and Tools Against the Exploitation of Children Today (PROTECT) Act, Rep. Thomas Feeney proposed what became known as the

"Feeney Amendment." Despite opposition from the defense bar, current and former Commission members, the President of the American Bar Association, and Chief Justice William Rehnquist, the amendment survived and was adopted (Bibas, 2004). In addition to adding five-year mandatory sentences for child pornography receipt and distribution offenses, the Amendment eliminated some downward departures and directed the Commission to increase other sentences. It also directly amended the child pornography guidelines, further increasing penalties. All of this went on without any of the empirical support that was to be the hallmark of the Sentencing Guidelines. Since the guidelines were mandatory, the Feeney Amendments, in the words of Sen. Kennedy, had "nothing to do with protecting children, and everything to do with handcuffing judges and eliminating fairness in our federal sentencing system" (Schneider, 2004, p. 540).

In its decision in *United States v. Booker* (2005), the U.S. Supreme Court struck down the "mandatory" nature of Sentencing Guidelines and made them advisory. It held that courts should consider the guidelines in a framework of all relevant facts, sentencing purpose, and parsimony and "Impose a sentence sufficient, but not greater than necessary." A spate of decisions followed, including *Rita v. U.S.* (2007), holding that a downward departure is appropriate if the guideline itself is unsound or fails to treat the defendant's characteristics in the proper way; *Gall v. U.S.* (2007), holding that sentencing courts must consider the "history and characteristics" of the defendant, including even those excluded by guidelines; and *Kimborough v. U.S.* (2007), holding that a judge may disagree if guidelines fail to reflect empirical data and national experience.

In 2011, federal prosecutors recommended a below-guideline sentence in 17.7 percent of child pornography cases. Another 47.9 percent of child pornography cases received below-guidelines sentences from federal judges. In 65.5 percent of all child pornography cases in 2011, courts sentenced offenders to below-guidelines sentences, a rate almost 50 percent higher than the below-guidelines percentage for all offense types (Debold & Tirschwell, 2012. Please see USSC, *Preliminary Quarterly Data Report, 4th Quarter Release through Oct. 31, 2011*, Tables 1 & 5 as cited therein). "Prosecutors and judges are not taking these actions because they feel that child pornography is a non-serious offense. It is because, even after a full appreciation of the harms caused by the crime, they cannot rely on the guidelines recommendation to give even a rough approximation of a sentence that serves the purpose of sentencing" Debold & Tirschwell, 2012, p. 2) As previously noted, the harms contemplated by Congress simply have not been shown to exist in the teen sexting world.

■ SCOPE OF THE ISSUE

The actual size and scope of electronic media use is difficult to track and catalog. The following statistics are provided only for purposes of understanding the incredible scope of the use and growth of technology. In 1993, the Internet carried approximately 1 percent of the world's telecommunications traffic. By 2000, that figure had grown to 51 percent, and by 2007, it had reached 97 percent (Hilbert & López, 2011). As of June 30, 2012, Internet World Stats estimated that there were 2.4 billion Internet users worldwide and 244 million in the United States (Internet World Stats, 2013). The venture capitalist firm Kleiner, Perkins, Caufield and Byers, in its Internet trends for 2013 report, (Meeker & Wu, 2013) finds 1.1 billion Facebook users and 5 billion global mobile phone users, of which 1.5 billion are smartphone subscribers (219 million in the United States alone).

Even more difficult to actually assess is the amount of the Internet activity related to pornography. A recent publication attempted to provide a systematic, empirically based estimate of the number of pornographic websites and the amount of Web searches for pornographic content (Ogas & Gaddam, 2011). They found that in 2010, of the million most trafficked websites in the world, 42,337 (or about 4 percent) were sex related. In addition, about 13 percent of all Web searches were for erotic content. While these numbers may seem low, it is important to remember that the study found that between seven million and 16 million persons visited the five most popular porn sites each month. Predicting how many of these visits were by adolescents would not be possible. A 2010 report from the Pew Internet & American Life Project, however, found that 93 percent of teens ages 12 to 17 go online, with nearly two thirds (63 percent) doing so several times a day, and 93 percent of young adults ages 18 to 29 go online (Zickuhr, 2010).

■ **THE LAW**

As of mid-2013, at least 18 states had laws relating to sexting, the practice of sending explicit phone messages or pictures of minors (Hinduja & Pathin, 2013). The content of such acts arguably varies across states, but the statutes all target evolving technology formats becoming ubiquitous in transmitting inappropriate material to minors. Since 2009, several states have updated and enacted legislation to reflect the increasing prevalence of child pornography transmitted via various digital formats, including sexting" (*2012 Sexting Legislation*, 2012). Of the 18 states that have legislation, Arizona, Connecticut, Florida, Hawaii, Illinois, Louisiana, Missouri, Nebraska, Nevada, New Jersey, New York, North Dakota, Pennsylvania, Rhode Island, South Dakota, Texas, Utah, and Vermont address minors specifically as perpetrators (Hinduja & Pathin, 2013).

Several of these statutes stipulate punishments if found guilty. Punishments range from the rehabilitative, such as community service and counseling, to felony charges and mandatory sex offender registration. The following represent a cross-section of the statutes in effect:

- *Florida*: Provides that a minor commits the offense of sexting if he or she knowingly uses a computer or other device to transmit or distribute a photograph or video of himself or herself which depicts nudity and is harmful to minors, or knowingly possesses such photograph or video that was transmitted or distributed to a minor from another minor; provides that transmission or distribution of multiple photographs or videos is single offense if such photographs and videos were transmitted or distributed in same 24-hour period; provides that possession of multiple photographs or videos that were transmitted or distributed by a minor is single offense if such photographs and videos were transmitted or distributed by the minor in same 24-hour period; provides that act does not prohibit prosecution of a minor for conduct relating to material that includes depiction of sexual conduct or sexual excitement or for stalking (Fla. Stat. § 847.0141, 2012).

- *Illinois*: Provides that a minor shall not distribute or disseminate an indecent visual depiction of another minor through the use of a computer or electronic communication device. The statute provides that a minor who violates any of these provisions may be subject to a petition for adjudication and adjudged a minor in need of supervision. The statute further provides that a minor found to be in need of supervision under this provision may be: (1) ordered to obtain counseling or other supportive services to address the acts that led to the need for supervision; or (2) ordered to perform community service (Section: 705 Ill. Comp. Stat. A. § 405/3-40, 2010).

- *Missouri*: Exempts youths aged 19 or younger who plead guilty or *nolo contendere* to, or were convicted of, or found guilty of [sexting] from being included in the sexual offender registry if he or she meets certain conditions (Mo. Rev. Stat. A. § 573.023 and Mo. Rev. Stat. A. § 589.400, 2009).

- *New York*: Creates an educational reform program and a diversionary program for certain juveniles (under the age of 19 at the time and both sender and receiver not more than 5 years apart in age) who are criminally charged with certain offenses involving the creation, exhibition or distribution of a photograph depicting nudity through the use of an electronic communication device, an interactive wireless communications device or a computer (N.Y. SOS LAW § 458-1, 2011).

- *Pennsylvania*: Amends the Crimes and Offenses Code and the Judiciary and Judicial Procedure Code. The statute provides for the offense of dissemination of prohibited materials by minors. The statute further provides for expungement of juvenile records (18 Pa C.S. § 6312, 2011). However, in *In re C. S., 2012 Pa. Dist. & Cnty. Dec. LEXIS 403 (Pa. County Ct. 2012)*, a trial court decision held it properly dismissed sexual abuse of children (18 Pa.C.S. § 6312) and related charges against a female juvenile because the child pornography statutes as applied to teenage sexting failed to provide a teenager of ordinary intelligence fair notice of what is prohibited. The Court found that the statute was "void for vagueness reasons." (Please see House Bill 321, 2013, which purports to respond to the Court's criticism.)

- *Rhode Island*: Prohibits the use of a computer or other telecommunication device to transmit an indecent visual depiction of himself or herself to another person, which is commonly known as sexting, by minors; provides that any violation of this act is deemed to be a status offense and shall be referred to the family court (R.I. General Laws § 11-9-1.4, 2012).
- *Utah*: Provides penalties for minors that distribute pornographic material or deal in material harmful to a minor; provides that a non-minor who solicits a person younger than 18 to distribute pornographic material or deal in material harmful to a minor is guilty of a third-degree felony and is subject to specified penalties; provides enhanced penalties for subsequent violations (Utah Code A. § 76-10-1204 and Utah Code A. § 76-10-1206, 2009).

Even though 18 states have formally codified statutes addressing minors in possession of child pornography, nearly all states have attempted to enact legislation tackling the issue (*2011 Legislation Related to "Sexting,"* 2012). Topics covered within the proposals vary widely. Several states approach the issue from an educational perspective, such as mandating that information be provided by schools as part of "safety programs" to reduce sexting. Similarly, some proposals suggest that schools disseminate information to parents. Other bills discuss the importance of post-infraction counseling and community service. All proposals highlight the severity of the infraction and deeming such acts as criminal. However, many proposals have stalled in committee or failed to be enacted.

Internationally, the discussion of minors in possession of child pornography varies across countries. In North America, Canada asserts that the issue is much less prevalent than in the United States, but prosecutions have occurred. In 2007, an Alberta teen avoided being jailed for possessing and disseminating child pornography after emailing photos of his ex-girlfriend to others. The teen pleaded guilty to a reduced charge of "corrupting morals." The prosecutor in that case remarked that the defendant was fortunate to walk away with a conditional discharge (Blais, 2007). The Canadian Criminal Code prohibits sending nude photos of a minor or to a minor. Specifically, Section 163(1) proscribes making, distributing, possessing, or accessing the prohibited material as criminal. According to Canadian Parliamentary history, the objective of the provision is to ban possession of child pornography, which harms and potentially exploits children (Casavant & Robertson, 2007). However, the Supreme Court of Canada clarified the boundaries of the provision in *R. v. Sharpe* (2001); specifically, the court narrowed the scope of the provision by explicitly excluding from its ambit two categories of material that were deemed private in nature and that posed no harm to children, namely "self-created expressive material" and "private recordings of lawful sexual activity." The ruling delineated between consensual sexual exploration (two adolescents sharing personal pictures between each other) and disseminated pictures of one individual without his or her permission. The latter act would be punishable under the clarified boundaries (*R. v. Sharpe*, 2001).

Overall, however, legal authorities have prioritized educating minors about the risks associated with sending sexually explicit material to other minors. In the absence of many prosecutions of minors engaging in sexting behaviors in Canada, the applicability of the Code's child pornography provisions remains unclear. Similarly, elsewhere in North America sexting or the sending of indecent material continues to be much less prevalent, let alone prosecuted. If mentioned at all, the sending of such material from a minor to another minor continues to be prohibited with unclear punishments.

The European Union has explicitly addressed the behavior. Lawmakers acknowledge that it is a growing concern in schools and other organizations who work with children across the EU. The prevalence of the behavior varies by country. A recent EU Kids Online survey found that 15 percent of 11- to 16-year-olds have received peer-to-peer sexual/suggestive images, and 3 percent say they have sent or posted such messages. The highest risk of sexting is encountered in Romania, the Czech Republic, and Norway, followed by France, Estonia, and Lithuania. In half of the countries across Europe, the risk of receiving sexual messages is below average, with Italy having the lowest level (Lobe & Livingstone, 2011). Overall, the findings suggest that the majority of children across countries have not encountered sexting. Nevertheless, it is illegal to create, transmit, or possess a sexual image of a minor per the 1989 UN Convention on the Rights of the Child, entered into force on September 2, 1990 (see Article 34c on the exploitative use of children in pornographic performances and materials) ratified by all EU Member States (UN Convention on the Rights of the Child, 1989).

In the United Kingdom, minors who have in their possession an indecent image of another minor would technically be in possession of an indecent image of a child, which is an offense under the Protection of Children Act of 1978 and the Criminal Justice Act of 1988. Again, much like Canada, there is a dearth of charges for such behavior, and subsequent punishments have not been examined. Thus, there has been little call to reform the law.

Conversely, both New Zealand and Australia are confronting sexting with evolving legislation. The parliament in Victoria has been told that new laws should be introduced to deal with sexting; currently the act is classified as child pornography if depicting someone aged under 18, even if the person pictured took the images himself or herself, and the offender must register on the sex offender database. A parliamentary inquiry has heard that young people are at risk of being placed on the register when its real intent is to monitor adults, and several legislators argue there should be a lesser offense covering consensual sexting between minors, rather than child pornography (*Inquiry into Sexting*, 2013). In Australia in 2007, 32 teenagers in Victoria were charged with child pornography offenses as a result of sexting (Porter, 2008). The charges resulted from Commonwealth Law, Part 10.6 of the Criminal Code Act 1995, which makes it an offense to access, transmit, publish, possess, control, supply, or obtain child pornography (Criminal Code Act, 1995).

■ WHAT WE KNOW ABOUT THE EFFECT OF NEGATIVE SANCTIONS

Law enforcement agencies in the United States made 1,906,600 arrests of persons under age 18 in 2009. As of February 24, 2010, approximately 71,000 juvenile offenders were held in residential placement facilities in the United States. When incarceration rates from around the world are compared, the United States incarcerates 336 per 100,000 youth. The next two closest countries are South Africa (69 per 100,000 youth) and New Zealand (68 per 100,000 youth) (*OJJDP*, 2011). Studies of youth released from residential corrections programs in the United States find that 70 to 80 percent of youth are rearrested within two or three years. Of the six states reporting juvenile or adult arrests within two years of release (from juvenile placement), none showed a rearrest rate of less than 68 percent. Virtually all states reporting three-year rearrest rates converge at about 75 percent (*OJJDP*, 2011).

A 20-year study followed 779 low-income youth in Montreal with annual interviews from age 10 to age 17, then tracked their arrest records in adulthood. Researchers also interviewed the teenagers' parents, schoolmates, and teachers. The study accounted for variables such as family income, single-parent-home status, and earlier behavior problems (such as hyperactivity) that are known to affect delinquency risk. Those adjudicated individuals who entered the juvenile justice system even briefly—for example, being sentenced to community service or other penance, with limited exposure to other troubled youth—were twice as likely to be arrested as adults, compared with youths with the same behavior problems who remained outside the system. Being put on probation, which involves more contact with misbehaving peers, in counseling groups or even in waiting rooms at probation offices, raised teens' odds of adult arrest by a factor of 14. The emerging consensus on the characteristics of effective programming for young offenders are as follows: punitive sanctions without services do not have a significant effect on reoffending; when services are matched to youths' criminogenic needs, they lower the chance of repeat offending; and mixing high-risk youth with low-risk youth can make low-risk youths worse (Gatti, Tremblay, & Vitaro, 2009).

Punishment and sanctions do not deter juvenile reoffending and, in some cases, may even increase it. In a recent research summary of 548 intervention studies, Lipsey (2009) reported that punishment increased recidivism rates by an average of 8 percent. Punitive sanctions without services have no impact on reoffending and actually cost more money. If risk is defined as risk for reoffending—engaging in future delinquent offenses, not minor violations such as truancy or violations/offenses that relate to substance abuse, Latessa (2013) has found that not a single reviewer of studies of the effects of official punishment (custody, mandatory arrests, increased surveillance, etc.) has found consistent evidence of reduced recidivism.

■ CONCLUSIONS

Clearly, using existing child pornography laws to address adolescent sexting is not an effective means of addressing any social issues that may be raised by the practice. The laws in many instances, particularly with respect to federal law, were not designed to respond to empirically recognized or identified risks. The enormous volume of Internet material available nowadays and the rapid ability to disseminate this material calls for a re-examination of laws related to these topics. Sanctioning adolescents has been shown to exacerbate reoffending rather than to curb it. Doing so when the risk of exploiting the subjects (who are often both perpetrator and victim) is not high is counterproductive. In this volume, authors will address issues related to today's digital world and its impact on adolescent sexual development, sexting, cyber-bullying and its relationship to adolescent suicidal ideation and behavior, social networking, and the relationship between juvenile Internet use and sex offending. We will also offer suggestions, based on such empirical data as do exist, for developing strategies to address issues where they cause harm, and help clinicians, educators, policymakers, and parents understand that much sexualized behavior in children and adolescents is a normal reaction and not cause for concern. We will endeavor in areas such as commercial sexual exploitation of children and Internet-based offending to offer strategies for addressing the risks created for children and adolescents.

As we have noted, applying negative sanctions to adolescents begins a spiral toward ongoing criminal justice involvement. If, as will be discussed, we are dealing with normal developmental growth, then criminalizing the conduct may indeed result in long-term harm to the individuals, to their families and communities, and to society as a whole. It is hoped that this chapter will provide information on the disparate forces that affect societal response to a rapidly expanding digital universe.

■ DISCLOSURES

Sara J. Brady has no conflicts of interest to disclose.
Fabian M. Saleh has no conflicts of interest, disclosures, and material support to report.
Richard Cody has no conflicts of interest to disclose.
Albert J. Grudzinskas, Jr. has no conflicts of interest to disclose.
Jonathan Clayfield did not disclose any conflicts of interest.

■ NOTES

1. The Free Speech Coalition is the trade association for the adult entertainment industry. Retrieved September 24, 2013, from: http://www.freespeechcoalition.com/about-us.html

2. Section 503 of the Act amended 18 U. S. C. §2252A to add a new pandering and solicitation provision, relevant portions of which now read as follows:

"(a) Any person who—

"(3) knowingly—

"(B) advertises, promotes, presents, distributes, or solicits through the mails, or in interstate or foreign commerce by any means, including by computer, any material or purported material in a manner that reflects the belief, or that is intended to cause another to believe, that the material or purported material is, or contains—

"(i) an obscene visual depiction of a minor engaging in sexually explicit conduct; or

"(ii) a visual depiction of an actual minor engaging in sexually explicit conduct,

"shall be punished as provided in subsection (b)." §2252A(a)(3)(B) (2000 ed., Supp. V)

■ REFERENCES

2011 Legislation Related to "Sexting" (2012, January 23). Retrieved on March 20, 2013, from http://www.ncsl.org/issues-research/telecom/sexting-legislation-2011.aspx

2012 Sexting Legislation (2012, December 14). Retrieved March 21, 2013, from http://www.ncsl.org/issues-research/telecom/sexting-legislation-2012.aspx

Ashcroft v. Free Speech Coalition, 535 U.S. 234 (2002).

Bibas, S. (2004). The Feeney Amendment and the continuing rise of prosecutorial power to plea bargain. *Journal of Criminal Law and Criminology, 94*. Available at: http://www.questia.com/PM.qst?a=o&se=gglsc&d=5008140708 Accessed Sept. 24, 2013.

Blais, T. (2007, October 2). *Teen who shared nude cell photos of girl avoids jail.* Retrieved March 20, 2013, from http://cnews.canoe.ca/CNEWS/Crime/2007/10/02/pf-4543498.html

Casavant, L., & Robertson, J. R. (2007). *The evolution of pornography law in Canada.* Retrieved March 21, 2013, from http://www.parl.gc.ca/content/lop/researchpublications/843-e.pdf

Comprehensive Crime Control Act of 1984, Title II.

Criminal Code Act of 1995, Australian Government, Act No. 12 of 1995. Retrieved March 21, 2013, from http://www.comlaw.gov.au/Series/C2004A04868

Criminal Justice Act (1988). Retrieved March 23, 2013, from http://www.legislation.gov.uk/ukpga/1988/33/contents

Debold, D., & Tirschwell, E. A. (2012). *Written testimony of the Practitioners Advisory Group: A Standing Advisory Group of the U.S. Sentencing Commission, Feb. 13, 2012.* Last accessed Sept. 24, 2013; available at: http://www.ussc.gov/Legislative_and_Public_Affairs/Public_Hearings_and_Meetings/20120215-16/Agenda_15.htm

Elias, J., & Victor, D. (2010, April 15). *Susquenita High School officials being investigated for handling of images in "sexting" case.* Retrieved March 20, 2013, from http://www.pennlive.com/midstate/index.ssf/2010/04/susquenita_high_school_officia.html

Fagan, P. J. (2009). Perspectives on sex and normality. In F. M. Saleh, A. J. Grudzinskas, Jr., J. M. Bradford, & D. J. Brodsky (Eds.), *Sex offenders: Identification, risk assessment, treatment, and legal issues* (pp. 3–11). New York: Oxford University Press.

Florida House Bill 75, Regular Session (2011). Offense of Sexting. Fla. Stat. § 847.0141, 2012.

Friedrich, W. N. (2003) Studies of sexuality in non-abused children. In J. Bancroft (Ed.), *Sexual development in children* (pp. 107–120). Bloomington: Indiana University Press.

Gatti, U., Tremblay, R. E., & Vitaro, F. (2009). Iatrogenic effect of juvenile justice. *Journal of Child Psychology & Psychiatry, 50*(8), 991–998.

Gall v. U. S., 552 U.S. 38 (2007).

Goodridge v. Dept. of Public Health, 798 N.E.2d 941 (Mass. 2003).

Grudzinskas, A. J., Brodsky, D. J., Federoff, J. P., Zaitchik, M., DiCataldo, F., & Clayfield, J. C. (2009). Sexual predator laws and their history. In F. M. Saleh, A. J. Grudzinskas, Jr., J. M. Bradford, & D. J. Brodsky (Eds.), *Sex offenders: Identification, risk assessment, treatment, and legal issues* (pp. 386–411). New York: Oxford University Press.

Hilbert, M. & López, P. (2011). The world's technological capacity to store, communicate, and compute information, *Science, 332*, 60–65.

Hinduja, S., & Patchin, J. (2013). *State sexting laws*. Cyberbullying Research Center. Retrieved Sept. 24, 2013, from http://www.cyberbullying.us/state_sexting_laws.pdf

Howley, S. (Feb. 15, 2012). Written testimony before the U.S. Sentencing Commission, citing Claudio Violato, Elizabeth Oddone-Paolucci & Mark Genius, eds. *The Changing Family and Child Development* (pp. 48–59). Aldershot, England: Ashgate Publishing Ltd. 2000.

Hyde, HM: (1960) *The Trials of Oscar Wilde* William Hodge And Company; 5th edition, London.

Illinois House Bill 4583, 96th General Assembly, 1st Regular Session (2010). Electronic Harmful Material.

Internet World Stats (2012) World internet usage and population statistics. Retrieved December 10, 2013 from http://www.internetworldstats.com/stats.htm

Inquiry Into Sexting. Parliamentary Paper No. 230, Session 2010-2013. Retrieved March 21, 2013 from http://www.parliament.vic.gov.au/images/stories/committees/lawrefrom/isexting/LRC_Sexting_Final_Report.pdf

Jacobellis v. Ohio, 378 US 184 (1964). Justice Stewart, concurring.

Jackson, S. (1990). Demons and the innocents: Western ideas on children's sexuality, I: Historical perspective. In M. E. Perry (Ed.), *Handbook of sexology* (Vol.: Childhood and Adolescent Sexology, pp. 23–49). Amsterdam: Elsevier Press.

Khadaroo, S. T. (May 5, 2011) Phoebe Prince bullies sentenced, but how do they make things right? *Christian Science Monitor*. Accessed Sept. 24, 2013, at http://www.csmonitor.com/USA/2011/0505/Phoebe-Prince-bullies-sentenced-but-how-do-they-make-things-right

Kimborough v. U.S., 552 U.S. 85 (2007).

Latessa, E. J. *What works and what doesn't in reducing recidivism: The principles of effective intervention.* Presented at Center for Criminal Justice Research, Division of Criminal Justice, University of Cincinnati. Last accessed: Sept. 24, 2013 Available at: www.uc.edu/criminaljustice.

Lawrence v. Texas, 539 U.S. 558, 559 (2003).

Lipsey, M. W. (2009). The primary factors that characterize effective interventions with juvenile offenders: A meta-analytic overview. *Victims & Offenders, 4*, 124–147.

Lobe, B., & Livingstone, S. (2011). *Cross-national comparison of risks and safety on the Internet: Initial analysis from the EU Kids Online Survey of European children.* Retrieved March 21, 2013, from http://www.lse.ac.uk/media@lse/research/EUKidsOnline/EU percent20Kids percent20II percent20 percent282009-11 percent29/EUKidsOnlineIIReports/D6 percent20Cross-national.pdf

Massachusetts General Laws, Ch. 71, § 37O, 2013.

Masslive (May 30, 2013). Massachusetts may update anti-bullying law created following Phoebe Prince, Carl Walker-Hoover suicides. Accessed Sept. 24, 2013, at http://s.masslive.com/4etXamE

Meeker, M. & Wu, L, (2013) Internet trends. Kleiner, Perkins, Caufield and Byers, Accessed Dec. 10, 2013 at http://www.kpcb.com/insights/2013-internet-trends

Michaels, S. (2008, Oct. 10). *Teen charged with sending nude pics of herself.* Retrieved March 21, 2013, from http://abcnews.go.com/TheLaw/story?id=5995084&page=1

Miller v. Mitchell, 598 F.3d 139 (2010).

Missouri House Bill 62, 95th General Assembly, 1st Regular Session. Mo. Rev. Stat. A. § 573.023 and Mo. Rev. Stat. A. § 589.400, 2009.

New York SOS LAW § 458-1, 2011. New York Assembly Bill 8170, General Assembly 2011-2012.

OJJDP Statistical Briefing Book: Census of Juveniles in Residential Placement 2010 (2011). P. 4. Last accessed: Sept. 24, 2013. Available at: http://www.ojjdp.gov/ojstatbb/corrections/qa08201.asp?qaDate=2010.

Ogas, O., & Gaddam, S. (2011). *A billion wicked thoughts: What the world's largest experiment reveals about human desire.* New York: Dutton: Penguin Group.

Pennsylvania Senate Bill 1211, Regular Session 2009-2010.

Pilkington, E. (2009, Jan. 14). *Sexting craze leads to child pornography charges.* TheGuardian.com. Retrieved March 20, 2013, from http://www.theguardian.com/world/2009/jan/14/child-pornography-sexting

Porter, L. (2008, Aug. 10). *Malice in Wonderland.* Retrieved March 21, 2013, from http://www.theage.com.au/news/technology/malice-in-wonderland/2008/08/09/1218139163632.html?page=fullpage#contentSwap1

Protection of Children Act (1978). Retrieved March 23, 2013, from http://www.legislation.gov.uk/ukpga/1978/37/body

R. v. Sharpe, 2001 SCC 2, (2001) 1 S.C.R. 45 at para. 123.

Rhode Island General Law § 11-9-1.4, 2012. House Bill 5094, Regular Session 2011. An Act Relating To Criminal Offenses—Children.

Rita v. U.S., 551 U.S. 338 (2007).

Schneider, E. T. (2004). Comment: The Feeney Amendment: Handcuffing our federal judges. *27* Hamline L. Rev. 536.

Seto, M. C. (2012). Testimony before the U.S. Sentencing Commission, Feb. 15, 2012, 20-28 citing Seto, M., Hanson, R.K. & Babchishin, K.: Contact sexual offending by men arrested for child pornography offenses, *Sexual Abuse: A Journal of Research and Treatment*, 23, 124–145 (2011).

Solem v. Helm, 463 U.S. 277 (1983).

Sutherland, E. H. (1950). The diffusion of sexual psychopath laws. *American Journal of Sociology*, 56, 142–148.

Teen sues Pennsylvania school district in sexting case, claiming principal looked at her nude photos (2010, May 20). Retrieved March 21, 201,3 from http://www.pennlive.com/midstate/index.ssf/2010/05/teen_sues_pennsylvania_school.html

U.S. Sentencing Guidelines Manual, Ch. 1 Pt. A (2011), p. 1.

United States v. One Book Entitled Ulysses by James Joyce, 72 F.2d 705, 706 (2d Cir. 1934).

United States v. Booker, 543 U.S. 220 (2005).

United States v. Williams, 553 U.S. 285 (2008).

United States v. Windsor, 570 U.S. ___, (2013).

UN Convention on the Rights of the Child, General Assembly resolution 44/25 (1989). Retrieved on March 20, 2013, from http://www.unicef.org/crc/

Utah House Bill 14, 58th General Assembly, 1st Regular Session (2009). Material Harmful to Minors Amendments, Utah Code A. § 76-10-1204 and Utah Code A. § 76-10-1206, 2009.

Wisconsin vs. Phillips. La Crosse County Case Number 2008 CF 000309 (2008).

Wisconsin v. Phillips (Sept. 15, 2008). Digital Media Law Project. Retrieved March 21, 2013, from, http://www.dmlp.org/threats/wisconsin-v-phillips

Zickuhr, K. (2010). Generations 2010: Generations, teens, seniors, e-mail, blogs, podcasting, religion, & banking. Pew Research Center. Accessed Dec. 10, 2013 at http://pewinternet.org/Reports/2010/Generations-2010.aspx

2 Understanding the World of Digital Youth

■ ANDREW J. HARRIS

Within a relatively brief window of time, digital communications have assumed an increasingly prominent role in our daily lives. Beginning with the rise of the commercial Internet in the 1990s, and continuing with the expansion of the interactive Web (sometimes referred to as "Web 2.0") that began in the mid-2000s, we have experienced dramatic changes in the way we consume, access information, and interact with one another. These changes have accelerated even further with recent developments in mobile computing technology and its attendant production of an "always on" society and a persistent flow of data and information.

Amidst this rapidly shifting landscape, researchers and commentators have paid considerable attention to the ways in which digital communication technology has affected the behaviors, norms, interactions, and values of adolescents. A common series of narratives has focused on the negative insidious effects of technology on young people's ability to connect with others, engage with society, forge meaningful relationships, pay attention, and think critically. Alternatively, some have suggested that "the kids are alright" and that the Web 2.0 era has ushered in unprecedented opportunities for learning, engagement, and interaction.

Contemporary youth culture has been characterized by the emergence of what Mizuko Ito and colleagues have termed "networked publics"—modes of interaction in which traditional modes of teen social engagement (e.g. friendship, dating, courtship, self-expression) are being reshaped and redefined through communication technology (Ito et al., 2009). This emerging normative framework serves as a vital point of reference for practitioners and policymakers seeking to promote balanced and appropriate responses to technology-mediated sexual behavior and expression among youth.

This chapter will explore the dynamic relationship between youth development, communication technology, norms of social interaction, and popular culture. It begins with a brief discussion of the digital revolution and its transformational effects within the broader society. Following a review of trends and patterns of communication technology usage among millennial teens and young adults, we then turn to the primary focus of the chapter—the way in which this technology has interacted with core elements of the adolescent experience. The primary emphasis will be on the role of technology in the social lives of teens, specifically the manner in which digital communications have transformed peer relationships and interactions. This, in turn, will provide vital context for subsequent chapters' exploration of specific online sexual behaviors, their social and developmental correlates, and related practice and policy responses.

■ THE RAPIDLY SHIFTING DIGITAL LANDSCAPE

Over the past two decades, the digital revolution has produced profound changes in modern society, with these changes happening at an increasingly accelerated pace. In terms of breadth and magnitude, consider the following statistics:

- In 1993, the Internet carried approximately 1 percent of the world's telecommunications traffic. By 2000, that figure had grown to 51 percent, and by 2007, it had reached 97 percent (Hilbert & López, 2011).
- In the first decade of the millennium, the number of worldwide Internet users grew from 361 million in 2000 to 1.9 billion in 2010—a sixfold increase. By 2012, there were an estimated 2.1 billion email users, 2.4 billion Internet users, and 634 million active websites across the globe.
- In October 2012, the social network Facebook, despite being less than seven years old, surpassed 1 billion users worldwide—over 12 percent of the world's population.
- During 2012, Facebook users generated an average of 2.7 billion "likes" per day. In a typical month, 800 million unique users visited YouTube and viewed 4 billion hours of video. YouTube users also uploaded 72 hours of new video content every minute (http://www.youtube.com/t/press_statistics).
- In mid-2011, Twitter reported transmitting over 200 million tweets per day, enough to fill a 10-million-page book, or 8,163 copies of Tolstoy's *War and Peace* (http://blog.twitter.com/2011/06/200-million-tweets-per-day.html). One year later, in mid-2012, the company reported that this figure had **doubled** to 400 million per day (http://marketingland.com/twitter-400-million-tweets-daily-improving-content-discovery-13581).

The breadth and volume of our digital activities, however, tell only part of the story. Equally important is the transformative effects that these activities have had on the way in which people interact, consume, create, learn, self-express, engage with their communities, and process information.

These effects have become particularly pronounced in the years since 2004, when analysts at the first "Web 2.0" conference noted a shift from a top-down "software as service" model to a bottom-up, consumer-driven "web as platform" approach (O'Reilly & Battelle, 2009). Led by standard-bearers such as Facebook, YouTube, Wikipedia, and Twitter, Web 2.0 technologies have permeated the communication landscape, transforming the domains of work, education, creative expression, social interactions, entertainment, commerce, and civic engagement (Kaplan & Haenlein, 2010).

The growing ubiquity of Web 2.0 has been amplified by an expansion in mobile computing technology. Data from the Pew Internet and American Life Project indicate that, as of February 2012, 88 percent of American adults own cellphones, and almost half own smartphones capable of accessing the mobile Web. Moreover, a substantial majority of adult cellphone owners use their phones for purposes other than making phone calls—over three quarters use them for taking pictures, 80 percent send and receive text messages, and more than half use their phones to access the Internet and/or email. The growing mobile Web, along with the emergence of tablets and ultraportable computers, has untethered the world of the Internet, contributing to an "always on" culture in which technology is increasingly embedded in our daily lives.

■ EVALUATING SOCIETAL IMPACTS

The Web is no longer a collection of static pages [that] describe something in the world. Increasingly, the Web is the world—everything and everyone in the world casts an "information shadow," an aura of data which, when captured and processed intelligently, offers extraordinary opportunity and mind-bending implications. (O'Reilly & Battelle, 2009, p. 2)

There is little argument that the technology has transformed human interactions in fundamental ways. The question of whether these transformations have been for the better, however, remains a matter of perspective.

Web 2.0 has certainly produced its share of passionate boosters who cite the promise of the interactive Web to improve society by challenging traditional power structures (Rheingold, 2008), producing new modes of learning and engagement (Jenkins, 2009), and providing vehicles for collective action (Shirky, 2009). Along these lines, technology and social media have indeed facilitated the sharing of information and ideas and have provided expanded opportunities for discourse. Moreover, technology may strengthen certain social relationships and ties by providing a platform for interaction and augmenting networks of social supports. For example, adult users of social media tend to have significantly higher levels of social ties and higher levels of engagement with community organizations (Smith, 2013). Additionally, the Internet offers the potential for individuals to connect with networks of social support related to specific life challenges, such as dealing with illness or loss—networks that might not otherwise be as readily accessible.

On the other side of the coin, many have attributed a range of negative effects to the changing technological landscape. Some have cited the isolating effects of digital technology, suggesting that the technology is leading us to neglect one another's emotional needs and devalue personal interaction. In an era in which multitasking has become *de rigueur*, and in which traditional boundaries between work life and home life have dissolved, the manner in which mobile devices and the Internet may distract us from personal relationships emerges as a vital concern (Turkle, 2012). Others have pointed to potentially insidious effects of the Internet on our cognitive functioning—Nicholas Carr, in his book *The Shallows*, argues that the Internet may be changing us in fundamental ways, including alterations in the structure and functioning of our brains. Carr argues that while the Internet may be arguably making us more "efficient" in our consumption of information, this has come at the price of compromising our brains' capacity for reflection, focus, and deep critical perspective (Carr, 2012).

The next generation of the web, Web 3.0—sometimes referred to as the "semantic Web"—promises further transformation, as our devices become increasingly customized and more tightly integrated into our daily decisions. As with the rise of the social Web, these changes carry both promise and potential perils and also herald a significant shift in social norms and expectations. Notably, as we move into the Web 3.0 era, we can expect continued debate over the tradeoffs between the convenience afforded by these technologies and the privacy of our personal information.

■ THE WORLD OF DIGITAL YOUTH

Amidst these changes, and as social media and mobile communications have become increasingly embedded in our daily lives, young people have emerged as avid and nimble adopters of emerging technology. While the digital revolution has surely altered the norms, attitudes, and behaviors of "premillennial" adults, it has fundamentally shaped and defined those of teens and young adults coming of age in the new millennium. The research literature on the magnitude and nature of these effects has been growing rapidly—for current purposes, a number of trends are of particular note.

Teens are increasingly "plugged in"

First, the Internet is a ubiquitous presence in the lives of most teens. As of 2011, over 95 percent of teens in the United States indicated that they were Internet users, with a substantial majority indicating that they accessed the Internet several times per day (Pew Internet & American Life Project, 2012). While there remains a socioeconomic and regional "digital divide," the expansion of Internet access in schools and rural areas has narrowed the access gap considerably.

Beyond access to the Internet, teens have also experienced greater access to mobile technology. As of 2013, 86% of U.S. teens between 12 and 17 had their own cellphones. Consistent with trends observed within the adult population, teens are also increasingly connected to the mobile Web—as of 2013, 44 percent of teens had access to smartphones that provide mobile access to the Internet. Industry projections suggest that these proportions will continue to grow, commensurate with the increased reliability and access and reduced costs of mobile broadband (eMarketer, August 2013).

Notably, the average age of mobile access has also shown a steady decline. While most youth continue to receive their first cellphones at the ages of 12 or 13, along with the transition to middle school, survey data suggest that a growing proportion of youth receive their phones at younger ages. A 2009 Pew survey of teens aged 12 to 17 indicated that none of the 17-year-olds had received cellphones prior to the age of 11, and fewer than 6 percent of 15- and 16-year-olds had done so. In contrast, 28 percent of the 12-year-olds surveyed had received their phone prior to the age of 11, suggesting a significant change in the age of such technological immersion over a brief window of time.

Texting is a dominant mode of interaction

Second, teens talk with their thumbs. Texting via cellphones has become a normative mode of social interaction among teens and has emerged as the preferred manner in which most teens communicate.

- Nearly two thirds of teens indicate that they exchanged text messages daily with people in their lives, outpacing cellphone calling (39 percent), face-to-face socializing outside of school (35 percent), social network messaging (29 percent), instant messaging (22 percent), and email (6 percent).
- In 2011, the median teen sent approximately 60 texts per day—a 20 percent increase from levels observed just two years earlier. Compared to boys and to younger teens, girls aged 14 to 17 represent the most avid texting cohort, with a median of over 100 texts per day.
- 2011 data from Nielsen indicate that teens with mobile phones aged 13 to 17 sent or received a average of 3,705 text messages per month. This was more than double the rate for the 18-to-24 age group (1,707 per month); five times the rate in the 25-to-34 age group (758 per month); and 10 times the rate in the 45-to-54 age group (349 per month).

When asked about the appeal of texting as a primary mode of communication, more than half of teens cite the quickness or ease of use, with smaller proportions indicating that texting provides them with the opportunity to think about their responses (16 percent) and that it gives them more privacy (11 percent) (Common Sense Media, 2012). We will explore the dynamics and implications of these motivations in the next section of this chapter.

Social network use is central to teens' lives

Third, teens love their social media. Over 90 percent report having participated in a social network, and two thirds report such participation on a daily basis. While Facebook remains the dominant platform for the majority of teen social network users, teens have also reported increasing use of other platforms such as Twitter, MySpace, and Google Plus.

Despite this saturation of social media use among teens, youth are not monolithic in their patterns of use. For example:

- Survey data suggest that approximately one quarter of teens appear to be heavy users of social networks, another quarter quite sporadic in its use, and the remaining half somewhere in between.
- While boys and girls are fairly consistent in terms of general use of social media, their patterns of use have shown significant differences. For example, compared to boys, girls are more than twice as likely (22 percent vs. 10 percent) to use the microblogging site Twitter; boys are three times more likely to have an account on YouTube; and girls are heavier users of video chat and photo sharing applications.
- Ethnic differences have been observed in relation to the types of platforms used. For example, a 2012 survey indicated that white youth tend to favor sites such as Facebook, while MySpace use was more common among Hispanic youth and African-American youth tend to favor microblogging sites such as Twitter.

Teens embrace a range of social media technologies

Fourth, augmenting their general use of common social networking platforms such as Facebook, teens have embraced social media in other ways. As Web 2.0 technologies have become more ubiquitous, they have created new opportunities for young people to engage with one another with increasing efficiency.

Photo sharing via social networks and mobile social media applications is a pervasive teen practice, particularly among teenage girls. Among 12- to 17-year-olds, 88 percent of girls and 71 percent of boys report posting photos or videos to social network sites, 79 percent of girls and 60 percent of boys reported having "tagged" others in posted photos, and 83 percent of teens reported commenting on friends' pictures.

Teens are also increasingly interacting with each other via video through tools such as iChat, Skype, Facetime, and Google Hangouts. Thirty-seven percent of teens aged 12 to 17 (33 percent of boys and 42 percent of girls) report having used such technology (Lenhart, 2012). The expansion of video use has been driven largely by technological factors that have made video chat increasingly accessible. Industry projections estimate that these figures will continue to grow well into the future. Hence, while text-based communications via SMS and instant messaging remain a dominant form of interaction for certain purposes, video-based interactions also seem to be staking out a place among the pantheon of adolescents' digital communications.

Teens use social media to connect to their broader culture

Fifth, teens have harnessed social media to connect and interact with the broader society and culture. Twenty-seven percent of teens have created and posted videos to YouTube and other online video sites; 13 percent reported streaming live video to the Internet; and Twitter use has grown exponentially, increasing from 16% of teens in 2011 to 24% in 2013 (Lenhart, 2012; Madden et al. 2013). The context of these activities, as well as their associated implications for youth identity and development, will be addressed as part of the next section.

■ TECHNOLOGY AND THE ADOLESCENT EXPERIENCE

The figures and trends cited above leave little question that digital communications have become a ubiquitous presence in the lives of teens, and that young people are nimble adopters of new media technologies. The numbers, however, tell only a small part of the story. Critically, one must also consider the **context** within which these technologies are employed and how they interact with the adolescent experience. Such an analysis requires looking beyond patterns of adoption and usage and toward a deeper understanding of how digital communication technology interacts with the essential elements of teens' developmental experiences such as learning, pursuing autonomy, and forging identity and relationships. The remainder of this chapter examines the nexus between emerging communication technology and the adolescent experience.

An evolving understanding

While the rapid pace of change surrounding the digital environment has created a "moving target" for researchers, recent years have produced a growing research literature examining the ways in which central facets of the adolescent experience—experimentation, identity development, engagement with the broader society, exploration of friendship and intimacy—have been transposed into the digital era.

Within this growing body of research, two initiatives in particular have provided significant insights concerning the opportunities and occasional perils of growing up in the rapidly changing digital environment—the MacArthur-funded Digital Youth Project and the Pew Internet and American Life Project.

The Digital Youth Project, funded through the MacArthur Foundation, drew upon the work of a multidisciplinary team of researchers who conducted a comprehensive ethnographic study of teens' experiences growing up in the age of new media. The study interviewed over 800 youth and young adults on matters relating to the role of communication technology in their social relationships, daily activities, learning, and personal growth and exploration. The study also conducted over 5,000 hours of observations of young people's social interactions and other activities within online environments (Ito et al., 2009).

The Pew Internet and American Life Project provides a rich array of survey data pertaining to the use of digital communication technology among both teens and adults in the United States. As the digital era has unfolded, Pew has conducted regular surveys of teens and adults based on nationally representative phone-based samples. Beyond revealing general trends in usage, the data derived from the Pew surveys also delved into the manner in which teens use digital technology in their social relationships. Coupled with interviews and ethnographic research such as that conducted through the MacArthur project, these data provide valuable perspectives on the emerging role of technology in the lives of U.S. teenagers.

Learning, engagement, and participatory culture

In 2006, media theorist Henry Jenkins and colleagues published a monograph describing the role of Web 2.0 in promoting the ideals of a "participatory culture" in which young people become active agents—rather than passive consumers—of information, culture, and knowledge. Building on his prior work related to participatory culture within offline fan communities, Jenkins argued that the opportunities linked to Web 2.0 technologies presented a new paradigm for self-expression, education, and civic engagement (Jenkins, 2006).

The growth in participatory culture has been made possible, in large part, by technologies that remove many of the traditional barriers between creators and consumers of media, particularly those related to time, money, and expertise. For example, the blogging platforms and Web publishing tools have allowed teens to establish online platforms for sharing their ideas and perspectives with the broader world, without the need for Web design expertise. Initiatives such as Wikipedia have provided platforms for the crowd sourcing of information and knowledge. Inexpensive access to the hardware and software allowing the production of video or musical content—along with the development of platforms such as YouTube that permit the sharing of such content—have provided new outlets for creative expression that allow anyone with a computer and the desire to become active participants in shaping popular culture.

For teens, these and related developments have created immense opportunities for exploration of interests, self-expression, learning, and societal engagement—opportunities that simply were not available to prior generations.

Exploring interests—Web 2.0 has presented spaces for young people to pursue their interests and passions. James Gee refers to these as "affinity spaces"—venues of informal learning in which participants are joined by a common series of interests and or purpose. Among their defined attributes, affinity spaces welcome a broad range of participants ranging from "newbies" to masters; defy boundaries of age, race, class culture, ethnicity, or gender; thrive on content generated through user interactions; and maintain porous leadership boundaries (Gee, 2005).

Translated into adolescent processes of exploration and emerging self-identity, affinity spaces can be immensely empowering. Rather than being defined by age, appearance, or other characteristics, one achieves standing based primarily on knowledge, expertise, and contributions to the group. The MacArthur researchers—referring to youth engagement with affinity spaces as "geeking out"—note that this type of engagement can provide adolescents who might otherwise be socially marginalized with a viable outlet for self-expression, socialization, and interaction with others who have similar interests. Moreover, the egalitarian nature of affinity spaces means that youth may be on equal footing with older and more experienced participants, and may find viable outlets for learning and development.

Informal learning—Beyond their role in teens' emerging self-identity and self-efficacy, affinity spaces may empower young people to serve as agents for their own learning and development. Jenkins notes that the informal, self-directed learning that occurs within the context of affinity spaces carries significant implications for systems of formal education. He suggests that schools must look beyond themselves as purveyors of knowledge and toward models where they are capable of leveraging the opportunities presented by the new digital landscape. Along similar lines, Cathy Davidson has argued that the massive changes in the way young people interact with and learn from technology calls for nothing short of a revolution in the way our schools and educational systems view the learning process (Davidson, 2012).

Public engagement—The rise of Web-enabled participatory culture has also afforded young people opportunities to engage with their communities and the broader society. The nature and extent of this engagement has emerged as a matter of some debate—based on certain types of indicators, some have argued that young people are increasingly more self-absorbed and alienated from the public sphere. Bennett distinguishes between two schools of thought in this regard—the "disengaged youth" and the "engaged youth" paradigms (Bennett, 2008). The disengaged youth perspective maintains that young people have become increasingly removed from mainstream social institutions, as indicated by measures such as declining voting behaviors and public affairs news consumption. The alternative "engaged youth" perspective suggests that such metrics do not account for other ways in which youth have engaged with society. According to this perspective, young people, lacking trust in public institutions and maintaining a general cynicism about political discourse and the mainstream political landscape, have engaged with society on a different level and have sought out alternative channels of engagement. In the words of Bennett, this paradigm "implicitly emphasizes generational changes in social identity that have resulted in the growing importance of peer networks and online communities."

The reality appears to lie somewhere in between. Citing data pointing to an "activation gap" between youths' desire to engage with their communities and the actual extent of this engagement, Rheingold suggests that the most viable path forward is to develop modes of engagement that allow young people to translate their voices from the private to the public sphere. Drawing a linkage between participatory engagement, young peoples' identity development, and new media literacy, he suggests that one's "voice, the unique style of personal expression that distinguishes one's communications from those of others, can be called upon to help connect young people's energetic involvement in identity-formation with their potential engagement with society as citizens. Moving from a private to a public voice can help students turn their self-expression into a form of public participation" (Rheingold, 2008a, p. 25).

Defining culture—One prominent feature of Web 2.0 has been the role of social media on the shaping of popular culture. By providing both the tools for that creation and repurposing of creative content, and the outlets for distributing that content, technology has helped to redefine the rules through which cultural touchstones are developed and diffused across society. Nowhere has this been more apparent than in the explosive growth of YouTube, which has simultaneously served as a source of entertainment, an outlet for disseminating creative content, and both a reflection and shaper of popular culture. Young people have indeed been at the forefront of driving this trend and have embraced online video as a dominant medium for entertainment, sharing with friends, and self-expression.

Friendship and peer connections

Having addressed the broader contexts of adolescents' learning and societal engagement, we now turn to an issue of paramount concern to most teenagers—peer relationships. The establishment and maintenance of peer relationships has long been recognized as central to the adolescent experience, with the ebbs and flows of these relationships defining the contours of teenagers' lives and sense of well-being. Given this, it is not surprising that teens have embraced social media as a means of social bonding and connection.

A common adult narrative surrounding teenagers' use of technologies such as texting and social media has been that these forms of communication have substituted for face-to-face interaction, leading teens to adopt a more superficial view of friendship and social connection. Yet despite commonly held notions that social media have **supplanted** "real world" relationships, it is perhaps more accurate to suggest that social media **augment** such relationships. Indeed, the vast majority of teenagers' online interactions are with peers they know from familiar settings such as schools, clubs, religious organizations, and sports activities (Ito et al., 2010).

Viewed through this lens, social media may possess certain positive attributes. First, in contrast with offline "hangout" venues, which are typically constrained by factors such as time, location, and transportation logistics, online venues provide opportunities for interaction that transcend these constraints. Online social spaces allow teens to maintain connections with their peers from virtually any location and at virtually any time, expanding opportunities for interaction and—at least potentially—enriching the depth of teens' social lives.

Second, social networks may expand social opportunities by redefining the boundaries that have traditionally existed across groups within familiar social settings such as schools. Although teens continue to maintain inner circles of friends, social media have expanded teens' web of social connections to encompass a broader peer network. While these extended notions of friendship and connection have often produced some measure of eye-rolling on the part of many adults (e.g., the idea that Facebook "friends" aren't really friends), this phenomenon may be more alternatively viewed as a positive expansion of teens' social horizons.

Third, by extending the opportunities for peer engagement, social media may, under appropriate conditions, alleviate some of the common teen anxieties surrounding social relationships and interactions. When asked about the impacts of social media use on their well-being, higher proportions of teens cite positive impacts than negative ones. According to a 2012 survey conducted by Common Sense Media, more than one in four teens say that social networking makes them feel less shy and more outgoing; one in five say it makes them feel more confident, more popular, and more sympathetic to others; and one in seven say it makes them feel better about themselves. In contrast, 5 percent or fewer teens indicated that social networking makes them feel less outgoing, worse about themselves, more depressed, less confident, and less popular. These negative sentiments are indeed cause for concern, as will be discussed shortly. However, for current purposes it should be noted that young people tend to view the impact of social media on their well-being in generally positive terms.

Results from the Common Sense survey also challenge the notion that social media have led teens to devalue face-to-face interaction. In fact, the data strongly suggest that teens are generally aware of the disruptive potential of social media—significantly higher proportions of teens say that they prefer face-to-face interactions to texting as a mode of communication; nearly half expressed frustration with their friends' use of texting and social media while in their company; and more than a third indicate that they sometimes wished that they could go back to a time when there was no Facebook.

Notably, the survey results also suggest that teens recognize the potential impact of technology on their family life and are concerned about their parents' digital behaviors—more than one in four youth indicated that their parents may have addictions to their mobile devices that are comparable to their own. This finding challenges two pervasive notions—first, that teens are desensitized to the potential effects of digital technology on relationships; and second, that these types of effects are somehow confined to youth.

Perils and negative impacts

The above examination challenges common narratives holding that digital communications invariably impede youths' positive social development and make teens more disconnected from peers and others. The benefits of social media in the lives of teens—improvements in certain metrics of well-being, expansion of venues for interaction among friends, and the extension of social circles—all may be viewed as positive byproducts.

At the same time, however, one must also recognize the various risks of negative social experiences that may be attributed to, or amplified by, social media. Some of these experiences may be related to deliberate meanness and aggression, while others may reflect less obvious and perhaps more insidious effects.

Overt aggression and meanness

The first series of risks to youth involve overt manifestations of aggression, meanness, and cruelty in digital environments—a topic that has attracted significant research attention in recent years (MTV, Pew). Data from these and other studies suggest that exposure to aggressive and mean behavior is a fairly routine part of teenagers' online social experience.

- 2011 survey data from Pew suggest that 88 percent of teens report having witnessed mean or cruel behavior occurring on social networking sites, with 12 percent indicating that they witnessed such behavior "frequently," 29 percent "sometimes," and 47 percent "once in a while."
- Approximately 9 percent of teens reported being bullied via text message and 8 percent in an online setting in the previous 12 months. By contrast, 12 percent reported having been bullied in person during that period. These data suggest that while online aggression (aka cyber-bullying) may affect many youth, it is more common that teens are victims of bullying within offline settings.
- Just over two thirds of teens surveyed (69 percent) believe that people are mostly kind on social network sites, compared to 20 percent who believed that people are mostly unkind. These effects, however, appeared to vary by demographics, with black teens, teens in urban environments, and younger teen girls (12 and 13) more likely to report that people are mostly unkind.

Certainly, peer-based meanness and aggression is not a new phenomenon within the teen experience. Indeed, many have suggested that online bullying and aggression may have much in common with offline aggression. Nevertheless, online settings present a unique series of challenges and issues.

Unrelenting nature of online conflicts—The first unique challenge stems from the "always on" nature of social media and digital communications, and the associated impact on the dynamics of peer conflict. Prior to the growth of social media, teens had built-in downtime from their social relationships and interactions. In cases involving conflict between teens, this provided a natural "decompression" period in which youth might have time and inclination to reflect, gather perspective, and seek guidance. Social media, by virtue of their relentlessly persistent nature, have undermined this mode of de-escalation and may easily contribute to an intensification of conflict. As such, digital communication venues may intensify peer-based social conflicts by depriving teens of the downtime that might otherwise dissipate the tension surrounding these conflicts.

Public dynamics of online conflicts—A related phenomenon involves the public and open nature of social network activity and the attendant potential for other teens to become involved in interpersonal conflicts. Particularly as technology has evolved, interactions that were once bilateral in nature have become increasingly open to a broader group of participants. Conflicts tend to increasingly play out in public spaces such as via Twitter feeds and Facebook walls. Not only does this enhance the potential volatility of conflict situations, but it also potentially amplifies harm by fostering greater shame and embarrassment experienced by youth on the receiving end of online aggression.

Porous boundaries of offline and online—A further consideration concerns the fact that the barriers between online and offline bullying behaviors are often quite porous. That is, many acts of online aggression may be closely linked to patterns of physical or psychological aggression that are manifested in offline environments. This presents particular challenges to educational systems, which most often deal with the fact that conflicts within school settings typically spill over into online venues outside of school.

More subtle impacts

> Because we're often using our computers in a social context, to converse with friends or colleagues, to create "profiles" of ourselves, to broadcast our thoughts through blog posts or Facebook updates, our social standing is, in one way or another, always in play, always at risk. (Carr, 2011, p. 118)

The effects of social media on the dynamics of overt meanness and aggression are indeed cause for concern. These effects, however, are not the only social landmines facing teens engaged with online peer interactions. Beyond their potential role as conduits for direct meanness and cruelty, online interactions may affect youth negatively in more subtle ways.

The above quote from Nicholas Carr captures a core paradox related to teen online experiences—at the same time that technology-mediated social relationships may mitigate teens' anxieties surrounding presentation of their "social selves," they also may amplify normal adolescent struggles surrounding their self-image and sense of belonging. The 2012 Common Sense Media teen survey indicated that more than one in three teenage girls and one in five teenage boys reported being stressed out about how they look in online photos, and that 45 percent of girls and 24 percent of boys indicated that they worried about people posting ugly pictures of them online.

When populating their pages on social networks, youth and adults alike tend to favor positive imagery. Although research suggests that social network participants' self-portrayals tend to be fairly accurate in their general representations (Back et al., 2010), there is also a tendency for people to emphasize the positive and de-emphasize the negative. For example, shared photos are more likely to depict smiling faces than frowning ones, and status updates are more likely to convey control than to expose vulnerability. Teens value social media precisely because they permit this type of manipulation of their persona—far more so than would be the case in the offline world.

From the perspective of the image creator, such manipulation might be viewed as a positive attribute of social media—they afford one the opportunity to contemplate and craft one's "outward-facing" image, similar to the way one might choose clothing or hairstyle. Yet from the perspective of those observing these images, the effects may be far from benign. Although on a cognitive level, most teens implicitly understand that online personas may be crafted and sugarcoated, there are likely significant subconscious impacts on teens' sense of their own happiness and well-being. To this general point, research has suggested that frequency of Facebook use may be negatively associated with one's sense of happiness in relation to others and one's sense of life's overall fairness (Kross et al., 2013).

Online interactions may also interact with, and in some cases exacerbate, teens' fear of social isolation. Being "left out" is a major source of teen social anxiety and inclusion is part of a fundamental need (Hartup, 1996). The highly public nature of online networks increases the likelihood that teens will become aware of activities from which they may have been excluded. Indeed, 47 percent of surveyed teens (57 percent of girls and 28 percent of boys) indicate that they sometimes feel left out when viewing pictures of others. To compensate, teens' online social participation may become something akin to a compulsion, driven by their concerns about missing out on activities within their social circle. To quote Carr again, "If they stop sending messages, they risk becoming invisible." (Carr, p. 118)

In sum, the opportunities afforded by social media for one to craft one's self-image and present it in the most positive light may indeed provide certain benefits for teens seeking to forge their identity. Yet at the same time, we must recognize that teens viewing the images of others may not always be fully attuned to their sugarcoated nature and may in turn experience amplified feelings of anxiety and insecurity.

▪ INTIMACY AND SEXUALITY

Beyond the forging of friendships, the establishment and exploration of intimacy emerges as a central element of the adolescent experience. Just as social media may carry both positive and negative implications for teens' general peer interactions, an equivalent set of phenomena may be observed in teens' pursuit and exploration of intimate relationships. As with peer friendships, dating, romance, and intimacy in the digital era is best understood as a confluence between the generation-agnostic realities of the adolescent experience and the shifting norms and behaviors among the millennial generation of teens.

In Chapter 5, we will address the shifting modes of sexual expression as mediated by digital technology, focusing on a constellation of behaviors commonly referred to as "sexting." For current purposes of providing context for other discussions in this volume, we briefly present two factors for consideration—the ways in which digital communication has altered the contours of dating and courtship, and some ways in which the digital era has affected cultural norms surrounding sexuality.

The new world of dating and courtship

The researchers from the MacArthur digital project focused a significant part of their analysis on examining the rituals and practices of digital youth surrounding the forging of intimate relationships (Pascoe, 2009). Framing the examination of the role of social media in teens' intimate relationships, C. J. Pascoe chronicles the evolution of dating practices during the twentieth century. She notes that "dating" as we know it is a relatively recent form of courtship and that adolescent relationships had been heavily mediated by families for most of modern history.

Pascoe notes the emancipating effects of technology on giving youth greater autonomy in the pursuit of intimate relationships, in particular drawing parallels between the rise of the automobile during the postwar era and the more recent rise of social media. Just as the automobile emancipated teens from the constraints of the home environment, the rise of social media has provided teens with venues in which teens can "meet people, flirt, date, and break up beyond the earshot and eyesight of their parents and other adults while also doing these things in front of all their online friends." (Pascoe, 2009, p. 145)

The MacArthur findings remind us that we are operating in a fundamentally different era in terms of both parental supervision and peer relationships. Regarding the former, mechanisms of parental monitoring have been greatly diminished—prior to the advent of mobile phones and digital social media, teens depended on shared, home-based landlines as primary vehicles of communication. This technology, by being confined to the home space, afforded parents at least a marginal level of ability to monitor the activities of their teenagers. The expansion of cellphone adoption and the "silent" medium of texting, along with the growth of online social networking, has emancipated teens from the watchful eyes of their parents. What this means, quite simply, is that teenagers are far more autonomous than young people in prior generations.

As for the latter, romantic relationships and the dynamics behind them have become increasingly visible within the public sphere of the peer group. Not only may the status of one's relationships may be clearly stated in one's Facebook profile, but the significant connectivity of social networks has made it increasingly the case that teenagers' relationships often unfold within the context of social networks. Similarly, the process of disengaging from a relationship is also often a public event. In the aftermath of such breakups, teenagers typically remain within the social circle of their former relationship and remain attuned to that person's continued activities, including new romantic relationships.

Thus, the rise of social media has created an important paradox in the realm of teenagers' exploration of dating and intimacy—their activities are simultaneously **more private** in that they are insulated from parental supervision and **more public** in that they often unfold within spaces accessible by peers.

The dynamics of romance and courtship are also affected by a similar range of factors noted earlier in our discussion of friendship and peer relationships. The "always on" culture promoted by texting, social networking, the availability of video chat, and a constant barrage of new apps and mobile technology has profoundly altered the manner in which teens interact with one another. In the context of romance and courtship, this capacity creates an environment of persistent communication, providing little "breathing space" that may be essential to the building and maintenance of healthy relationships.

All of these factors—insulation from parents, the pervasive nature of social media, limitations on privacy within the peer group, and the public nature of breakups—converge to create a challenging environment within which teenagers must navigate their emerging explorations of intimacy and romantic attachment.

Digital media, sex, and popular culture

Another set of issues involves the ways in which the new media landscape has affected cultural notions of intimacy and sexuality. Shifting norms of sexuality and sexual expression are certainly not unique to the digital era and have been sources of intergenerational conflict for quite some time. There are, however, certain unique challenges that have been presented by the rise of the Internet.

First, the Internet has expanded access to sexually explicit content and pornography. This increased access, coupled with the reality of teens' sexual identity development and exploration, has meant that teens are far more likely to be exposed to explicit sexual material than teens in prior generations. A study by Mitchell and colleagues indicated that the percentage of youth experiencing unwanted exposure to pornography grew significantly between 2000 and 2005—this increase was particularly pronounced for those in the youngest age cohort (those between the ages of 10 and 12), for whom such exposure more than doubled, growing from 9 percent to 19 percent (Mitchell, Finkelhor, & Wolak, 2003). Another study of college students indicated that 93 percent of males and 62 percent of females reported exposure to online pornography during adolescence (Sabina, Wolak, & Finkelhor, 2008). Coupled with the exponential growth of Internet adoption since 2005 among youth of all ages, it is likely that children and teenagers in 2013 have been exposed to sexually explicit content at even greater rates.

Second, there is indeed an intersection between digital technology, celebrity culture in the era of YouTube, and shifting modes of sexual expression. Teenagers are routinely exposed to stories of celebrity sex tapes that show up online, "sexting" among celebrities, and sexual content on prime-time TV. Related to this, sexual content and humor has become far more accessible and has fundamentally altered the ways in which adolescents, particularly girls, view the dynamics and expectations associated with sexual relationships (Kim et al., 2007; Tolman et al., 2007).

In a later chapter, we will explore how these factors may translate into certain unhealthy or risky teen digital behaviors in the form of "sexting." For current purposes, however, it should be recognized that these developments—increased exposure to explicit sexual content and implicit cultural acceptance—are far from benign. Rather, they carry significant implications for the ways in which youth perceive "normative" sexuality and in turn view their own notions of healthy relationships and their own sexual identities.

■ CONCLUSION: THE WORLD OF DIGITAL YOUTH IN CONTEXT

While much is made of the "digital divide," this appears to be less a function of the use of digital and mobile communications, which also seems to be growing significantly among adults, but rather a function of the roles of digital communication in their broader lives. By their nature, teens are predominantly focused on social interactions with their peers, while adults come with a more diverse array of concerns, including those related to work and family.

Clearly there are a range of critical issues related to youth safety and well-being in the digital age. Under certain circumstances, digital media may be used for overt expressions of aggression. Additionally, when coupled with broader cultural messages, the dynamics of the online environment may contribute to adolescents' feelings of inadequacy, depression, and other factors related to teen anxiety. Moreover, the "always on" nature of digital communications may under certain circumstances produce new problems that are not inherent to offline environments.

At the same time, we must acknowledge the opportunities that social media provide to youth in expanding their horizons, finding their place in society, engaging in self-expression, and augmenting their friendships and intimate relationships. As such, parents, educators, policymakers, industry, and those concerned with the well-being of youth are wise to remain attuned to both the promises and perils of the online environment. Ultimately, our policies and practices should be guided by a few basic principles—minimizing harm, recognizing opportunities for engagement and growth, and providing teens with the foundation for developing healthy and robust social relationships.

■ DISCLOSURE

Andrew J. Harris has no conflicts to disclose.

■ REFERENCES

Back, M. D., Stopfer, J. M., Vazire, S., Gaddis, S., Schmukle, S. C., Egloff, B., & Gosling, S. D. (2010). Facebook profiles reflect actual personality, not self-idealization. *Psychological Science, 21*(3), 372–374. doi:10.1177/0956797609360756

Bennett, W. Lance. "Changing Citizenship in the Digital Age." Civic Life Online: Learning How Digital Media Can Engage Youth. In W. Lance Bennett. The John D. and Catherine T., eds. *MacArthur Foundation Series on Digital Media and Learning* (pp. 1–24). Cambridge, MA: The MIT Press. doi: 10.1162/dmal.9780262524827.001

Carr, N. (2011). The shallows: What the Internet is doing to our brains. WW Norton & Company.

Common Sense Media (2012). Social Media, Social Life: How Teens View Their Digital Lives. Accessed January 15, 2013 from http://www.commonsensemedia.org/research/social-media-social-life

Davidson, C. N. (2012). *Now you see it: How technology and brain science will transform schools and business for the 21st century* (p. 352). Penguin Books. Retrieved from http://www.amazon.com/Now-You-See-Technology-Transform/dp/014312126X

Emarketer (2013). US Cellphone and Smartphone Users, By Age. www.eMarketer.com.

Gee, J. P. (2005). Semiotic social spaces and affinity spaces. In: *Beyond communities of practice* (pp. 214–232). Cambridge: Cambridge University Press.

Hartup, W. W. (1996). The company they keep: Friendships and their developmental significance. *Child Development, 67*(1), 1–13.

Hilbert, M., & López, P. (2011). The world's technological capacity to store, communicate, and compute information. *Science, 332*(6025), 60–65.

Ito, M., Baumer, S., Bittanti, M., Boyd, D., Cody, R., Herr-Stephenson, B., et al. (2009). *Hanging out, messing around, and geeking out: kids living and learning with new media.* Cambridge: MIT Press.

Jenkins, H. (2006). *Fans, bloggers, and gamers: Exploring participatory culture.* NYU Press.

Jenkins, H. (2009). *Confronting the challenges of participatory culture: Media education for the 21st century.* The MIT Press.

Kaplan, A. M., & Haenlein, M. (2010). Users of the world, unite! The challenges and opportunities of Social Media. *Business horizons, 53*(1), 59–68.

Kim, J. L., Lynn Sorsoli, C., Collins, K., Zylbergold, B. A., Schooler, D., & Tolman, D. L. (2007). From sex to sexuality: Exposing the heterosexual script on primetime network television. *Journal of Sex Research, 44*(2), 145–157.

Kross, E., Verduyn, P., Demiralp, E., Park, J., Lee, D. S., Lin, N., & Ybarra, O. (2013). Facebook use predicts declines in subjective well-being in young adults. *PloS one, 8*(8), e69841.

Lenhart (2012). Teens and Online Video. Pew Internet & American Life Project. Accessed November 7, 2013 from http://www.pewinternet.org/Reports/2012/Teens-and-online-video.aspx

Madden, M. Lenhart, A., Cortesi, S., Gasser, U., et al. (2013). Teens, Social Media, and Privacy. Pew Internet & American Life Project. Accessed November 7, 2013 from http://www.pewinternet.org/Reports/2013/Teens-Social-Media-And-Privacy.aspx

Mitchell, K. J., Finkelhor, D., & Wolak, J. (2003). The Exposure Of Youth To Unwanted Sexual Material On The Internet A National Survey of Risk, Impact, and Prevention. *Youth & Society, 34*(3), 330–358.

O'Reilly, T., & Battelle, J. (2009). Web squared: Web 2.0 five years on. *Web 2.0 Summit*. Retrieved from http://gossgrove.com/sites/default/files/web2009_websquared-whitepaper.pdf

Pascoe, C. J. (2009). Intimacy. In M. Ito, ed. *Hanging out, messing around, and geeking out: kids living and learning with new media*. Cambridge: MIT Press.

Pew Internet and American Life Project (2012). Teen and Young Adult Internet Use. Accessed November 7, 2013 from http://www.pewresearch.org/millennials/teen-internet-use-graphic/

Rheingold, H. (2008a). Using Social Media to Teach Social Media. *New England Journal of Higher Education, 23*(1), 25–26.

Rheingold, H. (2008b). "Using Participatory Media and Public Voice to Encourage Civic Engagement." Civic Life Online: Learning How Digital Media Can Engage Youth. In W. Lance Bennett. The John D. and Catherine T, eds. *MacArthur Foundation Series on Digital Media and Learning* (pp. 97–118). Cambridge, MA: The MIT Press. doi: 10.1162/dmal.9780262524827.097

Sabina, C., Wolak, J., & Finkelhor, D. (2008). The nature and dynamics of Internet pornography exposure for youth. *CyberPsychology & Behavior, 11*(6), 691–693.

Shirky, C. (2008). *Here comes everybody: The power of organizing without organizations*. Penguin.

Smith, A. (2013). Civic Engagement in the Internet Age. Pew Reseaerch Center. Accessed 11/7/13 from http://pewinternet.org/Reports/2013/Civic-Engagement.aspx

Tolman, D. L., Kim, J. L., Schooler, D., & Sorsoli, C. L. (2007). Rethinking the associations between television viewing and adolescent sexuality development: Bringing gender into focus. *Journal of Adolescent Health, 40*(1), 84–89.

Turkle, S. (2012). *Alone together: Why we expect more from technology and less from each other*. Basic Books.

3 Sexual Development and Behavior in Children and Adolescents

■ H. MARTIN MALIN AND
FABIAN M. SALEH

■ INTRODUCTION

The study of sexual development of children and adolescents, particularly the development of sexual behaviors, is one of the more difficult and risky of all academic pursuits. It therefore should come as no surprise that our knowledge of childhood and adolescent sexual development is incomplete. Additionally, much of what we believe we know may or may not be accurate.

In this chapter, we present a comprehensive review of the extant literature on "normal" sexuality and sexual development and behavior in children and adolescents. First, we discuss the sources of information concerning child and adolescent sexual development and some methodological limitations of performing such research, including the plethora of sociocultural obstacles and constraints inherent in such work. Next, we focus on the biological and psychosocial aspects of the trajectory of sexual development, from the perinatal and prepubertal acquisition of sexual behavior and knowledge to the sexual behaviors seen in puberty and throughout adolescence. We conclude with a review of current assessment methods, which help distinguish sexual behaviors that are "normal" from those that are "abnormal."

■ SOURCES OF INFORMATION ABOUT SEXUAL DEVELOPMENT AND METHODOLOGICAL ISSUES

Research about child and adolescent sexuality is premised upon demonstrable evidence that sexual behaviors are present in the normal developmental sequences of all primates, including humans. In contrast, one of the most pervasive and deeply held beliefs in twenty-first-century America and, to a greater or lesser degree elsewhere in industrialized cultures, is that children who have not been sexually abused are normally asexual until puberty intrudes upon their state of prelapsarian innocence (Jackson, 1990).

For many individuals, the notion that prepubertal children normally engage in behaviors adults would label as sexual or display some degree of sexual knowledge, absent a history of sexual abuse, is an anathema. Yet research has clearly demonstrated that even young children exhibit a broad range of sexual behaviors in the absence of a demonstrated abuse history and that even sexually intrusive behavior displayed by children may not always be indicative of pathology (Friedrich, 2003).

Cultural imperatives abound concerning what are, or should be, appropriate levels of sexual knowledge for non-adults. There is also a widespread cultural belief, despite evidence to the contrary, that discussing sexual matters with children and adolescents may incite unhealthy premature interest in sexual matters or cause significant trauma or at least unnecessary distress (Lenderyou, 1994). Clearly such is not the case with formal sex education curricula. In a literature review of the impact of sex education programs on adolescents, Visser and van Bilsen (1994) found that sex education increased knowledge about sexuality and often brought about a more liberal and tolerant attitude toward sexuality but did not appear to have an impact on adolescent sexual intercourse. More recent investigations suggest that sex education, far from having a negative impact on children and adolescents, reduces risky sexual behaviors and postpones the age of first intercourse in both males and females (Mueller, Gavin, & Kulkarni, 2008).

While it is clear that talking with children and adolescents about sex in the context of formal sex education poses no particular risk for distress or trauma, the traumatic effects of research inquiring about sexual knowledge and practices is less well documented. O'Sullivan and colleagues (2000) conducted a Reaction-to-Study interview of 98 boys (ages 7 to 13) and their mothers following a study on the development of problem sexual behaviors as part of a longitudinal study of disruptive behaviors in high-risk boys. While a significant number of the boys were reticent to talk about sexual matters, participants generally reported a positive experience with the interview overall. The authors concluded that "significant distress on behalf of children who participate in interviews on sex seems unwarranted" (O'Sullivan, Meyer-Bahlburg, & Wasserman, 2000).

Much research on Western childhood sexuality comes from Northern European and Scandinavian countries, where attitudes toward sexuality are more permissive than in the United States. Therefore, results from these studies may not be generalizable to other cultures (Gordon & Schroeder, 1995). Several ethnographic studies of non-Western cultures include observations of childhood sexual behavior, and while anthropology has not focused extensively on children's sexuality, childhood sexual behavior has been recorded in many cultures. This includes, for example, Trobriand Islanders (Malinowski, 1927), the Samoans (Mead, 1928, 1933), the Canela (Crocker & Crocker, 1994), the Mehinaku (Gregor, 1985), and the Sambia (Herdt, 1993). The broad outlines of sexual developmental patterns appear not to be culture-bound (Currier, 1981), although Montgomery (2009) points out that there is a large gap in our knowledge about how children understand their own sexual experiences. She cautions that childhood sexual experience and understanding of that experience must be considered within its cultural context (Montgomery, 2009).

Much of our current knowledge about the behavioral aspects of developmental sexology comes from studies that rely heavily upon retrospective self-reports

(Kinsey, Pomeroy, & Martin, 1948; Kinsey, Pomeroy, Martin, & Gebhard, 1953; Ramsey, 1950; Rotheram-Borus et al., 1992a, 1992b). In the case of the Kinsey "Male Volume," retrospective data on male children included reports of sexual behavior by "trained" participant-observers (Kinsey et al., 1948), a circumstance that has occasioned much controversy ("Allegations," n.d.).

Other investigators, as well as Kinsey and his colleagues, have also sought parents' or caregivers' reports of childrens' observed sexual behaviors (Achenbach, 1991; W. N. Friedrich, Grambsch, Broughton, Kuiper, & Beilke, 1991; Gunderson, Melas, & Skar, 1981; Rosenfeld et al., 1984; Sears, Macoby, & Levin, 1957). While this approach has yielded considerable information, it is not without significant limitations (Meyer-Bahlburg, & Steel, 2003).

The current barriers to research on child and adolescent sexuality are largely, but not exclusively, sociocultural. This includes the belief among a myriad of gate-keepers that children are incapable of providing informed consent to participate in research on their own behalf. Another such belief is rooted in the Romantic vision of the child as pure and innocent (Higonnet, 1998), therefore asexual. According to this belief, "premature" exposure to sexual matters may lead to spiritual, emotional, and/or physical damage. In more modern dress, concerns about child abuse also contribute to the difficulty of conducting research about childhood sexuality (Montgomery, 2012). Research questions or protocols may be construed by parents or children as innately abusive.

In addition, sex research with children and adolescents, as with adults, is technically difficult. Except in the case of very young children, the socialization process ensures that sexual behavior occurs largely in private, so that direct observation is an unlikely event. Even with the youngest of children, direct observation of sexual behavior is typically limited to individuals, such as parents, preschool workers, and nannies, who care for the child on a regular basis and assist in bathing, toileting, and feeding. It is unusual for these caregivers, even if they recognize a behavior as sexual, to systematically observe and report on the behaviors encountered.

A few investigators have attempted to gather information from children by direct questioning (Broderick, 1966; Elias & Gebhard, 1969; Ramsay, 1943, 1950). Given current social norms, conducting additional studies of this type appears unlikely. Furthermore, children themselves, especially younger children, may not be particularly amenable to study by direct questioning since it is not clear that how a child conceptualizes and describes sexual behaviors is congruent with the meaning intended by an adult questioner (Volbert, 2000). In general, interviewing children and adolescents about sexual knowledge or behavior is more problematic than it is with adults (O'Sullivan et al., 2000).

A further source of difficulty in conducting research on child and adolescent sexuality is funding. Support for research on child and adolescent sexuality is a significant barrier to research since public and private granting agencies may be reticent to underwrite research seen by their boards or constituents as controversial (O'Sullivan et al., 2000). Additionally, since much research on human development is dependent upon funding administered by institutions of higher learning, Institutional Review Boards (IRBs), charged with protecting human subjects and, not incidentally, limiting liability to their respective institutions, may also mirror social reticence surrounding the study of childhood and adolescent sexuality and impede research (Sieber & Baluyot, 1992). Ceci found that proposed research into "socially sensitive topics" is twice as likely to be rejected by IRBs as research investigating less socially sensitive questions (Ceci, Peters, & Plotkin, 1985).

Not all aspects of sexuality in children or adolescents seem equally socially problematic to investigate. Studies of physical development and maturation are perhaps the least controversial for investigation and often yield information from which behavioral information may be inferred (Smith, Udry, & Morris, 1985; Udry, 1990; Udry, Talbert, & Morris, 1986). Studies of sexual patterns in childhood and adolescence, focusing more narrowly on behaviors absent the context of abuse-generated pathology, are more controversial. Research in developmental sexology thus tends to bifurcate into "acceptable" and "unacceptable" areas of study that mirror social values about "acceptable" and "unacceptable" sexual behaviors at a given age or stage. Accordingly, the knowledge base of the less value-laden anatomical and physiological trajectories of sexual development is more comprehensive and mature than the knowledge base of the more value-laden psychobehavioral trajectories.

■ STAGES OF SEXUAL DEVELOPMENT

For convenience, child and adolescent sexual development may be examined in narrowly defined age ranges, as are other developmental phenomena, including a prenatal period, infancy (birth to 2 years), early childhood (3 to 5 years), late childhood (6 to 10 years), early adolescence (11 to 13 years), middle adolescence (15 to 17 years), and late adolescence (18 and 19 years).

Puberty and early adolescence are often considered to be synonymous and may be operationally defined as the one or two years of rapid growth preceding the acquisition of the ability to reproduce. Most commonly, in girls, the onset of puberty is defined as thelarche (onset of breast development) and sexual maturity is marked by menarche approximately two years later. For most girls, however, menarche does not precisely coincide with the ability to reproduce since mature ova may not be produced for another two years or more. In boys the onset of puberty is less precise but is generally agreed to be semenarche, as evidenced in ejaculation during masturbation or nocturnal emission. The presence of mature spermatozoa in urine is generally considered evidence of male sexual maturity and the endpoint of puberty in males.

However, with the exception of birth, which marks the boundary between the prenatal and infancy phases of development, there are no clear demarcations between developmental phases, and individual variation within broad phases of development can be significant. Studies in developmental sexology do not always confine themselves to such narrow age ranges, often using samples of convenience spanning several years in age. To complicate matters further, data are not always reported in easily comparable age ranges.

Prenatal stage

Much of prenatal sexology is concerned with anatomical sequencing in utero, under the control of the genome and fetal hormonal and maternal hormonal environments.

Genetic sex is determined at fertilization, and differentiation of genital morphology begins around the fifth week of gestation with migration of germ cells from the yolk sac to the undifferentiated gonads. Mullerian ducts develop in the sixth week and, in males, the seminiferous tubules differentiate in the seventh week. In males, the Mullerian ducts begin to regress in week eight and the first Leydig cells begin to synthesize testosterone. Masculinization of the genital ridge is observable by week 10. In females, ovaries begin to develop by week eight and produce estradiol, which supports germ cell development but does not materially influence genital development since maternal estrogens are overwhelmingly available to the fetus irrespective of sex.

It is now commonly accepted, if not universally known even among professionals, that the neurological and genital capacity for sexual arousal to orgasm exists in children from before birth. Ultrasound examinations have demonstrated that fetuses suck their toes and fingers and male fetuses touch their penises. Erections are commonly seen in ultrasound images (Hitchcock, Sutphen, & Scholly, 1980), and masturbation in utero has also been observed in sonographic studies of a seven-month fetus (Meizner, 1987). Giorgi and Siccardi (1996) observed on sonography what appeared to be masturbation to orgasm in a 32-week female fetus, noting that she touched the region of her clitoris with her hand repeatedly for 30- to 40-second intervals, displaying short, rapid movements of her pelvis and legs, after which she stopped for a few minutes. After approximately 20 minutes of this behavior, which was also observed by the mother, the fetus displayed contractions of trunk and limb muscles, followed by tonic–clonic movements of the whole body, after which she "relaxed and rested. " While such apparent masturbation to orgasm in utero may be phenomenologically quite different from its homologs in postnatal life, Giorgi and Siccardi point out that female sexual response is distinct from reproductive function and "does not need a full sexual maturity to be explicit"(Giorgi & Siccardi, 1996).

Infancy (Birth to 2 Years)

Both male and female infants display evidence of sexual arousal at birth, with erections continuing for male infants and female infants displaying vaginal lubrication (Martinson, 1981). Infants and toddlers explore their genitals during bathing, diaper changes, or other times when they are permitted access to them. As they learn to talk, they learn the names, both proper and slang, for genitalia, as they also learn the names of other body parts. The antecedents to gender constancy are also established in infancy. Infants and toddlers will remove their own clothing and appear to enjoy nudity (Gordon & Schroeder, 1995).

Although it is common to think of intentional genital stimulation at this age as simply one facet of a broader pleasure-seeking imperative, genital pleasure during infancy appears to be qualitatively similar, if not largely identical, to the sexual response cycle observable later in childhood and adolescence. The observation that infants experience orgasm through masturbatory activity is not new. In the late nineteenth and early twentieth centuries, influential physicians, including Moll, Stekel, and Freud, wrote about infant genital arousal, and as early as the eighteenth century, Vogel described "postural" masturbation to orgasm in an infant (Janssen, 2007). In more modern times, a number of investigators have reported on the observation of orgasms in infants (Borneman, 1990; Kinsey et al., 1948). More current research, which we review next, adds to the observations of these earlier writers.

Masturbatory behavior in infants can be difficult to recognize because musculoskeletal development and lack of fine motor coordination may preclude the use of the hands (Martinson, 1981; Nechay, Ross, Stephenson, & O'Regan, 2004). Indeed, infantile masturbation (gratification behavior, sometimes called unhappily labeled "gratification disorder") sometimes leads to unnecessary invasive neurological workups because clinicians, responding to worried caregivers, have failed to recognize the characteristic postures and movements of infantile masturbation, believing them to be epileptiform or other malign movement disorders (ddenise625, April 27, 2012; Yang, Fullwood, Goldstein, & Mink, 2005).

Martinson (1981) postulates that because infants and young children lack the fantasy content and the ability to concentrate typically present at a more advanced age, the ability to experience sexual arousal is present only at the physiological-reflexive level. Ajlouni and colleagues (2010) explored the hormonal triggers for masturbation in infants and young children referred to pediatric neurology clinics, measuring dehydroepiandrosterone sulfate, 17-hydroxyprogesterone, free testosterone, estradiol, dehydroepiandrosterone, sex hormone-binding globulin (SHBG), and androstenedione. Case and control groups were comparable for all measures except estradiol levels, which were lower in the case group, leading him to conclude that low estradiol is a possible trigger for masturbation in this group (Ajlouni, Daoud, Ajlouni, & Ajlouni, 2010).

Early Childhood (3 to 5 Years)

Children in early childhood engage in a variety of behaviors adults would label as sexual, sometimes incurring sanctions from uncomfortable caregivers. Hugs and kisses are generally well tolerated or even encouraged in this age group, while talk about private body parts, playing house or doctor, and displaying or touching their own genitals may be less welcome. Masturbation, sometimes to orgasm, appears to be relatively common in early childhood (Kinsey et al., 1948, 1953; Larsson & Svedin, 2001). In one study involving 60 preschool teachers in nine Norwegian kindergartens, 85 percent reported observing children engaged in masturbation, with 23 percent reporting that they had observed masturbation to orgasm among their students in this age group (Gundersen, Melas, & Skar, 1981). Sex play with peers and siblings is also common at this age, as is sexual rehearsal play, sometimes with simulated intercourse (Gordon & Schroeder, 1995). Sexual rehearsal play is a behavioral stratagem shared with other primates and is readily observable across cultures (Ford & Beach, 1951; Money, 1990). Rarely do children in early childhood ascribe sensory or sexual functions to genitalia, instead explaining them as integral to excretory functions or, in some cases, relating them to pregnancy and birth but not copulation or sexual pleasure (Gordon, Schroeder, & Abrams, 1990).

Three-year-olds can easily identify their own biological sex correctly as well as the sex of others. Some of this knowledge appears to be culture-bound (Goldman & Goldman, 1982), and sexual distinctions may be made on the basis of clothing, hairstyles, or body decoration rather than by differences in genital morphology. By the age of 4, however, most children are aware of genital differences, have incorporated gender constancy based upon genital differences, and are familiar with the names of genitals, although both boys and girls are more likely to have correct information about male than female genitals (Bem, 1989; Bosinski, 1989; Gordon et al., 1990).

While the repertoire of sexual behaviors in early childhood is typically somewhat narrow, some children in this age group display a more comprehensive range of sexual behaviors, including oral–genital contact and penetrative behaviors. Age-atypical sexual knowledge and behaviors are generally seen as indicators of sexual abuse (W. N. Friedrich, 1993), but there is not universal agreement about what constitutes age-typical sexual knowledge and behaviors (Volbert, 2000). Friedrich, in a study of a normative sample of non-abused children 2 to 12 years old, found that in the preschool 2- to 6-year-old cohort some reports of age-atypical behavior that at first report would have been judged to be "quite deviant" were found, on follow-up, to be "benign" (W.N. Friedrich, 2003).

In a study of 1,114 children aged 2 to 12 screened for absence of sexual abuse, Friedrich and colleagues confirmed a broad range of sexual behaviors, as reported by primary female caregivers, with adult behavioral correspondence, including gender role behavior, self-stimulation, sexual anxiety, sexual interest, sexual intrusiveness, sexual knowledge, and voyeuristic behavior (Friederich, Fisher, Broughton, Houston, & Shafran, 1998). Such behaviors included touching fathers' genitals and mothers' or other women's breasts, touching their own genitals, deliberately exposing their genitals to other children or adults in such activities as playing house or doctor, or attempting to see other people nude or partially clothed. Rosenfeld and colleagues found that parents in his sample reported that 30 to 45 percent of children under 10 years of age touched their mother's breasts or genitals at least once (Rosenfeld, Bailey, Siegel, & Bailey, 1986).

Friedrich and colleagues found that 2-year-old children are observed by their caregivers to be relatively more sexual than their early adolescent counterparts and become increasingly sexual up to age 5, when observed sexual behaviors decline. Another decrease in observed behavior occurs after age 9 and does not increase until age 11 in girls and age 12 in boys, when there is increasing interest in the opposite sex (Friedrich et al., 1998). A number of investigators have pointed out that lower levels of observed sexual behavior may be a function of children's increasing secrecy about genitally focused sexual activities, including increasing awareness of shame and modesty (Griffin, 1995; Meyer-Bahlburg & Steel, 2003).

Later Childhood (6 to 9 Years)

Children in middle and late childhood consistently and correctly assign gender on the basis of genitalia. With increasing age, there is increasing knowledge of the sexual components of reproduction and pregnancy as well as knowledge about masturbation, mating behavior in humans and other animals, and the mechanics of intercourse and birth.

Sexual rehearsal play continues in this stage, including a variety of games with a sexual focus such as "spin the bottle" or "truth or dare," and peers assume an increasingly larger role in the acquisition of sexual knowledge and values. Fantasy, based upon experimentation or exposure to erotic media, augments the masturbation experience, rendering it more richly complex. At the same time, publicly observable sexual behaviors, including masturbation, diminish as modesty, embarrassment, the internalization of social proscriptions against public nudity or genital exposure, and sometimes frank punishment, coalesce to drive sexual expression into hiding (Griffin, 1995). Children in later childhood may dream about sex and become more interested in media with a sexual content (Gordon & Schroeder, 1995).

Early Adolescence (10 to 13 Years)

Early adolescence is marked by the onset of pubertal biological processes that will culminate in anatomical sexual maturity and the ability to produce mature gametes. There is a considerable body of knowledge about the biological and environmental factors associated with onset of puberty, and its regulation by the pituitary–hypothalamic axis, as well as biosocial influences (Hopwood et al., 1990; Sanders & Reinisch, 1990). In Western culture, the average age at thelarche (Tanner stage 2) is 10.4 years for Caucasian girls, 9.5 years for African-American girls, and 9.8 years for Mexican-American girls. Caucasian boys in the West begin puberty, as marked by Tanner 2 stage penile growth and pubic hair distribution, at 12.0 years, African-American boys at 11.2 years, and Mexican-American boys at 12.3 years. Typically, girls begin to menstruate by age 12 or 13, although there is a wide range of normal. Most girls will begin to menstruate by age 16 and most boys will ejaculate by age 15 (Sun et al., 2002). It is important to emphasize the wide range of normal for these experiences among individual children and adolescents. These individual differences add to the complexity of understanding typical development and thus detecting statistical and/or clinical deviance.

In the sexual repertoire, early adolescents have a working knowledge of sexual intercourse, although they may not yet have experienced it. They also generally have some knowledge, at least academic, about contraception and sexually transmitted diseases. With the onset of puberty, sexual fantasy plays an increasingly important role in sexual expression. Recalled onset of first sexual fantasy is generally between 11 and 13 years old, with men recalling earlier onset of fantasy than women (Leitenberg & Henning, 1995).

Masturbation continues as the predominant sexual outlet in early and middle adolescence, although a significant number of adolescents engage in sexual intercourse for the first time at about age 12 (Finkel & Finkel, 1981; Scott-Jones & White, 1990). Approximately 43 percent of males and 37 percent of females in this developmental stage masturbate (Reece et al., 2010b).

Middle Adolescence (14 to 17 Years)

In middle adolescence, as with early adolescence, increases in sexual behavior, social factors, as well as hormonal factors affect sexual expression and the onset of specific sexual behaviors (Silovsky & Swisher, 2008). Contemporary theories about antecedents of specific sexual behavioral milestones throughout the span of childhood and adolescence generally postulate multivariate, integrative biopsychosocial influences (Crockett, Bingham, Chopak, & Vicary, 1996; Udry, 1990).

Biologically the onset of puberty has a genetic component, evidenced, for example, by a significant correlation of age at menarche between mother and daughter (Garn, 1980), and early menarche is correlated a lower age for first coitus in girls (B. C. Miller et al., 1997). Dopamine receptor genes may also be associated with age at coitarche (W. B. Miller et al., 1999), and testosterone level and pubertal stage predict the initiation of sexual intercourse in early adolescent age boys (Halpern, Udry, Campbell, & Suchindran, 1993).

A variety of social indicators have been identified that predict onset of some sexual behaviors. Several studies, for example, have found that both pubertal milestones and the sexual behavior of best friends predicted the onset of specific sexual behaviors in middle adolescence (Billy & Udry, 1985; Smith et al., 1985). As Subrahmanyam and colleagues point out elsewhere in this volume (Chapter 4), the digital worlds that children and adolescents inhabit co-construct the childhood and adolescent sexual developmental processes (see also Subrahmanyam, Smahel, & Greenfield, 2006). This includes, for example, adolescents' experimentation with sexual talk and behaviors in online contexts such as social networking sites and chat rooms.

Beginning sexual intercourse is normative by end of middle adolescence, with approximately two thirds of American teenagers having experienced intercourse by the 12th grade (Crockett, Rafaelli, & Moilanen, 2003). Unfortunately, not all such experiences are voluntary. In one national survey of 7,643 sexually experienced women aged 15 to 44, 20 percent of those who initially had intercourse before 15 years of age said their first intercourse was not voluntary (Chandra, Martinez, Mosher, Abma, & Jones, 2005), as did 4 percent of women who first had intercourse at 20 years or older (Chandra, Martinez, et al., 2005).

Rates of recent oral sex are relatively low among 14-year-olds (4.3 percent female partners for young men and 6.6 percent male partners for young women) but increase with age (Reece et al., 2010b). Data from the National Survey on Family Growth indicate that 32.6 percent of females and 37.5 percent of males aged 15 to 17 have engaged in heterosexual oral sex. The numbers double in the 18- and 19-year-old cohort (65.6 percent of females and 65.9 percent of males) (Copen, Chandra, & Martinez, 2012).

Most sexual behaviors engaged in by adults, including anal sex, are observed in 14- to 17-year-olds, although generally not at the same rates. In 14- and 15-year-olds, 1 percent of males and 4 percent of females have engaged in receptive anal sex within the preceding year, and the incidence in 16- and 17-year-olds is approximately the same, with a slight increase to 5 percent for females. The incidence within the preceding year for insertive penile–anal intercourse is about 3 percent for 14- and 15-year-old boys, increasing to about 5 percent in the 16- and 17-year-old group, but the incidence nearly doubles to 11 percent in the 20- to 24-year-old group and peaks at 27 percent in the 25- to 29-year-old cohort (Reece et al., 2010a).

While sex with partners is normative in this developmental stage, sexual behavior involving a partner among middle adolescents at any given time is the exception rather than the rule. Thus, although 40 percent of 17-year-old boys said they engaged in vaginal intercourse in the preceding year, only 27 percent said they did so in the preceding 90 days (Reece et al., 2010b). In another study, approximately 45 percent of 15- to 19-year-old males said they had no partnered sex within the preceding 12 months, while approximately 30 percent said they had a single female partner and approximately 22 percent had two or more female partners. For women in the same age group, 42.9 percent reported no male partners in the preceding 12 months, 30.5 percent reported one male partner, and 16.8 percent reported two or more male partners (Chandra, Mosher, Copen, & Sionean, 2011).

Same-sex contact is also frequently observed in this age group, although a significant number of adolescents remain uncertain about their sexual orientation.

Remafedi, studying junior and senior high-school students in Minnesota, found that 88.2 percent of males and females self-identified as heterosexual, 1.1 percent self-identified as bisexual or homosexual, while 10.7 percent said they were not sure about their sexual orientation (Remafedi, Resnick, Blum, & Harris, 1992). Awareness of sexual gender orientation, the attraction to same- and/or opposite-sex partners, typically manifests before puberty and precedes partnered sexual behavior (Seto, 2012).

Mosher and colleagues (2005) found that 2.4 percent of males aged 15 to 19 had engaged in same-sex behaviors in the preceding 12 months while 7.7 percent of females reported same-sex sexual contact in the previous 12 months (Mosher, Chandra, & Jones, 2005).

Late Adolescence (18 to 21 Years)

By late adolescence, it is common for individuals of both sexes to be engaged in a greater variety of sexual behaviors on an ongoing basis with increasing incidence compared with younger age cohorts. In a study of 5,865 subjects aged 14 to 70+, Reece and colleagues (2010) found significant increases in most sexual behavior measures in their 18- and 19-year-old and 20- to 24-year-old cohorts compared with their 14- and 15-year-old and 16-and 17-year-old cohorts. For example, while 62 percent of males and 40 percent of female 14- and 15-year-olds acknowledged masturbating in the preceding year, 75 percent of male and 45 percent of female 16- and 17-year-olds, 81 percent of male and 60 percent of female 18- and 19-year-olds, and 83 percent of male and 64 percent of female 20- to 24-year-olds masturbated in the past year (Reece et al., 2010b).

With respect to coitus, 9 percent of male and 11 percent of female 14- and 15-year-olds engaged in penile–vaginal intercourse in the preceding year, while 30 percent of both male and female 16- and 17-year-olds, 53 percent of male and 62 percent of female 18- and 19-year-olds, and 63 percent of male and 80 percent of female 20- to 24-year-olds engaged in penile–vaginal intercourse in the last year (Reece et al., 2010b).

Masturbation continues to be an important sexual outlet for both males and females in late adolescence, with 83 percent of 20- to 24-year-old men and 64 percent of women having masturbated alone within the preceding year and 44 percent of males and 36 percent of females having masturbated with a partner. Oral sex is also an important outlet in this age group, with 63 percent of men and 70 percent of women receiving oral sex from an opposite-sex partner in the preceding year and 55 percent of men and 74 percent of women performing oral sex on an opposite-sex partner. For women, late adolescence is the age of the highest frequency of receptive anal sex, with almost a quarter of women acknowledging penile–anal penetration within the preceding year (Reece et al., 2010b).

■ NORMAL OR ABNORMAL: CURRENT ASSESSMENT METHODS

Distinguishing between normal and abnormal sexual behaviors in childhood and adolescence is of great interest to clinicians and others who work with sexually abused children as well as to the criminal justice system. Unfortunately, this is not so reliable a determination as it is often supposed. Friedrich (2003) notes that sexually intrusive behavior has made the criminalization of children who display such behaviors commonplace while, at the same time, policy and treatment recommendations are routinely based on "little research guidance" (W. N. Friedrich, 2003).

Sexually abused children and adolescents sometimes display sexual behaviors that are deemed inappropriate for their developmental stage, leading to the conclusion that these behaviors were learned in an abusive context. Such abnormal sexual behavior is widely believed to correlate with sexual abuse. Techniques for assessment that attempt to distinguish between normal and abnormal sexual behavior in children and adolescents are, therefore, important in the prevention and treatment of child sexual abuse (W. N. Friedrich, Urquiza, & Beilke, 1986).

Currently, there are only two well-standardized screening instruments for childhood sexual behaviors, the Sexual Problem Scale (SPS) derived from the Child Behavior Checklist (CBCL) (Achenbach, 1991), and the Child Sexual Behavior Inventory (CSBI-II) (W. L. Friedrich, 1997). The SPS currently consists of six items, four dealing specifically with sexual behavior and two dealing with cross-gender behavior. Of the four sexual behavior items, two deal with masturbation, one inquires about "sex problems," and one focuses on "thinking about sex too much." The SPS has been criticized for poor psychometric properties and has little utility as a broad screening instrument for problematic sexual behavior in children and adolescents (Meyer-Bahlburg & Steel, 2003).

Friedrich initially used the CBCL in research on sexually abused children (W. N. Friedrich et al., 1986) and found that these children engaged in significantly more sexual behavior than comparison groups of non-abused children or psychiatric outpatient children (Friedrich, Urquiza, et al., 1986). Subsequent work led to the development of the CSBI, now in its second edition, which better demonstrates the relationship between age-inappropriate sexual behavior in children and adolescents and sexual abuse (W. L. Friedrich et al., 1992; W. N. Friedrich, 2000).

The CSBI-II is a 36-item instrument to be scored by parents or caregivers that inquires, using a four-point scale ranging from "never" to "at least once a week," how often certain sexual behaviors have occurred recently or in the last six months. The CSBI, in its original English and translated versions, has undergone extensive factor analytic studies leading to possible areas of additional fruitful exploration of underlying cross-cultural dimensions of sexual behavior (Schoentjes, Deboutte, & Freidrich, 1999). Cross-cultural studies using some or all of the items on the CSBI have demonstrated the importance of context when considering sexual behavior in children and adolescents (Friederich, Sandfort, Oostveen, & Cohen-Kettenis, 2000; Larsson, Svedin, & Friederich, 2000; Larsson & Svedin, 2002).

■ SUMMARY

Considerable evidence now supports the conclusion that sexual behavior, as well as physical sexual maturation, unfolds in a developmental continuum from intrauterine life throughout childhood and adolescence. While the meanings of observed sexual behaviors may vary across the lifespan, it is clear that the biological substrate for sexual expression is present very early in life.

It is also clear that sexual development, while constrained to a degree by biological trajectory, both affects and is affected by the elements of culture. Technology has played an important role in extending our ability to observe sexual unfolding and it has also affected the process itself. Our culture continues to grapple with the implications. What are we to make, for example, of findings from polysomnography that an average of two to three hours of nocturnal penile tumescence is normal in prepubescent males (Francouer, 1990), or that ultrasonography consistently reveals erections in utero (Hitchcock et al., 1980), as well as activities in both apparently normal female and male fetuses that investigators describe as intrauterine "masturbation" (Meizner, 1987) or "sexual behavior" (Giorgi & Siccardi, 1996)? These technologies, widely used for the past two decades, would seem to have produced clear and convincing evidence that sexual capacity and behavior do not simply spring forth at puberty but are part of a lengthy developmental process.

Even more strikingly, as the contents of this volume attest, the ascendance of the Internet culture with its attendant technologies has had a significant impact on sexual development, and there is every reason to believe that this particular cultural development has already profoundly affected the developmental trajectory of sexual behavior and will continue to do so. Yet the era of widespread use of personal computers and ready access to an HTTP-addressed World Wide Web (W3) is barely a generation old.

While research has demonstrated that elevated levels of sexual behaviors, particularly age-incongruent behaviors, can point toward sexual abuse in some children, sexual expression in childhood and adolescence is entirely normative rather than inherently pathological (W. N. Friederich, 2003). Developmental sequencing in the absence of abuse progresses in an orderly and largely predictable fashion throughout childhood and adolescence in all life domains, including the sexual domain, although considerable individual variance exists. Such variance persists into adulthood to the end of life.

Sexual behaviors appear in tandem with, and to some degree depend upon, biological sequencing. Solo masturbation, the first observable sexual behavior, begins in utero, once genital and neurological competence permits, and is a constant in sexual behavior patterns for most individuals throughout the lifespan. Until the decade and a half from 25 to 40, when both men and women are somewhat more likely to have engaged in vaginal intercourse in the preceding year than in masturbation, the incidence of masturbation is consistently greater than for any other sexual behavior. In the fifth, sixth, and seventh decades of life masturbation returns to its place as the most frequently reported sexual behavior for a preceding year (Reece et al., 2010b).

Despite our increasing understanding of pediatric sexology, much-needed research continues to be difficult to accomplish, both because of sociocultural strictures and the need to develop better research strategies. The remedy to both of these impediments appears to lie in continuing efforts to educate social gate-keepers about the normative nature of child and adolescent sexual development and its attendant behaviors and to challenge unwarranted assumptions about the inappropriateness of sex research with children and adolescents. When cultural thought leaders are satisfied that sexual behavior in childhood and adolescence is not inherently pathological and that well-designed research in developmental sexology is needed to further our understanding of the processes involved, it seems reasonable to expect a gradual shift in political will to support further investigation. Additional research is fundamental to our ability to intervene appropriately when things go awry and to informing our strategies for ameliorating such damage, as might have been done when normal developmental processes have been disrupted.

Technology will continue to illuminate the processes and patterns of sexual development as well as influence them and will inform our cultural beliefs about what is normal as well as what is acceptable and desirable sexual behavior. It is hoped that a more widespread understanding of the normative processes and behaviors of pediatric developmental sexology, as they are now understood, will lead to a greater willingness to entertain more extensive research that could further increase our ability to nurture our children, protect them against sexual violence, and care for both victims and perpetrators of sexual abuse.

■ DISCLOSURE

H. Martin Malin and Fabian M. Saleh have no conflicts of interest to disclose.

■ REFERENCES

Achenbach, T. M. (1991). *Manual for the Child Behavior Checklist/4-18 and 1991 Profile.* Burlington, VT: University of Vermont Department of Psychiatry.

Ajlouni, H. K., Daoud, A. S., Ajlouni, S. F., & Ajlouni, K. M. (2010). Infantile and early childhood masturbation: Sex hormones and clinical profile. *Annals of Saudi Medicine, 30*(6), 471–474. doi: 10.4103/0256-4947.72271

Allegations about childhood data in the 1948 book, *Sexual Behavior in the Human Male.* Retrieved from http://from www.iub.edu/~kinsey/about/controversy 2.htm.

Bem, S. L. (1989). Genital knowledge and gender constancy in preschool children. *Child Development, 60*(3), 649–662.

Billy, J. O., & Udry, J. R. (1985). The influence of male and female best friends on adolescent sexual behavior. *Adolescence, 20*(77), 21–32.

Borneman, E. (1990). Progress in empirical research on children's sexuality. In M. E. Perry (Ed.), *Childhood and adolescent sexology* (Vol. vii, pp. 201–210). Amsterdam: Elsevier.

Bosinski, H. (1989). [Current status of sex education of preschool children]. *Arztliche Jugendkunde, 80*(5), 290–297.

Broderick, C. B. (1966). Socio-sexual development in a suburban community. *Journal of Sex Research, 2*, 1–24.

Ceci, S. J., Peters, D., & Plotkin, J. (1985). Human subjects review, personal views, and the regulation of social science research. *American Psychologist, 40*, 994–1002.

Chandra, A., Martinez, G. M., Mosher, W. D., Abma, J.C., & Jones, J. (2005). Fertility, family planning, and reproductive health of U. S. women: Data from the 2002 National Survey of Family Growth. *Vital Health Statistics, 23*(25), 73.

Chandra, A., Mosher, W. D., Copen, C., & Sionean, C. (2011). Sexual behavior, sexual attraction, and sexual identity in the United States: data from the 2006–2008 National Survey of Family Growth. *National Health Statistics Report*, (36), 1–36.

Copen, C., Chandra, A., & Martinez, G. (2012). Prevalence and timing of oral sex with opposite-sex partners among females and males aged 15–24 years: United States, 2007–2012. *National Health Statistics Report*, (56), 1–14. Hyattsville, MD: National Center for Health Statistics.

Crocker, W., & Crocker, J. (1994). *The Canela: Bonding through kinship, ritual and sex.* Fort Worth, TX: Harcourt Brace College Publishers.

Crockett, L. J., Bingham, C. R., Chopak, J. S., & Vicary, J. R. (1996). Timing of first sexual intercourse: the role of social control, social learning, and problem behavior. *Journal of Youth & Adolescence, 25*(1), 89–111.

Crockett, L. J., Rafaelli, M., & Moilanen, K. L. (2003). Adolescent sexuality: Behavior and meaning. In G. R. Aams & M. D. Berzonsky (Eds.), *Blackwell handbook of adolescence* (pp. 371–392). Malden, MA: Blackwell Publishing Ltd.

Currier, R. L. (1981). Juvenile sexuality in global perspective. In L. L. Constantine & F. M. Martinson (Eds.), *Children and sex: New findings, new perspectives* (p. 17). Boston: Little, Brown and Company.

ddenise625. (April 27, 2012). *Gratification behavior episode.* Retrieved from http://www.youtube.com/watch?v=95x8jav9_1A

Elias, J., & Gebhard, P. H. (1969). Sexuality and sexual learning in children. *Phi Beta Kappan, 50*, 401–405.

Finkel, M. L., & Finkel, D. G. (1981). Sexual and contraceptive knowledge, attitude and behavior of male adolescents. In F. Furstenberg, R. Lincoln & J. Menken (Eds.), *Teenage sexuality, pregnancy and childbearing* (pp. 327–335). Philadelphia: Temple University Press.

Ford, C. S., & Beach, F. A. (1951). *Patterns of sexual behavior.* New York: Harpers.

Francouer, R. T. (1990). Religion and childhood. In M. E. Perry (Ed.), *Handbook of sexology* (Vol. vii, p. 83). Amsterdam: Elsevier.

Friedrich, W. L. (1997). *The Child Sexual Behavior Inventory: Professional manual.* Odessa, FL: Psychological Assessment Resources.

Friedrich, W. L., Grambsch, P., Damon, L., Hewitt, S. K., Koverola, C, & Lang, R. A. (1992). Child Sexual Behavior Inventory: Normative and clinical comparisons. *Psychological Assessment, 4,* 303–311.

Friedrich, W. N. (1993). Sexual victimization and sexual behavior in children: a review of recent literature. *Child Abuse & Neglect, 17*(1), 59–66.

Friedrich, W. N. (2000). Children and adolescents who are sexually abusive of others. *Journal of the American Academy of Child & Adolescent Psychiatry, 39*(7), 809–810. doi: 10.1097/00004583-200007000-00005

Friedrich, W. N. (2003). Studies of sexuality of nonabused children. In J. Bancroft (Ed.), *Sexual development in childhood* (pp. 107–120). Bloomington: Indiana University Press.

Friedrich, W. N., Fisher, J., Broughton, D., Houston, M., & Shafran, C. R. (1998). Normative sexual behavior in children: A contemporary sample. *Pediatrics, 101*(4), 108.

Friedrich, W. N., Grambsch, P., Broughton, D., Kuiper, J., & Beilke, R. L. (1991). Normative sexual behavior in children. *Pediatrics, 88*(3), 456–464.

Friedrich, W. N., Sandfort, T. G. M., Oostveen, M. D., & Cohen-Kettenis, P. T. (2000). Cultural differences in sexual behavior: 2- to 6-year-old Dutch and American children. *Journal of Psychology & Human Sexuality, 12*(1/2), 117–129.

Friedrich, W. N., Urquiza, A. J., & Beilke, R. L. (1986). Behavior problems in sexually abused young children. *Journal of Pediatric Psychology, 11*(1), 47–57.

Garn, S. M. (1980). Continuities and change in maturational timing. In O. G. Brim & J. Kagan (Eds.), *Constancy and change in human development* (pp. 113–162). Cambridge, MA: Harvard University Press.

Giorgi, G., & Siccardi, M. (1996). Ultrasonographic observation of a female fetus' sexual behavior in utero. *American Journal of Obstetrics & Gynecology, 175*(3 Pt 1), 753.

Goldman, R., & Goldman, G. (1982). *Children's sexual thinking: A comparative study of children aged 5–15 in Australia, North America, Britain and Sweden.* London: Routledge & Kegan Paul.

Gordon, B. N., & Schroeder, C.S. (1995). *Sexuality: A developmental approach to problems.* New York: Plenum Press.

Gordon, B. N., Schroeder, C. S., & Abrams, J. M. (1990). Children's knowledge of sexuality: a comparison of sexually abused and nonabused children. *American Journal of Orthopsychiatry, 60*(2), 250–257.

Gregor, T. (1985). *Anxious pleasures: the sexual lives of an Amazonian people.* Chicago: Chicago University Press.

Griffin, S. (1995). A cognitive-developmental analysis of pride, shame, and embarassment in middle childhood. In J. P. Tangney & K. W. Fischer (Eds.), *Self-conscious emotions: the psychology of shame, guilt, embarassment and pride* (pp. 219–236). New York: Guilford.

Gundersen, B. H., Melas, P S., & Skar, J. E. (1981). Sexual behavior of preschool children: teachers' observations. In L. L. Constantine & F. M. Martinson (Eds.), *Children and sex: new findings, new perspectives* (pp. 45–62). Boston: Little, Brown and Company.

Gunderson, B. H., Melas, P. S., & Skar, J. E. (1981). *Sexual behavior of preschool children.* Boston: Little, Brown and Company.

Halpern, C. T., Udry, J. R., Campbell, B., & Suchindran, C. (1993). Testosterone and pubertal development as predictors of sexual activity: a panel analysis of adolescent males. *Psychosomatic Medicine, 55*(5), 436–447.

Herdt, G. H. (1993). Semen transactions in Sambia culture. In G. Herdt (Ed.), *Ritualized homosexuality in Melanesia* (pp. 167–211). Berkeley: University of California Press.

Higonnet, A. (1998). *Pictures of innocence: the history and crisis of ideal childhood.* London: Thames and Hudson, Ltd.

Hitchcock, D. A., Sutphen, J. H., & Scholly, T. A. (1980). Demonstration of fetal penile erection in utero. *Journal of Perinatology-Neonatology, 4,* 59–60.

Hopwood, N. J., Kelch, R. P., Hale, P. M., Mendez, T. M., Foster, C. M., & Beitins, I. Z. (1990). The onset of human puberty: Biological and environmental factors. In J. Bancroft & J. M. Reinisch (Eds.), *Adolescence and puberty* (pp. 29–49). New York: Oxford University Press.

Jackson, S. (1990). Demons and innocents: Western ideas on children's sexuality in historical perspective. In M. E. Perry (Ed.), *Handbook of sexology* (Vol. Childhood and Adolescent Sexology, pp. 23–49). Amsterdam: Elsevier.

Janssen, D. F. (2007). First stirrings: cultural notes on orgasm, ejaculation, and wet dreams. *Journal of Sex Research, 44*(2), 122–134. doi: 10.1080/00224490701263595

Kinsey, A. C., Pomeroy, W. B., & Martin, C. E. (1948). *Sexual behavior in the human male.* Philadelphia: Saunders.

Kinsey, A. C., Pomeroy, W. B., Martin, C. E., & Gebhard, P. H. (1953). *Sexual behavior in the human female.* Philadelphia: Saunders.

Larsson, I., & Svedin, C. G. (2001). Sexual behaviour in Swedish preschool children, as observed by their parents. *Acta Paediatrica, 90*(4), 436–444.

Larsson, I., & Svedin, C. G. (2002). Sexual experiences in childhood: young adults' recollections. *Archives of Sexual Behavior, 31*(3), 263–273.

Larsson, I., Svedin, C. G., & Friederich, W. N. (2000). Differences and similarities in sexual behavior among preschoolers in Sweden and USA. *Nordic Journal of Psychiatry, 54,* 251–257.

Leitenberg, H., & Henning, K. (1995). Sexual fantasy. *Psychological Bulletin, 117*(3), 469–496.

Lenderyou, G. (1994). Sex education: A school-based perspective. *Journal of Sexual and Marital Therapy, 9,* 127–144.

Malinowski, B. (1927). *Sex and representation in savage society.* London: Routledge & Kegan Paul.

Martinson, F. M. (1981). Eroticism in infancy and childhood. In L. L. Constantine & F. M. Martinson (Eds.), *Children and sex: new findings, new perspectives.* Boston: Little, Brown and Company.

Mead, M. (1928). *Coming of age in Samoa: a psychological study of primitive youth for Western civilization.* New York: William Morrow.

Mead, M. (1933). *From the South Seas: studies of adolescence and sex in primitive societies.* New York: William Morrow.

Meizner, I. (1987). Sonographic observation of in utero fetal "masturbation." *Journal of Ultrasound in Medicine, 6*(2), 111.

Meyer-Bahlburg, H. F. L., & Steel, J. L. (2003). Using parents as a source of information about the child. In J. Bancroft (Ed.), *Sexual development in childhood* (Vol. VII, pp. 34–53). Bloomington: Indiana University Press.

Miller, B. C., Norton, M. C., Curds, T., Hill, E. J., Schvaneveldt, P. L., & Young, M. H. (1997). The timing of sexual intercourse among adolescents: Family, peer and other antecedents. *Youth & Society, 29*(1), 54–83.

Miller, W. B., Pasta, D. J., MacMurray, J., Chiu, C., Wu, H., & Comings, D. E. (1999). Dopamine receptor genes are associated with age at first sexual intercourse. *Journal of Biosocial Science*, *31*(1), 43–54.

Money, J. (1990). Four tutorials in pediatric sexology. In M. E. Perry (Ed.), *Childhood and adolescent sexology* (Vol. VII). Amsterdam: Elsevier.

Montgomery, H. (2009). *An introduction to childhood: anthropological perspectives on children's lives*. Oxford: Wiley-Blackwell.

Montgomery, H. (2012). Child sexual abuse: an anthropological perspective. In G. Rousseau (Ed.), *Children and sexuality: from the Greeks to the Great War*. Palgrave Macmillan.

Mosher, W. D., Chandra, A., & Jones, J. (2005). Sexual behavior and selected health measures: men and women 15–44 years of age, United States, 2002. *Advance Data*, (362), 1–55.

Mueller, T. E., Gavin, L. E., & Kulkarni, A. (2008). The association between sex education and youth's engagement in sexual intercourse, age at first intercourse and borth control use at first sex. *Journal of Adolescent Health*, *42*, 89–96.

Nechay, A., Ross, L. M., Stephenson, J. B., & O'Regan, M. (2004). Gratification disorder ("infantile masturbation"): a review. *Archives of Diseases of Childhood*, *89*(3), 225–226.

O'Sullivan, L. F., Meyer-Bahlburg, H. F. L., & Wasserman, G. (2000). Reactions of inner-city boys and their mothers to research interviews about sex. In T. G. M. Sandfort & J. Rademakers (Eds.), *Childhood sexuality: Normal sexual behavior and development* (pp. 81–103). Binghamton, NY: Haworth Press, Inc.

Ramsay, G. V. (1943). The sexual development of boys. *American Journal of Psychology*, *56*, 217–233.

Ramsey, G. V. (1950). *Factors in the sex life of 291 boys*. Doctoral dissertation, Indiana University, Bloomington, IN.

Reece, M., Herbenick, D., Schick, V., Sanders, S. A., Dodge, B., & Fortenberry, J. D. (2010a). Background and considerations on the National Survey of Sexual Health and Behavior (NSSHB) from the investigators. *Journal of Sexual Medicine*, *7*(Suppl 5), 243–245. doi: 10.1111/j.1743-6109.2010.02038.x

Reece, M., Herbenick, D., Schick, V., Sanders, S. A., Dodge, B., & Fortenberry, J. D. (2010b). Sexual behaviors, relationships, and perceived health among adult men in the United States: results from a national probability sample. *Journal of Sexual Medicine*, *7*(Suppl 5), 291–304. doi: 10.1111/j.1743-6109.2010.02009.x

Remafedi, G., Resnick, M., Blum, R., & Harris, L. (1992). Demography of sexual orientation in adolescents. *Pediatrics*, *89*(4 Pt 2), 714–721.

Rosenfeld, A., Bailey, R., Siegel, B., & Bailey, G. (1986). Determining incestuous contact between parent and child: frequency of children touching parents' genitals in a nonclinical population. *Journal of the American Academy of Child Psychiatry*, *25*(4), 481–484.

Rosenfeld, A., Siegel-Gorelick, B., Haavik, D., Duryea, M., Wenegrat, A., Martin, J., & Bailey, R. (1984). Parental perceptions of children's modesty: a cross-sectional survey of ages two to ten years. *Psychiatry*, *47*(4), 351–365.

Rotheram-Borus, M. J., Meyer-Bahlburg, H. F., Rosario, M., Koopman, C., Exner, T. M., Henderson, R., …Gruen, R. S. (1992a). Lifetime sexual behaviors among runaway males and females. *Journal of Sex Research*, *29*, 15–29.

Rotheram-Borus, M. J., Meyer-Bahlburg, H. F., Rosario, M., Koopman, C., Haignere, C. S., Exner, T. M., …Gruen, R. S. (1992b). Lifetime sexual behaviors among predominantly minority male runaways and gay/bisexual adolescents in New York City. *AIDS Education & Prevention*, (Suppl), 34–42.

Sanders, S. A., & Reinisch, J.M. (1990). Biological and social influences on the endocrinology of puberty: Some additional considerations. In J. Bancroft & J. M. Reinisch (Eds.), *Adolescence and puberty* (pp. 50–62). New York: Oxford University Press.

Schoentjes, E., Deboutte, D, & Freidrich, W. (1999). Child Sexual Behavior Inventory: A Dutch-speaking normative sample. *Pediatrics*, *104*, 885–893.

Scott-Jones, D., & White, A. B. (1990). Correlates of sexual activity in early adolescence. *Journal of Early Adolescence*, *10*, 221–238.

Sears, R. R., Macoby, E. E., & Levin, H. (1957). *Patterns of child rearing*. Evanston, IL: Row, Peterson.

Seto, M. C. (2012). Is pedophilia a sexual orientation. *Archives of Sexual Behavior*, *212*(41), 231–236.

Sieber, J. E., & Baluyot, R. M. (1992). A survey of IRB concerns about social and behavioral research. *IRB*, *14*(2), 9–10.

Silovsky, J. F., & Swisher, L. M. (2008). Sexual development and behavior problems. In M. L. Wolraitch, D. D. Drotar, P. H. Dworkin, & E. C. Perrin (Eds.), *Developmental-behavioral pediatrics: Evidence and practice* (pp. 805–825). Philadelphia: Mosby Elsevier.

Smith, E. A., Udry, J. R., & Morris, N. M. (1985). Pubertal development and friends: a biosocial explanation of adolescent sexual behavior. *Journal of Health & Social Behavior*, *26*(3), 183–192.

Subrahmanyam, K., Smahel, D., & Greenfield, P. (2006). Connecting developmental constructions to the Internet: identity presentation and sexual exploration in online teen chat rooms. *Developmental Psychology*, *42*(3), 395–406. doi: 10.1037/0012-1649.42.3.395

Sun, S. S., Schubert, C. M., Chumlea, W. C., Roche, A. F., Kulin, H. E., Lee, P. A., …Ryan, A. S. (2002). National estimates of the timing of sexual maturation and racial differences among US children. *Pediatrics*, *110*(5), 911–919.

Udry, J. R. (1990). Hormonal and social determinants of adolescent sexual initiation. In J. Bancroft & J. M. Reinisch (Eds.), *Adolescence and puberty* (pp. 70–87). New York: Oxford University Press.

Udry, J. R., Talbert, L. M., & Morris, N. M. (1986). Biosocial foundations for adolescent female sexuality. *Demography*, *23*(2), 217–230.

Visser, A. P., & van Bilsen, P. (1994). Effectiveness of sex education provided to adolescents. *Patient Education & Counseling*, *23*(3), 147–160.

Volbert, R. (2000). Sexual knowledge of pre-school children. *Journal of Psychology & Human Sexuality*, *12*(1/2), 5–26.

Yang, M. L., Fullwood, E., Goldstein, J., & Mink, J. W. (2005). Masturbation in infancy and early childhood presenting as a movement disorder: 12 cases and a review of the literature. *Pediatrics*, *116*(6), 1427–1432. doi: 10.1542/peds.2005-0532

4 Adolescent Sexuality on the Internet: A Developmental Perspective

■ DAVID SMAHEL AND
KAVERI SUBRAHMANYAM

■ ADOLESCENT SEXUALITY ON THE INTERNET: OLD ISSUES, NEW FORMS

Adolescence is a period of transition—biological, cognitive, and social (Hill, 1983; Steinberg, 2008), and the Internet has become an important context within which youth deal with the changes occurring in their life. Perhaps the most fundamental transition of adolescence is the onset of puberty and subsequent sexual development, the focus of this book. In this chapter, we describe some of the different ways that adolescents use the Internet and newer tools to explore their sexuality, and we point out the challenges and opportunities they encounter as they do so. First, we present our co-construction model, which we have proposed to understand the relation between adolescents' online behavior and their development. Then we describe the characteristics of online environments that are relevant to the expression and exploration of sexuality online. Finally, we describe the different ways that adolescents engage in online sexual exploration in the service of their sexual development.

■ THEORETICAL FRAMEWORK: THE CO-CONSTRUCTION MODEL

In earlier work, we have suggested that the Internet and other digital media are becoming an important social context for adolescents (Subrahmanyam & Smahel, 2011; Subrahmanyam, Smahel, & Greenfield, 2006), along the lines of the more traditional contexts such as the peer group, family, and schools. Why is this? First, peer communication is one of the most popular uses of technology among youth (Subrahmanyam & Greenfield, 2008). Secondly, these new media also connect youth to the other contextual influences in their lives, such as their leisure activities and even their families. Consequently, we have proposed that online communication forms may provide a promising venue for adolescents to manage the developmental tasks before them such as their adjusting to their developing sexuality, constructing a coherent identity, and forming intimate relationships (Subrahmanyam, Greenfield, & Tynes, 2004; Subrahmanyam, Smahel, & Greenfield, 2006). In our co-construction model, we seek to connect adolescents' digital worlds to the developmental processes in their lives. Since the Internet and other digital contexts are interactive, adolescent users are essentially constructing and co-constructing their online environments such as those that populate chat rooms and social networking sites. Consequently, we expect that youth will bring the people and issues from their offline worlds into their online worlds. Thus, we anticipate that core adolescent issues such as sexuality, identity, intimacy, and interpersonal connection will feature prominently in their online contexts. Per the co-construction model, we expect to see psychological connectedness between online and offline worlds— this connectedness can involve typical and healthy adolescent behaviors such as exploring one's sexuality and identity online. However, it can also involve problem behaviors as in the case of youth who engage in substance abuse offline and risky behavior online such as meeting and interacting with strangers.

Even though we expect there to be connectedness between online and offline worlds, this does not mean that the two are mirror images of each other. This is because online communication environments have unique features such as their disembodied users, potential for anonymity, and text-based nature (Subrahmanyam & Šmahel, 2011). Thus, even when youth use the Internet to deal with core concerns such as sexuality and identity, we expect that they will do so in novel and creative ways that capitalize on the opportunities and adapt to the challenges of online communicative environments. When using online venues to enact real-life issues, they may do so differently and with different intensities, and thus these online behaviors might be similar, exaggerated, or even reversed from their offline counterparts.

With the co-construction model as our theoretical framework, the rest of this chapter will describe how young people use the Internet to deal with their developing sexuality (described in detail in the previous chapter). We begin by examining the characteristics of online environments that support sexual activities more generally. The rest of the chapter presents some of the different ways that adolescents engage in online sexual exploration: searching for information about sexuality and sexual health, constructing and presenting sexual selves online, cybersex (sexual chatting between two or more individuals), and access to sexually explicit content. Where relevant, we also examine the opportunities and challenges that youth face as they engage in these online explorations in the service of their sexual development.

■ CHARACTERISTICS OF ONLINE ENVIRONMENTS RELEVANT TO SEXUALITY

Sexual content on the Internet is one of the most dominant aspects of the Web (Cooper, Delmonico, & Burg, 2000). Cooper and colleagues (Cooper, Putnam, Planchon, & Boies, 1999a; Cooper, Scherer, Boies, & Gordon, 1999b) have attempted to account for this by identifying three characteristics of online environments that support sexuality, notably problematic aspects of online sexual behavior. The three features are called the *Triple A Engine*:

(1) Accessibility—the Internet provides easy and unfettered access to vast amounts of information, sexual and nonsexual. Since the early days when Cooper and colleagues identified this element, the Internet also provides easy access to applications for communicating about sexual matters such as social networking sites, chat rooms, or private messaging systems.

(2) Affordability—the Internet has made it cheap to access pornography and sexual communication; one needs only an Internet connection to access them.

(3) Anonymity—while online, one can be as anonymous as one chooses to be, including when engaging in online sexual communication. At the time that Cooper proposed the *Triple A Engine*, online anonymity was the norm, particularly in text-based environments. However, in recent years, as text has given way to pictures, video, and audio, anonymity is much harder to attain while online. While there are online contexts (e.g., bulletin boards, websites with sexual content) where one can be anonymous, most of the more popular communication applications today involve interaction with friends and acquaintances rather than strangers (Reich, Subrahmanyam, & Espinoza, 2012), and so anonymity does not hold up as much anymore for many online communication tools.

In addition to these characteristics, other characteristics of online contexts relevant to sexuality include disembodiedness as well as self-disclosure and disinhibition (Subrahmanyam & Šmahel, 2011). Disembodiedness, or the lack of information about the face and body, is an important characteristic of many online contexts and presents challenges to sexuality because cues for physical appeal such as age, gender, race, or physical appearance (height, weight, etc.) are not readily available. Even when information about the body may be available, such as via photographs, face-to-face cues such as gesture, gaze, and other elements of body language may still be missing. Of course tools such as webcams and camera phones provide these cues indirectly, and many applications (e.g., social networking sites) allow users to exchange such information easily via pictures and video clips. Disinhibited behavior and high levels of self- disclosure are another characteristic of many online environments (Joinson, 2007), thus providing perfect venues for sexual exploration and presentation.

■ ONLINE SEXUAL EXPLORATION

The rest of the chapter describes adolescents' use of the Internet and other digital technologies such as cellphones to deal with their changing bodies, growing interest in sex, and the developmental task of constructing their sexual selves. As noted earlier, these digital contexts provide quick and easy access to information stores, allow users to create content of their own, and allow them to interact with other users. Adolescents are not only consumers of sexual content; they are also actively engaged in constructing many aspects of the sexualized environment in which they are immersed (Greenfield, 2004). In the next sections, we examine the four ways in which adolescents engage in online sexual exploration: (1) searching for information about sexuality and sexual health, (2) constructing and presenting their emerging sexual selves, (3) engaging in sexual conversations or cybersex, and (4) accessing sexually explicit content. Although online sexual exploration is very similar in spirit to its offline counterpart, we will show that it takes on new forms as youth adapt to the characteristics of online environments.

■ SEARCHING FOR INFORMATION ABOUT SEXUALITY AND SEXUAL HEALTH

For adolescents, coping with their developing sexuality is a fundamental developmental challenge. Sexual maturation entails an increased sexual drive and interest in sex (Weinstein & Rosen, 1991), and youth spend "time talking about sex, telling jokes, using sex slang, and exchanging sex-oriented literature" (Rice, 2001, p. 385). They are also sexually active; in one study of 15- to 17-year-old youths in the United States, 36 percent of boys and 39 percent of girls reported that they had vaginal intercourse (Mosher, Chandra, & Jones, 2005). Research also suggests that adolescents are more likely to be sexually active as they grow older (Cubbin, Santelli, Brindis, & Braveman, 2005). Although the actual numbers of sexually active adolescents depends on a number of factors such as demographics (e.g., ethnicity, geographic location), year of data collection, definition of sexual behavior (e.g., oral intercourse, vaginal intercourse), assessment questions or measures, the bottom line is that a lot of youths are engaging in sexual intercourse, often at earlier ages than in previous eras (Steinberg, 2008).

One way that adolescents seek to understand and control their sexual feelings and growing interest in sex is by searching for information about sex. Not surprisingly, parents and other adults are not the preferred sources for information about sex, and the primary source of information about sex that adolescents turn to are their peers, followed by the media (Ward, 2004).

Mass media such as television, magazines, and movies have always been an important source of information about sex (Borzekowski & Rickert, 2001; Brown, 2002; Brown, Childers, & Waszak, 1990; Johnson Vickberg, Kohn, Franco, & Criniti, 2003; Steele, 1999; Ward, 2004). As the media landscape has changed, the particular media source that adolescents have relied on has also changed. As an example, in earlier eras *Playboy* and similar magazines were the media form that many youth turned to; today, pornography and other kinds of sexually explicit material are widely available online. We address this issue in detail in a subsequent section.

Here we examine adolescents' use of the Internet for information and support in the areas of health and sexuality. Not only does the Internet provide free, easy, and virtually unlimited access to vast amounts of publicly available information, it also allows individuals to connect and interact with other individuals, including both peers who are experiencing the same issue or have experienced it as well as experts in the field (e.g., WebMD) (Linares & Subrahmanyam, 2012). Finally, it affords the opportunity to store and access personal medical information via online accounts or briefcases and can be used in the service of health and well-being.

Survey studies confirm that youth use the Internet for health information, and such use has been increasing over time (Borzekowski & Rickert, 2001; Rideout, 2001; Roberts, Foehr, & Rideout, 2005). The 2005 Kaiser report, which surveyed a sample of U.S. 8- to 18-year-olds, noted that half of the youth respondents had searched for health information online (Roberts et al., 2005). These trends are not unique to the United States; youth in other industrialized countries (Cole, Suman, Schramm, Zhou, Salvador, Chung, & Lee, 2008) and even Ghana (Borzekowski, Fobil, & Asante, 2006) report using online health resources. What kinds of health information do youth search for online? An early content analysis of online teen health bulletin boards found that the most frequent topics in the discussion were sexuality and relationships. It is clear that youth turn to online contexts for information about sexual health. The same service hosted two bulletin boards—one on general teen issues and one on sexual health—and there were twice as many discussion threads in the sexual health bulletin board (Suzuki & Calzo, 2004).

It is important to keep in mind that adolescents are not a monolithic group and their use of online contexts for sexual health information does vary by age and gender (Gilbert, Temby, & Rogers, 2005; Rideout, 2001). For instance, adolescent girls in the Kaiser report were more likely to report that they had searched for information on a sexual health topic (e.g., pregnancy and birth control) (Rideout, 2001). An online survey of a teen STD prevention site reported that adolescent boys had searched for information on puberty and teen sexuality, whereas adolescent girls had searched for information on contraception, relationships/dating, general and specific STD information such as prevention, symptoms, testing, transmission, and treatment, teen pregnancy, and virginity. In the same study, younger teens (13- and 14-year-olds) searched for information about puberty, whereas older teens (15- to 17-year-olds) sought specific information about sexuality such as contraception, general STD information, STD symptoms and transmission, and teen pregnancy (Gilbert et al., 2005).

The above data clearly indicate that youth turn to online contexts such as websites and bulletin boards for information about their developing sexuality and sexual health in general. Researchers have speculated that because of its potential for anonymity, adolescents may find the Internet appealing for sensitive topics that they may not be comfortable talking to adults about (Gray et al., 2005; Suzuki &

Calzo, 2004). Other advantages include its availability any time of day or night and the ability to draw on a wider network of people than one's face-to-face network, particularly via interactive forums such as bulletin boards (Subrahmanyam & Šmahel, 2011). Online health resources are not without their challenges—research suggests that teens are not very good at searching for and finding the information they need. There are also credibility concerns with regard to online health information, and we do not know whether teens consistently take into account credibility considerations when looking for health information online.

Recently, there have been attempts to harness young people's affinity for digital tools to empower them in the area of sexual health information (Collins, Martino, & Shaw, 2011). In the SEXINFO program, the San Francisco Department of Public Health implemented a text-messaging intervention for African-American youth (Levine et al., 2008). The program targeted 18- to 24-year-olds using posters, street marketing, and banner ads on *Yahoo!* with messages such as "text SEXINFO" for sexual health information and referrals or "text B2 if u think ur pregnant" for basic information and referrals for consultation. Levine and colleagues reported that the messaging service received 4,500 texts in first 25 weeks of service and appeared to reach the target demographic of African-American youth. A statewide version of the program called HOOKUP provided 13- to 24-year-olds with information about sexual health and Title X clinics that provide low-cost sexual and reproductive health services. After nine months, there were 2,826 subscribers in California and 33% received clinic referrals (Braun, Howard, & Madsen, 2010). Other programs include use of text messaging to inform youth when STI results were ready (Winston, 2010), soap opera programs via handheld computers to influence cognition and behavior related to sexual risk for HIV (Jones, 2008), and a viral video delivered via cellphone with a message about HIV testing for young men (Freimuth et al., 2009). Although there are no data about the effectiveness of these interventions, they attest to the growing role of the Internet in adolescent sexual development.

■ CONSTRUCTING AND PRESENTING SEXUAL SELVES ONLINE

Sexuality is a developmental issue that is present throughout the life cycle, but it becomes especially salient during adolescence; not surprisingly, and as we will show here, it features prominently in adolescents' online lives as well (Subrahmanyam & Šmahel, 2011; Subrahmanyam, Smahel, & Greenfield, 2006). Online contexts and other digital tools have themselves been changing rapidly in the last several years, and so have the ways in which adolescents use them to present and explore their sexuality. Accordingly, we first describe how youth presented and constructed their sexuality in early online applications such as chat rooms and then describe their sexual presentation in subsequent online applications such as social networking sites and text messaging.

Early research: chat rooms

Internet chat rooms were the first generation of online communication applications that were popular among youth. They provided a text-based space where users could interact with others while remaining anonymous and disembodied. Furthermore, when chat rooms first emerged on the digital scene, not every youth was online and accessed chat rooms; consequently, those who did visit chat rooms were able to meet and interact with people outside their offline circle of peers. Although many chat rooms had no adult monitor, some had monitors who ensured that the conversation was civil, safe, and not obscene or sexually explicit. Thus the chat rooms, particularly the unmonitored ones, afforded a rare window into adolescents' online sexual exploration—how they used chat rooms and the different tools within them (e.g., nicknames, avatars) to present and thus construct their sexual selves (Subrahmanyam, Greenfield, & Tynes, 2004; Subrahmanyam, Smahel, & Greenfield, 2006).

We report in some detail the results of our work on public teen chat rooms so the reader can get a picture of youth online exploration that is very difficult to obtain today as online contexts have become more private. To understand the culture of chat rooms, we first used qualitative discourse methodology to micro-analyze a transcript from an online teen chat room monitored by an adult (Subrahmanyam et al., 2004). We found that the chat users discussed a broad range of sexual topics and concerns, such as abortion, premarital sex, and birth control methods (e.g., condoms). The extract below reveals the teen participants' preoccupation with sexual issues and also highlights how the anonymous chat space encouraged the participants to talk frankly and openly about sex

> 548. Immaculate ros: sex sex sex that all you think about?
> 559. Snowbunny: people who have sex at 16 r sick:-(
> 560: Twonky: I agree
> 564. 0oo0CaFfEiNe: no sex until ur happily married…thatz muh rule
> 566. Twonky: I agree with that too
> 567. Snowbunny: me too caffine!

Keep in mind that because the conversations occurred in the main public chat room, even those who were not contributing to the conversation could nonetheless passively participate by "lurking." We replicated these results in a larger study, wherein we analyzed 10 hours of teen chat conversations that yielded more than 12,000 utterances (Subrahmanyam et al., 2006). Our analysis of the content/ themes of their utterances revealed that approximately 5 percent of the conversation threads contained sexual themes (e.g., ANY HOT CHICKS WANNA CHAT PRESS 69) and 3 percent consisted of obscene language (e.g., *my dick*). We also coded utterances in terms of whether they were sexually implicit (*who wants to chat with a hot and sexy 13/f/ct press 12345?*) or explicit (*any hot, horny or wet*

ladies wanna chat with a cute 18 m from canada pic on file if so pm me or press 123).
We found that 3 percent of the utterances were sexually implicit and 3 percent were
explicit. Together these results indicate that within the teen chat space, there was
one sexual comment per minute and less than one obscenity per minute, a very
high rate of exposure for the youth participants, and one likely to be higher than
that found in their face-to-face conversations. Similarly, analysis of the nicknames
showed that 20 percent of all of the nicknames were sexualized; they were categorized as either sexually implicit (*RomancBab4U* or *Snowbunny2740*) or sexually
explicit (*SexyDickHed* or *Da1pimp6sur*). Keep in mind that only 28 percent of the
nicknames contributed a sexual utterance. Nonetheless, the majority (72 percent)
of participants in the chat space had access to the sexual content because the interactions occurred in the public space.

Interestingly, the trends in sexual expression within the chat rooms paral-
leled offline developmental ones. Chat participants who presented themselves as
older also produced more explicit sexual utterances (Subrahmanyam et al., 2006).
Those who presented themselves as females were more likely to use implicitly
sexual nicknames; such nicknames attract sexual attention passively and subtly
and parallel trends in offline behavior. Female identity (via feminine nicknames
such as *Lilprincess72988*) was also associated with implicit sexual communication,
whereas masculine identity (via masculine nicknames such as *Vikingdude123*)
was associated with explicit sexual communication. These results suggest that teen
chat users who wanted to present a sexualized presence did so by adopting sexualized nicknames.

Post-chat room technology and research

Applications that have emerged after chat rooms such as instant messaging,
social networking sites (e.g., Facebook), and mobile phones are much more private. Even social networking sites, the most public of all, allow users to choose
and limit who is privy to their public communications. Youth are now more
informed about privacy issues, and research has suggested that they do use the
privacy controls offered by online applications such as blogs and social networking sites and most teens do not engage in risky behavior (e.g., talking to
strangers) on these sites (Hinduja & Patchin, 2008; Reich, Subrahmanyam, &
Espinoza, 2012; Subrahmanyam, Garcia, Harsono, Li, & Lipana, 2009). Thus, it
is no longer as practical to conduct the kind of research that we did with chat
rooms. Nonetheless, there is a small body of work that has begun to examine
adolescents' construction of their sexuality in these newer digital contexts, and
we describe this next.

It appears that youth are using these newer digital tools to exchange sexually
suggestive content. In one non–peer-reviewed survey, sexually suggestive content
was defined as including sexually explicit text messaging and nude or seminude
personal pictures or videos captured on a cellphone or digital camera and sent via

personal texts, emails, and instant messages (National Campaign to Prevent Teen and Unplanned Pregnancy & Cosmogirl.com, 2008). Keep in mind that electronic content can easily be forwarded, and thus such sexually suggestive messages may reach many more individuals than the originally intended recipients. One particular kind of digital sexual messages that we focus on here is that of *sexting*, "the sending of sexually explicit text or pictures via cell phone" (Subrahmanyam & Šmahel, 2011); others have defined it more broadly as an "electronic distribution of text messages, one's own photographs or one's own video with sexual content, which occurs via virtual electronic media, especially the Internet" (Kopecky, 2012, p. 39). Sexting by youth has raised a lot of public concern, and some U.S. and Czech youth who have engaged in sexting have even been prosecuted on criminal charges related to possession and transmission of pornography (Galanos, 2009; Kopecky, 2012). Clay Calvert discusses these matters in greater detail (see Chapter 5).

In a survey of 11- to 17-year-old Czech youth conducted in 2011, 73 percent reported that publishing and sending suggestive photos of oneself was dangerous; 10 percent reported that they had sent sexually suggestive materials ("sexy" nude or seminude picture) to someone else, with girls and youth over 15 more likely to do so. The most frequent motives for sending such material included boredom, making intimate contact with the opposite sex, self-representation, under the influence of a group, to arouse the recipients, and unplanned or accidental (Kopecky, 2012). Given the limited survey data on adolescents' sexting, we also report data from another survey of slightly older youth (mean age of 20.70 years). In this survey, conducted on U.S. Hispanic female college students, 20 percent of the respondents reported that they had sent erotic or nude pictures of themselves at least once (Ferguson, 2011).

Adolescents also use social networking sites as they construct their sexual selves. In a content analysis of 142 publicly available MySpace profiles of 16- and 17-year-olds, 21 percent self-presented information about their sexual activity (Moreno, Parks, & Richardson, 2007). There is some indication that males may be more likely to post "self-promoting and risqué" pictures and comments related to sex and alcohol on their social networking sites, whereas females are more likely to post "romantic or cute pictures" (Peluchette & Karl, 2008); it is important to note that this was a survey study among college students. These new forms of sexually self-produced material are collectively referred to as "sexually explicit user-generated content (SEUGC)" (Sirianni & Vishwanath, 2012). We could not find any empirical research on adolescents, but a study of U.S. college students suggested that factors that triggered and motivated the likelihood of creating and sharing SEUCG were as follows: viewing pornography, sexual self-efficacy (defined as "the belief in one's ability to perform sexually and to give sexual pleasure to their partners"), and entertainment and arousal (Sirianni & Vishwanath, 2012). Although the participants ranged in age from 17 to above 30, the majority (88 percent) were between 17 and 21 years of age, so the implications of their results are worth noting. Participants who created and shared SEUGC believed that the expected outcomes of doing so would be beneficial to them and consequently did not consider any potential negative repercussions, including adverse social consequences.

These recent findings, along with the earlier research on chat rooms, confirm that youth are indeed using digital media to construct and present their sexual selves and may do so in ways that are not evident to parents and researchers. For the purposes of research and public policy, it is important to note that as the technologies and their capabilities change, so will the particular behaviors (text-based chat conversations vs. sexualized images), but their core purpose, such as sexual exploration or construction, will remain the same.

While there is no question that a small but significant number of adolescents are creating and sharing SEUGC, less is known about the psychological characteristics that are associated with such practices, and their effect on adolescents' intimate relationships. Again, we turn to research on college students for some guidance. Weisskirch and Delevi (2011) surveyed college students (mean age 22, range 18 to 30 years) and found that among those respondents in relationships, attachment anxiety predicted the likelihood of sending texts soliciting sexual activity. Attachment anxiety was also more generally associated with acceptance of sexting and an expectation that it was normative in a relationship and would also enhance the quality of the relationship (Weisskirch & Delevi, 2011). In another survey study of college students (mean age 20.5, range 18 to 36 years), texting, sexting, and attachment in the context of committed romantic relationships, Drouin and Landgraff (2012) found that the frequency of text messaging was associated with secure attachments, whereas the frequency of sexting was associated with insecure attachment, and in particular with attachment avoidance. The authors speculated that their participants engaged in sexting in place of casual sex and possibly as a way to engage in a sexual relationship without intimacy.

■ CYBERSEX: SEXUAL ACTIVITIES ONLINE

The *Triple A Engine* (Accessibility, Affordability, Anonymity) (Cooper et al., 1999a, 1999b) described earlier in this chapter makes online contexts a perfect venue for other kinds of online sexual exploration, including online sexual activities, cybersex, or virtual sex. Researchers have defined cybersex and virtual sex in different ways, ranging from a more general definition that includes anything sexual such as viewing pornographic content to a narrower one entailing online sexual communication between people (Subrahmanyam & Šmahel, 2011). We use the term "cybersex" more narrowly and define it as sexual chatting/talking between two or more individuals that may or may not include role playing and masturbatory activities for one or more of them (e.g., Noonan, 2007; Saleh, 2009; Whitty & Carr, 2006). When the term was introduced, cybersex mainly involved text-based interactions; with the advent of video and voice, it now includes talking about sex and sexual experiences as well as experimenting with sex on the Internet (Sevcikova & Konecny, 2011), such as the use of webcams while engaging in sexual activities. Delmonico and Griffin (2008, p. 432) have noted that webcams are "used by teens to experiment with seductive, voyeuristic, and exhibitionistic sexual behaviors that were not as readily available prior to the availability of webcams."

Even though the particular form of cybersex may have changed with the technology, we believe that Turkle's (1997) comments about its lure remain relevant:

> Many people who engage in netsex say that they are constantly surprised by how emotionally and physically powerful it can be. They insist that it demonstrates that truth of the adage that ninety percent of sex takes place in the mind. This is certainly not a new idea, but netsex has made it commonplace among teenage boys, a social group not usually known for its sophistication about such matters. (p. 21)

Given the topic of adolescent sexuality and the challenges of human subjects review when studying such sensitive topics with minors in the United States, it is no surprise that there is very little research on its nature and prevalence among U.S. youth. We therefore draw on research conducted outside the United States to inform our discussion. In a qualitative study of 15 Czech 12- to 22-year-olds who identified themselves as experienced Internet users, five participants reported that they had engaged in virtual dating and cybersex activities (Smahel, 2003). For these five participants, the Internet—either public chat rooms or the more private instant messaging—was also the venue of their first sexual experience. Based on a survey study of 692 Czech 12- to 20-year-olds, Vybíral, Smahel, and Divínová (2004) reported that 16 percent of participants had tried "virtual sex" on the Internet. Interestingly, there were no significant differences between males and females in this study with regard to participating in virtual sex. Very similar rates of virtual sex participation (16 percent for males and 15 percent for females) were found in another survey study of 681 12- to 20-year-olds (Smahel, 2006). Surprisingly, there were no age differences in the likelihood of engaging in cybersex, and 14 percent of 12- to 14-year olds, 16 percent of 15- to 17-year-olds, and 14 percent of 18- to 20-year-olds reported having done so. Also relevant here is the finding of one study showing that male adolescents were more likely to engage in sexual self-disclosure (which is the act of revealing information about sexuality online) and to respond to their cyberpartner's sexual self-disclosure (Chiou, 2006).

Adolescence is a period of sexual awakening; it is well known that in offline contexts, adolescents show an increased interest in sex, talk more frequently about sex, make more sexual jokes, and generally engage in sexual activities (Suler, 2008). Thus, their interest in and participation in cybersex is hardly surprising and is entirely consistent with the co-construction model as described earlier in the chapter. In fact, it appears that youth participate in cybersex as part of their desire to learn more about sex (Divinova, 2005). As a 15-year-old girl in Divinova's study responded: "when I was eleven years old, it was a perfect way how to get sexual information, which interested me a lot." Some youth may even initiate online relationships in order to engage in cybersex activities, and for some their first sexual encounter may actually happen online (Smahel, 2003). More recent research with 17-year-old Czech adolescents revealed that sexual experience offline was associated with the use of the Internet for sexual purposes, and sexually less experienced adolescents were less likely to use the Internet for sexual activities. For respondents who reported having offline sexual experiences, increased offline sexual activity was positively associated with discussing one's sexual experiences, engaging in virtual sex, and exchanging erotic photos (Sevcikova & Konecny, 2011). While admittedly preliminary and correlational, this study does seem to suggest that adolescents who are sexually active offline go online to continue with this sexual exploration rather than the reverse—that online cybersex opportunities are inviting or luring sexually inexperienced adolescents to participate in activities they are not involved with offline.

Regardless, adolescents' involvement in cybersex does raise concerns for parents, practitioners, and other adults in their life. For one, adults may view cybersex unfavorably and see it as superficial, artificial, or unnatural. Unlike youth, who are digital natives and have lived their whole life immersed in digital contexts, most parents of today's teens came of age before the Internet and are more akin to digital immigrants (Prensky, 2001). Thus, parents may be concerned about their teen's cybersex activities, which may seem perfectly natural to youth. Without research on this topic, we do not know whether cybersex is beneficial or harmful. Given that online contexts are here to stay and young people are very comfortable within them, we feel that they offer a relatively safe venue to gain sexual experience, as long as youth follow basic rules and protect their privacy by not revealing identifying information such as their name, address, telephone number, etc. (Divinova, 2005).

At the same time, one very valid concern about adolescent cybersex is its potential for compulsive or addictive behaviors. Internet addiction and Internet sex addiction are not officially recognized by the DSM-IV, and there is disagreement among researchers as to whether "addiction to the Internet" is possible. Terms such as "sexual addiction to the Internet" or "online sexually compulsive behavior" have been used to characterize excessive levels of cybersex (Subrahmanyam & Šmahel, 2011). Regardless, it is clear that excessive or problematic Internet use is possible, and virtual sexual behavior has been identified as an area of addictive behavior to which youth may be susceptible (Delmonico & Griffin, 2008). In Cooper and colleagues' (1999) description of the three types of Internet users who are engaged in extreme levels of online sexual activities, adolescents are likely to be considered as *hazardous users:* individuals who have no prior history of compulsive sexual behavior online but experience problems while going online. More research is necessary to determine the actual prevalence of compulsive cybersex behavior among youth, and to assess whether these youth may be at risk for online sexual solicitation and other predatory behaviors.

■ ACCESSING SEXUALLY EXPLICIT CONTENT ONLINE

Perhaps no other Internet-related topic has resulted in as much consternation, discussion, and hand-wringing as young people's access to sexually explicit material online. Commonly referred to as pornography, such material is readily available online. In 2006, it was estimated that there were 420 million pornography sites and every second, more than 28,000 Internet users across the world viewed pornography; worldwide, the revenue from the pornography industry reached almost $100 billion that year (FamilySafeMedia, 2006). Since the early days of the Internet, sites containing sexual and pornographic content have been among the most frequently visited webpages, and the keywords "sex" and "pornography" are two of the most frequently searched keywords (e.g., Cooper, Delmonico, & Burg, 2000). Cooper and colleagues report that 50 percent of males and 50 percent of females searched for the keyword "sex," and 96 percent of males and 4 percent of females searched the keyword "porn." In the following subsections, we examine the extent to which adolescents are exposed to sexually explicit content as well as the correlates and possible outcomes of such exposure.

Adolescents' exposure to sexually explicit content

Before we examine the research on this topic, it is worth noting that there is tremendous variation in what exactly is subsumed under the terms "sexually explicit," and different researchers have used different definitions of "sex," "pornography," and "sexually explicit material." (In Chapter 10 Lisa Murphy and colleagues consider the implications of these definitional challenges with respect to online child pornography.) Examples of the categories of online sexual content in one study included (a) pictures with clearly exposed genitals, (b) movies with clearly exposed genitals, (c) pictures in which people were having sex, (d) movies in which people were having sex, and (e) erotic contact sites (Peter & Valkenburg, 2006a). In a robust survey study of more than 25,000 children in Europe aged from 9 to 16 years (EU Kids Online), sexually explicit material was defined as follows: "In the past year, you will have seen lots of different images—pictures, photos, videos. Sometimes, these might be obviously sexual—for example, showing people naked or people having sex" (Livingstone et al., 2011). While this list is by no means exhaustive, it provides a sense of the kinds of content that are included under the term "sexually explicit." It is also important to know the particular definitions and questions in a study as they do have an impact on the results.

Per survey research, between 23 and 71 percent of adolescents report being exposed to sexually explicit materials (Flood & Hamilton, 2003; Livingstone et al., 2011; Lo & Wei, 2005; Mitchell, Finkelhor, & Wolak, 2003, 2005; Peter &

Valkenburg, 2006a, 2006b; Ybarra & Mitchell, 2005). The relatively higher rates of exposure are consistent with adolescents' developmentally appropriate interest in sexuality and with research, which indicates that they access offline pornography (Brown & L'Engle, 2009; Lo & Wei, 2005; Ybarra & Mitchell, 2005). In the EU survey study of more than 25,000 children, 12 percent reported seeing sexual images on television, film, or DVD, 7 percent in a magazine or a book, and 14 percent on any website (Livingstone et al., 2011). Despite adolescents' use of pornography and its seeming consistency with developmental demands in their life, adolescents may nevertheless feel ambivalent about it. In a Swedish study of 15- to 25-year-olds, the majority reported they had viewed pornography, yet 46 percent of females and 23 percent of males described it as "degrading." Males, particularly the youngest ones, reported more positive attitudes about pornography (Wallmyr & Welin, 2006). It is possible that opinions about pornography are changing—in the more recent EU Kids Online survey, only 4 percent of all children reported "being bothered" by seeing sexual images online (Livingstone et al., 2011).

In examining the research on youth exposure to sexually explicit material, it is important to distinguish between intentional and unintentional or accidental exposure, especially when considering younger adolescents. In the United States, in a nationally representative survey of 1,501 10- to 17-year-olds conducted in the fall of 1999 and spring of 2000, 25 percent of the respondents reported unwanted contact with online sexual images over the previous year (Mitchell et al., 2003). A majority (73 percent) of the incidents occurred when the respondents were surfing the Internet and 27 percent occurred when they opened an email or clicked on a link in an IM or in an email. Although most of the respondents did not experience negative reactions to the unwanted exposure, about 24 percent stated that they were "very/extremely upset about the exposure." Boys reported unwanted exposure more often than girls (57 vs. 42 percent) and older adolescents more often than younger. A little over 10 years later, on the EU Kids Online survey, 7 percent of all the children (or half of those who had seen any sexually explicit material online) reported seeing sexual images that were accidentally opened in pop-up windows. It appears that half of the exposure to online sexual explicit materials among youth is accidental, a challenging and vexing issue for parents, providers, and government policymakers who want to protect children from unwanted exposure (Livingstone et al., 2011).

The above-mentioned U.S. survey on 1,501 youth also asked respondents whether they had intentionally viewed sexual material on the Internet and traditional media (e.g., magazines) in the previous year. Almost 25 percent of adolescent males reported intentionally viewing sexual content compared to 5 percent of the female respondents (Ybarra & Mitchell, 2005). Not surprisingly, older youth stated they had looked at sexual sites more often; they also preferred online sexual content, whereas younger adolescents preferred more traditional exposure (such as X-rated videos) than those found on the Internet. The more recent EU Kids Online research revealed similar trends; younger youth more often

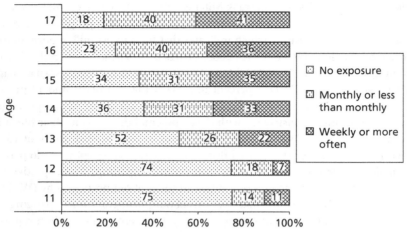

Figure 4.1 Frequency of viewing sites with sexual content among Czech adolescents. (Data from "Risks of Internet Use for Children and Adolescents" project, 2012.)

reported exposure in traditional media compared to online media, whereas older youth more often reported exposure on the Internet compared to offline media (Livingstone et al., 2011).

Other research similarly confirms that males and older adolescents access sexually explicit content at much higher rates than females and younger adolescents (Flood & Hamilton, 2003; Lo & Wei, 2005; Wallmyr & Welin, 2006), patterns that are consistent with offline developmental trends in sexual behavior. Figure 4.1, which presents data from an ongoing project titled "Risks of Internet Use for Children and Adolescents" (personal communication, Sevcikova & Smahel, 2012), nicely illustrates that the rate of viewing online sexual content increases with age.

To examine how broader societal attitudes about sex and adolescent sexual activity in particular may influence adolescents' access to inappropriate material, we examine the 2007 World Internet Project data (Fig. 4.2) and a longitudinal study of adolescents' exposure to sexually explicit material conducted in the Netherlands (Peter & Valkenburg, 2006a, 2006b, 2007, 2008a, 2008b). Starting from the year 2005, the Dutch researchers conducted an online survey on a sample of 745 Dutch adolescents between 13 and 18 years of age (Peter & Valkenburg, 2006a). In the six-month period prior to the survey, 71 percent of Dutch male adolescents and 40 percent of female adolescents reported exposure to some kind of sexually explicit materials. In the World Internet Project data, there was considerable variability across the countries, and the greatest proportion of youth who reported viewing sexually explicit content at least once a week were from the United States, Canada, and the Czech Republic. The rates of access were much lower than the Dutch data, even though the respondents in the World Internet Project were older and considered to be in late adolescence and emerging adulthood. The Netherlands

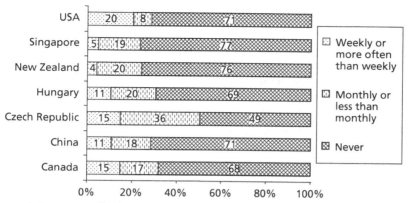

Figure 4.2 Frequency of looking at sites with sexual content among emerging adults in different countries (18 to 21 years old). (Data from World Internet Project, 2007.)

is considered sexually very permissive, and it is no surprise that the Dutch participants reported much higher rates of accessing sexually explicit content. On the other hand, the reason for the different rates could stem from differences in methodology, because the Dutch researchers used a very precise definition for sexually explicit materials; in contrast, the World Internet Project used only one question for assessing the rate of exposure. From a cross-country perspective, the EU Kids Online project (Livingstone et al., 2011) reveals that the rates of seeing sexual images on websites across countries ranged from 4 percent in Germany, 7 percent in Italy, and 11 percent in Spain to 29 percent in Finland, 29 percent in Estonia, and 34 percent in Norway. In comparison to the Dutch data (Peter & Valkenburg, 2006a), the average rate of exposure to online sexual material in the EU Kids Online survey was much lower, at 22 percent. Again, it's possible that this difference may be real or may stem from differences in measuring rates of access to sexual material.

Not surprisingly, all the projects have reported gender differences. Males generally reported greater access to sexually tinged content in the Dutch study and in most of the countries in the World Internet Project (United States, New Zealand, Hungary, and Canada). There were no gender differences in China and Singapore, and in general, young women in Western countries reported accessing sexual content less often than women in Asian countries. In sum, the research suggests that young people's online access of sexually explicit content parallels their offline patterns of sexual socialization.

Factors associated with access of sexually explicit material

Research on adolescents and youth in the United States suggests that sexually explicit media are viewed more frequently by African-American adolescents compared to white teens, youth of lower socioeconomic status, adolescents with less-educated parents, and higher sensation-seeking adolescents (Brown & L'Engle, 2009). Intentional exposure to pornography has been associated with delinquent behaviors and substance abuse in the previous year, and online sexual material seekers more often report clinical features associated with depression and less emotional bonding with their parents and family members (Ybarra & Mitchell, 2005). In a research on Czech early adolescents aged 11 to 15 years, it was found that high rates of sexual exposure were also associated with excessive Internet use, emotional problems, and high rates of sensation seeking (Sevcikova, Serek, Machackova, & Smahel, 2013). The Dutch study described earlier also revealed that adolescents were more likely to access sexual materials if they were sensation seekers, were less satisfied with their lives, used sexual content in other media, and had friends who were predominantly younger. Among female youth, greater sexual experience was associated with decreased exposure to online explicit sexual materials. In summary, we see that in addition to demographic factors such as age, gender, and ethnicity, problem behaviors in offline life as well as psychological well-being might predict whether an adolescent seeks sexually explicit materials.

Effects of accessing sexually explicit material

Although access to sexually explicit material may be becoming normative among youth, nonetheless it is important to examine the potential effects of such exposure on adolescent sexual behavior. This is particularly important as adolescents are at a formative stage of life with regard to the development of their sexuality. For example, there are legitimate concerns that exposure to pornographic content could distort teens' view about sexuality, influence their attitudes about sex and sexual behaviors, shape sexual arousal patterns, and create unrealistic expectations. An alternative hypothesis is that adolescents with more permissive attitudes and a greater interest in sex are simply more likely to access sexually explicit content in the first place. It is important to recognize that only longitudinal research can truly help to disentangle these alternative hypotheses, since correlational research attests only to an association and not to the direction of influence.

A study from Taiwan on 14- to 17-year-old middle- and high-school students suggests that exposure to online pornography was related to a greater acceptance of sexual permissiveness and a greater likelihood of engaging in sexually permissive behavior (Lo & Wei, 2005). Since the study was correlational, we cannot rule out the possibility that youth with permissive attitudes were simply more likely to access sexually explicit material. However, a longitudinal and prospective study of middle- and high-school students in the United States does address this possibility. For young males, increased exposure to sexually explicit media at a younger age predicted more permissive sexual norms two years later, whereas for females, greater exposure to explicit sexual media predicted less progressive gender role attitudes two years later (Brown & L'Engle, 2009). Interestingly, increased exposure to sexual media predicted higher sexual harassment perpetration for males two years later, but not for females. The study demonstrated that exposure to sexually explicit media (online and offline) was one of the strongest predictors of sexual attitudinal and behavioral measures two years later.

A related and similar question is whether adolescents' exposure to sexually explicit materials may be associated with recreational attitudes toward sex. Using data from the Dutch sample described earlier, the researchers found that adolescents' exposure to explicit online material was determined by the gender of the adolescent and that it was not directly related to recreational attitudes toward sex, but was surprisingly mediated by the extent to which adolescents evaluate sexual material as realistic (Peter & Valkenburg, 2006b). Adolescent users who accessed explicit material more frequently were predominantly male and tended to perceive this material as more realistic. It appears that viewing sexual material as realistic was associated with a recreational attitude toward sex.

Overall, the cross-sectional and limited longitudinal research suggests that that exposure to sexually explicit material is associated with more permissive attitudes, greater preoccupation with sex, and more casual sexual exploration. The Dutch researchers have argued that uncertainty is part of sexual development during adolescence and that sexually explicit materials could play an important role in the lives of adolescents. However, as we noted earlier, the Netherlands is much more liberal and much less restrictive when it comes to attitudes toward sex and sexually explicit material, and parents and public officials in other countries may not endorse this view. As the data from the World Internet Project and the EU Kids Online study showed, there is considerable diversity between countries with regard to online sexual exposure and attitudes toward sex. More research is necessary to identify the direction of influence between exposure and preoccupation with sexual content.

▪ ACCESSING SEXUALLY VIOLENT MATERIALS

One category of sexually explicit material that we address separately, and that can be extremely dangerous, is that of sexually violent materials, which are easy to find on the Internet. A report coming from the Australian Institute recommends distinguishing between "mainstream" pornography (i.e., commercially available pornographic videos) and the proliferation of violent and extreme material on the Internet (Flood & Hamilton, 2003). Violent sexual content is common in some stories, images, and videos circulating among certain Internet newsgroups and websites. Although the Internet provides too easy access to violent pornography and sexual materials, research regarding its influence on youth is scarce. The Australian report describes three types of online pornography, which focus on nonconsenting sexual acts: rape, bestiality, and "upskirts" (such sites provide voyeuristic pictures depicting views up the skirts of women) websites. The authors suggest that pornography use among adolescents and the consumption of violent portrayals are associated with sexually aggressive attitudes and behavior. This association may be particularly strong for 4 to 5 percent of Australian 16- and 17-year-olds, who reported watching X-rated videos and pornographic content online every week. The researchers suggest that the regular consumption of violent and extreme pornography content is a risk factor for boys and young men in the perpetration of sexual assault. Simply put, such habits may foster a greater tolerance for sexual violence. Such hypotheses should be verified in future research.

Other researchers have similarly warned that women may experience greater incidences of sexual violence because of easily accessible online sexual violence sites (Gossett & Byrne, 2002). They conducted a content analysis of 31 freely accessible websites containing violent pornographic material. Four sites from their sample specifically advertise the genuineness of their rape images, with one of the sites promising, "*Want a video of a real rape? This is no joke, they actually raped a girl and made this video*" (p. 696). The analysis revealed that the iconography of online pornography strongly emphasized the depiction of victims and the sexual representation of unequal power relations. Gossett and Byrne suggest that the online world provides an interactive experience in which Internet users are encouraged to see through the eyes of a rapist. In contrast to offline forms of pornography, online pornography can enhance the sense of power given to the user over such images. According to the authors, violent pornography is much more easily accessible on the Internet than it is or was in the physical world, and consequently may lead to an increase in such behavior in the physical world. Although there is no research to date on this issue, it is very likely that exposure to sexually violent imagery may well influence youths' attitudes and tolerance toward such types of behavior. Consistent with the co-construction model, youths who are already vulnerable offline may be particularly susceptible to these influences.

■ CONCLUSIONS

We have described the main ways that adolescents use technologies such as the Internet to help them with the developmental task of establishing their sexuality: searching for sexual health information, presenting their sexual selves, cybersex, and accessing sexually explicit content. In line with our co-construction model, we showed that adolescents use different online contexts for sexual exploration, a core offline concern. Although some age and gender trends in their online explorations parallel offline ones, we also saw that youth adapted their online sexual behaviors to capitalize on the particular characteristic of the online environment in question. While some adolescent online sexual activities (e.g., sexting, exposure to violent pornography) may pose risks, for the most part these online sexual activities appear to be a normal part of their sexual development. Research is only now beginning to examine the costs and benefits of such exploration, particularly with respect to pornography. The challenge for researchers is to study adolescent online sexual exploration and the effects of such exploration even as the technologies themselves change.

■ **ACKNOWLEDGMENTS**

Portions of this chapter were previously published in Digital Youth: The role of media and Development, 2011; Chapter 3 [Sexuality on the Internet: Sexual exploration, cybersex, and pornography] by Kaveri Subrahmanyam & David Smahel; With kind permission from Springer Science+Business Media B.V.

David Smahel acknowledges the support of the Czech Science Foundation (GAP407/11/0585) and the VITOVIN project (CZ.1.07/2.3.00/20.0184), which is co-financed by the European Social Fund and the state budget of Czech Republic.

■ **DISCLOSURE**

David Smahel and Kaveri Subrahmanyam has not reported any conflicts of interest

■ **REFERENCES**

Borzekowski, D. L. G., Fobil, J. N., & Asante, K. O. (2006). Online access by adolescents in accra: Ghanaian teens' use of the internet for health information. *Developmental Psychology, 42*, 450.

Borzekowski, D. L. G., & Rickert, V. I. (2001). Adolescent cybersurfing for health information: A new resource that crosses barriers. *Archives of Pediatric Adolescent Medicine, 155*, 813–817.

Braun R, Howard H, Madsen A. *Implementing a text-message-based sexual health information and clinic referral service for California youth.* Paper presented at: SexTech; February 26 & 27, 2010, San Francisco, CA.

Brown, J. D. (2002). Mass media influences on sexuality. *Journal of Sex Research, 39*, 42–45.

Brown, J. D., Childers, K. M., & Waszak, C. S. (1990). Television and adolescent sexuality. *Journal of Adolescent Health Care, 11*, 62–70.

Brown, J. D., & L'Engle, K. L. (2009). X-rated: Sexual attitudes and behaviors associated with US early adolescents' exposure to sexually explicit media. *Communication Research, 36*, 129.

Chiou, W. B. (2006). Adolescents' sexual self-disclosure on the Internet: Deindividuation and impression management. *Adolescence, 41*, 547–561.

Cole, J. I., Suman, M., Schramm, P., Zhou, L., Salvador, A., Chung, J. E., et al. (2008). *World Internet Project: International report 2009.* Los Angeles: Center for the Digital Future, USC Annenberg.

Collins, R. L, Martino, S. C., & Shaw, R. (2011). *Influence of new media on adolescent sexual health: Evidence and opportunities.* Working Paper, RAND. http://aspe.hhs.gov/hsp/11/AdolescentSexualActivity/NewMediaLitRev/index.shtml

Cooper, A., Delmonico, D. L., & Burg, R. (2000). Cybersex users, abusers, and compulsives: New findings and implications. *Sexual Addiction and Compulsivity, 7*, 5–29.

Cooper, A., Putnam, D. E., Planchon, L. A., & Boies, S. C. (1999a). Online sexual compulsivity: getting tangled in the net. *Sexual Addiction & Compulsivity, 6*, 79.

Cooper, A., Scherer, C. R., Boies, S. C., & Gordon, B. L. (1999b). Sexuality on the Internet: From sexual exploration to pathological expression. *Professional Psychology: Research and Practice, 30*, 154–164.

Cubbin, C., Santelli, J., Brindis, C. D., & Braveman, P. (2005). Neighborhood context and sexual behaviors among adolescents: Findings from the national longitudinal study of adolescent health. *Perspectives on Sexual and Reproductive Health, 37*, 125–134.

Delmonico, D. L., & Griffin, E. J. (2008). Cybersex and the e-teen: What marriage and family therapists should know. *Journal of Marital and Family Therapy, 34*, 431–444.

Divinova, R. (2005). *Cybersex—forma internetové komunikace. [Cybersex—form of Internet communication]*. Prague: Triton.

Drouin, M., & Landgraff, C. (2012). Texting, sexting, and attachment in college students' romantic relationships. *Computers in Human Behavior, 28*, 444–449.

FamilySafeMedia. (2006). Pornography statistics. Retrieved November 17, 2008, from http://www.familysafemedia.com/pornography_statistics.html.

Ferguson, C. J. (2011). Sexting behaviors among young Hispanic women: Incidence and association with other high-risk sexual behaviors. *Psychiatric Quarterly, 82*, 239–243.

Flood, M., & Hamilton, C. (2003). Regulating youth access to pornography. Discussion Paper Number 53. https://www.tai.org.au/documents/dp_fulltext/DP53.pdf.

Freimuth, V. S., Snyder, L., & Nadorff, P. G., (2009). *Assessing the viral transmission of HIV mobile media messages*. Paper presented at CDC Annual Conference on Health Communication, Marketing, & Media, Atlanta, GA.

Galanos, M. (2009). Is "sexting" child pornography? Retrieved July 16, 2009, from http://www.cnn.com/2009/CRIME/04/08/galanos.sexting/index.html

Gilbert, L. K., Temby, J. R. E., & Rogers, S. E. (2005). Evaluating a teen STD prevention web site. *Journal of Adolescent Health, 37*, 236–242.

Gossett, J. L., & Byrne, S. (2002). "Click here": A content analysis of Internet rape sites. *Gender & Society, 16*, 689–709.

Gray, N. J., Klein, J. D., Noyce, P. R., Sesselberg, T. S., & Cantrill, J. A. (2005). Health information-seeking behaviour in adolescence: The place of the Internet. *Social Science & Medicine, 60*, 1467–1478.

Greenfield, P. M. (2004). Inadvertent exposure to pornography on the Internet: Implications of peer-to-peer file-sharing networks for child development and families. *Journal of Applied Developmental Psychology: An International Lifespan Journal, 25*, 741–750.

Hill, J. P. (1983). Early adolescence: A research agenda. *Journal of Early Adolescence, 3*, 1–21.

Hinduja, S., & Patchin, J. W. (2008). Personal information of adolescents on the Internet: A quantitative content analysis of MySpace. *Journal of Adolescence, 31*, 125–146.

Joinson, A. N. (2007). Disinhibition and the Internet. In J. Gackenbach (Ed.), *Psychology and the Internet* (pp. 75–92). San Diego: Academic Press.

Johnson Vickberg, S. M., Kohn, J. E., Franco, L. M., & Criniti, S. (2003). What teens want to know: Sexual health questions submitted to a teen web site. *American Journal of Health Education, 34*, 2580264.

Jones, R. (2008). Soap opera video on handheld computers to reduce young urban women's HIV sex risk. *AIDS and Behavior, 12*, 876–884.

Levine, D., McCright, J., Dobkin, L., et al. (2008). SEXINFO: A sexual health text messaging service for San Francisco youth. *American Journal of Public Health, 98,* 393–395.

Kopecky, K. (2012). Sexting among Czech preadolescents and adolescents. *New Educational Review, 28,* 39–48.

Linares, D., & Subrahmanyam, K. (2012). E-health Behaviors. In Z. Yan (Ed.), *Encyclopedia of cyber behavior* (pp. 649–660). IGI Global: Hershey, PA.

Livingstone, S., Haddon, L., Görzig, A. & Olafssson, K. (2011). Risks and safety on the Internet: The perspective of European children. Full findings. London: LSE/EU Kids Online.

Lo, V.-h., & Wei, R. (2005). Exposure to Internet pornography and Taiwanese adolescents' sexual attitudes and behavior. *Journal of Broadcasting & Electronic Media, 49,* 221–237.

Mitchell, K. J., Finkelhor, D., & Wolak, J. (2003). The exposure of youth to unwanted sexual material on the Internet: A national survey of risk, impact, and prevention (Vol. 34, pp. 330–358).

Mitchell, K. J., Finkelhor, D., & Wolak, J. (2005). The Internet and family and acquaintance sexual abuse (Vol. 10, pp. 49–60).

Moreno, M. A., Parks, M., & Richardson, L. P. (2007). What are adolescents showing the world about their health risk behaviors on MySpace? *Medscape General Medicine, 9,* 9.

Mosher, W. D., Chandra, A., & Jones, J. (2005). Sexual behavior and selected health measures: Men and women 15–44 years of age, United States, 2002. Retrieved October 28, 2005, from http://www.cdc.gov/nchs/data/ad/ad362.pdf.

National Campaign to Prevent Teen and Unplanned Pregnancy, & Cosmogirl.com. (2008). Sex and tech: Results from a survey of teens and young adults. Retrieved July 16, 2009, from http://www.thenationalcampaign.org/sextech/PDF/SexTech_Summary.pdf

Noonan, R. J. (2007). The psychology of sex: A mirror from the Internet. In J. Gackenbach (Ed.), *Psychology and the Internet: Intrapersonal, interpersonal, and transpersonal implications* (2nd ed., pp. 93–139). Academic Press.

Peluchette, J., & Karl, K. (2008). Social networking profiles: An examination of student attitudes regarding use and appropriateness of content. *CyberPsychology & Behavior, 11,* 95–97.

Peter, J., & Valkenburg, P. M. (2006a). Adolescents' exposure to sexually explicit material on the Internet. *Communication Research, 33,* 178–204.

Peter, J., & Valkenburg, P. M. (2006b). Adolescents' exposure to sexually explicit online material and recreational attitudes toward sex. *Journal of Communication, 56,* 639–660.

Peter, J., & Valkenburg, P. M. (2007). Who looks for casual dates on the Internet? A test of the compensation and the recreation hypotheses. *New Media & Society, 9* (3), 455–474.

Peter, J., & Valkenburg, P. M. (2008a). Adolescents' exposure to sexually explicit Internet material and sexual preoccupancy: A three-wave panel study. *Media Psychology, 11,* 207–234.

Peter, J., & Valkenburg, P. M. (2008b). Adolescents' exposure to sexually explicit Internet material, sexual uncertainty, and attitudes toward uncommitted sexual exploration: Is there a link? *Communication Research, 35,* 579–601.

Prensky, M. (2001). Digital natives, digital immigrants. *On the Horizon, 9*(5), 1–6.

Reich, S. M., Subrahmanyam, K., & Espinoza, G. (2012). Friending, IMing and hanging out face-to-face: Overlap in adolescents' online and offline social networks. *Developmental Psychology, 48,* 356–368.

Rice, F. P. (2001). *Human development.* Upper Saddle River, NJ: Prentice Hall.

Rideout, V. (2001). Generation rx.Com: How young people use the Internet for health information. Retrieved December 18, 2008, from http://www.kff.org/entmedia/upload/Toplines.pdf.

Roberts, D. F., Foehr, U. G., & Rideout, V. (2005). Generation m: Media in the lives of 8-18 year-olds—report. Retrieved December 16, 2008, from http://www.kff.org/entmedia/7251.cfm.

Saleh, F. M. (2009). *Internet pornography and cybersex*. Paper presented at the American Society for Adolescent Psychiatry. Available at http://www.adolpsych.org/presentations09/Saleh-InternetPornographyandCybersex.pdf.

Sevcikova, A., Serek, J., Machackova, H., & Smahel, D. (2013). Extent matters: Exposure to sexual material among Czech adolescents. *Journal of Early Adolescence, 33*(8), 1048–1071.

Sevcikova, A., & Konecny, S. (2011). An exploration of the relationship between real-world sexual experience and online sexual activity among 17-year-old adolescents. *Cyberpsychology: Journal of Psychosocial Research on Cyberspace, 5*, Article 3.

Sirianni, J. M., & Vishwanath, A. (2012). Sexually explicit user-generated content: Understanding motivations and behaviors using social cognitive theory. *Cyberpsychology: Journal of Psychosocial Research on Cyberspace, 6*.

Smahel, D. (2003). *Psychologie a internet: děti dospělými, dospělí dětmi. [Psychology and Internet: children being adults, adults being children.]* Prague: Triton.

Smahel, D. (2006). *Czech adolescents' partnership relations and sexuality in the Internet environment*. Paper presented at the Society for Research on Adolescence Biennial Meeting. Available at http://www.terapie.cz/materials/smahel-SRA-SF-2006.pdf.

Steele, J. R., & Brown, J. D. (1995). Adolescent room culture: Studying media in the context of everyday life. *Journal of Youth and Adolescence, 24*, 551–576.

Steele, J.R. (1999). Teenage sexuality and media practice: Factoring in the influences of family, friends and school. *The Journal of Sex Research, 36*(4), 331–341.

Steinberg, L. (2008). *Adolescence*. New York, NY: McGraw-Hill.

Subrahmanyam, K., Garcia, E. C., Harsono, S. L., Li, J., & Lipana, L. (2009). In their words: Connecting online weblogs to developmental processes. *British Journal of Developmental Psychology, 27*, 219–245.

Subrahmanyam, K., & Greenfield, P. M. (2008). Communicating online: Adolescent relationships and the media. *The Future of Children, 18*, 119–146.

Subrahmanyam, K., Greenfield, P. M., & Tynes, B. M. (2004). Constructing sexuality and identity in an online teen chat room. *Journal of Applied Developmental Psychology: An International Lifespan Journal, 25*, 651–666.

Subrahmanyam, K., & Šmahel, D. (2011). *Digital youth: The role of media in development*. Advancing Responsible Adolescent Development series. New York: Springer Publishing.

Subrahmanyam, K., Smahel, D., & Greenfield, P. (2006). Connecting developmental constructions to the Internet: Identity presentation and sexual exploration in online teen chat rooms. *Developmental Psychology, 42*, 395–406.

Suler, J. (2008). *The psychology of cyberspace*. Retrieved August 20, 2008, from http://www-usr.rider.edu/~suler/psycyber/psycyber.html.

Suzuki, L. K., & Calzo, J. P. (2004). The search for peer advice in cyberspace: An examination of online teen bulletin boards about health and sexuality. *Journal of Applied Developmental Psychology, 25*, 685–698.

Turkle, S. (1997). *Life on the screen: Identity in the age of the Internet (1st ed.)*. New York: Touchstone.

Vybíral, Z., Smahel, D. & Divínová, R. (2004). Growing up in virtual reality—adolescents and the Internet. In P. Mareš (Ed.), *Society, reproduction, and contemporary challenges*. Brno: Barrister & Principal. Available at http://www.terapie.cz/materials/czech-adolescents-internet.pdf

Wallmyr, G., & Welin, C. (2006). Young people, pornography, and sexuality: Sources and attitudes. *Journal of School Nursing, 22*, 290–295.

Ward, L. M. (2004). *And TV makes three: Comparing contributions of parents, peers, and the media to sexual socialization.* Paper presented at the Society for Research in Adolescence.

Weinstein, E., & Rosen, E. (1991). The development of adolescent sexual intimacy: Implications for counseling. *Adolescence, 26*, 331–339.

Weisskirch, R. S., & Delevi, R. (2011). Sexting and adult romantic attachment. *Computers in Human Behavior, 27*, 1697–1701.

Winston, L. (2010). *Good, better, best: School-based STD screening in Washington, DC.* Department of Health, 2010.

Whitty, M. T., & Carr, A. (2006). *Cyberspace romance: the psychology of online relationships.* Basingstoke, England, and New York: Palgrave Macmillan.

Ybarra, M. L., & Mitchell, K. J. (2005). Exposure to Internet pornography among children and adolescents: A national survey. *CyberPsychology & Behavior, 8*, 473–486.

PART TWO

Adolescent Sexual Behavior in the Digital Age

5 Youth-Produced Sexual Images, "Sexting," and the Cellphone

■ CLAY CALVERT

■ INTRODUCTION

One of the most controversial categories of speech in the United States is sexual expression. During the twentieth century, censored sexual material ranged across media from printed books like *Ulysses* by James Joyce to spoken stand-up comedy routines by Lenny Bruce to mainstream Hollywood-produced films like *Carnal Knowledge* by Mike Nichols. More recently, producer Ira Isaacs was found guilty on five counts of obscenity in April 2012 by a Los Angeles jury relating to the distribution of films involving adults engaged in scatology and bestiality.

In the past seven or eight years, however, a new subset of sexual expression conveyed on a different medium emerged, to much media fanfare, called sexting. It initially "spurred a vigorous, if often sensational, discourse in the popular press" (Judge, 2012, p. 86). Indeed, Curnett (2012) adds that initial news media and talk show coverage "framed sexting as an epidemic in which teenage participants are psychologically traumatized and possibly guilty of producing child pornography" (p. 353).

Perhaps partly prompted by such sensational and high-profile attention that sexting garnered in 2009 and 2010 in the mainstream news media, a raft of scholars from a multitude of disciplines soon began attempting to provide a more dispassionate and objective examination of this phenomenon. At the same time, lawmakers across the United States considered—and, in some cases, adopted—statutes to address sexting. Yet by late 2013, gaining a firm grasp on all facets of this cultural, sexual, and technological phenomenon was still largely elusive.

That is principally because sexting is, quite literally, generations removed from adult movies like *Deep Throat* and *Behind the Green Door* shown during the porno-chic era of the 1970s in now-shuttered "dirty" movie theaters, and then later replayed at home during the 1980s on erstwhile cutting-edge technologies like the videocassette recorder. Indeed, as the times have progressed, so too have the technologies with which sexual content can be produced, disseminated, and consumed. Sexting, as this chapter illustrates, is a thoroughly twenty-first-century phenomenon that pivots not only on changing times and technologies, but also on shifting notions of who can or should produce and possess sexually explicit content and who, in turn, can or should be prosecuted and punished for it, assuming it even is harmful. In fact, as Karaian (2012) writes, often-alarmist news media coverage of sexting largely suggests it is "a significant and overwhelmingly harmful practice for youth and for teenage girls in particular" (p. 60).

Sexting, from an etymological perspective, is a provocative portmanteau that melds "sex" and "texting." From a cultural standpoint, it represents a combustible combination of carnality and technology—one in which individuals use cellphones, smartphones, webcams, and other modes of socially interactive digital technology to take and transmit sexually suggestive and/or explicit images of themselves or others. Although constituting only a small fraction of a much larger wave of amateur pornography that now floods the Internet and jeopardizes the business models of traditional commercial purveyors of adult content, sexting triggered something close to both a moral and legal panic in the United States toward the end of the first decade of the twenty-first century and into the early 2010s. That is because minors who sext, be it with other minors or adults, are possibly producing and purveying one of the most loathed and reviled forms of expression today—child pornography.

By taking sexually graphic photographs and/or webcam videos of their own genitalia and pubic areas, minors now can easily create their own child pornography, depending on the degree of explicitness and level of lasciviousness of the imagery. And by sending those same sexually charged images downstream to other minors on the Internet or via their smart phones, they move beyond the realm of creators and producers of child pornography to the province of distributors. In turn, minors who receive—be it unexpectedly or through active solicitation—explicit images of other minors might well possess child pornography. It's a trifecta of trouble, from production to dissemination to reception. Teens and their favorite mobile communication technologies, in brief, are pushing the boundaries of child pornography laws and other statutes.

For instance, a 17-year-old male student at Bridgman High School in Berrien County, Michigan, was charged in March 2012 with distributing sexually abusive material featuring a child after he allegedly texted a friend a photograph of a nude 14-year-old girl (Aiken, 2012, p. 1A). The girl, it turns out, had taken the photo of herself and had texted it, along with four other images, to the accused. In January 2012, two students at Palmyra Area High School near Hershey, Pennsylvania, faced criminal charges after a sexting incident in which a 17-year-old girl allegedly sent explicit photographs of herself to a 15-year-old boy who, in turn, allegedly showed them to other students at the school ("Two Palmyra teens charged," 2012). The girl was charged with open lewdness, while the boy who initially received her photos was charged with disorderly conduct.

In November 2011, three teenage students at Oak Park-River Forest High School near Chicago were charged with misdemeanor counts of distribution of harmful material after sharing a photograph of a nude minor that apparently had been forwarded from one boy to another (Dwyer, 2011, p. 14). Also in 2011, police in Saline, Michigan, near Ann Arbor, dealt with three separate reports of middle-school students sending and sharing sexually explicit images of themselves via cellphones and other mobile communication technologies (Aisner, 2011). Four students there were charged with disturbing the peace, including a 13-year-old boy who allegedly used his cellphone to send a girl a picture of his genitals.

Sexting, as these incidents indicate, is a very far cry from the now seemingly quaint sexual risk-taking activities of youth like skinny dipping in the backyard pool, streaking across campus, or flashing a passing trucker on a highway. Unlike those behaviors, the captured imagery of sexting leaves a permanent record of a minor's participation that can linger in perpetuity on the Internet or last for years stored on a smartphone or a computer hard drive. Ultimately, sexting can entangle a child in the juvenile and criminal justice systems for sexual foolishness. As Judge (2012) observes, "what is different about sexting is that a digital artifact of sexual behavior is created in the act: the potential circulation and permanence of this image introduce a range of troubling legal questions" (p. 91).

Exacerbating the problem is the fact that sexted images can, in the parlance of our times, go viral. This sometimes occurs when a young couple breaks up and a spurned and angered boyfriend blasts out sexted images of his ex-girlfriend for all of his friends and her enemies to ogle. Those recipients, in turn, may pass them on to still other minors, with the prospect of shame, embarrassment, and public ridicule growing exponentially larger for the ex-girlfriend with each further retransmission to an originally unintended and undesired audience. In 2013, some of those images were ending up on so-called revenge porn websites, which are dedicated to sexually explicit postings uploaded by disgruntled former paramours. Such abusive, nonconsensual sexting behavior by the angered boyfriend has been labeled *aggravated* sexting by one pair of researchers attempting to fashion a sexting typology (Wolak & Finkelhor, 2011, p. 3). The converse of aggravated sexting is *experimental*, in which minors take photos of themselves and then consensually send them to established boyfriends or girlfriends or to others in an effort to spark a romantic interest or to gain someone's attention (Wolak & Finkelhor, 2011, p. 3).

All of this makes it unsurprising that "sexting has challenged society's definitions of normal adolescent behavior, problematic sexual behaviors, and a felony sex crime. Several teenagers are now serving time for sending and receiving photographs of their peers" (Weiss & Samenow, 2010, p. 244). Such outcomes, in part, have caused the social-sexual phenomenon of sexting in the United States to provoke "moral panic level responses" (Lumby & Funnell, 2011, p. 285).

For example, a January 2012 telephone survey conducted for the C.S. Mott Children's Hospital at the University of Michigan and administered nationwide by Knowledge Networks, Inc. to a randomly selected, stratified group of adults age 18 and older found that 44 percent of those surveyed considered sexting among teens to be a "very serious" issue (C.S. Mott Children's Hospital, 2012). The same study also found that 81 percent of adults surveyed believed that teens who sext should attend an education program or receive some form of counseling, while 76 percent favored requiring schools to give all students and parents information about sexting. In addition, 75 percent of those surveyed supported requiring sexting teens to perform community service.

Rather than receive education and counseling, however, sexting minors—from creators to distributors to possessors—can be subject to the harsh punishments typically meted out under federal and state child pornography statutes to adult sexual predators who exploit defenseless children. This sordid sexual reality, with the prospect that minors' unbridled sexual exuberance and legal naïveté could unwittingly transform themselves into convicted felons and registered-for-life sex offenders, not surprisingly captured public attention. Perhaps public recognition of the gravity of criminal consequences is why the same C.S. Mott Children's Hospital survey noted earlier also found that "[m]ost adults do not favor legal consequences for sexting among minors. Only 44% of adults support fines (less than $500) for youth sexting, while 20% or less believe that sexting should be treated a sex crime or that teen sext offenders should be prosecuted under sexual abuse laws." The results mirrored the sentiment expressed in a 2010 *New York Times* article, which found a "growing consensus among lawyers and legislators that the child pornography laws are too blunt an instrument to deal with an adolescent cyberculture in which all kinds of sexual pictures circulate on sites like MySpace and Facebook" (Lewin, 2010, p. A1). Similarly, a July 2010 issue of the *FBI Law Enforcement Bulletin* cautioned against aggressive prosecution of all juvenile sexting incidents, noting that "[l]aw enforcement officers and prosecutors must keep in mind that juvenile sex and child pornography laws exist to protect young people. While the activity associated with juvenile sexting technically may violate criminal statutes, prosecutors must use discretion" (Bowker & Sullivan, 2010, p. 30). But moderate, level-headed approaches to sexting are not always the rule. As Leary (2010) observes, "any social problem that exists at the intersection of adolescence, sex, technology, and criminal law compels strong reactions from all sides" (p. 487).

The reactions, in fact, from some legal quarters proved exceedingly strong during the first decade of the twenty-first century. In a few instances, minors who created or received such self-produced child pornography via cellphones or the Internet were either threatened or charged with producing, distributing, and possessing child pornography by zealous prosecutors. This chapter later explores how lawmakers across the United States are struggling to play legislative catch-up with a teen trend that challenges the legislative intent underlying child pornography laws. Those laws originally were designed to protect minors from adults, not to prosecute them for what some see as youthful indiscretions and hormone-charged sexual excitement. As McElroy (2010) wrote, "[t]he purpose of child pornography laws is to protect children from sexual abuse and exploitation, not punish them. Thus, lawmakers and prosecutors who wish to punish teens to teach them the lesson that sexting is wrong should not seek retribution under statutes meant to protect minors" (p. 15). Because some prosecutors are seeking such retribution, however, minors' electronic exhibitionism is causing states to adopt new laws that, generally speaking, substantially lessen the punishment for minors who consensually sext with other minors when compared with the sanctions that otherwise would be mandated under extant child pornography laws.

Adults, of course, also engage in sexting. For instance, a recent study of 760 young adults in the United States ranging in age from 18 to 24 years found that 30 percent of those surveyed had sent a sext and 41 percent had received a sext (Gordon-Messer, Bauermeister, Grodzinski, & Zimmerman, 2012). Perhaps most famously among older adults, U.S. Representative Anthony Weiner from New York became embroiled in 2011 in a sexting scandal in which he sent or exchanged sexually suggestive messages and images with several women via Twitter and other new media technologies. Weiner ultimately resigned his political post after the aptly named "Weinergate" affair became comedic fodder for late-night talk show hosts and a serious distraction for fellow members of Congress, some of whom called for him to step down. In 2013, during an ill-fated run for mayor of New York City, Weiner admitted to more sexting. The Weiner scandal, in fact, caused the editor-in-chief of *Cyberpsychology, Behavior, and Social Networking* to call for more research on adult sexting and to address why married people text sexual messages and photos to someone other than their spouse (Wiederhold, 2011, p. 481). In addition to Weiner, former National Football League quarterback Brett Favre was entangled in a sexting scandal in 2010 after he allegedly sent sexual messages and lewd photos via his cellphone to a female football-sidelines reporter.

While such incidents are embarrassing for the adults involved and highly troubling from a moral perspective, the legal consequences are far more serious when minors are the protagonists. Sexting and minors thus are the focus of this chapter. This chapter initially examines the threshold, definitional problem of explicating sexting, including the multiple permutations and variations of youth-only sexting that make its study so difficult. The chapter then scrutinizes the real-world practice of youth-only sexting and its prevalence, providing the results of several surveys and summarizing the facts from some high-profile sexting incidents that helped to put this new genre of sexual expression on the public's radar screen. The chapter next explores some of the possible reasons why minors sext. The chapter then turns both to the First Amendment guarantee of free speech and to the pivotal exception to that constitutional safeguard carved out by the U.S. Supreme Court for child pornography. In particular, it analyzes how and when sexting by minors may fall within the reach of current child pornography statutes. Finally, the chapter focuses on the growing number of legislative responses to youth sexting, exploring how they address sexting through some very different approaches.

■ SEXTING BY MINORS AND ITS MULTIPLE VARIATIONS

A threshold problem with analyzing sexting is semantic. Sexting lacks a clear, coherent definition. Just as the word "pornography" carries no legal definition in the United States (in contrast to obscenity, which the U.S. Supreme Court defined in 1973) and means different things to different people, so too does sexting not possess an agreed-upon definition, be it legal or even colloquial. It thus has been observed that the "term has been defined in numerous ways by various stakeholders" (Lumby & Funnell, 2011, p. 285).

Broadly defined, sexting need not even involve imagery. It might consist solely of racy and risqué text-only messages, perhaps swapped between paramours or traded as a high-tech form of flirtation between sexually attracted individuals. Rather than passing love notes, in other words, a young couple or pair of possible partners might text their erotic passions and fantasies about each other in a series of steamy touch-screen messages.

When imagery is involved, however, the question then becomes whether sexting includes only explicit images of unclothed body parts such as breasts, genitalia, and pubic areas, or whether it more broadly encompasses all sexually suggestive or provocative images. For example, a sexually suggestive yet nonexplicit image might include an above-the-waist image of a 14-year-old girl wearing only a bra or covering her bare breasts with her hands. Using the term "sexually suggestive" to measure teens' sexting habits thus is problematic because it is vague and "open to wide interpretation" (Lumby & Funnell, 2011, p. 285).

The following are some examples of how sexting has been defined in both academic literature and survey research: "youth-produced sexual images," meaning "pictures created by minors (age 17 or younger) that depict minors and that are or could be child pornography under applicable statutes" (Wolak & Finkelhor, 2011, p. 2); "the sending and receiving of sexually explicit photos and/or text using cell phones with digital cameras" (Wysocki & Childers, 2011, p. 220); the transmission or reception by teens of "sexually suggestive nude or nearly nude photos or videos of themselves or of someone they knew on their cell phones" (Lenhart, 2009, p. 4); and "a colloquial term that refers to individuals sending explicit photographs or messages to others" (Ferguson, 2011, p. 239). Rather than having academics, researchers, and lawmakers impose their own definitions on sexting, Lumby and Funnell (2011) argue that those "interested in sexting ought to turn their attention to how those engaged in or associated with the activity of sexting define it for themselves" (p. 286).

While sexting lacks an agreed-upon legal definition, several states now use the term in statutory language. For instance, Florida Statute Section 847.0141 (2012), which took effect in October 2011, defines "the offense of sexting." By December 2012, the National Conference of State Legislatures reported that at least 20 states had adopted laws or resolutions to address sexting by minors and at least a dozen more were considering sexting bills that same year. As addressed later, not all of the states use the term "sexting" within their statutory language.

Even if a single definition of sexting eventually is universally agreed upon by either academic researchers or lawmakers, it still would not resolve the difficulties of studying this phenomenon. That is because there are multiple variations and permutations in which sexting may occur, even when considering just the minor-to-minor, youth-only sexting context and when excluding possible adult-to-minor and minor-to-adult sexting variations. For example, in some instances youth sexting may be completely consensual in terms of both the sender and the recipient. This would be the case when one minor, voluntarily and without coercion, takes a sexually explicit image of herself and then texts it to a willing-recipient boyfriend.

In other instances, however, the minor recipient may be unwilling and even offended to receive the image, or the initial taker may have been coerced or otherwise physically threatened by a boyfriend to take the image of herself against her will. Similarly, a minor at a slumber party who is stepping out of the shower may have her nude image surprisingly and jokingly taken by a friend, but then later find it posted online or texted to others. In brief, any one or all of the three steps or phases of sexted images—from their creation to their transmission to their reception—may be either consensual or nonconsensual. As Judge (2012) observes, "although the exchange of images may begin in an experimental or friendly context, it may abruptly shift to an aggravated one—especially given the vicissitudes of adolescent relationships, the normative increase in sexual energy during this period, and potent neurodevelopmental influences" (p. 89).

In addition to the variable of consensuality, sexting may be primary or secondary. A primary sexting incident occurs when the minor taking a sexted image is the same person who also appears in the image and who transmits it. It thus might also be considered *primary, self-sexting*, as there is unity of person among the taker, the depicted, and the transmitter of the image. Conversely, sexting may be secondary (incidents in which the sender is not the same person who took and initially transmitted the image in question but, instead, is a person who received it from someone else and then forwarded it on to others, without the permission or knowledge of the person who originally took it). This latter variety thus might also be classified as *secondary, downstream-sexting* (Calvert, 2009, p. 30; Calvert, Murrhee, & Steve, 2010, p. 10). Put differently, secondary sexting may be thought of as downstream sexting because someone other than the original sender of a sexted image is retransmitting it to a larger pool of recipients. Some or all members of that larger pool of recipients may not be individuals for whom the image was originally, or even ever later, intended. This would be the case, for instance, when a boy who has consensually received a sexted image taken and transmitted voluntarily by his girlfriend decides, without her knowledge, to show off the picture to his friends by texting it to them. The boy is a downstream sexter and his friends are downstream-sexting recipients.

▪ THE PROBLEM AND ITS PREVALENCE

It is fair to say that 2009 is the year when sexting first caused a full-blown news media frenzy in the United States, after starting to percolate the prior year. The *New York Times*, for instance, identified sexting as one of the top buzzwords for

2009 (Leibovich & Barrett, 2009). The stir that year was largely due to the triangulation of several factors and events, including (1) the release of survey data purporting to show the widespread nature of sexting among American teens; (2) a series of sexting incidents involving either brushes with the criminal justice system or personally tragic endings; and (3) public pushback to overly aggressive responses by law enforcement officials.

■ THE DATA

First and foremost among the variables that catapulted sexting to national prominence was a study released in December 2008 by CosmoGirl.com and the National Campaign to Prevent Teen and Unplanned Pregnancy called "Sex and Tech: Results From a Survey of Teens and Young Adults" (National Campaign to Prevent Teen and Unplanned Pregnancy, 2008). Its sponsors proudly touted it as the "first public study of its kind to quantify the proportion of teens and young adults that are sending or posting sexually suggestive text and images." The survey found that 22 percent of all teen girls surveyed—more than one out of five—said they had sent or posted either nude or seminude pictures or videos of themselves. The study also determined that 25 percent of teen girls and 33 percent of teen boys said they had had nude or seminude images that were originally meant for someone else shared with them.

Not surprisingly, those kind of figures generated sensational and attention-grabbing newspaper headlines, such as "Teen Girls are Hot for Texting Nude Pix, Sez Survey" in the December 11, 2008, edition of the *New York Daily News* (Boyle, 2008) and "Sex 'Cells' for Naked Teenagers; Naughty Cam Craze" in the January 25, 2009, edition of the *New York Post* (Cahalan, 2009). A front-page story in the December 10, 2008, edition of *USA Today* ran under the sub-headline, "Racy Pics, Messages Flying Among Young" (Jayson, 2008). That same day, the *Today Show* reported on the survey, and later that month, Bill O'Reilly featured the so-called "culture warriors"—Gretchen Carlson and Margaret Hoover—on *The O'Reilly Factor* discussing sexting and the survey's results. By March 2009, even staid National Public Radio program *All Things Considered* had aired a segment on teen sexting. Sexting, in brief, had thoroughly captured both print and broadcast media attention and the public imagination in a few short months, thanks largely to the results of one dataset.

A look behind the "Sex and Tech" survey, however, reveals that only 653 teens participated and those "teens" included many 18- and 19-year-olds—adults in the eyes of the law, at least when it comes to child pornography. In fact, of the teens surveyed, slightly more than half (51 percent) were 17 years of age or older. Furthermore, while the study reported that 22 percent of all teenage girls surveyed had sent or posted nude or seminude photos or videos of themselves, the figure dropped dramatically to 11 percent when the age range was narrowed from 13- to 19-year-olds to 13- to 16-year-olds. In addition, the "Sex and Tech" survey used an online panel that did not involve probability sampling. As Bialik (2009) wrote in a *Wall Street Journal* column about the survey, "many wonder whether the average person who signs up for such a panel can be representative of the broader population" (p. A9).

Some subsequent studies have produced different figures that suggest a lower prevalence of sexting among teens. For instance, the Pew Internet & American Life Project in December 2009 released the results of a nationwide telephone survey of 800 teens, ranging age from 12 to 17 years, that was conducted by Princeton Survey Research International between June 26 and September 24, 2009. The survey, called "Teens and Sexting: How and Why Minor Teens are Sending Sexually Suggestive Nude or Nearly Nude Images via Text Messaging," used both landline and cellphone telephone numbers. Two big-picture findings emerged: (1) 4 percent of cell-owning teens surveyed between the ages 12 and 17 years said they had sent sexually suggestive nude or nearly nude images of themselves to someone else via text messaging and (2) 15 percent of cell-owning teens within that same age range said they had received sexually suggestive nude or nearly nude images of someone they knew on their cellphone. The data also produced a gender-neutral finding—girls and boys were equally as likely to have sent a suggestive picture to another person.

A more recent telephone survey of 1,560 Internet users, ranging in age from 10 through 17 years, reached dramatically different results from both the "Sex and Tech" and "Teens and Sexting" surveys and, in particular, revealed that how one defines sexting makes a great deal of difference in the results (Mitchell, Finkelhor, Jones, & Wolak, 2012). That study found that if sexting is defined as youth creating *sexually explicit* images of themselves that include their naked breasts, genitals, or bottoms—the type of content that might rise to the level of illegal child pornography—the rate of involvement is only 1 percent. On the other hand, if sexting is more broadly defined as appearing in or creating *sexually suggestive* images, rather than explicit ones, then the figure rises to 2.5 percent. The authors acknowledged, however, that the actual figures could be somewhat higher because some minors may not self-disclose their sexting activities during a telephone interview.

The January 2012 nationwide survey of adults conducted for the C.S. Mott Children's Hospital defined sexting as "sending sexually explicit or nude photos or videos by cell phone." The survey found that 10 percent of parents reported their own teens as having received a sexted message on their cellphones, while 6 percent of parents said their teens have transmitted a sexted message.

Finally, an article published online in July 2012 in the *Archives of Pediatrics & Adolescent Medicine* determined that slightly more than 27 percent of the 964 public high-school students from the Houston area surveyed reported having sent a naked picture of themselves through text or email (Temple, Paul, van den Berg, Le, McElhany, & Temple, 2012). The authors found no significant difference between girls and boys when it came to sending sexts (p. E2). On the other hand, nearly 69 percent of girls surveyed said they had been asked to send a text, while only

42 percent of boys had been asked to transmit one. In terms of correlations with sexting among girls, the survey reported that "prevalence of having started dating, having had sex, having multiple sex partners, and using alcohol or drugs before sex were all higher among those who have sent, received, or asked for a sext than among those who had not engaged in those sexting behaviors" (p. E3). Among boys, however, the survey found "no significant association between having sent or received a sext and having multiple sex partners or using alcohol or drugs before sex" (p. E3).

The bottom line is that a consensus does not yet exist on how many or what percentage of American teens sext. The actual figures are likely to fluctuate depending upon how narrowly or expansively sexting is operationalized in any given survey instrument. In addition, the very real possibility that some teens won't reveal, either for fear of parental retribution or personal embarrassment, their own sexting habits on self-disclosure instruments further muddies efforts to pin down accurate sexting data.

■ HIGH-PROFILE SEXTING INCIDENTS AND PUBLIC PUSHBACK TO PROSECUTIONS

A second factor—one beyond the startling results of the "Sex and Tech" survey—that helped to shine media, public, and legislative spotlights on sexting was a series of relatively contemporaneous incidents. One involved the January 2009 charging of six minors—three girls, 14 and 15 years old, and three boys, 16 and 17 years old—from Greensburg Salem High School in Westmoreland County, Pennsylvania, with child pornography offenses. The girls allegedly took and sent nude or seminude photographs of themselves to the boys. A school district official stated that the students in question seemed desensitized, while the parents were in shock (Stiles, 2009). The decision to arrest the minors for child pornography offenses drew a swift rebuke from some quarters, with Ferguson (2009) calling it "a travesty of justice. Their behavior is injudicious and irresponsible but, like it or not, not unusual. Such behavior should be treated with firm parental discipline and love, not imprisonment" (p. H-4). Ultimately, five of the teens entered into consent decrees with juvenile authorities, while a sixth, who already had a juvenile record, was placed on a one-year probation. None was required to register as a sex offender.

In March 2009, news of another troubling sexting incident from a small, rural Pennsylvania community broke in national news media outlets, including the *New York Times* (Hamill, 2009, p. A21). This incident, unlike the one in Greensburg, spawned a civil rights-based lawsuit that ultimately worked its way up to a federal appellate court in 2010 (*Miller v. Skumanick*, 2010). The controversy began in October 2008 when officials in the Tunkannock Area School District, about 30 miles northwest of Scranton, reportedly discovered seminude and nude photos of teenage girls, many of whom were enrolled in the district, on several students' cellphones. Male students in the district apparently had been trading the photos on their own phones. They, in turn, ultimately surrendered their phones to George Skumanick, the District Attorney of Wyoming County.

In February 2009, the controversy heated up when Skumanick sent a letter to the parents of 20 students. In it, he threatened to bring felony child pornography charges against their children unless the minors agreed to attend a five-week, 10-hour education program designed by Skumanick in conjunction with two other agencies. That choice quickly caught the attention of the American Civil Liberties Union of Pennsylvania, which filed a federal lawsuit in March 2009 on behalf of three girls who appeared in two of the photographs on which Skumanick had set his prosecutorial sights. The other 17 minors, however, accepted Skumanick's terms and did not contest the matter.

According to the ACLU, neither of the two images in question came close to constituting illegal child pornography. One photo showed two of the girls, Marissa Miller and Grace Kelly, from the waist up wearing white opaque bras, with one girl talking on a cellphone and the other making a peace sign. They were 12 or 13 years old at the time the photo was taken. The other image depicted a 16-year-old girl identified only as Nancy Doe (a pseudonym used to protect her real identity) standing just outside of a shower, with a white, opaque bath towel wrapped around most of her body, but tied just underneath her bare breasts. Neither of the two photos depicted any sexual activity or revealed anything below the waist.

As described later in this chapter, there typically must be a lascivious exhibition of the genitals or pubic area for an image to constitute child pornography if no other sexual conduct, such as intercourse, bestiality, or masturbation, is depicted. Under the Pennsylvania law applicable in the Wyoming County case, an image rises to the level of child pornography only when there is a "lewd exhibition of the genitals or nudity if such nudity is depicted for the purpose of sexual stimulation or gratification of any person who might view such depiction" (18 Pa. Cons. Stat. § 6312 (g) (2013)). Nudity by itself, in other words, does not amount to child pornography. Despite these facts, Skumanick nonetheless claimed the bra-clad image of Miller and Kelly constituted child pornography because the two girls were "provocatively" posed, and he asserted that the topless image of Doe also was child pornography.

The ACLU asserted in its lawsuit on behalf of all three girls that the images were protected by the First Amendment freedom of speech and, in turn, that the girls possessed a constitutionally protected right to refuse to participate in the education program Skumanick had offered as an alternative to a child pornography prosecution. Skumanick, the lawsuit claimed, was retaliating against the girls simply for exercising a constitutionally protected right. In addition, the ACLU argued on behalf of Nancy Doe that requiring her to attend the education program in lieu of facing child pornography charges impermissibly usurped and violated her mother's fundamental right to raise her child without undue state interference.

Skumanick's threat to charge with the girls with child pornography was blasted by several news organizations. For instance, the editorial board of the *Philadelphia*

Inquirer opined that "criminal charges for this brand of adolescent stupidity are the equivalent of going nuclear. Convict a teen under child porn laws and he or she will be branded as a sex offender, forced to register under Megan's Law-style statutes, and basically scarred for life" ("Editorial," 2009, p. A10). Megan's Law statutes are named in honor of Megan Kanka, a seven-year-old New Jersey girl who was raped and murdered in July 1994 by a child molester who had moved across the street from the Kanka family without their knowledge. The statutes, which now exist in some form in all states, as well as at the federal level, are designed to alert local community members when registered sex offenders move into their neighborhoods.

While the sexting lawsuit of *Miller v. Skumanick* was under way, and perhaps demonstrating the unpopularity of his actions, Skumanick lost his re-election bid for Wyoming County District Attorney in November 2009. In April 2010, with the case having previously reached the appellate court level, U.S. District Judge James M. Munley issued a permanent injunction prohibiting the new district attorney, Jeff Mitchell, and his staff from ever initiating criminal charges against plaintiffs Marissa Miller, Grace Kelly, and Nancy Doe for the two photographs at issue (*Miller v. Mitchell*, 2010).

The case of a young Floridian named Phillip Alpert also gained widespread news media attention in 2009. Alpert was 18 years old when he emailed nude photographs of his former girlfriend—photos she had consensually taken of herself at age 16 and sent to him when he was 17—to about 70 people during a fit of anger. For that action, he ultimately pleaded guilty in 2008 to transmitting child pornography charges. Alpert, who received five years probation and was forced to attend so-called recovery meetings with convicted pedophiles as part of the terms of that probation, today is listed as a registered sex offender on the Florida Department of Law Enforcement's website. He will remain a registered sex offender until at least age 43, at which time he can petition the Florida courts to be removed from the list. There is no guarantee that such a petition would be granted.

During a May 2009 interview conducted by the author of this chapter and a colleague with Alpert and his attorney, Lawrence Walters, Alpert explained the impact on his life of being a registered sex offender:

> Any time I move, I have to register. There are also a lot of places I can't move to. My father's house, for example. I would be living with him right now, which would save a lot of money and frustration, but, unfortunately, he lives too close to a high school. Ironically, it is the high school I attended. (Richards & Calvert, 2009, p. 21)

Alpert also elaborated on what he perceived as the unjustness of his inclusion of the sex offender registry, stating that:

> [t]he list itself is designed so that you know who around your area...could be a danger to you or your children. If you saw me on that list, you would see, as my offense, the sending of child pornography. You would think, therefore, to keep your

children away from me. But I'm not a threat to your children. (Richards & Calvert, 2009, p. 23)

In addition to Phillip Alpert's case and the Pennsylvania sexting incidents in both Westmoreland and Wyoming counties, several other sexting events garnered media attention around the same time. One case centered on the suicide of 18-year-old Jessica Logan in July 2008. Logan, from Ohio, took a nude photograph of herself with her cell phone and sent it to her then-boyfriend, Ryan Salyers. After they broke up, however, he allegedly sent the image out to several other students. The image apparently soon went viral and was re-forwarded again and again, eventually reaching hundreds of students attending at least seven Cincinnati-area high schools. Some of the girls who received the image taunted Logan mercilessly, calling her names like "slut" and "whore" until finally she took her own life. The case, which gained national attention in March 2009 when Logan's mother went on the *Today Show* to describe her daughter's life and death to anchor Matt Lauer, illustrates how sexting can merge with another troubling, high-tech adolescent phenomenon, cyber-bullying.

Cyber-bullying, which like sexting lacks an agreed-upon definition, involves online aggression and "can include anything from the sending of private messages to the posting of public messages, photos, or videos about a targeted individual" (Law, Shapka, Domene, & Gagné, 2012, p. 664). New Jersey's youth sexting law, which took effect in April 2012, makes explicit reference to cyber-bullying, as it provides that minors who sext shall undergo a remedial education or counseling program in which they are to be made aware of "the possible connection between bullying and cyber-bullying and juveniles sharing sexually suggestive or explicit materials" (N.J. Stat. § 2A:4A-71.1 (2012)).

■ WHY MINORS SEXT

Academic literature on sexting, although sparse and only its infancy, is growing within a diverse range of disciplines. It can be found, for instance, in the realm of legal scholarship, as well as in the fields of psychiatry, psychology, cyber-psychology, human–computer interaction, and education. As this assortment of scholarly approaches intimates, sexting may carry not only legal consequences for minors but also possible developmental and psychological ones. A pivotal question is why minors choose to engage in sexting in the first place.

One major factor that contributes to teen sexting, according to Sadhu (2012), simply is access to technology and, in particular, "the dramatic increase in cell phone use and ownership by teenagers over the past few years" (p. 76). In fact, as Judge (2012) observes, "text messaging is the preferred form of basic communication among adolescents today, even ahead of cell calling" (p. 87).

This technology and its use, in turn, is deployed by minors who are experimenting with their own identities and may not perceive the risks and dangers involved with disseminating sexual images of themselves. As Sadhu writes, "[t]eenagers' tendency toward exhibitionism and narcissism, their desire for intimacy in relationships, their desire and preoccupation with sexual exploration, and the hope of creating their identities as individuals who are attractive and desired may make them more vulnerable to the allure of sexting" (p. 76). Judge (2012) elaborates on this point, writing that sexting "may be viewed as an emotionally driven behavior that is often impulsive and without a clear anticipation or understanding of the potential adverse consequences. An adolescent who speaks rationally about sexting when calm may nonetheless engage in the behavior (including in an aggravated manner) when emotionally aroused" (p. 90).

O'Keefe and Clarke-Pearson (2011) add that "[b]ecause of their limited capacity for self-regulation and susceptibility to peer pressure, children and adolescents are at some risk as they navigate and experiment with social media" (p. 800). Chalfen (2009) notes that girls often say that their boyfriends are asking for sexual photos or that girls "sext to specific boys they wish to know better" (p. 263).

A sex-saturated culture, replete with music, movies, video games, and television content that sexualizes young girls, also likely contributes to the normalization of sexting by girls. Durham (2008) writes that "kids are evidently getting the message that sexual behavior is appropriate at very early ages. As they enter the "tween years—eight to twelve—many of them begin to engage in sexual activity" (p. 48). Per objectification theory (Fredrickson & Roberts, 1997), as some girls start to self-objectify by viewing and treating their own bodies as objects to be ogled, evaluated, and desired by boys, it seems natural that they would send self-taken images of their nude or partially nude bodies to be the focus of boys' gaze.

The propensity to sext also may correlate with other risky behaviors. Dake, Price, Maziarz, and Ward (2012) surveyed more than 1,000 middle-school and high-school students and found that sexting was "highly associated with engaging in high risk sexual behaviors, including having had four or more sexual partners, engaging in oral and anal sex, as well as not using contraception at their last sexual intercourse" (p. 12). Sexting was also significantly associated with substance use activities such as smoking marijuana and drinking alcohol. They note, however, "that not all teens who sext are involved in sexual activity," suggesting that "for some teens, sexting might be an alternative to engaging in sexual activity" (Dake et al., p. 13).

In terms of the motivations for sexting, minors may consensually sext with each other when they are involved in an ongoing romantic relationship or to draw sexual attention to themselves among prospective romantic partners (Wolak & Finkelhor, 2011, p. 5). Conversely, minors may sext due to peer pressure or, worse, they may be coerced into sexting against their will, perhaps by a threat of harm from a boyfriend unless a sexual image is not forthcoming. In addition, minors may sext with an intent to cause harm, as when a boy sends out sexual images of his ex-girlfriend to classmates, intending to embarrass her. As noted earlier, this can be considered aggravated sexting (Wolak & Finkelhor, 2011, p. 5) and also a form of cyber-bullying.

▓ THE FIRST AMENDMENT AND CHILD PORNOGRAPHY

The First Amendment to the U.S. Constitution protects freedom of expression against government censorship, providing in relevant part that "Congress shall make no law...abridging the freedom of speech." Despite such seemingly absolute language about "no law" and the fact that "Congress" has been interpreted by the U.S. Supreme Court to include not only the U.S. Congress but also state and local governmental entities and officials, the First Amendment does not safeguard all forms of expression from censorship. In particular, the nation's high court has carved out multiple exceptions to freedom of speech since the First Amendment was adopted more than 220 years ago in 1791.

Among the categorical carve-outs of unprotected speech are fighting words, incitement to violence, true threats of violence, false advertising, obscenity, and, of most importance for this chapter, child pornography. In *New York v. Ferber* (1982), the Supreme Court wrote that "the exploitative use of children in the production of pornography has become a serious national problem" (p. 749). The case centered on the prosecution of the proprietor of a Manhattan bookstore named Paul Ferber who sold to an undercover police officer two films depicting young boys masturbating. When the case reached the U.S. Supreme Court, the issue the justices faced was simply framed: "To prevent the abuse of children who are made to engage in sexual conduct for commercial purposes, could the New York State Legislature, consistent with the First Amendment, prohibit the dissemination of material which shows children engaged in sexual conduct, regardless of whether such material is obscene?" (p. 753).

In answering that query in the affirmative, the Supreme Court made it clear that obscenity and child pornography are not the same type of content. States are entitled to greater leeway in the regulation of pornographic depictions of children than they are of sexual depictions of adults. Put differently, when minors are depicted in sexually explicit activity, the content need not rise to the level of obscenity, as defined by the U.S. Supreme Court in *Miller v. California* (1973), before states can prohibit it. The reason for this lesser standard, the Court stressed in *Ferber*, is that minors are harmed physiologically, emotionally, and mentally when they participate in child pornography. In addition, minors who engage in child pornography can face a lifetime of pain because "the materials produced are a permanent record of the children's participation and the harm to the child is exacerbated by their circulation" (*Ferber*, p. 759).

Since *Ferber*, the Supreme Court has held that the First Amendment does not protect the production, distribution, possession, and viewing of child pornography. As the Court reasoned in a case called *Osborne v. Ohio* (1990), "it is now difficult, if not impossible, to solve the child pornography problem by only attacking production and distribution" (p. 110).

The Supreme Court, however, has not provided a definition of child pornography, leaving it to the U.S. Congress and state legislative bodies to fashion their own definitions. This too is different from obscenity. The Court in *Miller v. California* fashioned a three-part test for obscenity in 1973 that focuses on whether the content (1) taken as a whole and applying contemporary community standards, appeals to a prurient interest in sex when considered from the perspective of an average adult; (2) is patently offensive as defined by the state legislature; and (3) lacks serious literary, artistic, political, or scientific value. This obscenity test is now incorporated into all state-level obscenity statutes.

In contrast to the judicially defined *Miller* test for obscenity, Congress statutorily classifies child pornography as images of those under 18 years of age engaged in "sexually explicit conduct" (18 U.S.C. §2256 (2013)). Sexually explicit conduct, in turn, includes a number of specific sexual acts, such as intercourse, masturbation, and bestiality, as well as a "lascivious exhibition of the genitals or pubic area of any person" (18 U.S.C. §2256 (2013)).

It is this last provision that is crucial for understanding why minors who sext can be charged with child pornography. In particular, federal law does not require a minor to be engaged in a sexual act with another person but simply mandates that an image features a lascivious exhibition of the genitals or pubic area. For instance, a 16-year-old girl who takes a close-up photograph of herself digitally stimulating her vagina and then sends it to her boyfriend via a cell phone has likely both created and disseminated child pornography. The boyfriend, in turn, probably possesses child pornography. Similarly, a 17-year-old boy who takes a close-up picture of himself touching his erect penis and sends it off to his girlfriend probably has created and disseminated child pornography.

The key term in the federal statute to decide whether or not the images are child pornography is "lascivious." Not every nude photograph of a minor constitutes a lascivious exhibition. If that were not the case, then innocuous and innocent images of a parent bathing her baby in a home bathtub would amount to child pornography. Instead, a lascivious exhibition is one that calls attention to the genitals or pubic area, such as a tightly focused shot, in order to excite lustfulness or sexual stimulation in the viewer. Many federal courts provide jurors in child pornography cases with a set of six factors to consider in reaching the lasciviousness determination: (1) whether the focal point of the picture is the minor's genitalia; (2) whether the setting or pose is customarily associated with sexual activity; (3) whether the minor's pose is unnatural given his or her age; (4) whether the minor is fully or partially nude; (5) whether sexual coyness or willingness to engage in sexual activity is suggested; and (6) whether the visual depiction is intended or designed to elicit a sexual response in the viewer. These elements frequently are referred to as the Dost factors, after the name of the defendant in the California federal district court decision from which they first arose, *United States v. Dost* (1986).

Another point must be considered under the federal child pornography statute, especially as it relates to sexting: an "exhibition" of the genitals or pubic area can occur even if a minor is wearing minimal clothing, such as a thong or skimpy bikini bottom. In other words, it is possible to have a lascivious exhibition of the genitals or pubic area when a minor is not fully nude. The seminal case that stands for this proposition is the opinion by the U.S. Court of Appeals for the Third Circuit in *United States v. Knox* (1994). The case centered on videotapes of young girls wearing bikinis, leotards, and underwear where the camera zoomed in on their pubic and genital areas to display close-up views for extended periods of time. In addition, the girls were "gyrating in a fashion not natural for their age" (p. 737). The appellate court concluded that the federal child pornography statute does not include a nudity requirement and that such exhibitions of minimally clothed pubic areas, as they were shot in the videos, were indeed lascivious. In terms of sexting, this means that a 14-year-old girl who captures a close-cropped shot or cellphone video of herself deeply rubbing her underwear-clad vagina in a sexually suggestive manner might be creating child pornography despite the fact that she is not nude.

Finally, the federal child pornography statutes do not exempt from their reach minors who create, distribute, or possess their own child pornography. In other words, they contain no age exemptions for younger perpetrators, and thus they would apply to typical sexting scenarios involving minors.

The punishment under federal law for creating and producing child pornography is severe. A first offense requires imprisonment of not less than 15 years and not more than 30 years (18 U.S.C. §2251 (2013)). Individuals who knowingly distribute or knowingly possess child pornography on a first offense are fined and imprisoned not less than five years and not more than 20 years (18 U.S.C. §2252 (2013) and 18 U.S.C. §2252A (2013)). It is the harshness of such penalties, as potentially applied to a pair of minors who consensually sext with each other as part of an ongoing romantic relationship, that seems unjust to many.

In addition to federal statutes outlawing child pornography, it is illegal to produce, distribute, and possess child pornography under the laws of all 50 states and the District of Columbia. Furthermore, an increasing number of states target the mere viewing of child pornography and other sexual imagery of minors, regardless of whether the individual possesses or controls the content.

Although states are not uniform in their definitions of child pornography, most track very closely the federal definition of sexually explicit conduct involving a minor. For instance, Connecticut defines sexually explicit conduct for purposes of its child pornography laws as "actual or simulated (A) sexual intercourse, including genital-genital, oral-genital, anal-genital, or oral-anal physical contact, whether between persons of the same or opposite sex, or with an artificial genital, (B) bestiality, (C) masturbation, (D) sadistic or masochistic abuse, or (E) lascivious exhibition of the genitals or pubic area of any person" (Conn. Gen. Stat. §53a-193 (2012)). Like the federal law, Connecticut's statute and others similar to it, such as Missouri Revised Statutes Section 573.010 (2012) and Mississippi Code Annotated Section 97-5-31 (2012), don't require sexual conduct by a minor but merely a lascivious exhibition of the minor's genitals or pubic area. They thus likely sweep up solo-shot sexted images by a minor of himself or herself that reveal the genitals or the pubic area in a sexually suggestive manner. Some states don't use the term "lascivious exhibition" but substitute more precise language. For instance, Washington Revised Code Section 9.68A.011 (2012) deploys the terminology "depiction of the genitals or unclothed pubic or rectal areas of any minor, or the unclothed breast of a female minor, for the purpose of sexual stimulation of the viewer." Florida, in contrast, does not use the term "lascivious" but instead opts for the phrase "actual lewd exhibition of the genitals" (Fla. Stat. §775.0847 (2012)). Similarly, Georgia employs the terminology "lewd exhibition of the genitals or pubic area" (Code Ga. Ann. §16-12-100 (2012)).

Despite such subtle nuances of definitional difference between the federal child pornography statutes and those of the states, the ramifications for violating the state laws often are equally as harsh as the federal punishments for child pornography. For example, Georgia generally mandates imprisonment for not less than five years nor more than 20 years and by a fine of up to $100,000 for the creation, distribution, and possession of child pornography (Official Code of Georgia Annotated Section 16-12-100 (g) (1) (2012)).

■ LEGISLATIVE RESPONSES TO SEXTING

By late 2013, more than 16 states had laws to address youth sexting, and other states were actively considering their own measures. There is little uniformity among the laws, however, other than that they all provide for far more lenient punishment for certain types of consensual sexting by minors than would be meted out under traditional child pornography laws.

To better understand the different approaches legislative bodies are taking with teen sexting, it initially is useful to break the current laws down into four components: (1) the definitions of the prohibited offense of sexting, including the age range of minors subject to the offense and whether or not the offense includes the transmission, reception, and/or possession of images; (2) the defenses or exemptions built into the sexting laws under which a minor could avoid any punishment; (3) the range of potential sanctions for a sexting offense, including different consequences for a first offense as compared to subsequent violations; and (4) possible language allowing for or precluding the possible prosecution of a sexting minor under additional and more serious criminal charges. Using these four components as an analytical tool, the following are three examples of state sexting laws. They illustrate different tacks taken to the problem, as well as the complex nuances and variations among the states in defining the offense of sexting. This is by no means a comprehensive review of all state sexting statutes, and more statutes likely will be adopted throughout the second decade of the twenty-first century.

Florida's sexting law, which took effect on October 1, 2011, is set forth at Florida Statute §847.0141 (2012). It is one of the most comprehensive sexting laws in the nation. In articulating the offense of sexting, it cross-references another Florida statute (Fla. Stat. §847.001 (2012)) to provide the meaning for such critical terms as minor (any person under the age of 18 years) and nudity (the showing of the genitals, pubic area, or buttocks with less than a fully opaque covering; the show-ing of the female breast with less than a fully opaque covering of any portion thereof below the top of the nipple; or the depiction of covered male genitals in a discernibly turgid state). In addition, Florida's sexting law incorporates the phrase "harmful to minors" from another state statute, which defines it as depictions of nudity, sexual conduct, or sexual excitement that: a) predominantly appeal to a prurient, shameful, or morbid interest; b) are patently offensive to prevailing stan-dards in the adult community as a whole with respect to what is suitable material or conduct for minors; and c) are without serious literary, artistic, political, or scientific value for minors (Fla. Stat. §847.001 (2012)).

Florida's sexting law includes separate provisions that address and distinguish between the offense of transmitting and distributing images, on the one hand, and the offense of possessing them, on the other. With regard to the former, the statute provides that a minor commits the offense of sexting if he or she knowingly "uses a computer, or any other device capable of electronic data transmission or distri-bution, to transmit or distribute to another minor any photograph or video of any person which depicts nudity…and is harmful to minors" (Fla. Stat. §847.0141 (2012)).

Several aspects of this seemingly simple statement must be unpacked to bet-ter understand its full reach and limitations. First, the offense applies only to minor-to-minor transmissions (the phrase "to another minor" indicates this), not to minor-to-adult or adult-to-minor exchanges. Second, the transmitted image or video in question apparently can be of either a minor or an adult, per the phrase "photograph or video of any person." The use of "any person" here also means that Florida's law does not distinguish between what this chapter earlier called *primary, self-sexting transmission* and *secondary, downstream-sexting transmission*. That is the case because "any person" sweeps up both minors who transmit images of themselves and minors who transmit images of others.

Third, a sexting offense involves more than just the conveyance of nude imag-ery; a nude image must also be one that is "harmful to minors" under the defini-tion of that phrase set forth earlier. Fourth, the offense applies to more than just the transmission of images via cellphones or smartphones; it also applies much more broadly to their conveyance through computers and "any other device capa-ble of electronic data." Fifth, the offense applies not simply to still photographs, but also to videos, as it uses the phrase "photograph or video."

Florida law recognizes that a minor may well transmit more than just one image of herself to another minor. In other words, during a night of sexting, a girl might transmit six different images of herself to a boy. Rather than punish the girl for six different transmission offenses, Florida's statute provides that the transmission of multiple photos or videos during the same 24-hour period is treated as a single offense. This single-offense provision certainly is favorable to transmitting minors.

Turning to the separate offense of possession, Florida provides that a minor commits the offense of sexting if he or she knowingly "possesses a photograph or video of any person that was transmitted or distributed by another minor which depicts nudity... and is harmful to minors." As with the offense of transmission, the possessed imagery can be of any person (a minor or an adult) and it must include not only nudity but nudity portrayed in such a way as to be harmful to minors. Also in the same fashion as the offense of transmission, the possession provision only applies to minor-to-minor sexting, as made evident by the phrase "transmitted or distributed by another minor." Finally, and in accord with the transmission offense, the law provides that the receipt of multiple photos or videos during the same 24-hour period shall be treated as a single offense.

There is, however, one critical difference between the transmission and possession offenses. Apparently recognizing a possible innocent-recipient possession scenario—one in which the minor possessor did not request the image and thus might be surprised to find it pop up on his or her smartphone or computer—the Florida legislature carved out an exemption to the offense of possession. In particular, a minor-possessor is not subject to an offense if three conditions are satisfied: (1) he did not solicit the photo or video; (2) he took reasonable steps to report it to his guardian, a school official, or a law enforcement officer; and (3) he did not further transmit the received image to anyone else. This trio of conditions is logical to protect the innocent recipient, yet one must wonder how likely it is that a minor who receives a sexted image on his phone would tell a parent or report it to a teacher or police officer.

In Florida, the possible punishments for the different offenses of transmission and possession are the same. They involve a three-level approach, in which both the designation of the offense and its corresponding consequences are ratcheted up for repeat violations. A first offense is considered noncriminal, with possible punishments including eight hours of community service or a $60 fine in lieu of service. On top of these consequences, judges have the option to order a first-time offender to participate in suitable training or instruction. The law does not, however, specify the precise nature of such training or instruction; presumably, it would be about the dangers of sexting.

A second offense is considered a first-degree misdemeanor, for which the maximum fine ramps up significantly to $1,000 under Florida Statute Section 775.083 (2012) and a maximum term of one year in prison per Florida Statute Section 775.082 (2012). Finally, a third-time sexting offense is treated as a third-degree felony subject to a fine of up to $5,000 and a maximum of five years in prison.

Florida lawmakers added a provision that allows prosecutors to file additional charges against a sexting minor, including the offense of stalking. In Florida, stalking includes cyberstalking, which is defined under Florida Statute Section 784.048 (1) (d) (2012) as engaging "in a course of conduct to communicate, or to cause to be communicated, words, images, or language by or through the use of electronic mail or electronic communication, directed at a specific person, causing substantial emotional distress to that person and serving no legitimate purpose." Based on this definition, it is clearly possible to envision how a minor who repeatedly sexts images of himself to the same girl could be targeted by law enforcement officials for both sexting and cyberstalking.

Before leaving Florida's statute, it is important to note what it does *not* include. In particular, there is no minimum age that a minor must have reached before he or she can be charged with either transmitting or possessing sexted imagery. Although it is highly doubtful that any technologically savvy five-year-old boys and girls will engage in sexting, there arguably is a difference in cognitive understanding between an 11-year-old who sexts and a 17-year-old who sexts, yet they are treated the same under Florida law.

Nevada Revised Statute Annotated Section 200.737 (2012) took effect in July 2011. It does not use the term "sexting" but nonetheless covers three variations of sexting activities by minors, two of which address the transmission of images and one of which centers on possession. Before addressing the differences among these three varieties of prohibited sexting, it first is useful to understand the terms and definitions they share. Commonalities include (1) defining minors as individuals under the age of 18 years; (2) employing the term "sexual image" to describe the forbidden content and, in turn, defining a sexual image as any visual depiction of "a minor simulating or engaging in sexual conduct or of a minor as the subject of a sexual portrayal"; and (3) prohibiting sexting via any "electronic communication device," which includes not only cellphones but also personal digital assistants, computers, and, more sweepingly, "any electronic device that is capable of transmitting or distributing a sexual image."

In a separate statute, Nevada defines the term "sexual conduct" mentioned above as "sexual intercourse, lewd exhibition of the genitals, fellatio, cunnilingus, bestiality, anal intercourse, excretion, sado-masochistic abuse, masturbation, or the penetration of any part of a person's body or of any object manipulated or inserted by a person into the genital or anal opening of the body of another" (Nev. Rev. Stat. Ann. §200.700 (2012)). The other key term used in the sexting statute to describe the type of prohibited content is "sexual portrayal," which Nevada defines as a "depiction of a person in a manner which appeals to the prurient interest in sex and which does not have serious literary, artistic, political, or scientific value" (Nev. Rev. Stat. Ann. §200.700 (2012)).

The first variety of sexting targeted by Nevada is the knowing and willful use of an electronic communication device by a minor to transmit or distribute a sexual image of himself or herself to another person. This is a primary, self-sexting transmission provision—it targets the transmission of self-taken sexual images, such as when a girl captures a sexual image of herself on a smartphone and then sends it directly to her boyfriend or a boy she likes. The self-sexting offense applies, however, regardless of the age of the individual to whom the self-taken sexual image is transmitted, as indicated by the use of the language "to another person" rather than "to another minor." The first variety of prohibited conduct thus includes both minor-to-minor and minor-to-adult sexting. This is a major difference from Florida's sexting transmission statute, which, as described earlier, applies only when a minor transmits an image "to another minor" (Fla. Stat. §847.0141, 2012).

The second variety of sexting regulated by Nevada is the knowing and willful use of an electronic communication device by a minor "to transmit or distribute a sexual image of another minor who is older than, the same age as or not more than 4 years younger than the minor transmitting the sexual image." This provision targets secondary, downstream-sexters (minors who receive photographs of other minors and then further transmit or forward them to others) because the image in question is not of the sender but "of another minor." What makes this provision particularly nuanced is its specificity of the requisite age-range difference between the minor who transmits the image in question and the minor who is depicted in it in order for there to be a sexting offense. In particular, the individual depicted in the image must not only be a minor—an individual under the age of 18 years—but must also be older than, the same age as or not more than four years younger than the minor who transmitted it.

The implications of this age-range proximity provision become more clear with an example. Consider a 16-year-old minor boy who willfully decides to transmit to others (Nevada's downstream-sexting transmission provision, it should be noted, is silent as to the age of the downstream recipients, so the "others" who receive it could be both minors and adults) a sexual image of his minor girlfriend. The provision would apply only if the depicted girlfriend was (1) 17 years of age (*older than the sender but still a minor*), (2) 16 years of age (*the same age as the sender*); or (3) 15, 14, 13, or 12 years of age (*not more than four years younger than the sender*). If the depicted girlfriend, however, is 11 years or age or younger (more than four years younger than the 16-year-old boy who transmits the image), then the downstream-sexting transmission provision would not apply. If this were the case—if the girlfriend was too young, relative to the sender's age—then the 16-year-old boy conceivably could be subject to Nevada's child pornography laws if the sexual image he sent was sufficiently explicit. Specifically, Nevada makes it a category B felony, subject to up to 15 years in prison and a $15,000 fine, to knowingly distribute child pornography.

The age-range proximity provision in Nevada's sexting statute is somewhat akin to so-called Romeo and Juliet provisions in the area of statutory rape that sometimes apply when both the alleged perpetrator and victim are minors separated by only a few years in age and who otherwise voluntarily engaged in sexual relations. In general, Romeo and Juliet provisions "allow for lessened penalties for certain sexual acts (such as oral sex) between teens who are close in age" (Hunter & Sharman, 2006, p. 17).

Finally, the third variety of sexting addressed under Nevada law relates to the possession of sexted images. It provides that a minor shall not knowingly and willfully possess a sexual image that was transmitted or distributed by another minor if the minor who is the subject of the sexual image is older than, the same age as or not more than four years younger than the minor who possesses the sexual image.

As with the downstream-sexting transmission provision, this possession provision includes an age-range proximity clause. In this instance, however, it is the age difference between the possessor of the image and the minor who is depicted in it that is key, rather than the age difference between the sender of the image and the portrayed minor.

As with Florida, Nevada recognizes the possibility of an innocent-recipient possession scenario in which the possessor did not request the image. The Nevada statute thus provides an affirmative defense to a possession charge if the image recipient (1) did not purchase, procure, solicit, or otherwise request the sexual image; (2) did not provide anyone else with access to the image, other than a law enforcement officer or school official; and (3) promptly and in good faith either took reasonable steps to destroy the image or reported it to school or law enforcement officials. If a student chooses to report the image to a school or law enforcement official, he or she must also give that official access to the image.

In contrast to Florida, however, Nevada's sexting statute does not include language that would treat the transmission or reception of multiple images during a 24-hour period as a single offense.

In terms of punishment, the Nevada law tracks Florida's to the extent that (1) first-time offenders are treated less severely than repeat offenders and (2) the punishments for both first-time offenders and repeat offenders are far less severe than those under state child pornography laws. When it comes to punishing minors for the transmission of sexual images, however, Nevada treats primary, self-sexting very differently from the offense of secondary, downstream sexting. In particular, a first-time offender under the primary, self-sexting transmission provision is designated merely as a "child in need of supervision." Thus, a 16-year-old girl who takes a sexual image of herself and then knowingly and willfully transmits it via cellphone to her boyfriend would fall into this category. The child-in-need-of-supervision classification typically is given to minors in Nevada who repeatedly skip school (truancy), run away from home, or habitually disobey reasonable and lawful demands of a parent (Nev. Rev. Stat. Ann. §62B.320, 2012). It also constitutes a less severe designation for a minor than delinquency (Nev. Rev. Stat. Ann. §62B.330, 2012), thus reducing the stigma attached to the offense. Furthermore, the Nevada's sexting statute specifies that first-time offenders are not to be classified as either sex offenders or juvenile sex offenders and, in turn, are not subject to the registration or community notification provisions associated with such designations.

There are two other reasons why the child-in-need-of-supervision classification is important. First, it places the sexting minor within the jurisdiction of juvenile court authorities when it comes to meting out punishment rather than within the authority of the adult criminal justice system. Second, a child in need of supervision cannot be "committed to or otherwise placed in a state facility for the detention of children or any other facility that provides correctional care" (Nev. Rev. Stat. Ann. §62E.420). In other words, incarceration of any kind is prohibited.

Typical penalties, instead, include small fines of not more than $100 and community service obligations (Nev. Rev. Stat. Ann. §62E.430).

Repeat primary, self-sexting offenders, however, are treated more harshly than first-time offenders and can be incarcerated. In particular, second and all further subsequent offenses for primary, self-sexting transmission in Nevada are treated as acts of delinquency and a court may order punishment consistent with that which could be given to an adult who commits a misdemeanor. This means that a repeat offender could be jailed for up to six months and/or fined a maximum of $1,000, although judges are allowed to substitute a fixed period of community service in lieu of all or part of such a sentence (Nev. Rev. Stat. Ann. §193.150). But even repeat offenders—like first-time offenders—cannot be classified as either sex offenders or juvenile sex offenders and cannot be made to register as such.

An initial offense of secondary, downstream-sexting transmission is treated much more seriously in Nevada than an initial offense for primary, self-sexting transmission. In particular, minors who transmit images of other minors, rather than images of themselves, are considered to have committed a delinquent act upon a first offense and thus can be jailed for up to six months and/or fined a maximum of $1,000. In other words, the possible punishment for a *first* offense of secondary, downstream-sexting transmission is treated the same as a *second* offense of primary, self-sexting transmission.

Rhode Island's youth sexting law, which took effect in July 2011, is found at that state's General Laws Section 11-9-1.4 (2012). As quickly becomes evident, it is far less comprehensive than the sexting laws of both Florida and Nevada. In particular, Rhode Island's statute addresses only the transmission—not the possession or reception—of sexted images. Specifically, it provides that "no minor shall knowingly and voluntarily and without threat or coercion use a computer or telecommunication device to transmit an indecent visual depiction of himself or herself to another person."

Four aspects of this seemingly simple statement require unpacking. First, as with Florida and Nevada, a minor is defined as any person under the age of 18 years. Second, and also in similar fashion to Florida and Nevada, Rhode Island's law addresses modes of sexting transmission beyond cellphones, sweeping up computers and other telecommunication devices. Third, and unlike Florida's statute that applies to the transmission of images of any person, the Rhode Island law applies only to self-sexted images (minors who take sexually explicit photographs of themselves and then send them to others), as it uses the term "transmit an indecent visual depiction *of himself or herself.*" In other words, the statute does not apply to downstream-sexting scenarios, such as when a minor who, after receiving a sexted image from another minor, forwards it to his friends. Because minors who forward indecent images of other minors are not covered by the new sexting statute, they risk prosecution under Rhode Island's child pornography statute, General Laws Section 11-9-1.3 (2012). Fourth, the phrase "indecent visual depiction" is defined as a "minor engaging in sexually explicit conduct," which, in turn, is defined as "actual masturbation or graphic focus on or lascivious exhibition of the nude genitals or pubic area of the minor." This means that the minor in the self-sexted image need not be engaged in sexual conduct with another person, but can simply be taking the type of solo-person images that fall within Rhode Island's definition of child pornography. That law, Rhode Island General Laws Section 11-9-1.3, defines child pornography as including both masturbation and a "graphic or lascivious exhibition of the genitals or pubic area."

In terms of punishment, Rhode Island classifies sexting as a mere status offense and refers the matter to the realm of family courts. Status offenses by minors typically include activities that would not be criminal if committed by adults, such as failing to attend school, running away from home, and breaking a curfew (Arthur & Waugh, 2009). The statute also makes it clear that under no circumstance shall a minor who violates Rhode Island's sexting law be subject to sex offender registration. Viewed collectively, these penalties are substantially less than those provided for under Rhode Island's child pornography statute, which makes those who knowingly transfer child pornography subject to up to 15 years in prison and a $5,000 fine.

Because the Rhode Island statute fails to address the reception by minors of sexted images of other minors, recipient-minors could be subject to generally applicable child pornography statutes.

Ultimately, as the laws of Florida, Nevada, and Rhode Island illustrate, there are multiple ways the legal system can approach sexting by minors. Over time, sexting laws may be amended to address situations unforeseen by lawmakers or to bring them into line with shifting societal conceptions of what constitutes punishable behavior.

■ SUMMARY

Sexting is a complex phenomenon that lacks an agreed-upon definition but has attracted widespread media, public, scholarly, and legal attention since 2008. Whether teen sexting waxes or wanes—whether it merely is a passing fad or takes a permanent place on the sexual landscape of minors—remains to be seen. Furthermore, whether laws designed to address it will have any effect on thwarting or mitigating sexting behaviors is unclear.

A few points, however, seemed apparent by late 2013. First, sexting comes in multiple variations, ranging from consensual to nonconsensual and from sexually suggestive to explicitly graphic. Second, not all sexted images of minors rise to the level of illegal child pornography. That determination necessarily hinges on a case-by-case basis, dependent upon the level of lasciviousness and explicitness of the imagery. Third, initial panic—moral and otherwise—over sexting, as well as over-aggressive prosecution of teens who engage in it, has largely subsided and been replaced by more dispassionate and moderate attempts to address it. Some of the sexting laws reflect this, as they provide for much more lenient punishment for minors than they would otherwise receive if convicted under generally applicable child pornography statues. Fourth, academic literature on the psychological and sociological causes and consequences of sexting will grow dramatically in the coming years. From such future knowledge one can hope that parents, educators, psychologists, lawmakers, prosecutors, and the news media all will gain a better understanding of sexting and how it should be addressed.

■ DISCLOSURE

Clay Calvert has no conflicts to disclose. He is employed and funded only by and through the University of Florida in Gainesville, Florida. He receives no grant support.

■ REFERENCES

18 U.S.C. §2251 (2013).
18 U.S.C. §2252 (2013).
18 U.S.C. §2252A (2013).
18 U.S.C. §2256 (2013).
Aiken, S. (2012, March 6). Student charged with "sexting." *The Herald-Palladium*, p. 1A.
Aisner, A. (2011, May 2). After sexting, incidents involving middle schoolers, Saline forum will look at cyber safety. *Ann Arbor News*, http://www.annarbor.com/news/after-sexting-incidents-involving-middle-schoolers-saline-schools-forum-will-look-at-cyber-safety
Arthur, P. J., & Waugh, R. (2009). Status offenses and the juvenile justice and delinquency prevention act: The exception that swallowed the rule. *Seattle Journal for Social Justice, 7*, 555–570.
Bialik, C. (2009, April 8). Which is epidemic—sexting or worrying about it? Cyberpolls, relying on skewed samples of techno-teens, aren't always worth the paper they're not printed on. *Wall Street Journal*, p. A9.
Bowker, A., & Sullivan, M. (2010, July). Sexting: risky actions and overreactions. *FBI Law Enforcement Bulletin*, 27–71.
Boyle, C. (2008, December 11). Teen girls are hot for texting nude pix, sez survey. *Daily News* (N.Y.), p. 3.
C.S. Mott Children's Hospital (2012). *National poll on children's health: For youth sexting: public supports education, not criminal charges.* Ann Arbor, MI: Author. Retrieved August 14, 2012, from http://www.mottnpch.org/sites/default/files/documents/032020 12youthsextingreport.pdf
Cahalan, S. (2009, January 25). Sex "cells" for naked teenagers; Naughty cam craze. *New York Post*, p. 3.
Calvert, C. (2009). Sex, cell phones, privacy and the first amendment: When children become child pornographers and the Lolita effect undermines the law. *CommLaw Conspectus: Journal of Communications Law and Policy, 18*, 1–65.
Calvert, C., Murrhee, K. C., & Steve, J. M. (2010). Playing legislative catch-up in 2010 with a growing, high-tech phenomenon: Evolving statutory approaches for addressing teen sexting. *University of Pittsburgh Journal of Technology Law & Policy, 11*, 1–60.
Chalfen, R. (2009). 'It's only a picture': Sexting, 'smutty' snapshots and felony charges. *Visual Studies, 24*(3), 258–268.

Code Ga. Ann. §16-12-100 (2012).

Conn. Gen. Stat. §53a-193 (2012).

Curnett, H. (2012). Flashing your phone: Sexting and the remediation of teen sexuality. *Communication Quarterly, 60*(3), 353–369. doi: 10.1080/01463373.2012.688728

Dake, J. A., Price, J. H., Maziarz, L., & Ward, B. (2012). Prevalence and correlates of sexting behavior in adolescents. *American Journal of Sexuality Education, 7*, 1–15. doi: 10.1080/15546128.2012.650959

Durham, M. G. (2008). *The Lolita effect: The media sexualization of young girls and what we can do about it.* Woodstock, NY: Overlook Press.

Dwyer, B. (2011, November 20). 3 students charged with sexting photo of naked girl. *Chicago Sun-Times,* p. 14.

Editorial: "sexting" overkill (2009, April 6). *Philadelphia Inquirer,* p. A10.

Ferguson, C. J. (2011). Sexting behaviors among young Hispanic women: Incidence and association with other high-risk sexual behaviors. *Psychiatry Quarterly, 82,* 239–243. doi: 10.1007/s11126-010-9165-8

Ferguson, C. J. (2009, January 25). Oversexted; Greensburg teens aren't child pornographers. *Pittsburgh Post-Gazette,* p. H-4.

Fla. Stat. §775.0847 (2012).

Fla. Stat. §784.048 (1) (d) (2012).

Fla. Stat. §847.001 (2012).

Fla. Stat. §847.0141 (2012).

Frederickson, B. L., & Roberts, T. (1997). Objectification theory: Toward understanding women's lived experiences and mental health risks. *Psychology of Women Quarterly, 21*(2), 173–206.

Gordon-Messer, D., Bauermeister, J. A., Grodzinski, A., & Zimmerman, M. (2012). Sexting among young adults. *Journal of Adolescent Health,* published online July 13, 2012. doi: 10.1016/j.jadohealth.2012.05.013

Hamill, S. D. (2009, March 26). Students sue prosecutor in cellphone photos case. *New York Times,* p. A21.

Hunter, D., & Sharman, P. (2006). Crimes and offenses, *Georgia State University Law Review, 23,* 11–25.

Jayson, S. (2008, December 10). In tech flirting, decorum optional; Racy pics, messages flying among young. *USA Today,* p. 1A.

Judge, A. M. (2012). "Sexting" among U.S. adolescents: Psychological and legal perspectives. *Harvard Review of Psychiatry, 20,* 86–96. doi: 10.3109/10673229.2012.677360

Karaian, L. (2012). Lolita speaks: "Sexting," teenage girls and the law. *Crime Media Culture, 8*(1), 57–73. doi: 10.1177/1741659011429868

Law, D. M., Shapka, J. D., Domene, J. F., & Gagné, M. H. (2012). Are Cyberbullies really bullies? An investigation of reactive and proactive online aggression. *Computers in Human Behavior, 28,* 664–672. doi: 10.1016/j.chb.2011.11.013

Leary, M. G. (2010). Sexting or self-produced child pornography? The dialogue continues—structured prosecutorial discretion within a multidisciplinary response. *Virginia Journal of Social Policy & the Law, 17*(3), 486–586.

Leibovich, M., & Barrett, G. (2009, December 20). Buzzwords: coining a not great year. *New York Times,* Week in Review, p. 3.

Lenhart, A. (2009). *Teens and sexting: How and why minor teens are sending sexually suggestive nude or nearly nude images via text messaging.* Pew Research Center. Retrieved August 13, 2012, from http://pewinternet.org/Reports/2009/Teens-and-Sexting.aspx.

Lewin, T. (2010, March 21). Rethinking sex offender laws for youths showing off online. *New York Times*, p. A1.

Lumby, C., & Funnell, N. (2011). Between heat and light: The opportunity in moral panics. *Crime, Media, Culture, 7* (3), 277–291. doi: 10.1177/1741659011417606

McElroy, M. C. (2010). Sextual frustrations: why the law needs to catch up to teenagers' texts. *Houston Lawyer, 48*, 10, 15, Nov.–Dec., 2010.

Miller v. California, 413 U.S. 15 (1973).

Miller v. Skumanick, 598 F.3d 139 (3d Cir. 2010).

Miller v. Mitchell, 2010 U.S. Dist. LEXIS 42512 (M.D. Pa. Apr. 30, 2010).

Mitchell, K. J., Finkelhor, D., Jones, L. M., & Wolak, J. (2012). Prevalence and characteristics of youth sexting: A national study. *Pediatrics, 129*(1), 1–8. doi: 10.1542/peds.2011-1730

National Campaign to Prevent Teen and Unplanned Pregnancy (2008). *Sex and tech: results for a survey of teens and young adult.* Retrieved May 7, 2012, from http://www.the-nationalcampaign.org/sextech

N.J. Stat. §2A:4A-71.1 (2012).

Nev. Rev. Stat. Ann. §62B.320 (2012).

Nev. Rev. Stat. Ann. §62B.330 (2012).

Nev. Rev. Stat. Ann. §200.700 (2012).

Nev. Rev. Stat. Ann. §200.737 (2012).

New York v. Ferber, 458 U.S. 747 (1982).

O'Keefe, G. S., & Clarke-Pearson, K. (2011). The impact of social media on children, adolescents, and families. *Pediatrics, 127*(4), 800–804. doi: 10.1542/peds.2011-0054

Osborne v. Ohio, 495 U.S. 103 (1990).

Richards, R. D., & Calvert, C. (2009). When sex and cell phones collide: Inside the prosecution of a teen sexting case. *Hastings Communications and Entertainment Law Journal, 32*, 1–39.

Sadhu, J. (2012). Sexting: The impact of a cultural phenomenon on psychiatric practice. *Academic Psychiatry, 36*(1), 76–81. doi: 10.1176/appi.ap.10100146

Stiles, B. (2009, January 13). Teens face porn charges in "sexting." *Tribune-Review*, A1.

Temple, J. R., Paul, J. A., van den Berg, P., Le, V. D., McElhany, A., & Temple, B. W. (2012). Teen sexting and its association with sexual behaviors. *Archives of Pediatrics & Adolescent Medicine*, published online July 2, 2012. doi: 10.1001/archpediatrics.2012.835

Two Palmyra teens charged in sexting incident (2012, January 4). *Lebanon Daily News*,

United States v. Dost, 636 F. Supp. 828 (S.D. Cal. 1986).

United States v. Knox, 32 F.3d 733 (3d Cir. 1994).

Weiss, R., & Samenow, C. P. (2010). Smart phones, social networking, sexting and problematic sexual behaviors—a call for research. *Sexual Addiction & Compulsivity, 17*, 241–246. doi: 10.1080/10720162.2010.532079

Wiederhold, B. K. (2011). Should adult sexting be considered for the DSM? *Cyberpsychology, Behavior, and Social Networking, 14*, 481–481. doi: 10.1089/cyber.2011.1522

Wolak, J., & Finkelhor, D. (2011, March). *Sexting: A typology*. Crimes Against Children Resource Center, 1–11.

Wysocki, D. K., & Childers, C. D. (2011). "Let my fingers do the talking": Sexting and infidelity in cyberspace. *Sexuality & Culture, 15*, 217–239. doi: 10.1007/s12119-011-9091-4

6

Chat Rooms and Social Networking Sites

■ CHARLES L. SCOTT

■ **INTRODUCTION**

The digital revolution has resulted in a simultaneous evolution in how adolescents meet and interact with others. Long gone are the days where youth form relationships under the watchful eyes of caring parents or other attentive adults. Instead, adolescents now interact in a virtual online world that consists of potential friends as well as possible foes. The term "Net Generation" reflects this trend, as juveniles' social lives are inextricably interwoven with the fibers of an expanding social media fabric (Tapscott, 1998).

Two important interactive Internet formats that adolescents use for the purpose of sexual expression and exploration are chat rooms and social networking sites (SNSs). This chapter highlights these formats with an overview of how juveniles' sexual behaviors are expressed in each. In addition, approaches designed to decrease the risk of harm to children and adolescents who use these particular Internet interactive tools are reviewed.

■ **CHAT ROOM OVERVIEW**

Chat rooms are online locations where different individuals can meet. Text messages are the primary form of communication in chat rooms and these messages are seen immediately once sent (Ybarra & Mitchell, 2008). Chat room communications often have a text code that represents words in an abbreviated manner. For example, the abbreviation "a/s/l" stands for the person's age/sex/location and provides useful information to other viewing participants (Greenfield & Subrahmanyam, 2003). To illustrate, the text "13/f/Atlanta" quickly alerts other chat room members that a 13-year-old girl from Atlanta has entered the room. Table 6.1 provides a glossary of some common abbreviations used in teen chat rooms.

Chat room participants typically create screen names (i.e., "identifiers") that appear when they enter the room. Having a screen name allows other members to directly address each other. Screen names may also communicate particular interests or characteristics. For example, the names "sexyteenwantsu" or "hotboyforhotgirl" both imply that the user is interested in having a sexual encounter. Some chat rooms allow alternate forms of screen identifiers, such as an avatar. An

TABLE 6.1. *Common Chat Room Abbreviations*

Term	Translation
ASL	Age, sex, location
ASLP	Age, sex, location, picture
CD9	Parents are around
F2F	Face to face
F2P	Free to play
IAG	I am gay
ILY	I love you
IRL	In real life
LMIRL	Let's meet in real life
NIFOC	Nude in front of computer
PAW	Parents are watching
PIR	Parents in room
POS	Parents over shoulder
P911	Parent emergency
TAW	Teachers are watching
WTGP	Want to go private?
WYCM	Will you call me?
53x	Sex

avatar is a graphical representation of the user and the avatar's selected appearance can communicate how the user wishes to be perceived. Because multiple individuals can simultaneously view personal information and postings, public chat rooms are among the least private forms of electronic communications (Subrahmanyam & Greenfield, 2008). Chat room participants can also speak privately with another chat room member by sending him or her a message not viewed by other members, a process often referred to as "instant messaging."

Although many chat rooms are available without costs, some chat rooms require a fee before the user can access the room. Chat rooms typically have names that identify the intended chat focus, thereby attracting individuals with a similar age, gender, or interest. For example, a chat room titled "TeenSexNow" will likely have a very different conversation focus and membership than a room titled "ChessTalk." Examples of chat rooms focused primarily on teenagers include TeenChat.com, AIM Chat, and Meebo Rooms. In sampling free chat rooms for teenagers, chat rooms that specifically promote a sexual content as the focus of the chat are easy to find.

Chat rooms can be divided into monitored and unmonitored chat rooms. In monitored chat rooms, the website provides a trained adult host who observes chat room members' communications and their adherence to conduct rules established by the service provider. Such rules typically involve prohibitions against abusive or threatening speech (to include hate speech), respect for fellow chat group members, and not impersonating a person or business or misleading other members for whatever reason. In monitored chat rooms, chat room members who use sexually or otherwise offensive language can be electronically evicted from the room (Tynes et al., 2004).

Developmental issues related to online chatting are similar to those adolescents experience offline. However, unlike in-person interactions, online chatting provides a sense of anonymity, with increased opportunities to discuss personal issues, such as one's sexual activity, interest, and orientation. In addition, participants do not typically have information about another person's age, gender, race, or physical attractiveness unless provided by the user (Subrahmanyam et al., 2006). Interestingly, adolescent boys and girls who utilize chat rooms disproportionately report psychological distress, a difficult living environment, and a higher likelihood of risky behaviors compared to nonusers (Beebe et al., 2004). Youth who feel isolated, desire attention, or enjoy risk taking may participate in chat rooms as a way to help meet those needs.

The popularity of chat rooms for juveniles appears to be declining. To illustrate, in 2000, 55 percent of online teens reported going to online chat rooms, whereas in 2006 only 18 percent of teens said they visited chat rooms (Lenhart et al., 2007). This shift may be accounted for, in part, by active public campaigns warning young users and their parents about the dangers of meeting strangers in this setting. This shift may also reflect changes in technology itself where youth may now interact face to face via media such as the chatting interface of Google, Facebook and other SNSs.

■ SNS OVERVIEW

SNSs are websites that permit users to share personal information about themselves and view personal information about others (Moreno & Kolb, 2012). In general, SNSs allow users to conduct three basic functions (Subrahmanyam & Greenfield, 2008):

1. Create a public or semipublic profile within a bounded system
2. Identify a list of other users with whom they share a connection
3. Examine their list of connections and those made by others within the system.

SNSs also allow users to post public information or updates about their life, comment about other people's posts, display pictures or videos, share Internet links of interest, play games, send private instant messages to other online members, or send a message to members offline that they can read when they sign on to the service. The popularity of SNSs is demonstrated by their explosive growth over the last decade. As of September 2012, Facebook was the world's largest SNS, with one billion members actively using the site every month. To put the enormity of this number in perspective, if Facebook were a nation, it would be the third largest nation in the world, behind China and India (Whittaker, 2012).

Online social networking is the most popular adolescent Internet activity, and this trend is increasing (Rideout et al., 2010). In November 2006, over 90 percent of U.S. youth ages 12 to 17 were using the Internet, with 55 percent of these adolescents creating a profile on an SNS. By September 2009, 93 percent of teenagers were using the Internet, with 73 percent using an online SNS (Lenhart et al., 2010).

Over one in five teenagers log on to their favorite SNS more than 10 times a day (Common Sense Media, 2009), and one in four teenagers use their cell phone to connect to a SNS (Hinduja & Patchin, 2007). Lenhart and colleagues (2010) reported that older online teens (ages 14 to 17) are more likely than younger teens (12 and 13) to use SNSs, though boys and girls are equally likely to use SNSs. In regard to common adolescent SNS activities, 86 percent of teen social network users post comments to a friend's page or wall and 83 percent of teen social network users add comments to a friend's pictures.

Many SNSs restrict membership based on the individual's age. In 1998, Congress passed the Children's Online Privacy Protection Act (COPPI) as a legislative response to concerns about children's privacy and safety online. COPPI requires parental consent whenever a website, such as an SNS, collects personal information on a child less than age 13 (Children's Online Privacy Protection Act of 1998). As a result of this legislation, many SNSs require that a child be at least 13 to sign up as a user, along with an agreement by the user that he or she meets the required age standard and is reporting his or her personal information accurately. For example, as of February 5, 2013, Facebook's Statement of Rights and Responsibilities specified the following in reference to the age of eligibility to use their site (Facebook Statement of Rights and Responsibilities, 2012): "You will not use Facebook if you are under 13" and "You will not provide any false personal information on Facebook, or create an account for anyone other than yourself without permission."

SNSs also vary regarding the extent to which the general public can automatically view the user's profile information. For example, MySpace automatically sets profiles of adolescents who are 14 or 15 years old to "private" to help minimize their personal information to public exposure. Facebook has a variety of options that allows the user to control whether or not the public or the user's Facebook friends can view his or her profile information. The exact age requirement and level of privacy afforded the user depends on the particular SNS. Table 6.2 summarizes the top 10 social networking sites, with associated descriptors and age requirements (Top 15, 2013).

Twitter is an online service that allows users to send and read text-based messages of up to 140 characters. These messages are known as "tweets." To some Twitter is a type of SNS, and to others it represents a forum where people can post their thoughts and responses to others' tweets, much like one would do on a blog. Hence, Twitter is sometimes referred to as "microblogging." In reality, Twitter has aspects of both communication systems. In contrast to other form of Internet communication, teenagers are not currently using Twitter in large numbers. Of Internet users ages 12 to 17, only 8 percent are using Twitter compared to 19 percent of adult Internet users. Girls ages 14 to 17 are the most likely teenage group to

TABLE 6.2. *Top 10 Most Popular Social Networking Sites, 2013*

Rank and Name	Characteristics	Estimated unique monthly visitors	Age requirement
1. Facebook	• Allows users to create personal profiles, search for profiles, and invite others to join • Allows application programming interface for third-party developers	750,000,000	13 and older
2. Twitter	• Debate whether or not a true SNS • An online environment where users can create profiles • Allows users to have a network of people they follow • Members send messages known as "tweets."	259,000,000	No longer has specific age requirement listed in terms of service though has developed "age screening" related to associated media
3. LinkedIn	• SNS developed for professionals • Provides a platform that allows members to collaborate on projects	110,000,000	Must be 18 years or older
4. Pinterest	• A pinboard-style photo-sharing website • Allows users to create and manage image collections and browse others' collections	85,500,000	13 or older
5. MySpace	• Ability to post blogs, news items, status updates, and user profiles • Bands and unsigned performers can debut new tracks and share information	79,500,000	13 or older
6. Google Plus +	• Multilingual social networking and identity service • Has social layers in contrast to a single site • Services include "circles," "hangouts," and "sparks"	65,000,000	Age determined by country of origination of account (13 in most countries)
7. DeviantArt	• Showcases user-made artwork • Includes journals, polls, groups, and portfolios	25,500,000	13 and older
8. LiveJournal	• Users keep a blog, journal, or diary. • Has various options for friend connections	20,500,000	13 and older
9. Tagged	• Has social games that encourage making new friends • Can send virtual gifts to friends	19,500,000	13 and older
10. Orkut	• Owned by Google and preferred online social network of Brazil • Very popular in India • No advertisements	17,500,000	13 or older

(Top 15, 2013)

use Twitter, with 13 percent of online girls ages 14 to 17 using Twitter, compared to 7 percent of boys that age (Lenhart et al., 2010). However, anecdotal and clinical evidence from contemporary teens suggests that more adolescents have migrated to media such as Twitter than these earlier estimates may capture. This potential discrepancy illustrates the difficulties of empirical research keeping pace with teens' rapidly changing preferences for different mediated technologies.

■ JUVENILE SEXUAL ACTIVITIES IN CHAT ROOMS AND SNSS

Adolescents utilize chat rooms and SNSs to engage in sexual discussions as well as to post messages, pictures, or videos that are sexually suggestive or have blatant sexual content. A youth's sexual postings may include attempts to be humorous, to respond to perceived peer or social pressures, to appear more mature to others online, or to adopt other identities that differ from his or her offline persona (Collins et al., 2011). Relative anonymity and unlimited possibilities to explore sexual issues have been theorized to potentially increase the likelihood that youth will make or receive sexual offers as compared to their viewing offline media (e.g., watching television or film) (National Campaign, 2008). Youth also use chat rooms and SNSs to gather information about prospective partners or to screen perspective dates. In one survey of 10- to 17-year-olds, 25 percent formed casual online friendships and 14 percent had developed close friendships or romantic relationships through the Internet (Wolak et al., 2002).

For some youth, discussing sex in chat rooms represents their first opportunity to explore a broad range of sexual topics, to include their own sexual identity (Subrahmanyam et al., 2004). In their study of teen chat room conversations, Subrahmanyam and colleagues (2006) reviewed the content of 10 monitored versus 10 unmonitored chat sessions that covered approximately 600 minutes of conversations. The content analysis of these 20 chat rooms found the following:

- Nineteen percent of screen nicknames were sexually suggestive.
- Five percent of chat room utterances contained a sexual theme.
- One sexual comment was made for every minute of chat room discussion.
- Males and females were equally likely to make sexual utterances, although males were more likely to make more explicit sexual comments.
- Explicit sexual utterances were more common when sites were unmonitored.
- Females were more likely to use implicit sexualized nicknames (e.g., RamancBab4U) and to use more implicit sexual communication as part of their chat than males.

SNSs provide additional mechanisms for youth to express their sexual interests in addition to chat room participation. For example, SNSs allow the user to upload photos and videos, which may be of a sexual nature. Research examining how often youth post sexual images through SNSs is limited by the fact that only public profile information is available for study (Collins et al., 2011). In their review of nearly 1,500 MySpace public profiles of adolescents who listed their age as 16 or 17, Hinduja and Patchin (2008) found that 5.4 percent posted a picture of themselves in a swimsuit or underwear, though whether or not such pictures were sexually suggestive is unclear.

In a subsequent study, Moreno and colleagues (2009) examined the MySpace public profile of 500 18-year-olds for sexual content. Sexual content was defined as displaying results of a completed sex survey, describing personal sexual preferences, posting pictures of underwear, disclosing personal sexual experiences, or downloading sexually suggestive icons. The authors found that 24 percent of profiles contained sexual content, with a trend for the women to display sexual content more often than men. Members who described their sexual orientation in terms other than "straight" were also more likely to make references to sexual behavior. In a follow-up study of 18-year-old MySpace users, Moreno and colleagues (2010) noted that users who had explicit sexual references in their profile (such as a revealing photograph or explicit language) were more likely to have friends who also had sexual references in their profiles.

Younger users also post sexual images to their SNS, though less frequently than older adolescents. In a survey of 635 teenagers (ages 13 to 19), 89 percent reported that they had a profile on a social networking site. Four percent of those surveyed answered that they had posted a nude or seminude picture or video on an SNS such as MySpace or Facebook or in a blog. Forty-three percent of teens in this survey acknowledged that they were pressured by their peers to post sexy pictures or video in their SNS profile (National Campaign, 2008).

Concerns have been raised that a youths' posting sexually suggestive pictures or other sexual content or revealing personal information through chat conversations, SNS activities, or tweets may increase the risk for unwanted sexual solicitation. Three surveys that specifically examine Internet solicitation of youth, the Youth Internet Safety Surveys (YISS-1, YISS-2, and YISS-3), involve cross-sectional, nationally representative telephone surveys of 4,561 Internet users ages 10 to 17. The surveys involve detailed structured telephone questionnaires about experiences with unwanted sexual solicitations, harassment, and unwanted exposure to pornography on the Internet (Jones et al., 2013).

In the surveys, unwanted sexual solicitation is defined as "requests to engage in sexual activities or sexual talk or to give personal sexual information that was unwanted or made by an individual ≥5 years, whether wanted or not." The three screening questions to determine if the youth has been sexually solicited are (Jones et al., 2012):

- "In the past year, did anyone on the Internet ever try to get you to talk online about sex when you did not want to?"
- "In the past year, did anyone on the Internet ask you for sexual information about yourself when you did not want to answer such questions? I mean

very personal questions, like what your body looks like or sexual things you have done?"

- "In the past year, did anyone on the Internet ever ask you to do something sexual that you did not want to?"

In addition to answering "yes" to any one of these three questions, youth who reported that they had an online sexual relationship with an adult were included in the study results. Solicitors who attempted to make or made offline contact with youth through regular mail, by telephone, or in person were defined as having made an "aggressive sexual solicitation."

In analyzing the data from YISS-3, Jones and colleagues (2012) found that unwanted sexual solicitations declined from 19 percent in 2000 to 13 percent in 2005, and to 9 percent in 2010. This decrease represents a 50 percent decline in unwanted sexual solicitations over the 10-year period studied. In contrast, aggressive solicitations did not change significantly (3 percent in 2000; 4 percent in 2005; and 3 percent in 2010). The authors provide three possible explanations for this decline in unwanted sexual solicitations via the Internet (Jones et al., 2012):

1. A migration of youth toward SNSs from chat rooms, where they are more likely to interact with people they know
2. Increased caution in chatting by youth with online strangers due to Internet education efforts
3. The potential impact of aggressive criminal prosecutions of adults in deterring all Internet participants from sexual solicitations of youth

Are some youth more likely to receive unwarranted sexual solicitations than others? In their review of youth Internet use between 2000 and 2005, Wolak and colleagues (2004) found the following factors were associated with higher rates of online sexual solicitation of youth:

- Exchanging personal information and photos.
- Talking about sex online.
- Harassing others online.

In addition to these factors, Mitchell and colleagues (2007) noted that youth who converse with people whom they first met online (in contrast to having known the person offline) were more at risk to receive a sexual solicitation.

Where a juvenile spends time on the Internet also appears to be associated with the likelihood that he or she will receive an unwanted sexual solicitation. In the Growing Up with Media study, the authors surveyed 10- to 15-year-olds who had used the Internet at least once in the prior six months. Of the 15 percent who reported receiving an unwanted online sexual solicitation in the prior year, the most common location for such incidents was through instant messaging (43 percent), chat rooms (32 percent), SNSs (27.1 percent), and email (21.6 percent) (Ybarra & Mitchell, 2008).

What is the likelihood that online sexual solicitation will result in an actual offline crime against the juvenile? The National Juvenile Online Victimization Study (NJOV) consists of three longitudinal studies conducted by the Crimes against Children Research Center at the University of New Hampshire to better understand a youths' risk of becoming a sexual victim through contacts made on the Internet (Wolak et al., 2012). These surveys do not clearly delineate the exact Internet forum where the offender met the youth victim; however, because the data include information from arrests involving officers who pose as juveniles in chat rooms, key findings from this study are included in this chapter.

The NJOV consists of three waves. Wave 1 (NJOV1) pertained to arrests for technology-facilitated crimes that occurred between July 1, 2000, and June 30, 2001, and Wave 2 (NJOV2) pertained to arrests during 2006. The NJOV3 longitudinal dataset includes data from 2,962 completed interviews. Phase I of each NJOV wave includes a national mail survey sent to law enforcement agencies, with Phase II of each wave consisting of telephone interviews to collect data from a national sample of the same local, county, state, and federal law enforcement agencies. The survey asked if arrests were made in cases involving attempted or completed sexual exploitation of a minor where at least one of the following occurred (Wolak et al., 2012):

1. The offender and victim met on the Internet
2. The offender committed a sexual offense against a victim on the Internet, regardless of whether or not they first met online

In their review of information collected through the NJOV for calendar year 2006, Wolak and colleagues (2009) found that arrests of online predators increased between 2000 and 2006. Most of these arrests involved offenders who solicited undercover investigators rather than actual youth. In fact, law enforcement made an estimated 615 arrests for crimes in which individuals 17 or younger were solicited for sex compared to an estimated 3,100 arrests for solicitations to investigators posing online as minors. The majority of individuals arrested for online sexual predatory behavior involved adolescents who were aware they were communicating with older adults seeking sex. Furthermore, most of the victims who arranged to meet the offenders did so with the expectation of engaging in sexual activity. The charged crimes typically involved non-forcible sexual activity that qualified as statutory rape. Only 5 percent of arrests involved sexual violence.

Wolak and colleagues (2009) also found that 73 percent of the online victims were ages 13 to 15; none was age 10 or younger. Most of the victims were girls. Important differences when comparing online crimes against children between 2000 and 2006 included the following:

- A change in the type of online social media used to contact children. In 2000, 80 percent of cases were initiated through contacts in chat rooms compared to 40 percent of cases in 2006. In 2000, no cases were reported as having made contact with a child through an SNS. In 2006, 33 percent of offenders were recorded as using an SNS to contact their child victim.

- Twenty percent of online offenders pretended to be minors in 2006 compared with only 5 percent of cases in 2000.
- Twenty-one percent of those arrested in 2006 possessed child pornography compared with 40 percent in 2000.

In the above study, there was no evidence that online predators were stalking or abducting unsuspecting youth victims based on information posted on their website, despite true cases that have been reported in the media where this has occurred. Furthermore, few of those arrested for online predation were registered sex offenders. Instead, the authors found that the vast majority of the cases involved older adolescents who were aware that they were communicating with an adult who was seeking sex with them (Wolak et al., 2009).

The NJOV3 survey found that arrests for Internet sex crimes with an identified youth victim doubled between 2006 and 2009. Most of this increase, however, involved offenders who used technology to facilitate sex crimes against victims they already knew face to face. As with the previous NJOV surveys, sex offenders who used the Internet to meet previously unknown victims (i.e., "online predators") accounted for only a small portion of arrests. Arrests of offenders who attempted to solicit sex from police posing as adolescents online declined from 2006 to 2009. It is unclear if this decrease was due to the diversion of resources to other types of investigations (such as investigation of suspects possessing child pornography) or from a true decline in the prevalence of offenders who attempt to solicit sex from minors online (Wolak et al., 2012).

■ JUVENILE "SEX OFFENDERS" IN CHAT ROOMS AND SNSS

Juvenile Prostitution

Juveniles can be arrested and charged for prostitution that occurs via the Internet. The promotion of juvenile prostitution through chat rooms or SNSs represents a serious form of juvenile solicitation and victimization, even when the juveniles describe that they were willing participants. Mitchell and colleagues (2011) describe that juvenile prostitution is a form of commercial sexual exploitation of children as adults are using them as commodities for financial profit. Juveniles may become involved in prostitution for a variety of reasons, to include preexisting traumatic histories making them vulnerable to online victimization, bartering sex for money or other financial gain to survive, wanting attention or love, or being coerced or pressured by others (Wells et al., 2012). Judge and Leary explore the effects of mediated technology on youth prostitution in greater detail in Chapter 9.

The story of Justin Berry illustrates how a youths' sexual exploration online can eventually lead to illegal prostitution. At age 13, Justin Berry hooked up his webcam to his computer with the hopes of meeting other teenagers through the Internet. Adult men watching Justin online began chatting with him though instant messaging services. Eventually, Justin was offered money to take off his shirt. One of Justin's Internet viewers helped Justin open a PayPal.com account so that he could receive payments for responding to sexual requests by members of his online audience. Over the course of five years, Justin increasingly sold images of his body through his webcam and computer, reaching an audience of more than 1,500 people willing to pay him. Justin also had face-to-face meetings with his online contacts, where he was paid to have sexual encounters. Justin eventually opened his own website titled "justinsfriends.com" that featured not only his own provocative pictures, but also those of other boys he had recruited. After turning age 18, Justin met with the FBI and turned over documentary evidence related to those involved in his webcam child pornography business in exchange for immunity (Eichenwald, 2005).

On April 4, 2006, Justin went before the Congressional Subcommittee on Oversight and Investigations, where he testified as follows:

I am not proud of the things I have done nor will I personally attempt to avoid responsibility for those decisions. While I did not comprehend the magnitude of what was happening when I was 13, as I grew older, I progressively became corrupted and acted in shameful ways. Still, I repeatedly attempted to pull away from this sick business, but each time I fell back into this criminal world that first seduced me and eventually controlled me. My experience is not as isolated as you may hope. This is not the story of a few bad kids whose parents paid no attention. There are hundreds of kids in the United States alone who are right now wrapped in this horror. (House Hearing, 2006)

Justin's testimony sadly proves true for juvenile prostitution through the use of chat rooms and SNSs. Wells and colleagues (2012) examined the role of the Internet in juvenile prostitution cases coming to the attention of law enforcement in conjunction with the National Juvenile Prostitution Study. The authors noted that 15 percent of the Internet prostitution cases involved the use of email, chat rooms, and text messages. In one case, a juvenile went to a Yahoo chat room titled "girls who need money," indicating that chat rooms can function as a forum to facilitate juvenile prostitution.

Criminal street gangs also use SNSs to recruit vulnerable high-school-age girls to work in their prostitution business. After a multi-agency state and federal investigation, the FBI announced that the leader of the Underground Gangster Crips pleaded guilty to various federal charges related to sex trafficking conspiracy. According to the FBI's investigation, the gang leader and his associates trolled SNSs to find attractive young girls. After a period of grooming, characterized by flattering the girl's looks or promises of money, the gang member arranged to meet the girl. Under pressure, and sometimes with the use of drugs and/or alcohol, the girls were lured into engaging in commercial sex with threats of violence if they didn't comply. On September 14, 2012, the gang leader was sentenced to 40 years in prison on charges related to these activities, and several of his fellow gang members also received prison sentences (Teen Prostitution, 2012).

Juveniles may also be subject criminal prosecution under child pornography laws that govern the posting of sexual images. In 2009, a 14-year-old New Jersey girl was charged with possession and distribution of child pornography after posting nearly 30 explicit nude pictures of herself on MySpace.com. The girl reportedly posted the picture to please her boyfriend. Although the charges were subsequently dropped, with counseling and probation required instead, this case highlights how many laws designed to protect children and adolescents from being harmed on the Internet may also result in their being labeled sexual offenders (Associated Press, 2009).

There are few data about juveniles who use chat rooms or SNSs to sexually solicit or prey on others. In their analysis of the Growing up with Media data described above, Ybarra and Bull (2007) found that 3 percent of 10- to 15-year-olds who used the Internet engaged in perpetrating unwanted sexual solicitation. All of these youth reported that they had also been a victim or perpetrator of online harassment. Depending on the jurisdiction, a juvenile could be criminally charged for his or her actions related to sexual solicitation or completed sexual activity. State statutes vary regarding the age of the juvenile perpetrator and the age difference required between juveniles to satisfy the legal definition of statutory rape. Many states have passed what are referred to as "Romeo and Juliet" laws, which serve to reduce or eliminate cases where there is a minimal age difference between the involved juveniles or sexual contact is considered rape only because of the lack of legally recognized consent (Nunziato, 2012).

Box 6.1 provides some sample questions specific to juveniles' activities in chat rooms and SNSs relevant to understanding their sexual involvement in these Internet forums.

■ MECHANISMS TO ADDRESS JUVENILE SEXUAL VICTIMIZATION IN CHAT ROOMS AND SNSS

User Age Verification

Despite many SNSs' explicit written age restrictions, such restrictions are relatively easy to violate. In a *Consumer Reports* survey examining the age of children using Facebook, researchers found the following in regard to Facebook's age restriction compliance (That Facebook friend, 2011):

- Of the 20 million minors using Facebook during the prior year, more than one third were younger than 13, in violation of Facebook's age restriction.

BOX 6.1 ■ Screening Questions for Chat Room and SNS Use

1. Are any of your screen names sexually suggestive in any way?
2. Have you ever chatted with someone online that you had not met offline?
3. Have you ever had a sexually oriented conversation online with someone you knew was an adult?
4. Has anyone online tried to get you to talk about sex when you didn't want to?
5. Has anyone online asked you sexual information about yourself?
6. Has anyone online asked you to do something sexual that you did not want to?
7. Have you ever initiated talking about sex online with someone else?
8. Have you ever had talked to someone offline that you met online?
9. Have you ever met someone offline that you met online?
10. Have you ever met someone offline for the purpose of engaging in sex that you met online?
11. Have you ever exchanged personal information and photos online with someone you did not know?
12. Have you ever posted pictures or videos of yourself that could be interpreted as sexually suggestive?
13. Have you ever harassed others online, such as calling them names or threatening them in some way?
14. Where do you spend most of your time on the Internet meeting others? (i.e. chat rooms, instant messaging, social networking sites, online games)
15. Have you ever been pressured to trade sex for money or something else you needed or wanted?

- More than 5 million youth using Facebook were under 10, and their Facebook accounts were largely unsupervised by their parents.

Several state attorney generals have pressured SNSs to verify the age of their users and/or to raise the minimal allowable age to access their sites (Emily & Angwin, 2006). However, numerous challenges emerge with a verification requirement, such as protecting the individual's privacy, preserving online freedom of speech and expression, and matching a myriad of records to verify any random person who could be residing anywhere in the world (Thierer, 2007).

Lawsuits attempting to hold SNSs liable for not verifying the age of their users have generally not been successful. In the 2008 case *Doe v. MySpace*, a 13-year-old girl (referenced as "Julie Doe" for privacy purposes) created a MySpace profile that falsely described her as an 18-year-old female (*Doe v. MySpace*, 2008). This deception allowed her to circumvent all safety features of the website and resulted in her profile being made public, a situation that would not have occurred had she accurately reported her age. Pete Solis, a 19-year-old male, subsequently contacted her through the site and eventually they communicated offline. They met in person for the first time on May 12, 2006, when Solis allegedly sexually assaulted her. Solis was indicted for second-degree sexual assault but claimed he was unaware of their age difference. Julie Doe and her mother filed a $30 million lawsuit against MySpace alleging that MySpace failed to implement basic safety measures to prevent sexual predators from communicating with minors through the SNS. In particular, the plaintiffs claimed that MySpace and its parent company, News Corporation, owed a legal duty to Julie Doe to institute and enforce appropriate security measures and policies that would substantially decrease the likelihood of danger and harm that MySpace posed to her.

The district court dismissed the claim, and on appeal the Fifth Circuit Court of Appeals affirmed the district court's ruling. In particular, the appellate court held that the 1996 Community Decency Act prohibits claims against Web-based interactive computer services based on their publication of third-party content (e.g., false user profiles) and therefore they were not liable for the sexual assault of Julie Doe (*Doe v. MySpace*, 2008). The U.S. Supreme Court declined to hear this case, thereby leaving the appellate court's decision standing. This court ruling indicates that there is limited, if any, liability for SNSs if users provide false information and thereby violate the site's terms of agreement.

Adults who engage sexually with minors they meet in SNSs have been likewise unsuccessful in suing SNSs for the site's failure to verify the minor's age, as illustrated by the case of *John Doe v. SexSearch.com* (2008). SexSearch.com is an Internet dating service that facilitates sexual encounters. The website notifies users before they register they must agree that they are at least 18 years old, in accordance with the site's Terms and Conditions. In the case of *John Doe v. SexSearch.com*, John Doe met a 14-year-old girl online who agreed to the Terms and Conditions and listed her age as 18 on her SexSearch profile. The two subsequently met in person at the girl's home, where they were sexually involved. The girl subsequently told police about her encounter with Doe, and he was arrested and charged with three counts of unlawful sexual conduct with a minor.

Doe then filed suit against SexSearch.com, alleging a wide variety of violations under Ohio law. In particular, Doe alleged that SexSearch.com permitted minors to become paid members and as a result they effectively delivered the underage girl to him. The Sixth District Court dismissed this claim, noting that the website never promised to verify ages of registered members and their Terms and Conditions stated that the site could not guarantee or assume responsibility for verifying the accuracy of users of their service. The court also emphasized that as a registered member, Doe was aware that users only had to check a box indicating that they were 18 or older without any verification.

Age misrepresentations are not limited to juveniles. Concerns have also been raised about adults who falsely claim that they are much younger or close to the youth's age with whom they are in contact. One purpose of posing as a teenager or younger child would be to gain the youth's trust, thereby increasing their chances of arranging a sexual encounter. An actual case where this occurred involves Michael Sebastian, a 29-year-old New Jersey resident who posed as a 17-year-old named Chris on Facebook. According to news accounts, Sebastian "friended" two 14-year-old girls on Facebook. He pled guilty to stalking one of the girls to a shopping center, where he lured her into his car and sexually assaulted her. He also exchanged sexually explicit text messages with the other 14-year-old girl, eventually picking her up from her house and driving her to a motel, where he provided her with alcohol and sexually assaulted her (Terruso, 2012).

Clearly there are cases where adults falsely pose as juveniles to facilitate their sexually victimizing a child or adolescent. But how common is this type of victimization? To help answer this question, Wolak and colleagues (2004) conducted a survey of 2,574 law enforcement agencies between October 2001 and July 2002 in regard to 129 sexual offenses against juvenile victims that originated with online encounters. The authors noted that 75 percent of the victims were 13- through 15-year-old teenage girls who met adult offenders in Internet chat rooms. Only 5 percent of the adult offenders lied about their age and pretended to be minors, and only 21 percent lied about their interest in having sexual relations with the minor. In other words, most offenders told their victims that they were adults who were interested in having a sexual relationship. Furthermore, most victims met and had sex with the adult they met online on more than one occasion. When the perpetrators did use deception, they did so primarily by promising love or romance when their primary intentions were sexual. The victims commonly reported that they felt they were in love or had close bonds with the adult perpetrator. This study emphasizes that age verification of adult users, alone, is unlikely to have a significant impact on sexual contact between adult perpetrators and juvenile victims who meet offline.

Laws Restricting Internet Access to Sex Offenders

The pressure to monitor potential sexual predators' activities in chat rooms and SNSs are not limited to Internet websites and parent companies. Increasingly, laws are being passed that limit sex offenders' activities in chat rooms and SNSs. In particular, federal and state legislation has been enacted that requires sex offenders to disclose their Internet identifiers to established registries so that they can be monitored and/or prevented from using certain SNSs. On the federal level, Congress passed the "Keeping the Internet Devoid of Sexual Predators Act of 2008," which was signed into law by President George Bush on October 13, 2008 (KIDS Act of 2008). Upon passage, co-sponsor Senator Chuck Schumer's press release provided the following statement ("President Bush Signs," 2008):

> Millions of teenagers log on to websites like MySpace and they, and their parents, shouldn't have to worry about running into these predators online...Sex offenders have no business joining social networking communities—especially those with teenage users—and our legislation will help keep them out. We know that many

predators are using the Internet to find victims. This legislation will take a big step toward keeping sexual predators out of the online neighborhoods our kids frequent.

The KIDS Act requires sex offenders to provide all Internet identifiers to the National Sex Offender Registry. In addition, this legislation requires the Attorney General to develop and maintain a secure system that SNSs can access to compare Internet identifiers stored in the registry with the Internet identifiers of their users. Critics of this legislation note that offenders could circumvent the legislation by not using any screen names that they have provided to the national registry. However, sex offenders who fail to register or update registration of email information are subject to up to 10 years' imprisonment under this legislation (KIDS Act of 2008).

Numerous states have passed similar laws requiring sex offenders to disclose their Internet identifiers to state sex offender registries, and many have attempted to implement even more restrictive requirements. Three state statutes targeted at online sexual offenders are provided below to illustrate the range of requirements and potential constitutional challenges to such legal mandates.

New York: Electronic Security and Targeting of Online Predators Act

On May 13, 2008, New York Governor David A. Paterson signed the Electronic Security and Targeting of Online Predators Act (e-STOP, 2008). E-STOP includes three components:

1. Requires convicted sex offenders to register their Internet accounts and identifiers with the state Division of Criminal Justice Services (DCJS)
2. Authorizes DCJS to release state sex offender Internet identifiers to SNSs and certain other online services to prescreen or remove sex offenders from using the site's services and notify law enforcement authorities and other government officials in conformity with state and federal law
3. Requires, as a condition of probation or parole, mandatory restrictions on Internet access for level 3 sex offenders (highest-level offender), for offenders whose victim was a minor, or for offenders who used the Internet to victimize a minor

Under e-STOP, sex offenders must notify DCJS within 10 days if they change any of their Internet identifiers or face penalties for failing to register. On April 28, 2011, Governor Cuomo announced that as of that date, e-STOP had resulted in the removal of more than 24,000 accounts and online profiles linked to registered sex offenders ("Governor Cuomo Announces," 2011). In December 2012, New York's Attorney General announced that 2,100 registered sex offenders had been banned from online gaming platforms resulting from an effort to further prevent sex offenders from interacting with children online in an operation known as "Operation Game Over" (Albanesius, 2012).

Indiana: Sex Offender Internet Offense

In 2008, Indiana passed legislation to ban sexually violent offenders from knowingly or intentionally using or accessing designated platforms of online communication that could be frequented by a person less than 18 years of age, such as SNSs, chat rooms, or instant messaging services. The legislation applied only to individuals found to be sexually violent predators or those who had been convicted of one or more of the following crimes: child molestation, child exploitation, possession of child pornography, vicarious sexual gratification, sexual conduct in the presence of a minor, child solicitation, child seduction, kidnapping of unrelated child less than age 18, or an attempt to commit or conspiracy to commit any of these crimes (Indiana Code, 2008). The legislation specified that registered sex offenders were not prohibited from using message boards and email services. The law, however, did not distinguish its application based on the age of the perpetrator's victims, how the crime was committed (i.e., whether or not it involved the use of the Internet), or the time since the offense was committed.

After this legislation was signed into law, Doe, an anonymous plaintiff, claimed that the statute violated his First Amendment right to free speech and requested that the court enjoin enforcement of the statute. Doe had been convicted for two counts of child exploitation. Doe noted that Indiana had already passed another law that prohibits persons 21 years or older from solicitation of children less than age 14 by using a computer network. The district court reasoned that the Indiana law was narrowly tailored because Doe was banned only from those websites where online predators have easy access to an endless pool of possible victims. District Judge Tanya Pratt determined that this statute left open numerous alternative channels of communication on the Internet and therefore did not violate Doe's First Amendment rights (*Doe v. Prosecutor*, 2012).

The American Civil Liberties Union of Indiana challenged the judge's ruling, and on January 23, 2013, the U.S. Seventh Circuit Court of Appeals struck down this law (*Doe v. Prosecutor*, 2013). This appellate court noted that the law targeted more activity than necessary to prevent the harm, and because it was not narrowly tailored the law violated the plaintiff's First Amendment rights.

Louisiana: "Unlawful Use or Access of Social Media"

Louisiana State Representative Jeff Thompson introduced a bill restricting sex offenders' use of social media after a man pretending to be a young girl reportedly lured a boy via the Internet and then murdered him. On June 14, 2011, Louisiana Governor Bobby Jindal signed into law the bill, entitled "Unlawful Use or Access of Social Media" (2011). This legislation unanimously passed the Louisiana Senate and banned certain categories of convicted sex offenders from using or accessing SNSs, chat rooms, and peer-to-peer networks. Five specific sex offenses were delineated: sex offenders convicted of having a victim who was a minor, indecent behavior with a juvenile, video voyeurism, computer-aided solicitation of minors, or pornography involving juveniles. Sex offenders found guilty of using social media could be sentenced to up to 10 years in prison or pay a maximum $10,000 fine for the first conviction and up to five to 20 years in prison or fines up to $20,000 for subsequent convictions.

In response to this law, two plaintiffs filed suit in the U.S. District Court, Middle District of Louisiana (*John Doe v. Bobby Jindal*, 2012). The plaintiffs challenged the law on the grounds that it violates the First Amendment's right to free speech and the Fourteenth Amendment's right to due process, which protects the public from vague criminal statutes. The plaintiffs argued that the definitions of SNSs, chat rooms, and peer-to-peer networks were so broad that the law effectively restricted registered sex offenders from accessing any Internet site where one can read or post comments. Examples of sites barred to convicted sex offenders under this legislation included CNN.com, NYTimes.com, USAJOBS.gov, and even the district court's own website.

In his 2012 holding, Chief Judge Brian Jackson ruled that the act was unconstitutionally overbroad and void for vagueness. In overturning this law, he wrote:

> Although the Act is intended to promote the legitimate and compelling state interest of protecting minors from Internet predators, the near total ban on Internet access imposed by the Act unreasonably restricts many ordinary activities that have become important to everyday life in today's world. The sweeping restrictions on the use of the Internet for purposes completely unrelated to the activities sought to be banned by the Act impose severe and unwarranted restraints on constitutionally protected speech. More focused restrictions that are narrowly tailored to address the specific conduct sought to be proscribed should be pursued. (*John Doe v. Bobby Jindal*, 2012, p. 17)

To address these constitutional concerns and maintain their goal of protecting youth from online sexual predators, Louisiana passed the following three laws that went into effect on August 1, 2012:

- House Bill 556: required sex offenders to provide law enforcement with changes to email and online user/screen names within three business days of the change (La. Rev. Stat. §15:542 2012).
- House Bill 249: required sex offenders to post notice of their convictions on "networking websites" that allow profile pages, photos, and the ability to send and receive messages (La. Rev. Stat. §15:542.1 (D). 2012).
- House Bill 620: narrowed the original definition of SNSs to include only those sites "the primary purpose of which is facilitating social interaction with other users of the website" (La. Rev. Stat. §14:91.5. 2012).

By narrowing the definition of an SNS, the Louisiana legislature attempted to address the court's concern that the previous definition was too broad. However, upon revisiting the prior statute, Louisiana passed the first bill in the nation that requires sex offenders to post that they are sex offenders when they enter an SNS. In reference to these enhanced requirements, Governor Jindal stated,

> Louisiana families should have the comfort of knowing their children are able to access the Internet without the threat of sex predators. We already restrict sex offenders from playgrounds, daycares, and schools, and they should not be allowed to prey on our children in our homes through our computers. As technology advances, so too must law enforcement's tools, so that we can stay ahead of the monsters that prey on our children. (Governor Jindal, 2012)

■ SUMMARY

Juveniles' sexual development and involvement with others are significantly linked to their interactions in an Internet world, a world that offers potentially positive and negative experiences. Over the last decade, juveniles have increasingly been using SNSs as their primary interactive Internet activity, with less time spent in chat rooms. Juveniles often utilize SNSs to post sexually suggestive comments, photos, or videos. Although research indicates that fewer juveniles are actually receiving unwanted online sexual solicitations than previously noted, concerns remain regarding their vulnerability to potential online sexual predators. Both federal and state laws have been enacted to help identify online sex offenders and prevent them from accessing chat rooms and SNSs likely to be accessed by youth. As juveniles advance through adolescence in chat rooms and SNSs, findings ways to keep their journey free of harm without unconstitutionally restricting the freedoms of others remains a challenge for this social and sexual brave new world.

■ DISCLOSURE

Albert J. Grudzinskas, Jr. has no conflicts of interest to disclose.

Barry Feldman has no conflicts of interest to disclose.

Charles L. Scott has absolutely no conflicts of any kind and he does not participate in any type of speaker's bureau or any other agency or business.

Fabian M. Saleh has no conflicts of interest to disclose.

Richard Cody has no conflicts of interest to disclose.

Simha E. Ravven has no conflict of interest to disclose.

■ REFERENCES

Albanesius, C. (Dec. 19, 2012). NY Removes 2,100 Sex Offenders From Online Gaming Platforms. http://www.pcmag.com/article2/0,2817,2413425,00.asp. Accessed January 26, 2013.

Associated Press (March 27, 2009). New Jersey girl, 14, arrested after posting nude pictures on MySpace. http://archive.firstamendmentcenter.org/news.aspx?id=21406. Accessed February 4, 2013.

Beebe, T. J., Asche, S. E., Harrison, P. A., et al. (2004). Heightened vulnerability and increased risk-taking among adolescent chat room users: Results from a statewide school survey. *Journal of Adolescent Health, 35,* 116–123.

Children's Online Privacy Protection Act of 1998. 15 U.S.C. §§ 6501-6506.

Collins, R. L., Martino, S. C., & Shaw, R. (April 2011). Influence of new media on adolescent sexual health: evidence and opportunities. WR-761. http://aspe.hhs.gov/hsp/11/adolescentsexualactivity/newmedialitrev/index.pdf. Accessed February 4, 2013.

Common Sense Media (2009). Is technology networking changing childhood? A national poll. San Francisco. www.commonsensemedia.org/sites/default/files/CSM_teen_social_media_080609_FINAL.pdf. Accessed January 29, 2013.

Doe v. MySpace, 528 F.3d 413 (5th Cir. 2008)

Doe v. Prosecutor, Marion County, S.D. Ind. (June 22, 2012).

Doe v. Prosecutor, Marion County, S.D. Ind. (7th Cir. January 23, 2013).

Doe v. SexSearch.com, 551 F.3d 412 (6th Cir. 2008)

Eichenwald, K. (Dec. 19, 2005). Through his webcam, a boy joins a sordid online world. *New York Times.* http://www.nytimes.com/2005/12/19/national/19kids.ready.html?pagewanted=all&_r=0. Accessed February 4, 2013.

Electronic Security and Targeting of Online Predators Act of 2008. http://criminaljustice.state.ny.us./legalservices/ch67.htm. Accessed February 4, 2013.

Emily, S., & Angwin, J. (June 23, 2006). MySpace receives more pressure to limit children's access to site. *Wall Street Journal.* http://online.wsj.com/public/article/SB115102268445288250-YRxkt0rTsyyf1QiQf2EPBYSf7iU 20070624.html?mod=tff main tff top. Accessed January 26, 2013.

Facebook Statement of Rights and Responsibilities (Dec. 11, 2012). http://www.facebook.com/legal/terms. Accessed February 5, 2013.

Governor Cuomo announced e-Stop law leads to removal of more than 24,000 social networking accounts and profiles linked to registered sex offenders (April 28, 2011). https://www.governor.ny.gov/press/042811estoplaw. Accessed January 26, 2013.

Governor Jindal signs new laws to crack down on sex offenders and gangs (May 23, 2012). http://gov.louisiana.gov/index.cfm?md=newsroom&tmp=detail&articleID=3436. Accessed February 4, 2013.

Greenfield, P. M., & Subrahmanyam, K. (2003). Online discourse in a teen chat room: new codes and new modes of coherence in a visual medium. *Applied Development Psychology, 24,* 713–738.

Hinduja, S., & Patchin, J. W. (2007). Offline consequences of online victimization: school violence and delinquency. *Journal of School Violence, 6,* 89–112.

Hinduja, S., & Patchin, J. W. (2008). Personal information of adolescents on the Internet: a quantitative content analysis of MySpace. *Journal of Adolescence, 31,* 125–146.

House Hearing, 109 Congress, Second Session, April 4, 2006, U.S. Government Printing Office, Washington DC, 2006

Indiana Code §35-42-4-12(e) (2008).

John Doe v. Bobby Jindal (M.D. La. Feb. 16, 2012).

Jones, L. M., Mitchell, K. J., & Finkelhor, D. (2012). Trends in youth Internet victimization: findings from three Youth Internet Safety Surveys 2000–2010. *Journal of Adolescent Health, 50,* 179–186.

Jones, L. M., Mitchell, K. J., & Finkelhor, D. (2013). Online harassment in context: trends from three youth Internet safety surveys (2000, 2005, 2010). *Psychology of Violence, 1,* 53–69.

KIDS Act of 2008. 42 U.S.C. §16915a.

La. Rev. Stat. §14:91.5. 2012.

La. Rev. Stat. §15:542.1 (D). 2012.

La. Rev. Stat. §15:542 2012.

Lenhart, A., Madden, M., Macgill, A. R., et al. (2007). *Teens and social media. The use of social media gains a greater foothold in teen life as they embrace the conversational nature of interactive online media.* Pew Internet and American Life Project, December 19, 2007. Available at: http://www.pewinternet.org/~/media//Files/Reports/2007/PIP_Teens_Social_Media_Final.pdf.pdf. Accessed January 3, 2013.

Lenhart, A., Purcell, K., Smith, A. et al. (2010). *Social media & mobile Internet use among teens and young adults.* Washington, DC: Pew Internet and American Life Project.

Mitchell, K. J., Jones, L. M., Wolak, J., & Finkelhor, D. (2011). Internet-facilitated commercial sexual exploitation of children: findings from a nationally representative sample of law enforcement agencies in the U.S. *Sexual Abuse: A Journal of Research and Treatment, 23*, 43–71.

Mitchell, K. J., Wolak, J., & Finkelhor, D. (2007). Trends in youth reports of sexual solicitations, harassment, and unwanted exposure to pornography on the Internet. *Journal of Adolescent Health, 40*, 116–26.

Moreno, M. A., Brockman, L., Rogers, C. B., et al. (2010). An evaluation of the distribution of sexual references among "top 8" MySpace friends. *Journal of Adolescent Health, 47*, 418–420.

Moreno, M. A., & Kolb, J. (2012). Social networking sites and adolescent health. *Pediatric Clinics of North America, 59*, 601–612.

Moreno, M. A., Parks, M., Zimmerman, F., et al. (2009). Display of health risk behaviors on MySpace by adolescents. Prevalence and associations. *Archives of Pediatric & Adolescent Medicine, 163*, 27–34.

National campaign to prevent teen and unplanned pregnancy and CosmoGirl.com. sex and tech: results from a survey of teens and young adults (2008). http:www.thenationalcampaign.org/sextech/pdf/sextech_summary.pdf. Accessed February 5, 2013.

Nunziato, D. C. (2012). Romeo and Juliet online and in trouble: criminalizing depictions of teen sexuality (c u l8r:g2g2jail). http://scholarcommons.law.northwestern.edu/ngtip/vol10/iss3/1. Accessed February 4, 2013.

President Bush signs Schumer bill to crack down on child predators on the internet-new law will mandate national email registry for sex offenders (Oct. 14, 2008). http://www.schumer.senate.gov/Newsroom/record.cfm?id=304293. Accessed January 26, 2013.

Rideout, V., Foehr, U., & Roberts, D. (2010). *Generation M2: Media in the lives of 8 to 18 years old.* Menlo Park, CA: Henry J. Kaiser Family Foundation.

Subrahmanyam, K., & Greenfield, P. (2008). Online communication and adolescent relationships. *The Future of Children, 18*, 119–146.

Subrahmanyam, K., Greenfield, P. M., & Tynes, B. (2004). Constructing sexuality and identity in on online teen chatroom. *Journal of Applied Developmental Psychology, 25*, 651–666.

Subrahmanyam, K., Smahel, D., & Greenfield, P. (2006). Connecting developmental processes to the Internet identity presentation and sexual exploration in online teen chat rooms. *Developmental Psychology, 3*, 395–406.

Tapscott, D. (1998). *Growing up digital: the rise of the net generation.* New York: McGraw Hill.

Teen Prostitution: Gang used social media sites to identify potential victims (Sept. 14, 2012). http://www.fbi.gov/news/stories/2012/september/teen-prostitution. Accessed February 4, 2013.

Terruso, J. (Aug. 3, 2012). Perth Amboy man gets 4 years in prison for assaulting teens he met on Facebook. http://www.nj.com/news/index.ssf/2012/08/perth_amboy_man_gets_4_years_i.html. Accessed January 26, 2013.

That Facebook friend might be 10 years old, and other troubling news (June 2011). *Consumer Reports*.http://www.consumerreports.org/cro/magainze-archive/2011/june/electronics-computers/state-of-the-net/facebook-concerns/index.htm. Accessed January 26, 2013.

Thierer, A. D. (March 21, 2007). *Social networking and age verification: many hard questions; no easy solutions*. Progress & Freedom Foundation Progress on Point Paper No. 14.5. http://dx.doi.org/10.2139/ssrn.976936. Accessed February 4, 2013.

Top 15 most popular social networking sites (February 2013). http://www.ebizmba.com/articles/social-networking-websites. Accessed February 4, 2013.

Tynes, B., Reynolds, L., & Greenfield, P. M. (2004). Adolescence, race, and ethnicity on the Internet: a comparison of discourse in monitored vs. unmonitored chat rooms. *Applied Developmental Psychology, 25*, 667–684.

Unlawful use or access of social media, LSA-R.S.14:91.5, June 14, 2011.

Wells, M., Mitchell, K. J., & Ji, E. K. (2012). Exploring the role of the Internet in juvenile prostitution cases coming to the attention of law enforcement. *Journal of Child Sexual Abuse, 21*, 327–342.

Whittaker, Z. (Oct. 4, 2012). Facebook hits 1 billion active user milestone. http://news.cnet.com/8301-1023_3-57525797-93/facebook-hits-1-billion-active-user-milestone/. Accessed January 29, 2013.

Wolak, J., Finkelhor, D., & Mitchell, K. (2004). Internet-initiated sex crimes against minors: implications for prevention based on findings from a national study. *Journal of Adolescent Health, 35*, 424.e11–424.e20.

Wolak, J., Finkelhor, D., & Mitchell, K. J. (2009). *Trends in arrests of "online predators."* Durham, NH: Crimes against Children Research Center, University of New Hampshire, pp. 1–10.

Wolak, J., Finkelhor, D., & Mitchell, K. J. (April 2012). *Trends in law enforcement responses to technology-facilitated child sexual exploitation crimes: the third National Juvenile Online Victimization Study (NJOV-3)*. http://www.unh.edu/ccrc/pdf/CV268_Trends percent20in percent20LE percent20Response percent20Bulletin_4-13-12.pdf. Accessed February 5, 2013.

Wolak, J., Mitchell, K., & Finkelhor, D. (2002). Close online relationships in a national sample of adolescents. *Adolescence, 147*, 441–455.

Ybarra, M. L., & Bull, S. S. (2007). Current trends in Internet- and cell phone-based HIV prevention and intervention programs. *Current HIV/AIDS Reports, 4*, 201–207.

Ybarra, M. L., & Mitchell, K. J. (2008). How risky are social networking sites? A comparison of places online where youth sexual solicitation and harassment occurs. *Pediatrics, 121*, e350.

7 Cybersexual Harassment and Suicide

FABIAN M. SALEH, BARRY N. FELDMAN, ALBERT J. GRUDZINSKAS, JR., SIMHA E. RAVVEN, AND RICHARD CODY

INTRODUCTION

During the 2008–2009 school year, some 7,066,000 U.S. students, 28 percent of all such students ages 12 through 18, reported they were bullied at school (National Center for Education Statistics, 2011). In another study, 43 percent of 13- to 17-year-olds reported being cyberbullied during the previous year (Moessner, 2007). Key findings of another national poll (Opinion Research Corporation, 2006) involving 1,000 youth below the age of 18 include the following:

- One third of all teens (ages 12 to 17) and one sixth of children (ages 6 to 11) have had mean, threatening, or embarrassing things said about them online; 10 percent of the teens and 4 percent of the younger children were threatened online with physical harm.
- 16 percent of the teens and preteens who were victims told no one about it.
- About half of children ages 6 to 11 told their parents.
- Only 30 percent of older kids told their parents.
- Preteens were as likely to receive harmful messages at school (45 percent) as at home (44 percent).
- Older children received 30 percent of harmful messages at school and 70 percent at home.
- 17 percent of preteens and 7 percent of teens said they were worried about bullying as they start a new school year.

Children found to be most at risk include those with mental health issues or who have a developmental disability; gay or lesbian adolescents, or those struggling with their sexuality; children who have recently moved to a new school; those perceived as outsiders by their peers; and adolescents who spend a lot of time online (American Academy of Child Adolescent Psychiatry, 2010).

In this chapter we will explore the developmental underpinnings of traditional bullying and the more contemporary manifestations of this phenomenon in cyber-bullying. We suggest that the emergence of cyber-bullying and media coverage that linked this form of bullying with the suicide of individual youths fostered renewed social concern in the topic, which has in turn spearheaded novel legal responses. These processes have occurred, however, when research on cyber-bullying remains in its early stages and thus in response to aspects of the digital revolution that remain poorly understood. We aim to critically evaluate extant empirical data about the relationship between bullying and an increased risk for suicidal behavior. We will review various legislative responses to bullying that have largely resulted from how the digital revolution configures the phenomenon of bullying. In this discussion we will consider the congruence between developmental research on bullying and emerging legal interventions. We conclude with a synthesis that includes implications for stake-holding professionals who work with youth.

■ WHAT IS BULLYING?

Olweus defined bullying or victimization in the following general way: "A student is being bullied or victimized when he or she is exposed, repeatedly and over time, to negative actions on the part of one or more other students. It is a negative action when someone intentionally inflicts, or attempts to inflict, injury or discomfort upon another—basically what is implied in the definition of aggressive behavior" (Olweus, 1978). He noted that negative actions need not be by words alone; they can be carried out by physical contact, by making faces or obscene gestures, and by intentionally excluding persons from a group. To use the term "bullying," he described the need for an imbalance in strength between the student who is exposed to the negative actions and therefore has difficulty defending himself or herself and the student or students who commit the harassing behavior (Olweus, 1993). While his comments were confined to student situations, the definition applies equally well to most social interactions and ages.

Both the bully and those being bullied may have serious, lasting problems, including physical health complaints, depression and anxiety, increased feelings of sadness and loneliness, changes in sleep and eating patterns, and loss of interest in activities they used to enjoy. Both parties may also suffer decreased academic achievement—grade point average and standardized test scores—and school participation. They are more likely to miss, skip, or drop out of school (Gruber & Fineran, 2008; Weir, 2001).

■ WHAT IS CYBER-BULLYING?

Defining cyber-bullying can be slightly more challenging and somewhat difficult to compare and contrast with "traditional bullying" given the varied methods with which it can be employed (Kowalski, Limber, & Agatston, 2008). Cyber-bullying utilizes an electronic medium and generally can be defined as "an aggressive intentional act carried out by a group or individual using electronic forms of contact repeatedly and over time against a victim who cannot easily defend him or herself" (Smith et al., 2008, p. 376, cited in Dooley, Pyzalski, & Cross, 2009). Cyber-bullying incorporates the aforementioned elements of traditional bullying, along with factors such as aggression/aggressor, power imbalance/power differential, and intentional behavior noted in traditional bullying definitions (see Olweus, 1993).

Other researchers suggest that repeated acts of aggression using electronic means should be called "online harassment" (Wolak, Mitchell, & Finkelhor, 2007). Of central importance when defining cyber-bullying is that the same elements central to face-to-face bullying are also inherent, though the methods employed are different. Kowalski and colleagues (2008) suggest that cyber-bullying is merely an electronic form of face-to-face bullying. Others, however, believe that cyber-bullying differs significantly from face-to-face bullying given the widespread messaging capabilities of electronic media when issues specific to repetition and power imbalances are examined (Dooley, Pyzalski, & Cross, 2009). Providing a detailed discussion of these contrasts in face-to-face bullying versus cyber-bullying methods is beyond the scope of this chapter. The current and future capacity of information and communication technology, to disseminate potentially psychologically harmful personal material and information, understandably has generated significant concern about the impact of both methods of bullying on the emotional and/or physical well-being of our young people.

Data from the Second Youth Internet Safety Survey indicates that cyber-bullying among preteens and teens has increased dramatically in recent years as young people spend more time socializing online (Ybarra & Mitchell, 2008). According to Patchin and Hinduja (2006), there are two major forms of cyber-bullying: (1) via personal computer, the aggressor can transmit emails and instant messages and post obscene, slanderous, and insulting messages to online "bulletin boards," or the aggressor can create websites to encourage and disseminate derogatory material/content; and (2) cellphones can be used to send insulting text messages. More recently, additional methods of transmission can be though Facebook, MySpace, Twitter, etc., and posting videos on YouTube.

■ BULLYING AND CYBER-BULLYING FROM A DEVELOPMENTAL PERSPECTIVE

To develop strategies to counter antisocial aspects of bullying behavior, it is important to understand the developmental antecedents of bullying behavior. As we have seen, cybersexual harassment can be characterized as a type of bullying behavior. Given the potentially profound negative impact of bullying on both victims—and also perpetrators—bullying can be seen as developmental processes gone awry.

In this section we will consider the historical development of the term "bully." We will then examine the literature on bullying from a developmental perspective to better understand how these behaviors change over the course of child and adolescent development, the impact of puberty, and long-term consequences of bullying. We will also examine characteristics of external structures (e.g., family, school, community) that support or discourage bullying.

As we have seen, bullying is generally defined as (1) aggressive behavior or "intentional harm doing" that (2) is carried out repeatedly over time in (3) an interpersonal relationship characterized by an imbalance of power. Bullying behavior may occur without apparent provocation and it can be physical, verbal, or indirect. Indirect aggression's principal forms are gossiping, spreading rumors, and persistent social exclusion (Smith et al., 2002; Smith & Monks, 2008; Olweus, 1993).

Smith and Monks (2008) define a bully as "an aggressive person who intimidates or mistreats weaker people." The etymology of the word "bully" shows an evolution from a word of praise and endearment to its current incarnation: from the 1530s, when it originally meant "sweetheart," as applied to either sex, from Dutch *boel* "lover, brother." The meaning deteriorated in the 17th century from "fine fellow," "blusterer," to "harasser of the weak." Perhaps this was by influence of *bull*, but a connecting sense between "lover" and "ruffian" may be found in "protector of a prostitute," which was one sense of *bully* (Barnhart, 1988).

Bullying between adolescents is found in vastly different cultural and geographic contexts. Rates are fairly consistent across continents and cultures, ranging from 29.9 to 40 percent (Williams & Veeh, 2012). Bullying behaviors in adolescents have been observed in India, South Korea, South Africa, Taiwan, Australia, and the United States (Williams & Veeh, 2012), as well as among the Arctic Utku Eskimo, Amazonian Yanomamo, and African mountain Ik groups (Volk et al., 2012). Historically, bullying is described in ancient Greece, ancient Rome, medieval China, medieval Europe, and Renaissance Europe (Volk et al., 2012). Physical, verbal and indirect social bullying (exclusion and isolation of individuals) are all described. While bullying is seen across cultures, it is difficult to compare terminology describing bullying across languages and cultures. Six groups of terms were identified across cultures: bullying (all types), verbal plus physical bullying, solely verbal bullying, social exclusion, solely physical aggression, and mainly physical aggression (Smith et al., 2002). Bullying behaviors are also seen in primates and other animals. "Dominant females gain access to food and male protection [through bullying] and their privileged status is passed down to their offspring" (Volk et al., 2012). Dominant male primates get better access to mating opportunities by "bullying females directly" or by bullying away male competitors (Volk et al., 2012).

It has been posited that bullying is an evolutionary adaptation to attain and control social and material resources in a context of limited resources (Volk et al., 2012). If social aggression is viewed from an evolutionary perspective, social dominance, attained through competition, may confer survival advantage. The outcomes of competition have structural importance in establishing hierarchies within social groups. As explained by Teisl and colleagues (2012), when individuals who are more dominant (as measured by repeated competitive successes), they are more socially visible and have greater influence on resource distribution. Though social hierarchy can reduce conflict, aggressive behavior is often a route to dominance, particularly in small children. Social dominance is not always maintained through aggression and may also be achieved through cooperation or combination of aggressive and pro-social approaches (Teisl et al., 2012).

In contemporary popular culture, bullying and cyber-bullying are prominent themes in many popular television shows and movies. The television show *Gossip Girl*, for example, is about a blog of the same name that discloses rivalries, secrets, and gossip, most of it sexual in nature, among a group of affluent Manhattan teens. *Mean Girls*, a 2004 comedy film, is based in part on the nonfiction book *Queen Bees and Wannabes* by Rosalind Wiseman, which describes how female high-school social cliques operate and the effect they can have on girls. Themes of bullying are ubiquitous in popular culture, from Stephen King's *Carrie* to Lucy bullying Charlie Brown in the classic comic strip *Peanuts*.

There may be both environmental and genetic bases to the development of bullying behaviors. A recent study of 1,000 sets of twins found significant heritability of bullying behaviors (Ball et al., 2008). Individual differences in temperament, which have both environmental and genetic underpinnings, play a role in the development of bullying behaviors. Research has found that bullies "exhibit a higher level of negative emotionality" than children who are not involved in bullying as either perpetrators or victims (Volk et al., 2012). Bullies also have deficits in behavioral regulation that make them less able to inhibit aggressive impulses (Volk et al., 2012).

While bullying can be strategic and even adaptive as a way to garner resources for the bully, it also has clear costs. Involvement in bullying, whether as victim or bully, has a serious impact on well-being. Youth involved as both bullies and victims (so-called "bully-victims") are particularly vulnerable, with meta-analytic data suggesting the most compromised psychosocial development for these youth (Cook et al., 2010). Bully-victims may have "the worst of both worlds," as they resemble victims in terms of being rejected and resemble bullies by being negatively influenced by the peers with whom they do interact.

Children involved in bullying as victims or as bullies tend to perform poorly in school and are at increased risk of developing poor physical health and psychiatric problems such as anxiety, depression, and psychotic disorders later in life (Jansen et al., 2012). Bullying can be seen as a relational problem in which one child asserts power over another through aggression (Pepler et al., 2006). As is implied in the etymology of the term, a close relationship between bully and victim can be seen. Pepler and colleagues (2006) found that 11- to 13-year-olds who reported bullying others were more likely to be involved in a romantic relationship and more likely to report being verbally and physically aggressive with their romantic partners than non-bullies. It is likely that among youths who bully, other peer relationships, non-romantic as well as romantic, are often characterized by physical, verbal, or indirect aggression.

There is a social cost to bullying for both boys and girls. Youth may experience less closeness and more conflict in their relationships, which continues into adulthood with more aggression in the workplace and in family life (Pepler et al., 2006). Bullies are at greater risk of behavioral problems and criminal behavior later in life. (Jansen et al., 2012). A recent meta-analysis of longitudinal studies of bullying found that, after controlling for other childhood risk factors, bullying perpetration predicted later criminal behavior, including shoplifting, theft, vandalism/property damage, violent offending, arrest, and police/court contact (Jansen et al., 2012).

The causal relationship between school bullying and psychopathology has been the subject of debate: Are youth with existent psychopathology bullied, or is bullying a cause of psychopathology? A 2006 prospective cohort study of bullying in two Korean middle schools examined the causal relationship between psychopathology and school bullying in a 10-month prospective cohort study. This study used multiple independent informants and statistical controls for identified confounders. Victimhood was found to be a cause of social problems in children. Perpetration predicted increased aggression and externalizing behaviors (Kim et al., 2006).

There are important developmental changes in the expression of aggression as children mature. Younger children are more likely to be direct in their aggressive behavior. They use verbal and physical aggression rather than indirect aggression (e.g., gossiping, social exclusion). Use of indirect aggression is characteristic of adolescents and older children (Smith & Monks, 2008). Younger children are also less likely to target the same child or children repeatedly and will more often target different children on different occasions. This may reflect a less fixed social hierarchy among younger children then older children and adolescents (Smith & Monks, 2008).

The frequency of bullying behavior generally declines from childhood to late adolescence (Smith, Madsen, & Moody, 1999). In a cross-national comparison of bullying in Norway, Sweden, England, Australia, and Ireland, a range of 14 percent (Ireland) to 32 percent (England) of 8-year-olds reported being bulled. Resurveyed at age 15, the prevalence of bullying had dropped to 1 percent and 9 percent, respectively. This decrease in bullying is well documented in many different contexts and is likely multifactorial. Children learn less aggressive ways of interacting with each other as they mature (Smith, Madsen, & Moody, 1999). There is a developmental progression from the use of primarily coercive strategies to more socially competent strategies to attain material and social resources. Among older children and adolescents, leaders are unlikely to rely solely on aggression to achieve dominance. They are more likely to employ pro-social strategies as well as aggressive ones to maintain positive social standing (Teisl et al., 2012).

Young children, up to age 5 or 6, are more likely to pursue dominance through aggressive/coercive means—with few consequences in terms of reduced likeability. As children reach middle childhood, coercive strategies become less socially effective and additional pro-social (i.e., cooperative) strategies are adopted. Pettit and colleagues (1990) found that aggression was associated with social dominance in first- and third-grade boys but that leadership behavior, including more pro-social behavior predicted dominance in the older, but not the younger, group. (See also Teis et al., 2012.)

Pro-social dominance strategies allow older children to balance resource attainment with maintenance of peer relationships. There are two main reasons for this shift in effective dominance strategies. First, there are increased negative consequences from peers of coercive behavior; and second, developmental changes in language skills, increased sophisticatation in social understanding, moral development and perspective taking allow children to develop more sophisticated and cooperative modes of maintaining leadership positions in social groups (Teisl et al., 2012). Opportunity to be bullied may also contribute to the decrease in bullying as children get older. Younger children "have more children who are older than them in school, who are in a position to bully them" (Smith, Madsen, & Moody, 1999).

Children's understanding of bullying versus "nasty behavior" becomes more nuanced as they get older (Smith & Monks, 2008). Several studies have found that younger children primarily differentiate between aggressive and non-aggressive behavior and are overly inclusive in their use of the term "bullying" to include fighting where there is not a power imbalance, while teens are able to discriminate fighting from physical and verbal bullying and social exclusion (Smith, 2002; Smith, Madsen, & Moody, 1999; Smith & Monks, 2008).

Several distinct developmental trajectories of bullying behavior have been described. In a longitudinal study of 871 Canadian children, four trajectories of bullying behavior were observed. The children were 10 to 14 years old at the study's onset and were followed for seven years. Approximately 10 percent of the sample engaged in consistently high levels of bullying over time; 13.4 percent initially engaged in moderate levels of bullying that desisted to almost none by the end of high school, 35.1 percent consistently engaged in moderate levels of bullying, and 41.6 percent almost never engaged in bullying (Pepler et al., 2008).

A constellation of bullying roles has been described in observational studies of group dynamics in children. A cross-sectional, observational study of 1,129 Dutch 9- to 12-year-olds examined bullying behavior and group dynamics. In addition to the primary bully and the victim, non-bullies had roles as well: reinforcers laugh and incite the bully and "provide bullies with an approving audience" (Olthof et al., 2011). They are assistants who join in after the ringleader has initiated bullying. Defenders provide help to the victim. There are outsiders as well, who actively avoid all involvement in bullying. In addition, there are uninvolved children who remain uninvolved without active avoidance (like outsiders). Those who helped the victims were relatively socially dominant themselves. Girls were more likely to be defenders of the bullied, or outsiders to the bullying ecosystem (Olthof et al., 2011).

At puberty, sexualized bullying behavior emerges. A major developmental task of adolescence is to learn to express sexual desire in socially acceptable ways (McMaster et al., 2002). McMaster and colleagues propose that sexual harassment emerges in the middle-school years as children reach puberty. Pepler and colleagues (2008) found that perpetration of cross-sex sexual harassment increases during early adolescence and is linked not only to puberty but also to changing composition of social groups, from small single-sex groups to larger groups with both boys and girls. Cross-gender sexual harassment among early adolescents may be, in part, a struggle to express sexual interest. Same-gender sexual harassment is thought to be solely aggressive in nature among majority heterosexual groups of youths (McMaster, et al., 2002). Same-gender harassment is "likely to entail homophobic insults, jokes, name-calling, and rumor spreading, as well as physical behavior such as might occur in hazing rituals" (McMaster et al., 2002).

In the 2002 study by McMaster and colleagues of peer-to-peer sexual harassment in early adolescence, boys were more likely to perpetrate sexual harassment than girls but were essentially equally likely to be a victim of sexual harassment. The most common sexual harassment acts, perpetrated by both boys and girls, were "sexual comments, jokes, gestures, or looks," homophobic slurs, rating "the parts of somebody's body that make them a boy or a girl." Girls were more likely to be victims of "sexual comments, jokes, gestures, or looks" and marginally more likely to be flashed by genitals or mooned by displays of buttocks. Boys were more often victims of homophobic slurs and having sexual pictures, messages, and photographs shown to them (McMaster, et al., 2002 at 95).

Aggressive behavior is generally less prevalent in girls. This may be due, in part, to girls exhibiting more indirect aggression, which is not as easily measured (Pepler et al., 2006). It may also be due to underreporting of aggressive behavior in girls. Girls may be less likely to acknowledge aggressive behavior because expression of aggression is less socially acceptable for girls. Playground observation has actually shown more gender balance in aggressive behavior than girls reported themselves (Pepler et al., 2006).

Among adolescents, much of the verbal bullying they engage in is sexualized in nature and much of the content is homophobic language. In a study of 14- and 15-year-olds in the United Kingdom, the most common pejoratives used in school were sexist (28 percent), referred to sexual behavior (23 percent), and were homophobic (10 percent) (Poteat & Rivers, 2010). Both heterosexually identified and lesbian, gay, bisexual, transgendered, or queer adolescents are the subjects of homophobic pejoratives. Homophobic discourse can be used to assert heterosexuality and enforce gender-normative behavior (Korobov, 2004). Homophobic pejoratives can be used, simply, as a put-down. As Poteat and Rivers (2010) explain, "When used as part of bullying, homophobic epithets may represent one way by which to stigmatize victimized students irrespective of their actual sexual orientation because sexual minorities remain a stigmatized and oppressed group in society" (see also Thurlow, 2001)

Sexual-minority adolescents are disproportionately subject to bullying and violence by peers, with profound negative effects. Sexual-minority and questioning youth are more likely than heterosexual youth to be victims of bullying and peer sexual harassment. In the 2005 Massachusetts Youth Risk Behavior Survey, sexual-minority youth, compared to their peers, were significantly more likely to have skipped school because they felt unsafe (13 vs. 3 percent), had been bullied (44 vs. 23 percent), had been threatened or injured with a weapon at school (14 vs. 5 percent), or had experienced dating violence (35 vs. 8 percent) or sexual contact against their will (34 vs. 9 percent) (Hightow-Weidman et al., 2011).

It can be difficult at times for adults (teachers, parents, healthcare providers) to recognize bullying when they see it or hear about it from children. There are generational differences in what is recognized as bullying (Smith & Monks, 2008). In Smith and Monk's study of developmental and cultural aspects of bullying, adults were less likely than children and adolescents to consider social and indirect aggression to be bullying. This may be related to recent work in schools to educate students about social and relational aggression. As Smith and Monks note, the generational differences of what constitutes bullying make for potential misunderstanding between children and adolescents and their parents and teachers and, perhaps, minimization of social and relational aggression. This is particularly important given the prevalence of this type of aggression in the cybersphere. According to a recent survey of Internet-using 10- to 15-year-olds, 33 percent reported online sexual harassment in the prior year, 15 percent reported an unwanted sexual solicitation online in the same time period, and 4 percent reported a sexual solicitation incident on a social networking site specifically (Ybarra & Mitchell, 2008).

Some individuals continue to rely on coercion and aggression after their peers have largely adopted more pro-social modes of interaction. What predicts continued bullying behavior? Early socializing experiences are important. Family violence, both domestic violence and child maltreatment, was associated with increased involvement in bullying, as bully, victim, or bully and victim (Bowes et al., 2009). Behavioral modeling by parents, siblings, and peers has an important impact on children's developing schemas of social interaction. Abuse has a profound effect. Child maltreatment has been linked to maladaptive, particularly aggressive, behavior in children. Children who are mistreated often struggle with emotional dysregulation. They also learn aggressive modes of interaction from those around them and anticipate reward from aggressive behavior, as they have observed in those around them (Teisl et al., 2012). In a study of African American fifth- through 12th-graders, the largest risk factor for bullying was family violence. Having been hit by a parent once or twice (odds ratio 1.70, confidence interval 1.22–2.22) and several times (odds ratio 2.44, confidence interval 1.45–3.11) were seen as risk factors; gang affiliation was also associated with bullying (Fitzpatrick,

Dulin, & Piko, 2007). Longitudinal studies of children "who later became bullies found that their parents provided less cognitive stimulation, emotional support and allowed more TV than other parents" (Ball et al., 2008). Bully-victims had harsh early home environments, witnessing and experiencing aggression.

Adolescents from families with lower socioeconomic status are more often victims of bullying and may face more severe mental health consequences compared to victims from more affluent backgrounds (Jansen et al., 2012). Low family and school neighborhood socioeconomic status have also been associated with an increased risk of being a bully or a bully-victim (Jansen et al., 2012). Parental depression (Bowes et al., 2009) has been associated with being involved in bullying. Larger school size was also positively associated with bullying (Fitzpatrick, Dulin, & Piko, 2007). Studies have also shown a genetic component to aggressive behavior (Ball et al., 2008).

Community violence can also model aggressive and coercive behavior. Not surprisingly, community and political violence can also affect children's and adolescents' behaviors. McGuckin and Lewis' review of bullying in Northern Ireland found that rates of victimization reported by elementary- and secondary-school students in Northern Ireland, were significantly higher than in the Republic of Ireland and England, where conflict was not as prevalent (McGuckin & Lewis, 1999). Cultural displacement, refugee status, and being a linguistic or ethnic minority may be risk factors for victimization. A 1999 study of Iranian refugee children in Sweden found that 3.5 years after arrival in Sweden, Iranian children reported exposure to bullying far more frequently than their Swedish peers (41 vs. 8.5 percent); however, this study did find that children's social adjustment improved over time (Almqvist & Broberg, 1999).

While adolescent aggression predicts relational difficulties and future legal problems for some, for many, adolescent aggression may be a developmental stage. Developmentally, adolescents are less able to overcome their aggressive impulses than adults and are more vulnerable to group pressure (Ash, 2012). In his discussion of adolescent culpability, Ash notes that adolescent aggression may be a time-limited phenomenon. Only 20 percent of adolescent violent offenders continue to offend in adulthood. There are also important differences in adolescent violent behaviors compared to adult violence. Adolescents typically offend in groups, while adults offend alone. Groups can exert significant peer pressure on adolescents both in terms of violent behavior and other verbal or indirect aggressive behavior. Ash asserts that adolescents are at particular risk of aggressive behavior and that this can be seen as a developmental state of "higher aggression or weakened self-control" (Ash, 2012).

Bullies also have distinct personality and psychological characteristics. They have a stronger need for social recognition than other children (Olthof et al., 2011). Surprisingly, they exhibit good theory of mind (the ability to understand others' mental states and understand that others have beliefs, desires, and intentions that are different from their own). They also have at least average social intelligence.

However, they have been found to lack moral awareness and empathy; and they are often perceived as popular by other children, but not liked.

■ BULLYING, CYBER-BULLYING, AND YOUTH SUICIDE: UNRAVELING THE CONNECTION

A number of myths and misconceptions exist regarding bullying and cyber-bullying and their impact on perpetrators and victims. A random sample of 1,963 middle-schoolers from one of the largest school districts in the United States completed a survey of Internet use and experiences; youth who had experienced bullying or cyber-bullying, reported more suicidal thoughts and were more likely to attempt suicide in contrast to those who had not experienced such behavior (Hinduja & Patchin, 2010). As we will explore, however, the empirical relationship between bullying and suicide is more complicated, since most children who are bullied do not attempt to commit suicide and no data causally link bullying to suicidal behavior. The increased risk, however, should not be ignored and speaks to the potentially serious consequences of bullying, cyber and otherwise, on youth outcomes.

Bullying and cyber-bullying have become the major focus of a widespread and continuing media campaign both nationally and internationally. There has been much speculation regarding the immediate and long-term effects of this behavior on aggressors, targets, and bystanders. Much discussion has been generated, and often information that has not been empirically demonstrated is believed to be valid. This section will provide a framework for understanding youth suicide and serve to untangle current misconceptions and inaccuracies surrounding the relationship between bullying and suicide.

Research has clearly demonstrated that negative events and experiences encountered during an individual's childhood can have adverse effects throughout the person's developmental history. One very notable and informative body of research derives from the Adverse Childhood Experiences (ACE) study. A collaboration between the Centers for Disease Control and Prevention and a large healthcare organization, the ACE study is one of the largest investigations ever conducted to assess associations between childhood maltreatment and later-life health and well-being. Findings from the ACE study suggest that certain childhood experiences are major risk factors for the leading causes of illness and death as well as poor quality of life in the United States. Included among these adverse childhood experiences is abuse (physical, sexual, verbal, and emotional). In fact, research based on ACE data has linked a large percentage of suicide attempts (50 percent of women and 33 percent of men) to childhood adversity (Afifi et al., 2008).

Progress in preventing and recovering from the nation's worst health and social problems is likely to benefit from an understanding that many of these problems arise as a consequence of adverse childhood experiences. An expanding body of research suggests that childhood trauma and adverse experiences can lead to a variety of negative health outcomes, including attempted suicide among adolescents and adults. Over a decade ago, Dube and colleagues (2001) reported a powerful graded relationship between adverse childhood experiences and risk of attempted suicide throughout the lifespan. They also noted that alcoholism, depressed affect, and illicit drug use, strongly associated with such experiences, seem to partially mediate this relationship. Estimates of the attributable risk associations caused by these experiences were large, suggesting that prevention of these experiences and the treatment of persons affected by them may lead to progress in suicide prevention (Dube et al., 2001).

■ YOUTH SUICIDE

Suicide is the third leading cause of death for young people (ages 15 to 24). In 2010, there were 4,600 completed suicides among this age group, and nearly 300 additional suicides recorded in the under-15 population. On average, a young person dies by suicide every 1 hour and 48 minutes (McIntosh & Drapeau, 2012).

Youth suicide data encompass the population between the ages of 10 and 19. Notably, this age group gives up the largest number of healthy years of life and therefore represents an important risk group for suicide prevention. Despite decreases in suicide rates among young people in recent years, upward trends were identified in the 10- to 19-year-old age group (Heron, 2012). For youth suicide, the impact of the death on parents, friends, and the community is significant.

Risk Factors for Youth Suicide

Risk factors are research-based, empirically validated characteristics and other variables that over long periods of time call our attention to the potential for suicide or suicidal behavior with those youth who engage in suicidal behavior versus those who do not. Risk factors do not establish a cause of suicidal behavior; they merely indicate an association. Risk factors can affect youth at different stages of their lives and put them at greater risk for developing and participating in negative behavior.

A multitude of risk factors are associated with youth suicide. In their review of the epidemiology of youth suicide, Cash and Bridge (2009) identify the following as major risk factors among adolescents: previous suicide attempt; psychiatric disorder, particularly major depressive disorder, bipolar disorder, conduct disorder, and substance use disorders (alcohol and drugs); and co-occurring psychiatric disorders, especially combinations of mood, disruptive, and substance abuse disorder. Additional risk factors include impulsive aggression (i.e., a tendency to react to frustration or provocation with hostility or aggression); availability of lethal means; feelings of hopelessness and worthlessness that typically are associated with depression; family history of depression or suicide; loss of a parent to death or divorce; family discord; physical and/or sexual abuse; absence of a support network, poor peer or parental relationships, and feeling socially isolated; and dealing with homosexuality in an unsupportive family or community or hostile school environment.

▪ BULLYING, CYBER-BULLYING AND THE RELATIONSHIP TO SUICIDAL IDEATION

Bullying has been defined earlier in this chapter. However, in the context of examining and clarifying connections between bullying, cyber-bullying, and suicide, the definition provided by Nansel and colleagues (2001) is also important when considering the impact of bullying behavior on the social functioning and social well-being of youth. They suggest that bullying is a specific type of aggression, consisting of intentionally harmful behavior perpetrated by one person or a group. Further, bullying consists of behavior(s) generally carried out repeatedly and over time, and includes a power differential between the bully and the victim (Nansel et al., 2001). When considering the potential psychological consequences of bullying behavior, the American Psychological Association (APA, 2004) identifies many forms of bullying: physical bullying; teasing or name-calling; social exclusion; peer sexual harassment; bullying about race, ethnicity, and religion, disability, sexual orientation, and gender identity; and cyber-bullying.

Bullying in schools has become widely viewed as an urgent social, health, and education concern and has moved to the forefront of public debate on school legislation and policy. Increasingly, elected officials and members of the school community have come to view bullying as an extremely serious and often neglected issue facing youths and local school systems (Swearer, Limber, & Alley, 2009). The focus on youth bullying has intensified over the past decade as a reaction to school violence that is often linked explicitly or by inference to bullying.

▪ VIOLENCE

An upsurge in school violence has dramatically increased awareness of the negative impact of all forms of bullying. Recent media reports have also detailed accounts of young people whose deaths were allegedly attributed to bullying and/or cyber-bullying. In 2008, we learned about the death of Lawrence King, a 15-year-old boy from Kansas, who was murdered by a 14-year-old schoolmate because of his perceived sexual orientation. Carl Hoover-Walker, a sixth-grader from Massachusetts, hanged himself in 2009, reportedly after repeated school bullying. Also in Massachusetts, the suicide of 15-year-old Phoebe Prince in 2010 led to the criminal prosecution of six teenagers for charges including statutory rape and civil rights violations. Her suicide, after months of bullying from school classmates, brought international attention to the problem of bullying in U.S. schools and led to the enactment of stricter antibullying legislation in Massachusetts. Later that same year, Tyler Clementi, an 18-year-old college freshman at Rutgers University, died by suicide. He was seen kissing another man on a computer webcam and was viewed doing so without his knowledge. The national media attributed Tyler's suicide to cyber-bullying by his roommate and another student. Despite being indicted for their roles in the webcam incidents, they were not charged with a role in the suicide itself.

Social media use has become so pervasive in the lives of American teens that having a presence on a social network site is almost synonymous with being online. Fully 95 percent of all teens ages 12 to 17 are now online, and 80 percent of those online teens are users of social media sites. Ninety-five percent of social media-using teens who have witnessed cruel behavior on the sites say they have seen others ignoring the mean behavior; 55 percent witness this frequently (Lenhart, et al., 2010). Adolescents who are targets of cyber-bullying are more than twice as likely to use tobacco, alcohol, and marijuana. According to the National Center on Addiction and Substance Abuse at Columbia University (2012), approximately one in five teens ages 12 to 17 report that someone has posted mean or embarrassing things about them on a social networking site. While many youths say they didn't mean what they said or were just joking, they are clearly underestimating the impact that such posts have on the peers who are the targets of these behaviors.

Between the times that the incidents recounted above occurred and now, there have been many additional reports of suicide among bullied teens. A review of these reports indicates that most of the suicides were known or presumed to be related to the sexual-minority orientation of the deceased individual. Understandably, these events received unprecedented attention from national and local media, bloggers, advocates, social media, and filmmakers.

It has been over 13 years since the school shootings in Columbine, Colorado, which resulted in the deaths of 12 students and one teacher, brought attention to the potential dangers of bullying. Although multiple social factors were at play in this event, it rapidly caused teachers, parents, and other to become more vigilant about school-related bullying and to quash bullying whenever an opportunity to do so presented itself (Pridgen, 2009).

In addition to violence perpetrated by students against other students, bullying in general has been linked to increased suicidal behavior. Specifically, bullied youths and bullies alike were found to be at increased risk for suicidal ideation, attempts, and completed suicides (Swearer, Limber, & Alley, 2009). Students who experienced frequent bullying behaviors in high school did not report developing later depression or suicidality, but students who experienced bullying behaviors *and* depression or suicidality were more impaired four years later (Klomek, Kleinman, Altschuler, et al., 2011). This indicates that bullying alone does not *cause* suicidal behavior, but bullying should instead be considered in conjunction with other risk factors for suicide. Based on our review of the myriad developmental antecedents of bullying behavior and the association between bullying and suicidality, we recommend that clinicians and other stakeholders understand suicidal ideation among bullies, victims, or bully-victims in developmental context and in relation to a child's overall functioning, not merely the experience of bullying.

Some adolescents may experience distress at being targets of bullying and/or cyber-bullying, yet others may not. Most teens who experience bullying and/or cyber-bullying do not engage in suicidal behavior (Hinduja & Patchin, 2010). Bullying behavior *alone* likely will not lead to youth suicide, since youths who do complete suicide typically had other social and emotional issues in their lives (Hinduja & Patchin, 2010). Bullying and/or cyber-bullying tend to exacerbate instability and feelings of hopelessness and helplessness for adolescents already struggling with stressful life situations. In addition, as noted earlier, such stressors and adverse experiences during childhood can have serious ramifications for future adjustment. The connection to suicide is clearly related to the presence of these additional factors.

Suicide is a significant public health issue, and one that is considered to be mostly preventable. While there is a need for further research on bullying and how it affects both targets and aggressors, we now know that it does not *directly cause* suicidal behavior in adolescents. It is evident, however, that suicide awareness and prevention education is necessary to reduce morbidity and mortality rates in this population. Researchers should examine risk factors and vulnerability variables that affect youth. Recent research has identified that future risk can be related to being a target of bullying and/or cyber-bullying. Future research should also examine the impact of bullying and cyber-bullying on segments of the adolescent populations struggling with depression and other mental health issues and other segments of the youth population who experience marginalization for reasons related to their race, ethnicity, or sexual orientation.

▪ LEGAL RESPONSES TO BULLYING

Increased media attention on bullying may have several positive effects. Foremost is the overall recognition that bullying can cause serious harm. Public awareness and attention have also increased regarding the disproportionate burden of bullying borne by youth based on their actual or perceived sexual orientation, such that sexual-minority individuals have a documented greater risk for suicidal ideation and rates of attempt. There has also been renewed attention on passing federal antibullying legislation (e.g., Safe Schools Improvement Act of 2013). Heightened awareness of the impact of bullying has generated increased activity to develop and implement antibullying programming, both at state and local levels. Overall, public attention on bullying has generated compelling national and grassroots conversations.

Conversely, there are multiple negative ramifications of the media-generated linkages of bullying to suicide. The general public is frequently exposed to inflammatory rhetoric and sensationalized headlines about suicide "epidemics" and "bullycide"; both terms distort the actual connections between bullying and suicide. Media and online coverage of suicide should be informed by using "best practices." One best-practice example is to avoid reporting that the death by suicide was preceded by a single event (e.g., a recent job loss, divorce, or bad grades); such reporting leaves the public with an understanding of suicide that is overly simplistic and misleading. Other best practices for reporting a suicide death should describe suicide as a public health issue and should include advice from suicide prevention experts regarding risk factors and warning signs for suicide. While some suicide deaths may be newsworthy, the manner in which media outlets report suicide can either contribute to contagion (a cluster effect) or encouraging others to seek help (AFSP Media Guidelines, 2012).

The public attention has also spawned the development of a variety of legal responses to the perceived problems. As we have noted, without the empirical support necessary to provide evidence on which to base practice, the effectiveness of some of these responses may be called into question. All 50 states have attempted to address the issues raised by bullying by enacting some form of specific antibullying legislation. Not all states specifically spell out or address cyber-bullying, however (National Conference of State Legislatures, 2010). While there is currently no federal law to directly address bullying, the topic is covered under several areas of discriminatory harassment when it is based on race, national origin, color, sex, age, disability, or religion. A school that fails to respond appropriately to harassment of students in a protected class may, for example, be violating one or more civil rights laws enforced by the Department of Education and the Department of Justice, including Title IV and Title VI of the Civil Rights Act of 1964, Title IX of the Education Amendments of 1972, Section 504 of the Rehabilitation Act of 1973, and Titles II and III of the Americans with Disabilities Act, Individuals with Disabilities Education Act (IDEA).

States have taken a variety of approaches to dealing with the issues raised by bullying behaviors. Many have passed specific antibullying legislation, and others have used existing criminal law to address the issues. States with a specialized statute approach share several factors in antibullying legislation. This includes a clear statement of the purpose for the law that details the detrimental effects of bullying and outlines the kind of prohibited conduct. In addition to definitions, this may include a prohibition against taking any sort of retaliation by perpetrators or school officials against persons who report bullying behavior. It may also include a prohibition against "passing on" harmful or demeaning material created by someone else by electronically forwarding the material. Most statutes include a statement of scope including defining whether or not the conduct to be prohibited must occur only on school grounds, or whether bullying that occurs on school property, buses, or school-provided technology can be included.

Statutes also detail the role of criminal justice or law enforcement agencies. Most define the consequences for engaging in prohibited conduct. Some take a criminal justice approach; others take a rehabilitation and recovery approach, including statutes that require services for the perpetrator as well as for the victim. Most require some recordkeeping protocols by school systems or by criminal justice agencies to track repeat offenders and to permit the collection of data to assess trends. These provisions are often phrased in a way that permits public access and scrutiny, thereby supporting transparency and accountability by stakeholders.

Effective statutes include an education and information-dissemination component as well as a referral process if the issues cannot be addressed with school-based resources. An excellent overview of the types of statutes available can be found on the following website supported by the U.S. Department of Education: http://www.ed.gov/about/office/list/opepd/ppss/index.html.

Massachusetts General Law is representative of efforts to provide a comprehensive approach to in-school bullying. It defines bullying as:

> the repeated use by one or more students of a written, verbal or electronic expression or a physical act or gesture or any combination thereof, directed at a victim that: (i) causes physical or emotional harm to the victim or damage to the victim's property; (ii) places the victim in reasonable fear of harm to himself or of damage to his property; (iii) creates a hostile environment at school for the victim; (iv) infringes on the rights of the victim at school; or (v) materially and substantially disrupts the education process or the orderly operation of a school. For the purposes of this section, bullying shall include cyber-bullying. (M.G.L., c. 71 § 370)

The same statute further defines cyber-bullying as:

> bullying through the use of technology or any electronic communication, which shall include, but shall not be limited to, any transfer of signs, signals, writing, images, sounds, data or intelligence of any nature transmitted in whole or in part by a wire, radio, electromagnetic, photo electronic or photo optical system, including, but not limited to, electronic mail, Internet communications, instant messages or facsimile communications. Cyber-bullying shall also include (i) the creation of a web page or blog in which the creator assumes the identity of another person or (ii) the knowing impersonation of another person as the author of posted content or messages, if the creation or impersonation creates any of the conditions enumerated in clauses (i) to (v), inclusive, of the definition of bullying. Cyber-bullying shall also include the distribution by electronic means of a communication to more than one person or the posting of material on an electronic medium that may be accessed by one or more persons, if the distribution or posting creates any of the conditions enumerated in clauses (i) to (v), inclusive, of the definition of bullying. (M.G.L., c. 71 § 370)

The statute then provides that each school district must create a plan to counteract bullying in its district:

> Each school district, charter school, non-public school, approved private day or residential school and collaborative school shall develop, adhere to and update a plan to address bullying prevention and intervention in consultation with teachers, school staff, professional support personnel, school volunteers, administrators, community representatives, local law enforcement agencies, students, parents and guardians. (M.G.L., c. 71 § 37O)

Finally, the statute provides—in pertinent part—that each plan should include, but not be limited to:

> (i) descriptions of and statements prohibiting bullying, cyber-bullying and retaliation; (ii) clear procedures for students, staff, parents, guardians and others to report bullying or retaliation; (iii) a provision that reports of bullying or retaliation may be made anonymously; provided, however, that no disciplinary action shall be taken against a student solely on the basis of an anonymous report; (iv) clear procedures for promptly responding to and investigating reports of bullying or retaliation; (v) the range of disciplinary actions that may be taken against a perpetrator for bullying or retaliation; provided, however, that the disciplinary actions shall balance the need for accountability with the need to teach appropriate behavior; (vi) clear procedures for restoring a sense of safety for a victim and assessing that victim's needs for protection; (vii) strategies for protecting from bullying or retaliation a person who reports bullying, provides information during an investigation of bullying or witnesses or has reliable information about an act of bullying...; and (x) a strategy for providing counseling or referral to appropriate services for perpetrators and victims and for appropriate family members of said students. The plan shall afford all students the same protection regardless of their status under the law. (M.G.L., c. 71 § 37O)

■ CONCLUSIONS

There are numerous developmental milestones that offer an opportunity for a resort to violence as a means to achieving legitimate developmental goals. The acquisition of resources and the gaining of preferred sexual status both have historic precedent in human development. The onset of a digital media that permits bullying without the need for face to face confrontation has expanded the ability of actors to engage in conduct that achieves the same goals without exposure to the risks attendant to normal human interaction. Legislatures responding to public demand have attempted to craft legislation that while stemming the abusive nature of these interactions permits the on-going social development. One side effect of these efforts is the sensationalization of events that may otherwise have gone un-noticed.

The American Foundation for Suicide Prevention reports that research studies worldwide determined that certain types of news coverage can increase the likelihood of suicide in vulnerable individuals. The magnitude of the increase is related to the amount, duration, and prominence of coverage. The risk of additional suicides increases when the story explicitly describes the suicide method or uses dramatic/graphic headlines or images, and when repeated/extensive coverage sensationalizes or glamorizes a death. Media reporting on suicide, if done carefully, even briefly, can change public misperceptions and correct myths, which can encourage those who are vulnerable or at risk to seek help (AFSP Media Guidelines, 2012). More often than not, media and online news sources provide a detailed description of the events preceding a youth suicide with bullying involved. This also underscores a wider narrative of death by bullying.

Sensationalized reporting of cyber-bullying and bullying-related deaths erroneously puts the focus on bullying rather than serving to raise awareness of other risk factors that create and/or contribute to vulnerability. Clearly, vulnerable youth populations include sexual minorities, gender-nonconforming individuals, and youth with disabilities. Research indicates that sexual-minority youths are at greater risk to have attempted suicide than their peers, even after controlling for other suicide risk factors (i.e., depression, alcohol abuse, family history of suicide attempts) and prior victimization. While sexual orientation potentially represents a risk variable for suicidal behavior, research has not demonstrated a greater risk of *completed* suicide. Public opinion, as perpetuated through the media, is led to believe otherwise.

■ REFERENCES

Afifi, T. O., Enns, M. W., Cox, B. J., Asmundson, G. J. G., Stein, M. B., & Sareen, J. (2008). Population attributable fractions of psychiatric disorders and suicidal ideation and attempts associated with adverse childhood experiences. *American Journal of Public Health, 98,* 946–952.

Almqvist, K., & Broberg, A. G. (1999). Mental health and social adjustment in young refugee children 3 1/2 years after their arrival in Sweden. *Journal of the American Academy of Child & Adolescent Psychiatry, 38,* 723–730.

American Academy of Child Adolescent Psychiatry (2010). Bullying Resource Center. Last accessed June 4, 2013, at http://www.aacap.org/cs/Bullying.ResourceCenter/bullying_faqs

American Foundation for Suicide Prevention (2012). Guidelines for reporting on suicide. Last accessed June 4, 2013 at http://www.afsp.org/news-events/for-the-media/reporting-on-suicide

American Psychological Association (2004). APA resolution on bullying among children and youth. Adopted APA Council of Representatives. Last accessed June 4, 2013 at http://www.apa.org/about/policy/bullying.pdf

Ash, P. (2012). But He Knew It Was Wrong: Evaluating adolescent culpability. *Journal of the American Academy of Psychiatry & the Law, 40*, 21–32, at p. 24.

Ball, H. A., Arseneault, L., Taylor, A., Maugham, B., Caspi, A., & Moffitt, T. E. (2008). Genetic and environmental influences on victims, bullies and bully-victims in childhood. *Journal of Child Psychology and Psychiatry, 49*, 104–112, at p. 109.

Barnhart, R. K. (Ed.) (1988). *Barnhart dictionary of etymology.* New York: H.W. Wilson Co.

Bowes, L., Arsenault, L., Maughan, B., Taylor, A., Caspi A., & Moffitt, T. E. (2009). School, neighborhood, and family factors are associated with children's bullying involvement: A nationally representative longitudinal study. *Journal of the American Academy of Child & Adolescent Psychiatry, 48*, 545–553.

Cash, S. J & Bridge, J. A. (2009). Epidemiology of youth suicide and suicidal behavior. *Current Opinions in Pediatrics, 21*(5), 1–15.

Cook, C. R., Williams, K. R., Guerra, N. G., Kim, T. E., & Sadek, S. (2010). Predictors of bullying and victimization in childhood and adolescence: A meta-analytic investigation. *School Psychology Quarterly, 26*, 65–83.

Dooley, J. J., Pyzalski, J., & Cross, D. (2009). Cyber-bullying versus face-to-face bullying: A theoretical and conceptual review. *Journal of Psychology, 217*(4), 182–188.

Dube, S. R., Anda, R. F., Felitti, V. J., Chapman, D., Williamson, D. F., & Giles, W. H. (2001). Childhood abuse, household dysfunction and the risk of attempted suicide throughout the life span: Findings from Adverse Childhood Experiences Study. *Journal of the American Medical Association, 286*, 3089–3096.

Fitzpatrick, K. M., Dulin, A. J., & Piko, B. F. (2007). Not just pushing and shoving: school bullying among African American adolescents. *Journal of School Health, 77*, 16–22.

Gruber, J. E., & Fineran, S. (2008). Comparing the impact of bullying and sexual harassment victimization on the mental and physical health of adolescents, *Sex Roles, 58*, 13–14.

Heron, M. (2012). Deaths: Leading Causes for 2009. National Vital Statistics Report, 61 (7) Hyatttsville, MD. Last accessed: June 4, 2013 at http://www.cdc.gov/nchs/data/nvsr/nvsr61/nvsr61_07.pdf

Hightow-Weidman, L. B., Phillips, G., Jones, K. C., Outlaw, A. Y., Field, S. D., & Smith, J. C. (2011). Racial and sexual identity-related maltreatment among minority YMSM: Prevalence, perceptions, and the association with emotional distress. *AIDS Patient Care and STDs, 25*, S39–S45.

Hinduja, S., & Patchin, J. W. (2010). Bullying, cyber-bullying, and suicide. *Archives of Suicide Research, 14*, 206–221.

Jansen, P. W., Verlinden, M., Domisse-van Berke,l A., Mieloo, C., van der Ende, J., Veenstra, R., Verhulst, F. C., Jansen, W., & Teimeier, H. (2012). Prevalence of bullying and victimization among children in early elementary school: Do family and school neighbourhood socioeconomic status matter? *BMC Public Health, 12*, 494.

Kim, Y. S., Leventhal, B. L., Koh, Y., Hubbard, A., & Boyce, T. (2006). School bullying and youth violence causes or consequences of psychopathologic behavior? *Archives of General Psychiatry, 63*, 1035–1041.

Klomek, A. B., Kleinman, M., Altschuler, E., Marrocco, F., Amakawa, L., & Gould, M. (2011). Suicidal adolescents' experiences with bullying perpetration and victimization during high school as risk factors for later depression and suicidality. *Journal of Adolescent Health, 53*, 537–542.

Korobov, N. B. (2004). Inoculating against prejudice: a discursive approach to homophobia and sexism in adolescent male talk. *Psychology of Men and Masculinity, 5*, 178–189.

Kowalski, R. K., Limber, S. P., & Agatston, P. W. (2008). *Cyberbullying: Bullying in the digital age.* Malden, MA: Blackwell Publishing.

Lenhart, A., Purcell, K., Smith, A., & Zickuhr, K. (2010). *Social media & mobile internet use among teens and young adults.* Pew Internet and American Life Project, Washington, D.C.

McGuckin, C., & Lewis, C. A. (2003). A cross national perspective on school bullying in Northern Ireland: A supplement to Smith et al. (1999). *Psychological Reports, 93,* 279–287.

McIntosh, J. L., & Drapeau, C. W. (2012) U.S.A. suicide 2010: Official final data. American Assoc. of Suicideology, Washington, D.C. Last accessed June 4, 2013 at http://www.suicidology.org

McMaster, L. E., Connolly, J., Pepler, D., & Craig, W. M. (2002). Peer-to-peer sexual harassment in early adolescence: A developmental perspective. *Development and Psychopathology, 14,* 91–105, at p. 93 & 95

Moessner, C. (2007). Cyber-bullying *Trends & Tudes, 6:4,1–5,* Last accessed June 4, 2013, at http://us.vocuspr.com/Newsroom/ViewAttachment.aspx?SiteName=NCPCNew&Entity=PRAsset&AttachmentType=F&EntityID=103393&AttachmentID=0f59e5b2-844e-41f2-b03e-11e5298fbce7

Nansel, T. R., Overpeck, M., Pilla, R. S., Ruan, W. J., Simons-Morton, B., & Scheidt, P. (2001). Bullying behaviors among U.S. youth: Prevalence and association with psychological adjustment. *Journal of the American Medical Association, 289*(16), 2094–2099.

National Center for Education Statistics. Student Reports of Bullying and Cyber-Bullying: Results from the 2009 School Crime Supplement to the National Crime Victimization Survey. U.S. Dept. of Education, August, 2011. NCES 2011–336.

National Center on Addiction and Substance Abuse (2012), Annual Report: Addiction: a predictable and treatable disease. Columbia University, New York, NY

National Conference of State Legislatures (2010). Cyber-bullying and the States. Denver, CO. Last accessed June 5, 2013; http://www.ncsl.org/issues-research/justice/cyberbullying-and-the-states.asox

Olthof, T., Goossens, F. A., Vermande M. M., Aleva, A. A., & van der Meulen, M. (2011). Bullying as strategic behavior: Relations with desired and acquired dominance in the peer group. *Journal of School Psychology, 49,* 339–359, at p. 342.

Olweus, D. (1978). *Aggression in the schools: Bullies and whipping boys.* Washington, D.C.: Hemisphere (Wiley) at p. 1173.

Olweus, D. (1993). *Bullying at school: What we know and what we can do.* Malden, MA: Blackwell Publishing.

Opinion Research Corporation. (2006). Teen Caravan. Fight Crime, Invest in Kids: Cyber Bully—Teen. Last accessed June 4, 2013; http://www.fightcrime.org/wp-content/uploads/sites/default/files/reports/cyberbullyingteen_2.pdf

Patchin, J., & Hinduja, S. (2006). Bullies move beyond the schoolyard: A preliminary look at cyberbullying. *Youth Violence and Juvenile Justice, 4*(2), 148–169.

Pepler, D. J., Craig, W. M., Connolly, J. A., Yuile, A., McMaster, L., & Jiang, D. (2006). A developmental perspective on bullying. *Aggressive Behavior, 32,* 376–384.

Pepler, D., Jiang, D., Craig, W., & Connolly, J. (2008). Developmental trajectories of bullying and associated factors. *Child Development, 79,* 325–338.

Pettit, G. S., Bakshi, A., Dodge, K. A., & Coie, J. D. (1990). The emergence of social dominance in young boys' play groups: Developmental differences and behavior correlates. *Developmental Psychology, 26,* 1017–1025.

Poteat, V. P., & Rivers, I. (2010). The use of homophobic language across bullying roles during adolescence. *Journal of Applied Developmental Psychology, 31,* 166–172, at p. 167.

Pridgen, B. (2009). Cyberbullying: Bullying in the Digital Age, *Journal of the American Academy of Child & Adolescent Psychiatry, 48,* 344–346.

Safe Schools Improvement Act S.403—113th Congress (2013-2014). Introduced by Sen. Bob Casey.

Smith, P. K., Cowie, H., Olaffson, R. F., & Liefooghe, P. D. (2002). Definitions of bullying: A comparison of terms used, and age and gender differences, in a fourteen-country international comparison. *Child Development, 73,* 1119–1133.

Smith, P. K., Madsen, K. C., & Moody, J. C. (1999). What causes the age decline in reports of being bullied at school? Towards a developmental analysis of risks of being bullied. *Educational Research, 4,* 267–285.

Smith, P. K., & Monks, C. P. (2008). Concepts of bullying: developmental and cultural aspects. *International Journal of Adolescent Medicine & Health, 20,* 101–112, at p. 102.

Swearer, S., Limber, S., & Alley, R. (2009). Developing and implementing an effective anti-bullying policy. In Swearer, S., Espelage, D., & Napolitano, S. (Eds.), *Bullying Prevention and Intervention: Realistic Strategies for Schools* (pp. 39–52). New York, New York: The Guilford Press.

Teisl, M., Rogosch, F. A., Oshri, A., & Cicchetti, D. (2012). Differential expression of social dominance as a function of age and maltreatment experience. *Developmental Psychology, 48,* 575–588.

Thurlow, C. (2001). Naming the "outsider within": homophobic pejoratives and the verbal abuse of lesbian, gay and bisexual high-school pupils. *Journal of Adolescence, 24,* 25–38.

Volk, A. A., Camilleri, J. A., Dane, A. V., & Marini, Z. A. (2012). Is adolescent bullying an evolutionary adaptation? *Aggressive Behavior, 38,* 222–238. at p. 230.

Weir, E. (2001). The health impact of bullying. *CMAJ, 165*(9), 1249.

Williams, J. H., & Veeh, C. A. (2012). Editorial: Continued knowledge development for understanding bullying and school victimization. *Journal of Adolescent Health, 51,* 3–5.

Wolak, J., Mitchell, K., & Finkelhor, D. (2007). Does online harassment constitute bullying? An exploration of online harassment by known peers & online only contacts. Special issue of *Journal of Adolescent Health, 41,* S51–S58.

Ybarra, M. L., & Mitchell, K. J. (2008). How risky are social networking sites? A comparison of places online where youth sexual solicitation and harassment occurs. *Pediatrics, 121,* 350.

8 Juveniles, the Internet, and Sexual Offending

■ CYRIL BOONMANN,
ALBERT J. GRUDZINSKAS, JR., AND
MARCEL AEBI

John is a 17-year-old high-school student. He lives with his parents. He has few friends in school, and according to his classmates he is a loner. John is under a lot of pressure. He wants to be successful on the junior basketball team. His ex-girlfriend recently broke up with him because she was in love with someone else. Since the breakup John has had recurring episodes of depressed mood, and he has begun to watch a lot of Internet pornography. With time, he finds most of the mainstream pornography artificial and boring. To get aroused he looks for more extreme pornographic material, such as child pornography and violent pornography, which he then downloads.

A few weeks later, John creates a fake profile on a social media platform. He contacts peers and asks them for contact information and erotic pictures of girls. He receives a naked picture and mobile phone number of a 16-year-old girl. John contacts her by text message and asks her about intimate details of her sex life. She is completely surprised by the messages, which she finds disturbing, but she does not know how to respond. She feels ashamed and tries to stop John asking her about such intimate details. John sends her the nude picture he has of her and threatens to upload the picture to the Internet if she does not cooperate and tell him explicit details of her sex life. The girl feels scared and tells John some intimate details. John masturbates during their sexual texting. When the girl talks about the incident with her best friend, her friend advises her to go to the police. John is easily identified by the number of his cellphone and is arrested for sexual harassment and sexual coercion the next day. He confesses immediately and is referred for a forensic psychiatric assessment.

■ INTRODUCTION

The case of John is an example of how the Internet and other new communication technologies can be misused for sexual offending behavior. For instance, the Internet can be used as a market for illegal child pornography where files are distributed and downloaded by adults as well as by juveniles. Internet platforms and smartphones allow new possibilities for sexual solicitation and harassment. Therefore, the Internet has become a challenge for judicial and forensic institutions.

Since the commercialization of the Internet in 1993 (Lo & Wei, 2005), the production, marketing, and sale of pornography on the World Wide Web have become a multibillion-dollar business. Access to sexually explicit material on the Internet is simple, anonymous, and largely free. This triple-A engine of accessibility, anonymity, and affordability of online sexual content (Cooper, 1998) has increased public concern for possible negative effects of Internet pornography in general, and for youth in particular. There is some evidence that juveniles who committed a sexual offense (JSOs) had been exposed to sexual behaviors or pornography more often than juveniles who committed general offenses (Seto & Lalumière, 2010). In the general population, adolescents' use of pornography is linked to self-reported sexual delinquent behavior. However, most of this research has been conducted on traditional forms of pornography (e.g., magazines, videotapes). Because juveniles' sexual attitudes and behaviors were found to be influenced to a higher degree by Internet content than by conventional forms of sexual content (Lo & Wei, 2005; Lo, Wei, & Wu, 2010), research has increasingly focused on the role of Internet pornography in sexually disruptive behaviors in juveniles.

From a clinician's point of view scientific knowledge on online sexual behavior and Internet pornography in juveniles is needed. The availability of sexually explicit material on the Internet and the possibilities of online social media platforms for sexual contacts increase juveniles' risk not only for illegal activities but also for sexual compulsive behaviors and social isolation. Furthermore, some juveniles with sexually deviant interests use the Internet for downloading child pornography or for sexual solicitation. The possession of child pornography has been considered as a criterion for pedophilia in the *Diagnostic & Statistical Manual of Mental Disorders* (DSM-V; www.dsm-5.org).

This chapter will provide an overview of the availability of pornography and sexual content on the Internet and the use of and exposure to Internet pornography by juveniles in general, and JSOs in particular. Use of pornography is defined as active sexual behavior. The term "pornography exposure" is used when the person showed no clear intention to consume pornography. Two important issues in the field of juvenile sexual delinquent behavior and the Internet will be discussed: (1) use of or exposure to Internet pornography as a possible risk factor for juvenile sex offending behavior and (2) online sexual offenses committed by juveniles (e.g., downloading of child pornography, sexting). Throughout the discussions in this chapter, the reader should remember that social desirability could have had an effect on the responses to sensitive questions about sexual behavior and the use of or exposure to sexual content in children and adolescents (Paul, 2009). This chapter will end with a summary and discussion of the results, clinical impressions, and recommendations for future research. For a discussion of the implications for sentencing in North America of persons convicted of possessing child pornography please see Chapter 1.

▪ **METHOD**

Different databases (Web of Science, PsycInfo) were searched for relevant papers. The following keywords, or combinations of key words, were used for this search: you*, juvenile* adolescen*, sex*, offen*, Internet, porn*, solicit*, harass*, download* and self-victim*. All abstracts were examined to determine whether the paper contained information about juveniles (preferably up to 18 years, but in exceptional cases up to 20 years) and the use of or exposure to pornography or online sexual offending (e.g., child pornography, sexting, soliciting). Subsequently, relevant articles in the retrieved papers were also included. It should be taken into account that this chapter is not a systematic review.

▪ **RESULTS**

Juveniles and Internet Pornography

Over the last 10 years, research has shown an increase of child and adolescent exposure to Internet pornography (Short, Black, Smith, Wetterneck, & Wells, 2012). The Internet can have both positive and negative effects for sexuality and sexual development (Braun-Courville & Rojas, 2009; Flood, 2007; Hill, 2011; Luder et al., 2011; Short et al., 2012). On the one hand, the positive effects are that (1) it can be educational and can provide sexual health information; (2) it enables the development of communities and subcultures with shared sexual interest, especially for sexual minorities (e.g., homosexuals, transgendered individuals), which can ease someone's coming-out process; (3) it can decrease prejudice and stereotyping of sexual minorities; (4) it can enhance the spectrum of sexual fantasies and provide an opportunity to experiment with sexuality in the safety of one's own environment; and (5) in the case of cybersex, it excludes the risk for sexually transmitted diseases (STDs) (Braun-Courville & Rojas, 2009; Hill, 2011). On the other hand, exposure to sexuality on the Internet may also have potentially harmful effects, especially for children and adolescents (Braun-Courville & Rojas, 2009; Flood, 2007, 2009): (1) it can easily upset children who are not ready to encounter explicit sexual content; (2) Internet pornography can lead to a more liberal sexual attitude and a greater belief that peers are sexually active (which in turn may lead to a younger age of first sexual activity, in some cases before someone is ready for it); (3) Internet pornography can disgust or trouble children, adolescents, and adults if the sexual attitudes or behaviors shown are outside their societal or cultural norms; (4) it can influence children's and adolescents' acceptance of sexual interests and behaviors in a negative way (e.g., a distorted view of sex, supportive attitudes toward sexual aggression and sexually violent behavior [Hill, 2011; Malamuth, Addison, & Koss, 2000; Seto, Maric, & Barbaree, 2001]) (Flood, 2007, 2009; Hill, 2011).

Several studies have addressed the issue of the use of or exposure to Internet pornography in juveniles in the general population. Deliberate (or wanted) use of pornography can be caused by curiosity, interest in sexual information, or the search for sexual stimulation. Accidental (or unwanted) exposure to pornography may result from pop-ups or unsolicited emails, ambiguous terms (with sexual and nonsexual meaning) in search engines, or improperly guessing/mistyping of a website address (Flood, 2007). The use of Internet pornography is less common than the exposure to Internet pornography. Studies reported that 8 to 26 percent of children and adolescents between 10 and 20 years used Internet pornography deliberately (Bleakley, Hennessy, & Fishbein, 2011; Flood, 2007; Luder et al., 2011; Mitchell, Finkelhor, & Wolak, 2003; Skoog, Stattin, & Kerr, 2009; Wolak, Mitchell, & Finkelhor, 2007), whereas 25 to 72 percent of juveniles in the general population were exposed to unwanted Internet pornography (Flood, 2007; Luder et al., 2011; Mitchell et al., 2003; Rideout, 2001; Wolak et al., 2007). In general, boys and older youths more often used Internet pornography and were more frequently exposed to Internet pornography than girls and younger juveniles (Bleakley et al., 2011; Bonino, Ciairano, Rabaglietti, & Cattelino, 2006; Flood, 2007; Lo et al., 2010; Lo & Wei, 2005; Luder et al., 2011; Mitchell et al., 2003; Sabina, Wolak, & Finkelhor, 2008; Shek & Ma, 2012; Ybarra & Mitchell, 2005). Exposure prior to the age of 13, however, was uncommon (Sabina et al., 2008). Deliberate use of Internet pornography was related to rule-breaking or delinquent behavior and substance use (Wolak et al., 2007; Ybarra & Mitchell, 2005). Unwanted exposure, on the other hand, was associated with the use of file-sharing programs to download images, online harassment, offline victimization, and symptoms of depression (Wolak et al., 2007).

In summary, the Internet can have both positive as well as negative effects on sexuality in juveniles. The use of Internet pornography in juveniles is less common than the unwanted exposure to sexually explicit materials. Boys and older juveniles more often use or get exposed to Internet pornography than girls and younger youths. Although research is limited, the use of Internet pornography seems to be related to externalizing problem behavior, whereas exposure to Internet pornography appears to be associated with internalizing problem behavior.

Juvenile Sex Offending and Internet Pornography

Psychological theories, forensic psychiatric theories, and criminological theories suggest that pornography may directly influence sexual offending. According to the social learning theory, juveniles learn social behavior from one another via observation, imitation, and modeling (Bandura, 1977). Youths who have been exposed to pornography may initiate sexual behaviors with younger children and/or peers independent of their agreement. The desensitization theory may explain the habituation regarding sexual aggression and sexual deviance and may also explain the web crawling for more extreme forms of pornography such as pictures of sexual violence or child pornography (Seto et al., 2001). Research in delinquent and nondelinquent adult samples consistently found that frequent use and the use of violent pornography were related to sexually aggressive outcomes and should be considered in the assessment and treatment of sexual offenders (Kingston, Malamuth, Federoff, & Marshall, 2009). However, research in adolescents is less consistent (Barbaree & Marshall, 2006) and therefore needs another review on Internet pornography and its relation to juvenile sexual offending. After a review of the studies addressing the prevalence of the use of pornography and exposure in JSOs, studies that address the relation between the use of and exposure to pornography and sexual offending behavior will be summarized.

An overview of empirical studies that report the prevalence of the use of and exposure to pornography in forensic samples of JSOs in the last 25 years is shown in Table 8.1. Both the use of and exposure to conventional forms of pornography as well as Internet pornography (in bold) are listed.

As far as we are aware, exposure to Internet pornography in JSOs was examined in only one recent study. Burton, Leibowitz, and Howard (2010) analyzed the exposure to pornographic web content in 218 juveniles who were incarcerated because of a sexual offense (mean age 16.6 years). One out of three youths had been exposed to Internet pornography in childhood and two out of three youths had been exposed to Internet pornography during adolescence. It was also reported that 5 to 12 percent of them had been exposed to deviant types of Internet pornography (e.g., child pornography, violent pornography). However, exposure to Internet pornography was not as prevalent as exposure to conventional forms of pornography, such as pictures and videos (Burton et al., 2010). Other studies on exposure of conventional pornography in JSOs reported percentages between 42 and 97 percent (Becker & Stein, 1991; Ford & Linney, 1995; Wieckowski, Hartsoe, Mayer, & Shortz, 1998).

TABLE 8.1. *Use of Pornography or Exposure in Forensic Samples of JSOs*

No.	Year	Authors	Sample size	Mean age (in years)	Information source	Frequency of use of pornography	Frequency of pornography exposure
1	1991	Becker & Stein	160	15.4	Self		89%
2	1993	Emerick & Dutton	76	15.09	Self and polygraph	Self: 26.8%; Polygraph: 77.6%	
3	1995	Ford & Linney	35	15.5	Self		42%
4	1998	Wieckowski et al.	30	13.9	Self		97%
5	2001	Zolondek et al.	485	N/A (11–17)	Self	31.6%	
6	2008	Alexy et al.	160	13.01	Self	50%	
7	2010	Burton et al.	218	16.6	Self		74.0–90.6% **63.5%**
8	2011	Carpentier et al.	351	15.8	Self	51.6%	

Note: The frequency of Internet pornography is shown in bold figures.

As previously noted, research on the use of Internet pornography in JSOs, is also scarce. Studies, however, did report on the use of pornography in JSOs in general, sometimes including Internet pornography. In a study published before the "Digital Revolution" it was shown that 27 percent of JSOs admitted to having used pornography (Emerick & Dutton, 1993). More recent studies found that 32 to 52 percent of juvenile delinquents who sexually offended had used pornography (Alexy, Burgess, & Prentky 2009; Carpentier, Leclerc, & Proulx, 2011; Zolondek, Abel, Northey, & Jordan, 2001). Over the last decade the use of Internet pornography in JSOs increased. This trend has to be interpreted with caution, however, as the report of the use of pornography largely depends on sample characteristics (e.g., age, judicial status) and the assessment methods used (mainly based on self-report). Furthermore, confessing to the use of pornography seems highly dependent on social desirability (Emerick & Dutton, 1993). For example, feelings of shame and the fear of consequences may lead to underreporting of the use of pornography.

Given the limited number of studies that addressed the presence of Internet pornography in JSOs, it is not surprising that no study specifically tested the effect of Internet pornography on juvenile sexual offending. There is some research that compared the use of and exposure to pornography between sexually and generally offending youths and normal controls in forensic and community samples. However, only one study considered Web-based pornography (Burton et al., 2010). As longitudinal studies are needed to examine possible causal effects, none of the following studies is able to test the causal effect of Internet pornography or pornography in general for sexually offending behavior in juveniles. In a meta-analysis in delinquent populations, Seto and Lalumière (2010) found that JSOs were significantly more likely to be exposed to pornography than nonsexual offenders (effect size d = 0.27, CI = 0.05–0.49). Burton and colleagues (2010) found that JSOs were also more exposed to Web-based pornography than nonsexually delinquent youths. Other studies have addressed the use of and exposure to pornography and their possible relation to sexual offending in community samples (Bonino et al., 2006; Kjellgren, Priebe, Svedin, & Långström, 2010). In a study in 14- to 18-year-olds, Bonino and colleagues (2006) found that the use of pornographic magazines and films was linked to self-reported sexual harassment and violent sexual behavior. The authors concluded that the use of pornography in juveniles is related to more tolerance for sexual aggression and unwanted sex. Similarly, Kjellgren and colleagues (2010) found that the daily use of pornography and exposure to violent pornography in a general population sample of 17- to 20-year-olds was significantly higher in youths who reported sexually coercive behaviors than in normal controls. However, no differences were found between sexually coercive juveniles and juveniles with conduct problems. In sum, use of and exposure to pornography seems to be related to sexually offending behavior but may also be related to delinquency in general.

In conclusion, research on the use of and exposure to Internet pornography in JSOs is scarce. In line with research in the general population, the use of pornography in general (including Internet pornography) is less common than the exposure to pornography. Due to a lack of longitudinal research it is not known whether the use of or exposure to pornography can be said to be a causal factor for sexual offending. JSOs, however, were more exposed to pornography than general offending youths. Subsequently, the use of and exposure to pornography was related to sexually offending behavior as well as general offending behavior in general population samples.

Juvenile Online Sexual Offending

In addition to the use of and exposure to Internet pornography in JSOs who committed their offense in the *real world*, the Internet is also an environment for delinquent sexual behaviors (e.g., downloading of child pornography). Although it is assumed that adults generally commit most sex offenses on the Internet, research shows that youths also account for a substantial part of these types of crime. For example, a study by the National Center for Missing and Exploited Children (Finkelhor, Mitchell, & Wolak, 2000) showed that online sexual solicitation was carried out by minors in 48 percent of the cases. Still, research on online sexually delinquent behavior of adolescents remains limited. Three types of sexually problematic Internet behaviors will be discussed (in line with Quayle, 2007): (1) producing, trading, and downloading child abuse (i.e., child pornography), (2) sexting or self-victimizing behavior, and (3) soliciting, grooming, or sexually harassing behavior.

Child Pornography

During the last decade there has been an increase in the number of arrests for crimes involving the possession of child pornography. A study in New Zealand based on cases of child pornography offenders (primarily Internet child pornography) investigated by the Department of Internal Affairs Censorship Compliance Unit reported that 24 percent of the offenders (N = 106) arrested for the possession of child pornography were under the age of 20 (14 percent of the offenders were under the age of 18) (Carr, 2004). In 2009 the study was updated, this time with 318 child pornography offenders: 14 percent of the offenders were under the age of 20 (Sullivan, 2009). Based on data from the National Juvenile Online Victimization Study (a national sample of more than 2,500 U.S. law enforcement agencies), the number of juvenile offenders (individuals younger than 18) arrested for child pornography in the United States was smaller (3 to 5 percent of the total) (Wolak, Finkelhor, & Mitchell, 2011a). Overall the number of arrests increased from 1,713 in 2000 to 3,672 in 2006. This was also the case for juvenile offenders: 3 percent (N = 14) in 2000 and

5 percent (N = 28) in 2006. However, it is unknown whether the availability or use of child pornography between 2000 and 2006 increased, or whether there was more attention by law enforcement to this type of offender (Wolak et al., 2011a).

With the growing number of juveniles arrested for the possession of child pornography, it is of interest to consider the characteristics of these offenders and to compare them with juvenile offenders who committed other sexual offenses. Moultrie (2006) examined seven male juvenile arrestees (age 13 to 16) referred to the Taith Service (a partnership of judicial authorities and forensic mental health institutions) between 2001 and 2004 for the possession and/or distribution of child pornography and compared them with juvenile offenders who committed other sexual offenses. As the number of juveniles arrested for possession of child pornography was very small, comparison with the other offender group was rather difficult. Although Moultrie (2006) did not report any level of significance, the authors of this chapter will try to interpret and extrapolate from these results. The juvenile Internet child pornography offenders possessed from 15 to "several hundreds" images. With respect to demographic characteristics, juvenile Internet child pornography offenders generally were Caucasian males. They did not differ from other JSOs in terms of gender and ethnicity/race. Offense characteristics showed that two of the juveniles who were arrested for Internet child pornography offenses also committed other harmful sexual behavior: (1) indecent photography of local children and (2) assault of a younger sister and another young girl. One juvenile Internet child pornography offender was arrested for a nonsexual crime: credit card fraud to access child pornography. However, compared with other JSOs, they had less often committed other harmful sexual behavior and nonsexual offenses. With respect to abuse, juvenile offenders of Internet child pornography did not report sexual or physical abuse, in contrast to other JSOs, who did report sexual and physical abuse. Child pornography offenders and other sexual offenders did not differ in history of emotional abuse, which was high in both groups. Internet child pornography arrestees had fewer learning difficulties, health problems or a disability, behavioral problems, and prior contact with social services than juveniles who committed other sex offenses. However, they did report more emotional loneliness than other JSOs. Both groups did not differ in poor self-esteem and cognitive distortion (Moultrie, 2006). These results suggest that juvenile Internet child pornography offenders have fewer problems in general than other JSOs (Table 8.2). However, these tentative results need to be replicated in larger samples.

Building on Moultrie's (2006) research, Aebi and colleagues (2013) studied juveniles (age 10 to 18) convicted for the possession and/or distribution of child pornography in Zurich, Switzerland, between 2000 and 2008 (N = 54). These offenders had downloaded and/or saved digital pictures or videos of sexual abuse with children on their computer or mobile phone. Juvenile possessors of

TABLE 8.2. *Overview Results, Moultrie (2006)*

	Juvenile Internet child pornography offenders (N = 7)	Other sex offenders (N = 209)
Demographic information		
- Gender (% males)	100%	93%
- Race (% Caucasian)	86%	97%
Static background factors		
- Other sexual harmful behavior	29%	61%
- Nonsexual offenses	14%	25%
- Sexual abuse	0%	51%
- Physical abuse	0%	38%
- Emotional abuse	43%	51%
- Learning difficulties	0%	51%
- Health problems/disability	14%	44%
- Behavioral problems	14%	38%
- Prior contact social services	0%	38%
Assessment		
- Poor self-esteem	29%	26%
- High emotional loneliness	57%	34%
- High cognitive distortion	29%	26%

child pornography had a mean age of 15.3 (SD = 1.4 years). Fifty percent of these offenders had also downloaded other illegal sexual pictures or videos. The number of illegal pictures or videos ranged from one up to 400. Juvenile possessors of child pornography were found to be heterogeneous in regard to the time frame and frequency of child pornography consumption. However, on average, they were downloading pornographic materials over a longer period of time and more frequently than other juvenile problematic pornography possessors (e.g., juvenile possessors of bestiality). Furthermore, juvenile possessors of child pornography significantly differed from sexual contact offenders regarding their demographic background and criminal behaviors. They were less likely to have been placed outside their family, which may indicate a less burdened familial context when compared with sexual contact offenders. Both prior and subsequent offending were found less often in juvenile possessors of child pornography compared to sexual contact offenders. Whereas delinquent behaviors and antisocial attitudes play a major role in juveniles who were convicted for sexual contact offenses (Aebi, Vogt, Plattner, Steinhausen, & Bessler, 2012; Butler & Seto, 2002), these factors were less important in juvenile possessors of child pornography. Due to the low rate of sexual reoffending in both child pornography possessors and contact offenders, no differences were found between these two groups. Consistent with research in adult child pornography possessors (Seto, Hanson, & Babchishin, 2011), a low rate of subsequent sexual offenses by juvenile child pornography offenders was found (Aebi et al., 2013).

In conclusion, between 3 and 14 percent of the offenders arrested for the possession of child pornography are juveniles. In general, juvenile Internet child pornography offenders seem to have fewer problems than juveniles who committed other sexual offenses. However, it is assumed that they show more emotional loneliness. With respect to criminal history and reoffending, Internet child pornography offenders show less previous and subsequent offending behavior than other JSOs. No differences in sexual criminal history or sexual reoffending were found, mainly because of the small number of juvenile Internet child pornography offenders.

Sexting

Sexting is the production and distribution of sexual images of oneself through a cellphone or the Internet (Calvert, 2009; Mitchell, Finkelhor, Jones, & Wolak, 2011; Wolak, Finkelhor, & Mitchell, 2011b; Zhang, 2010). In 2007 Quayle discussed adolescents' self-victimizing sexual problem behavior through new technologies (i.e., sexting). Due to of a lack of research about this topic she reported four cases of adolescents who took indecent pictures of themselves or recorded their sexual activities and posted these files on open Internet sites. Although child pornography laws are necessary for the protection of children, these laws are now also being used to prosecute children and adolescents who practice sexting (Calvert, Murrhee, & Steve, 2010; Zhang, 2010). Instead of being educated about the possible risks of the Internet and the negative consequences of their immature and irresponsible behavior, the aforementioned juveniles may also be in danger of being prosecuted for the production, possession, and distribution of child pornography (Zhang, 2010). The pictures and videos could also be available for family and friends, educational institutions, and (future) employers, thereby jeopardizing the future of these juveniles (Mitchell et al., 2011).

Although sexting receives a lot of media attention, research on this topic is still in its infancy (Judge, 2012). In a nationally representative survey of 800 U.S. adolescents in the general population (12 to 17 years old), Lenhart (2009) reported that 4 percent of the adolescents with a cellphone had sent sexual images (nude or nearly nude) of themselves to someone else and that 15 percent of the adolescents had received such images of someone they knew. Sending as well as receiving was more prevalent in older than in younger teenagers (Lenhart, 2009). Based on a U.S. national telephone survey on Internet use among 1,560 adolescents (12 to 17 years old), 3 percent of the respondents reported they created or appeared in nude or nearly nude images and 7 percent reported receiving these kinds of images (Mitchell et al., 2011). The rate of adolescent sexting decreased from 3 percent to 1 percent when it was defined as *creating images of themselves that included their naked breasts, genitals, or bottom* (Mitchell et al., 2011, p. 17). Another recent prevalence study based on self-report data of 948 U.S. public high-school students (14 to 19 years old) showed that 28 percent had ever sent a naked picture of themselves (Temple et al., 2012). In addition, 31 percent had asked someone and 57 percent had been asked to send someone a sexual picture. Boys were more likely to have asked someone to send them a sext, whereas girls were more likely to be asked for it. In line with Lenhart (2009), older teenagers were more likely to send sexual images than younger adolescents. In general, sexting behavior was associated with dating and having had sex. Only in girls was sexting also related to risky sexual behavior (Temple et al., 2012).

Although common among adolescents, only a small subgroup of juveniles has been arrested for sexting (Calvert et al., 2010). To determine whether these juveniles constitute a specific subgroup with more delinquent behavior, Wolak and colleagues (2011b) conducted a national survey of U.S. law enforcement agencies on youth-produced sexual images. These agencies handle about 1,750 such cases every year. Sexual images are divided into two categories: aggravated (67 percent) and experimental[1] (33 percent) (Wolak & Finkelhor, 2011; Wolak et al., 2011b). Images in the aggravated category had additional criminal features next to the production, possession, or distribution. This category was subdivided into images with adults involved[2] (54 percent of the aggravated category and 36 percent of the total sample) and images with youths only[3] (46 percent of the aggravated category and 31 percent of the total sample). In 62 percent of the aggravated cases where adults were involved, 36 percent of the aggravated youth-only cases, and 18 percent of the experimental cases an arrest occurred. These data suggest that most youth-produced sexual images that come to the attention of the police do not lead to an arrest (Wolak et al., 2011b).

In conclusion, sexting is common in juveniles. Juveniles more often receive rather than send these images. It is assumed that sexting is related to sexually risky behavior in girls but not in boys. Finally, although about 1,750 cases of sexting come to the attention of law enforcement agencies in the United States every year, most cases do not lead to an arrest. A major part of the cases that lead to an arrest include additional criminal features beyond the sexting behavior.

Soliciting

Research on soliciting, grooming, or sexual harassment behavior on the Internet has mainly focused on adult offenders and juvenile victims. In a study by Finkelhor and colleagues (2000) about the online experiences of 1,501 juvenile Internet users, one in five juveniles who used the Internet on a regular basis was sexually solicited. In 48 percent of the cases the offender was also a juvenile. As research in this field is limited, scholars should focus on (1) the prevalence of this kind of behavior in adolescents in the general population as well as in juvenile delinquent populations, (2) the characteristics of these juveniles, and (3) similarities and differences compared to non-soliciting juvenile Internet users in general as well as non-soliciting JSOs. This knowledge will enable us to offer soliciting juveniles the appropriate care and will prevent them from persistent offending behavior.

Summary

Juveniles in general are frequently exposed to conventional forms of pornography as well as Internet pornography, deliberately or by accident. Exposure to Internet pornography in juveniles is more common than the use of Internet pornography. Boys and older youths used Internet pornography or were exposed to Internet pornography more often than girls and younger youth. While the use of Internet pornography was more related to externalizing problems, the exposure to Internet pornography appears to be associated with internalizing problems.

In general, research on Internet pornography in JSOs is limited. Juveniles who committed a sexual offense were exposed to Internet pornography during childhood in 31 percent of the cases studied and during adolescence in 64 percent of the cases studied. Between 5 and 12 percent had ever been exposed to deviant types of pornography. However, JSOs were more frequently exposed to conventional forms of pornography than to Internet pornography. Compared to generally offending youths, JSOs were more often exposed to pornography. In general population samples, the use of or exposure to pornography was related to sexual offending behavior as well as general offending behavior.

This chapter also discussed three types of online sexual offenses: child pornography, sexting, and online sexual harassment. First, although most of the online child pornography offenders are adults, juveniles are responsible for 3 to 14 percent of this type of offending. In general, such offenders seem to have fewer problems than juveniles who committed other types of sex offenses, although they seem to have more internalizing problems (e.g., emotional loneliness). With regard to offending behavior, they do not seem to have an offending history and show low rates of reoffending, sexually as well as nonsexually. Second, sexting, the production and distribution of sexual picture of oneself by means of a cellphone or the Internet, is common in juveniles. More juveniles reported they had received a sext than that they had sent one. Only in girls was sexting associated with risky sexual behavior. Most of the sexting behavior that came to the attention of law enforcements involved aggravated sexual content. These cases do not generally lead to an arrest. Most cases that do lead to an arrest include additional criminal features beyond the sexting behavior. Finally, online sexual harassment behavior committed by juveniles is limited. Although 48 percent of the online sexual harassers are juveniles, research has mainly focused on grooming behavior of adults.

■ DISCUSSION

Today, young people are increasingly engaged in new media and Internet content such as social media platforms, chat rooms, and websites. With the rise of these new technologies, the use of and exposure to Internet pornography as well as online offending behavior has also increased (Short et al., 2012). Juveniles spend a significant amount of time on the Internet; they are therefore at risk to use or be exposed to illegal pornography and to commit online sexual offenses (Carr, 2004). Forensic experts and criminologists are faced with new ways of sexual offending. For researchers and practitioners working with JSOs, this has also raised difficult challenges, such as: What is the effect of Internet pornography on juvenile sexual offending? What kind of online sexual offenses do juveniles commit? (Quayle, 2007).

Due to the importance of the Internet for young people, and the association of pornography and sexual offending, this chapter reviewed empirical studies on the relation of Internet pornography to JSOs. This chapter also examined online sexually offending behavior of juveniles. Research in this field is limited. Most studies that consider pornography in JSOs are still based on conventional forms of pornography (e.g., magazines or movies). Outcome studies on the possible effects of Internet pornography on juveniles mainly focused on sexuality and mental health, but not on sexually aggressive behavior. Although there is a significant body of research on JSOs in general, the role of the Internet on adolescents' sexually offending behavior is still not well understood. Accordingly, the existing body of research does not allow well-founded recommendations for clinical practice.

Given the large amount of free sexual content on the Internet, the use of and exposure to pornographic materials may have increased in youth in general, and more specifically in JSOs. From community and clinical studies there is some evidence that pornography is linked to sexually offending behavior in juveniles. However, the mechanism of Internet pornography on sexual offending in juveniles is not well understood. As the viewing of Internet pornography is common in juveniles in general, this may not be distinctive for sexual offending in juveniles. Future research on Internet pornography in JSOs should therefore focus on the frequency of the use of pornography or exposure to pornography as well as the type of pornography (e.g., violent pornography).

Although some of the mass media have raised concern that Internet pornography may encourage juveniles to commit sexual offenses to a greater degree than conventional pornography, most scientific studies did not show a stronger relationship between Internet pornography and sexually offending behavior. However, research specifically focusing on Internet pornography is important for at least two reasons. First, Internet pornography may more strongly influence sexual attitudes and behaviors than conventional pornography (Lo & Wei, 2005; Peter & Valkenburg, 2008). Secondly, it is hard to control the Internet; therefore, it may include more deviant and violent content than more conventional forms of pornography. Longitudinal studies that assess pornography, especially Internet pornography, are necessary to understand the development of the use of and exposure to pornography by juveniles from adolescence to adulthood. Will the use of Internet pornography and exposure remain stable (high and low), increase or decrease with age? This knowledge may also enlarge our insight in the relation between the use of or exposure to Internet pornography in juveniles and possible future sexual offending.

With respect to online sexual offending in juveniles, research is still limited. Juvenile online child pornography offenders seem to differ from juveniles who committed other sexual offenses; online offenders report fewer problems, although they seem to have more internalizing problems (e.g., emotional loneliness) (Moultrie, 2006). Juveniles who commit Internet child pornography offenses do not seem to be at high risk for reoffending (Aebi et al., 2013). Future research should replicate the aforementioned results in larger populations and should extend the research on the characteristics of online child pornography offenders, also compared to other JSOs. Only then can researchers target the effectiveness of treatment of juvenile online child pornography offenders.

It is important that laws initially designed to protect children and adolescents (Zhang, 2010) should not be used to prosecute juveniles. Only in case of aggravated sexting behavior where other offending behavior is displayed (e.g., forceful sex) should juveniles be prosecuted. This seems to be true for most jurisdictions (Wolak et al., 2011b). Finally, because one in two perpetrators of online sexual harassment behavior is a juvenile (Finkelhor et al., 2000), future research should also target this offending behavior in juveniles.

Considerations for Clinical Practice

When juveniles are assessed because of sexually as well as generally offending behavior, it should be taken into account that the new media are a dominant and influential activity in youths (Quayle, 2007). As can be seen in the case of John that introduced this chapter, young people are not only passive consumers of Web content (e.g., by downloading or watching pictures) but are also social actors who create and change the Internet (e.g., by communicating over social media platforms). Due to laptops, tablets, and smartphones, the Internet is omnipresent in the lives of youth. Internet experts, social and mass media experts, child and adolescent psychologists and psychiatrists, youth social workers, and forensic experts must take into account how juveniles use these new technologies and how they affect their lives.

Given the possible relation of the use of and exposure to pornography and sexual offending as well as the widespread access to the Internet, we suggest that the following issues should be considered in assessment and treatment for all JSOs (Table 8.3). As it is assumed that offending juveniles in general could profit from specific treatment for JSOs (Zimring, Jennings, Piquero, & Hays, 2009), these issues should also be considered in general juvenile offender assessment. Existing instruments for the assessment and treatment of JSOs already include many of these issues (e.g., Multidimensional Inventory of Development, Sex, and Aggression [MIDSA]; Knight, 2011). To gain more insight into the role of the use

TABLE 8.3. *Internet, Social Media, and Internet Pornography Use in the Assessment and Treatment of JSOs*

Internet	Do you have access to the Internet and what kind of device do you use (e.g., laptop, tablet computer, smartphone)?
	How much time do you spend on the Internet each day?
Social media	Do you use social media platforms to contact others for friendship and sexual relationships?
	Do you use chat rooms for sexual issues?
	Do you display sexually aggressive behavior on social media platforms and/or chat rooms?
Internet pornography	Do you use or have you been exposed to Internet pornography?
	How often do you use Internet pornography?
	How much time do you spend on Internet pornography every week?
	What kind of Internet pornography do you use (e.g., heterosexual, homosexual, violent pornography, child pornography)?
	Do you use Internet pornography for curiosity and/or sexual gratification?
	Do you masturbate while watching Internet pornography?

of and exposure to Internet pornography in future online and real-life sexual and general offending, longitudinal research is needed (e.g., by means of the MIDSA).

More extensive assessment of the use of the Internet, social media, and the use of and exposure to Internet pornography is necessary for online JSOs. Present guidelines for the assessment and treatment of JSOs (Miner et al., 2006; Shaw, 1999) mainly target juveniles who have committed sexual contact offenses. It can be argued that the existing framework (e.g., the MIDSA) is sufficient for online JSOs: assessment and treatment already target relevant factors about individual and developmental (e.g., mental health problems, sexual maturation), family (bonding, parental skills), and environmental (e.g., social isolation, sexual relationships) issues. However, there are some specific issues concerning offending behavior that should be considered in online JSOs. Quayle (2007) has proposed a number of helpful questions for juveniles who downloaded illegal sexual images. These questions concern downloading (e.g., How many images were accessed and where were the images accessed?), trading (e.g., Have images been exchanged with other Internet users?), and producing (e.g., Have images been created through scanning or digital camera?) images. The assessment of online offenders should also include the specific characteristics of their online sexual behaviors. Special attention is needed to detect compulsive use of pornography in juvenile online offenders. The pleasure that some youths receive from the consumption of pornography may lead to addictive behaviors (Sussmann, 2007). Some youths with insufficient coping skills may use sexual stimulation as a way of solving problems (Van den Eijnden, Meerkerk, Verhulst, Spijkerman, & Engels, 2008). Finally, the use of child pornography as a recently suggested criterion for pedophilia in the DSM-V (www.dsm-5.org) (Seto, 2010) should lead to careful assessment of youth who have frequently downloaded such material for their deviant sexual desires.

■ DISCLOSURE

Cyril Boonmann, Albert J. Grudzinskas, Jr., and Marcel Aebi have no conflicts of interest to declare. Marcel Aebi has received grants from the Swiss Federal Institute of Justice for the evaluation of a juvenile sex offender treatment program.

■ NOTES

1. A boy (14 years old) and a girl (12 years old) who were boyfriend/girlfriend who sent each other sexual pictures/videos of themselves for a couple of weeks (Wolak & Finkelhor, 2011; Wolak et al., 2011b).

2. A girl (14 years old) who was in a sexual relationship with her step-uncle (38 years old). After six months of Internet communication (including sexual communication and exchange of sexual pictures), they met face to face and took sexually explicit pictures of themselves and each other (Wolak & Finkelhor, 2011; Wolak et al., 2011b).

3. A girl (13 years old) sent a topless picture of herself to her boyfriend (14 years old). When they broke up, the boyfriend sent the picture to some peers, who, in turn forwarded the pictures (Wolak & Finkelhor, 2011; Wolak et al., 2011b).

■ REFERENCES

Aebi, M., Plattner, B., Ernest, M., Kaszynski, K., & Bessler, C. (2013). Criminal history and future offending of juveniles convicted of the possession of child pornography. *Sexual Abuse: A Journal of Research and Treatment*. E-pub ahead of print. doi: 1079063213492344

Aebi, M., Vogt, G., Plattner, B., Steinhausen, H. C., & Bessler, C. (2012). Offender types and criminality dimensions in male juveniles convicted of sexual offenses. *Sexual Abuse: A Journal of Research and Treatment, 24*(3) 265–288. doi: 10.1177/1079063211420449.

Alexy, E. M., Burgess, A. W., & Prentky, R. A. (2009). Pornography use as a risk marker for an aggressive pattern of behavior among sexually reactive children and adolescents. *Journal of American Psychiatric Nurses Association, 14*, 442–453. doi: 10.1177/1078390308327137

Bandura, A. (1977). *Social learning theory*. New York: General Learning Press.

Barbaree, H. E., & Marshall, W. L. (2006). *The juvenile sex offender*, 2nd ed. New York: The Guilford Press.

Becker, J. V., & Stein, R. M. (1991). Is sexual erotica associated with sexual deviance in adolescent males? *International Journal of Law and Psychiatry, 14*, 85–95.

Bleakley, A., Hennessy, M., & Fishbein, M. (2011). A model of adolescents' seeking of sexual content in their media choices. *Journal of Sex Research, 48*(4), 309–315.

Bonino, S., Ciairano, S., Rabaglietti, E., & Cattelino, E. (2006). Use of pornography and self-reported engagement in sexual violence among adolescents. *European Journal of Developmental Psychology, 3*(3), 265–288.

Braun-Courvnille, D. K., & Rojas, M. (2009). Exposure to sexually explicit web sites and adolescent sexual attitudes and behaviors. *Journal of Adolescent Health, 45*, 156–162.

Burton, D. L., Leibowitz, G. S., & Howard, A. (2010). Comparison by crime type of juvenile delinquents on pornography exposure: The absence of relationships between exposure to pornography and sexual offense characteristics. *Journal of Forensic Nursing, 6*, 121– 129. doi: 10.1111/j.1939-3938.2010.01077.x

Butler, S. M., & Seto, M. C. (2002). Distinguishing two types of adolescent sex offenders. *Journal of the American Academy of Child and Adolescent Psychiatry, 41*(1), 83–90.

Calvert, C., Murrhee, K. C., & Steve, J. (2010). Playing legislative catch-up in 2010 with a growing, high-tech phenomenon: Evolving statutory approaches for addressing teen sexting. *University of Pittsburgh Journal of Technology Law & Policy, 11*, 1–60.

Calvert, C. (2009). Sex, cell phones, privacy and the first amendment: When children become child pornographers and the Lolita effect undermines the law. *CommLaw Conspectus: Journal of Communications Law and Policy, 18*, 1–65.

Carpentier, J., Leclerc, B., & Proulx, J. (2011). Juvenile sexual offenders: correlates of onset, variety and desistence from criminal behavior. *Criminal Justice and Behavior, 38*(8), 854–873.

Carr, A. (2004). *Internet traders of child pornography and other censorship offenders in New Zealand.* Wellington: Department of Internal Affairs Te Tari Taiwhenuam.

Cooper, A. (1998). Sexuality and the Internet: Surfing into the new millennium. *Cyberpsychology & Behavior, 1*, 181–187.

Emerick, R., & Dutton, W. A. (1993). The effect of polygraphy on the self report of adolescent sex offenders. *Annals of Sex Research, 6*, 83–103.

Finkelhor, D., Mitchell, K. J., & Wolak, J. (2000). *Online victimization: A report of the nation's youth.* Washington, DC: National Center for Missing and Exploited Children.

Flood, M. (2007). Exposure to pornography among youth in Australia. *Journal of Sociology, 43*(1), 45–60. doi: 10.1177/1440783307073934

Flood, M. (2009). The harms of pornography exposure among children and young people. *Child Abuse Review, 18*, 384–900. doi: 10.1002/car.1092

Ford, M. E., & Linney, J. A. (1995). Comparative analysis of juvenile sexual offenders, violent non-sexual offenders and status offenders. *Journal of Interpersonal Violence, 10*(1), 56–70. doi: 10.1177/088626095010001004

Hill, A. (2011). Sexualität in Zeiten des Internet. *Psychotherapeut, 56*, 475–484. doi: 10.1007/s00278-011-0866-8

Judge, A. M. (2012). "Sexting" among U.S. adolescents: Psychological and legal perspectives. *Harvard Review of Psychiatry, 20*(2), 86–96. doi: 10.3109/10673229.2012.677360

Kingston, D. A., Malamuth, N. M., Federoff, P., & Marshall, W. L. (2009). The importance of individual differences in pornography use: theoretical perspectives and implications for treating sexual offenders. *Journal of Sex Research, 46*(2–3), 216–232.

Kjellgren, C., Priebe, G., Svedin, C. G., & Långström, N. (2010). Sexually coercive behavior in male youth: Population survey of general and specific risk factors. *Archive of Sexual Behavior, 39*(5), 1161–1169.

Knight, R. (2011). The Multidimensional Inventory of Development, Sex, and Aggression (MIDSA), downloaded on October 3 from http://www.midsa.us/pdf/MIDSA_clinical_manual.pdf.

Lenhart, A. (2009). *Teens and sexting. How and why minor teens are sending sexually suggestive nude or nearly nude images via text messaging.* Washington, DC: Pew Research Center. Retrieved September 24, 2012, from http://pewinternet.org/Reports/2009/Teens-and-Sexting.aspx

Lo, V., & Wei, R. (2005). Exposure to internet pornography and Taiwanese adolescents' sexual attitudes and behavior. *Journal of Broadcasting and Electronic Media, 49*, 221–237.

Lo, V., Wei, R., & Wu, H. (2010). Examining the first-, second- and third-person effects of Internet pornography on Taiwanese adolescents: implications for the restriction of pornography. *Asian Journal of Communication, 20*(1), 90–103.

Luder, M. T., Pittet, I., Berchtold, A., Akre, C., Michaud, P. A., & Suris, J. C. (2011). Associations between online pornography and sexual behavior among adolescents: myth or reality? *Archives of Sexual Behavior, 40*(5), 1027–1035. doi: 10.1007/s10508-010-9714-0

Malamuth, N. M., Addison, T., & Koss, M. (2000). Pornography and sexual aggression: Are there reliable effects and how might we understand them? *Annual Review of Sex Research, 11*, 26–91.

Miner, M. H., Borduin, C. M., Prescott, D., Bovensmann, H., Schepker, R., Du Bois, R., et al. (2006). Standards of care for juvenile sexual offenders of the International Association for the Treatment of Sexual Offenders. *Sexual Offender Treatment, 1*(3).

Mitchell, K. J., Finkelhor, D., & Wolak, J. (2003). The exposure of youth to unwanted sexual material on the Internet: A national survey of risk, impact, and prevention. *Youth & Society, 34*(3), 330–358.

Mitchell, K. J., Finkelhor, D., Jones, L. M., & Wolak, J. (2011). Prevalence and characteristics of youth sexting: A national study. *Pediatrics, 129*(1), 13–20. doi: 10.1542/peds.2011-1730

Moultrie, D. (2006). Adolescents convicted of possession of abuse images of children: a new type of adolescent sex offenders? *Journal of Sexual Aggression, 12*, 165–174. doi: 10.1080/135526006823670

Paul, B. (2009). Predicting Internet pornography use and arousal: The role of individual difference variables. *Journal of Sex Research, 46*(4), 344–357.

Peter, J., & Valkenburg, P. M. (2008). Adolescents' exposure to sexually explicit Internet material, sexual uncertainty, and attitudes toward uncommitted sexual exploration. Is there a link? *Communication Research, 35*(5), 579–601.

Quayle, E. (2007). Assessment issues with young people who engage in sexually abusive behaviours through the new technologies. In M.C. Calder (Ed.), *Working with children and young people who sexually abuse: Taking the field forward* (pp. 217–229). Lyme Regis: Russell House Publishing Limited.

Rideout, V. (2001). *Generation Rx.com. How young people use the Internet for health information*. Menlo Park, CA: Henry J. Kaiser Family Foundation.

Sabina, C., Wolak, J., & Finkelhor, D. (2008). The nature and dynamics of Internet pornography exposure for youth. *Cyberpsychology & Behavior, 11*, 691–693.

Seto, M. C. (2010). Child pornography use and internet solicitation in the diagnosis of pedophilia. *Archives of Sexual Behaviors, 39*(3), 591–593. doi: 10.1007/s10508-010-9603-6

Seto, M. C., Hanson, R. K., & Babchishin, K. M. (2011). Contact sexual offending by men with online sexual offenses. *Sexual Abuse: A Journal of Research and Treatment, 23*(1), 124–145.

Seto, M. C., & Lalumiere, M. L. (2010). What is so special about male adolescent sexual offending? A review and test of explanations through meta-analysis. *Psychological Bulletin, 136*(4), 526–575. doi: 10.1037/a0019700

Seto, M. C., Maric, A., & Barbaree, H. E. (2001). The role of pornography in the etiology of sexual aggression. *Aggression and Violent Behavior, 6*, 35–53.

Shaw, J. A. (1999). Practice parameters for the assessment and treatment of children and adolescents who are sexually abusive of others. American Academy of Child and Adolescent Psychiatry Working Group on Quality Issues. *Journal of the American Academy of Child and Adolescent Psychiatry, 38*(12 Suppl), 55S–76S.

Shek, D. T. L., & Ma, C. M. S. (2012). Consumption of pornographic materials among Hong Kong early adolescents: A replication. *Scientific World Journal.* doi: 10.1100/2012/406063

Short, M. B., Black, L., Smith, A. H., Wetterneck, C. T., & Wells, D. E. (2012). A review of Internet pornography use research: Methodology and content from the past 10 years. *Cyberpsychology, Behavior, and Social Networking, 15*(1), 13–23.

Skoog, T., Stattin, H., & Kerr, M. (2009). The role of pubertal timing in what adolescent boys do online. *Journal of Research on Adolescence, 19*(1), 1–7.

Sullivan, C. (2009). *Internet traders of child pornography: Profiling research—Update (December 2009).* Wellington: Department of Internal Affairs Te Tari Taiwhenuam.

Sussmann, S. (2007). Sexual addiction among teens: A review. *Sexual Addiction & Compulsivity: The Journal of Treatment & Prevention, 14*(4), 257–278.

Temple, J. R., Paul, J. A., van den Berg, P., Donna Le, V., McElhany, A., & Temple, B.W. (2012). Teen sexting and its association with sexual behaviors. *Archives of Psychiatric and Adolescent Medicine, 166*(9), 828–833. doi: 10.1001/archpediatrics.2012.835

Van den Eijnden, R. J. J. M., Meerkerk, G.-J., Vermulst, A. A., Spijkerman, R., & Engels, R. C. M. E. (2008). Online communication, compulsive Internet use, and psychosocial well-being among adolescents: A longitudinal study. *Developmental Psychology, 44*(3), 655–665. doi: 10.1037/0012-1649.44.3.655

Wieckowski, E., Hartsoe, P., Mayer, A., & Shortz, J. (1998). Deviant sexual bahavior in children and young adolescents: frequency and patterns. *Sexual Abuse: A Journal of Research and Treatment, 10*(4), 293–303.

Wolak, J., & Finkelhor, D. (2011). *Sexting: a typology.* Durham, NC: Crimes Against Children Research Center.

Wolak, J., Finkelhor, D., & Mitchell, K. (2011a). Child pornography possessors: Trends in offender and case characteristics. *Sexual Abuse: A Journal of Research and Treatment, 23*(1), 22–42. doi: 10.1177/1079063210372143

Wolak, J., Finkelhor, D., & Mitchell, K. (2011b). How often are teens arrested for sexting? Data from a national sample of police cases. *Pediatrics, 129*(1), 1–9. doi: 10.1542/peds.2011-2242.

Wolak, J., Mitchell, K., & Finkelhor, D. (2007). Unwanted and wanted exposure to online pornography in a national sample of youth Internet users. *Pediatrics, 119*(2), 247–257. doi: 119/2/247 [pii]10.1542/peds.2006-1891

Ybarra, M. L., & Mitchell, K. J. (2005). Exposure to Internet pornography among children and adolescents: A national survey. *Cyberpsychology & Behavior, 8,* 473–486.

Zimring, F. E., Jennings, W. G., Piquero, A. R., & Hays, S. (2009). Investigating the continuity of sex offending: Evidence from the Second Philadelphia Birth Cohort. *Justice Quarterly, 26*(1), 58–76.

Zhang, X. (2010). Charging children with child pornography—Using the legal system to handle the problem of "sexting." *Computer Law & Security Review, 26,* 251–259. doi: 10.1016/j.clsr.2010.03.005

Zolondek, S. C., Abel, G. G., Northey, W. F., & Jordan, A. D. (2001). The self-reported behaviours of juvenile sexual offenders. *Journal of Interpersonal Violence, 16*(1), 73–85.

9

From the Streets to Cyberspace: The Effects of Technology on the Commercial Sexual Exploitation of Children and Adolescents in the United States

■ ABIGAIL M. JUDGE AND
MARY GRAW LEARY

■ INTRODUCTION

The commercial sexual exploitation of children (CSEC) in the United States is a challenging problem for professionals, researchers, and policymakers to address. The reasons for this complex landscape are several. First, on the ground, this assault on children takes many forms (e.g., child sexual abuse images, juvenile prostitution, child sex trafficking), which disguises its occurrence in the culture and makes it difficult to recognize. No matter the form, CSEC often involves psychologically complex relationships between child victims and exploiters, which may result in youth not self-identifying as victims and, thereby, further hiding the exploitation. Secondly, all forms of CSEC are crimes against children that occur in secret, hidden to some extent from mainstream society and law enforcement. These aspects of the crime affect victim identification and also limit research on the topic (Melrose, 2002). Thirdly, CSEC affects multiple disciplines such as the law, public policy, social work, and public health, and each of these disciplines brings to research and practice its own emphasis and concerns. The lack of agreement between disciplines and jurisdictions as to what constitutes CSEC can impede needed collaborations across professions and systems. The lack of a consensus definition also limits efforts to reliably measure the crime's nature and breadth. Without such a fundamental understanding, however, effective prevention, rehabilitation, and legal efforts risk missing their intended mark.

In addition to the definitional and systemic challenges that characterize this issue, digital and other mediated technologies (i.e., mobile communications devices, social media, other Internet applications) have revolutionized the industry of CSEC. Early theorists and researchers described the profound effects of the Internet on sexual behaviors overall (Cooper, 1998; Cooper et al., 1999; Turkle, 1997) as well as the symbiotic relationship between the Internet and the commercial sex industry in particular:

> Since its inception, the Internet has been associated with sexuality in a kind of synergistic dance, each fueling the transformation with the other. The influence of the Internet on sexuality is likely to be so significant that it will ultimately be recognized as the cause of the next "sexual revolution." (Cooper et al., 1999, p. 519)

The current volume explores aspects of this "synergistic dance" across a range of devices and domains, and this chapter describes these manifestations in CSEC. Not sexuality per se, CSEC is a sexual crime and the commodification of sexual activity with children. Accordingly, this chapter will provide an overview of CSEC and then describe the emergent role of technology on the crime's ecosystem. The discussion focuses on CSEC in the United States in part to raise awareness about its domestic scope and significance, although the authors recognize that the Internet and other technologies challenge the boundaries among domestic and international jurisdictions and may render this distinction less meaningful.

First, the chapter explores the different definitions of CSEC that various disciplines have proposed. While recognizing the imperfection of any one definition, the authors will adopt one in the interest of clarity. With this definition in mind, the chapter will then discuss the various forms of CSEC and provide a critical examination of available estimates. The next section explores the unique role that technology plays in the industry of CSEC. Although limited empirical research exists on the role of networked technologies in CSEC, other sources of data suggest its powerful effects (e.g., case law, law enforcement data, popular press stories, clinical reports). As boyd and colleagues have observed about juvenile prostitution, "Technology makes many aspects of human trafficking more visible and more traceable, for better and for worse" (boyd, 2012, p. 1). The potential for technology to enhance the visibility of CSEC has particular significance for juvenile prostitution, a phenomenon that has been described as hidden in plain site (Herman, 2003). Accordingly, this work aims to explore the nature and possible consequences of this increased visibility with respect to its effects on child victims, the challenges to the many involved systems, and the social consequences of a crime that commodifies sexual activity with minors for financial profit.

■ DEFINITIONS

At first, the definition of CSEC may seem readily apparent. Upon closer examination, however, the relationships among CSEC and child sexual abuse, noncommercial sexual exploitation, or child neglect become unclear. Policymakers have wrestled with such questions as: Is child sexual exploitation separate from child sexual abuse? Is it a form of child sexual abuse? What is necessary to transform sexual abuse of a child into a commercially exploitive act?

What may be clear is that sexual exploitation of children involves the act of unjustly using a child under the age of 18 in sexually manipulative activity for one's own benefit (Garner, 2004). By virtue of the modifier "commercial," CSEC signifies a more narrow term than the broad label of child sexual exploitation. CSEC includes such exploitation that is related to commerce or the buying and selling of the commodity of the child's sexualization (Garner, 2004). Such broad agreement is not sufficient, however, for understanding what is meant by CSEC. It leads only to further questions (e.g., What if the purchaser is not an adult? Is sexual activity in exchange for anything CSEC? Must the exchange be for something of value?). These questions can only be answered with a more precise definition.

Legal Definitions

Although the law is certainly not the only definitional source for CSEC, because the criminal law of any society often conveys what is generally accepted or generally condemned by the relevant community, it often forms the bedrock of other definitions. This is true in the area of CSEC. The role of children in society in general is often reflected in the law. For example, prior to the nineteenth century child abuse was not recognized as it is today as a crime warranting governmental intervention. Such matters were commonly thought to be concerns within the family. Indeed, the first prosecution for child abuse was brought within the context of the American Society Against Cruelty to Animals, because no such organization yet existed to protect children (American Humane Association, 2012). While unimaginable today, this reflected the societal view of children as neither particularly vulnerable nor equal in status to that of adults. In contrast, today every state has some form of child abuse laws, the U.S. Department of Justice (DOJ) has a section designed to protect children from exploitation (DOJ, 2012), and the U.S. Department of Health and Human Services has the Administration for Children and Families, whose work includes a federal response to child abuse and neglect (U.S. Department of Health and Human Services, 2012).

International Law

Although this chapter focuses on the domestic sexual exploitation of children, there is a logic to beginning the discussion regarding definitions of CSEC from an international perspective. First, this crime, like many in the twenty-first century that are directly affected by technology, is global in its scope. It is a crime that knows no international boundaries (ECPAT, 2008). Second, most discussions regarding the status and harm of children begin with the landmark international agreement, the United Nations Convention of the Rights of the Child

(UNCRC, 1989). Although the United States has not ratified the document (standing alone with Somalia), it is the most accepted international accord in United Nations history (United Nations Blog, 2012; United States Treaty Collection, 2013). Moreover, its principles pervade any discussion of the rights of children, even in the United States (see, for example, *Graham v. Florida,* 2010 as modified, *Miller v. Alabama,* 2012).

While the UNCRC does not define CSEC per se, the UNCRC terminology is often referenced as the basis of definitions found in later documents. The UNCRC calls on states to protect children from all forms of sexual exploitation and abuse, specifically noting that such a label includes any inducement to engage in "any unlawful sexual activity," as well as "the exploitive use of children in prostitution or unlawful sexual practices," and the "exploitive use of children in pornographic performances or material" (UNCRC, Article 34). This initial reference suggests that child sexual abuse and CSEC together include not only prostitution and unlawful sexual contact but also child pornography (also known as, and also referenced to in this chapter as, "child sexual abuse images") as a form of exploitation. Moreover, even in 1990, the international community understood that CSEC exists in many forms, including intrafamilial CSEC, when UNCRC stated that its reference to exploitation includes "sexual abuse when in the care of parents, legal guardians, or another person who has care of the child" (UNCRC, Article 19).

In 1996 the international community attempted to directly address CSEC at the First World Congress Against Commercial Sexual Exploitation of Children in Stockholm. This Congress produced a nonbinding international statement, the Stockholm Declaration of Action, which adopted a decidedly broad definition of CSEC. Recognizing that CSEC is a fundamental violation of children's rights and a "contemporary form of slavery," this Declaration stated that CSEC "comprises sexual abuse by the adult and remuneration in cash or in kind to a third person or persons" and includes situations in which the child is treated as a sexual and commercial object (First World Congress Against Commercial Sexual Exploitation of Children, paragraph 5). Its discussion of CSEC contained a clear recognition that such a label includes organized criminal formats composed not only of criminals but also several layers of intermediaries who facilitate the crime, as well as intrafamilial exploitation (paragraphs 7 and 8; Agenda for Action, paragraph 4). Thus, the notion of some form of remuneration to any party was explicitly introduced into the equation.

Therefore, by 1996 it was clear child pornography was a problem, but there was not definitional clarity as to the relationship between child pornography and child exploitation. The UNCRC placed child pornography and the prostitution of children under the umbrella of child exploitation and sexual abuse. Whether child pornography fell within only one or both of these labels was unclear, as was whether child sexual abuse and child exploitation were distinct and separate categories. The Stockholm Declaration clearly embraced an exchange of remuneration for sexual abuse as a form of CSEC. Whether child pornography also fell under the broader situation in which a child "is treated as a sexual and commercial object" was not apparent. However, taken together, the UNCRC and the Stockholm Declaration suggest that CSEC includes child pornography and commercial sexual acts such as, but not limited to, prostitution.

There have been several international documents that indirectly confirm this broad understanding of CSEC. The confirmation is "indirect" because the documents themselves do not explicitly define the term "CSEC." Rather, they define one of the components of CSEC very broadly. For example, in 1999 the International Labor Organization's (ILO) Convention on the Worst Forms of Child Labor placed within this category procuring children for prostitution, production of pornographic material, and production of pornographic performances (ILO, 1999). Similarly, in 2000 a major protocol was signed, the Protocol to Prevent, Suppress, and Punish the Trafficking of Persons, especially Women and Children (Palermo Protocol). This Protocol to the Treaty Against Transnational Organized Crime forms the basis of international Human Trafficking Law and offers the first comprehensive definition of human trafficking and more specifically sex trafficking. After 2000, both internationally and domestically, policymakers had become more aware of the contours of human trafficking. That awareness has led to an increased understanding that many children involved in what was earlier referred to the prostitution of children are victims of child sex trafficking. Therefore, in the present day, many have merged the two labels of "prostitution of children" and "child sex trafficking."

Under the Palermo Protocol, "trafficking in persons" includes "the recruitment, transportation, transfer, harbouring or receipt of a child for the purpose of exploitation" (Palermo Protocol, 2003). Exploitation includes, "at a minimum, the exploitation or the prostitution of others or other forms of sexual exploitation" (article 3a). Two points are critical here. First, prostitution and other sexual exploitation of children are included as a form of child sex trafficking. Second, the Protocol does not require "threat or use of force or other forms of coercion, of abduction, of fraud, of deception, of the abuse of power or of a position of vulnerability or of the giving or receiving of payments or benefits" if the victim is under 18 (article 3(c), (d)).

This shift in understanding CSEC, specifically a more victim-focused approach, continued in other international documents. It is unclear whether this represents a move to relabel CSEC into the more precise terms of child sex trafficking or the "sale of children" or is a more subtle recognition that CSEC is included under other forms of child abuse. However, it is likely academic to draw distinctions between the two. This move reflects a growing awareness that CSEC is a crime in which the child is the victim of the kind of abuse of her rights akin to slavery.

The next international document that shed light on the definition of CSEC was the Optional Protocol to the Convention of the Rights of the Child on the Sale of Children, Child Prostitution, and Child Pornography, which was signed in 2000 and entered into effect in 2002. According to the United Nations Treaty

Collections, the United States has signed this Protocol. Here, child prostitution is "the use of a child in sexual activities for remuneration or any other form of consideration" (Optional Protocol on the Sale of Children and Child Prostitution, 2000). Child pornography is defined equally as broadly to include "any representation by whatever means, of a child engaged in real or simulated explicit sexual activities or any representation of the sexual parts of a child for primarily sexual purposes" (Optional Protocol on the Sale of Children and Child Prostitution, 2000, Art. 2(c)). The "Sale of Children," therefore includes the offering, obtaining, procuring, or providing a child for either child prostitution or child pornography.

Further support for this international definition of CSEC, by virtue of its incorporation of a broad definition of exploitation and its conjoining of the prostitution of children/child sex trafficking and child pornography, is found in the Council of Europe's Convention on the Protection of Children Against Sexual Exploitation and Abuse. Here one observes a very expansive understanding of sexual exploitation. This Convention states that child sexual exploitation and abuse includes all of the following offenses outlined in Articles 18 to 23: sex abuse, child prostitution, various child pornography offenses, corrupting a child, and solicitation (Council of Europe's Convention on the Protection of Children Against Sexual Exploitation and Abuse, 2007). Because Article 18 is entitled "Sexual Abuse," it would seem that "Sexual Abuse" refers to that article and "Sexual Exploitation" includes the remaining prostitution, pornography, and corruption and solicitation offenses. Each offense is also defined rather broadly as well. Child prostitution includes not just recruiting or causing a child to engage in prostitution but also "profiting or otherwise exploiting a child for such purposes" (Art. 19). Combined with the expansive definition of prostitution in the Optional Protocol to the CRC including "remuneration or any other form of consideration," this casts a wide net (Optional Protocol on the Sale of Children and Child Prostitution, 2000; Art. 2(c)). Similarly, the definition of child pornography in the EU Convention on the Protection of Children follows the Optional Protocol's example of including depiction of children engaged "in real or simulated sexual activities" as well as depicting a "child's sexual organs primarily for a sexual purpose" (Convention on the Protection of Children Against Sexual Exploitation and Sexual Abuse, 2007; Art. 20, 20; Optional Protocol on the Sale of Children and Child Prostitution, 2000; Art. 2(c)).

The Rio de Janeiro Declaration and Call for Action to Prevent and Stop Sexual Exploitation of Children and Adolescents (2008; hereinafter Rio Declaration), a nonbinding international agreement to follow up on the Stockholm Declaration and Yokohama Global Commitment, solidifies this modern understanding of child sexual exploitation. This document explicitly states that " 'sexual exploitation of children and adolescents' is used to denote all forms of sexual exploitation and sexual abuse of people under the age of 18 in all settings: in the home and family, in schools and educational settings, in care and justice institutions, in the community and in the workplace" (p. 3).

Given the foregoing review of legal definitions, it would seem that internationally child sexual exploitation would include child pornography, child prostitution, and child sex trafficking. Commercial child sexual exploitation would refer to any of these actions where there is remuneration or consideration of any kind to any party.

Domestic Law

As this chapter will discuss, in the United States many agencies and nonprofit organizations have offered definitions of CSEC. Most, if not all, appear to draw from definitions in federal law. Therefore, that is a logical first source. However, textually federal law is somewhat inadequate, as the federal criminal code is intended to be narrower than a state code. Criminal codes on the state level are intended to include all forms of conduct sought to be condemned. However, for an action to become a federal crime, the federal government must have jurisdiction (28 USC §533 (2010)). The federal government cannot make an action a federal crime simply because it condemns the action. The federal government has jurisdiction only to regulate certain crimes. Federal crimes must implicate federal interests. Therefore, federal crimes do not reflect the complete list of activities condemned, but only those over which the federal government has jurisdiction. While federal child exploitation law does define its crimes, one must keep in mind it can treat as a crime only a limited amount of wrongful activity, the rest being left for the states.

The federal government has identified some areas in which there is a federal interest in CSEC. One is child pornography when it implicates interstate commerce. Indeed, the child pornography offenses in the federal criminal code are entitled the Sexual Exploitation of Children and the Sale of Children (18 U.S.C. §§2251, 2251A (2010)). However, in 2000 the federal government adopted criminal legislation regarding the trafficking in children, which was previously primarily handled in the format of "child prostitution" on the state level (or at times under the Mann Act statutes (18 USC §2421)). In so doing, the federal government explicitly criminalized child sex trafficking within its Trafficking Victims Protection Act (William Wilberforce Trafficking Victims Protection Reauthorization Act, 2008). It defined a commercial sex act as "any sex act, on account of which anything of value is given to or received by any person" (18 U.S.C. §1591(e) (2010)). Therefore, its definition of child sex trafficking can include the recruitment, harboring, transportation, provision, or obtaining of a child under 18 for a sex act for which anything of value is received by any person. In its official Findings for the TVPA, Congress adopted the same implicit category for CSEC to include prostitution, child pornography, and other sexual exploitation where something of value is transacted. It described the sex industry as involving "sexual exploitation of persons, predominantly women and girls, involving activities related to prostitution, pornography, sex tourism, and other commercial sexual services" (22 USC §7101(b)(2) (2010)).

This legal definition is confirmed by the DOJ's own definition of CSEC as "sexual abuse of a minor for economic gain. It involves physical abuse, pornography, prostitution, and the smuggling of children for unlawful purposes" (DOJ, 2007). Such a comprehensive definition is reflected in other federal government definitions such as the Department of Health and Human Services, Office of Refugee Resettlement (2012), and the State Department's Annual Trafficking in Person's Report (2012), which discussed Child Sex Trafficking as:

> When a child (under 18 years of age) is induced to perform a commercial sex act, proving force, fraud, or coercion against their pimp is not necessary for the offense to be characterized as human trafficking. (p. 33)

State Law

This broad definition of CSEC is also reflected in recent trends in state law. According to the Polaris Project (2012), which conducts an annual rating of state human trafficking laws, 49 states and the District of Columbia have human trafficking laws. However, the content and scope of these laws vary significantly. Regarding CSEC, only 47 have a sex trafficking provision (Polaris Project, 2012). Of those, 36 provide that force, fraud, or coercion is not necessary to prove trafficking of minors. Similarly, only 11 have any sort of provision that dictates a minor victim of CSEC cannot be prosecuted for prostitution. Among the most comprehensive definitions of CSEC on the state level is Washington's, which defines a commercial sex act as "any sex act or sexually explicit performance on account of which anything of value is promised to, given to, or received by any person" (Wash. Rev. Code Ann. §9A.40.010). Arizona also reflects this broad approach, defining CSEC as follows:

> Using, employing, persuading, enticing, inducing or coercing a minor to engage in or assist others to engage in exploitive exhibition or other sexual conduct for the purpose of producing any visual depiction or live act depicting such conduct; [or]...to expose the genitals or anus or the areola or nipple of the female breast for financial or commercial gain.
>
> Permitting a minor under the person's custody or control to engage in or assist others to engage in exploitive exhibition or other sexual conduct for the purpose of producing any visual depiction or live act depicting such conduct.
>
> Transporting or financing the transportation of any minor through or across this state with the intent that the minor engage in prostitution, exploitive exhibition or other sexual conduct for the purpose of producing a visual depiction or live act depicting such conduct. (Ariz. Rev. Stat. §13-3552)

It is clear, therefore, that both domestically and internationally, CSEC has been defined broadly. It goes well beyond "child prostitution" as traditionally understood. It includes any action in which a child is induced to engage in a sexual act, including a pornographic image or performance, and any form of remuneration is exchanged to any person. Because this definition is consistent with federal law, international law, and state trends, this will be the definition adopted in this chapter.

Civil Society

A brief review of civil society's literature reflects this broad understanding of definitions. The previously discussed ILO definition is such an example. Domestic civil society follows a similar path as these definitions often relate back to federal law. Three preeminent nonprofit organizations (Shared Hope International, ECPAT, and the Protection Project) include under the umbrella term CSEC four forms of abuse: child trafficking for sexual purposes, child prostitution, child pornography, and child sex tourism (Shared Hope International, 2006). The most comprehensive definition in American civil society comes from ECPAT (2008), which asserts that three "primary and interrelated" forms of CSEC are prostitution, pornography, and trafficking for sexual purposes, and other forms of CSEC include child sex tourism, child marriages, and forced marriages.

> The key element is that this violation of children and their rights arises through a commercial transaction of some sort…That there is an exchange in which one or more parties gain a benefit—cash, goods, or kind, from the exploitation of for sexual purposes of someone below the age of 18. (ECPAT, 2008)

This notion of "in kind" exchanges is critical to understanding CSEC because it then includes "survival sex," in which a minor may appear to be voluntarily engaging in a sexual act, but it is done in exchange for food, protection, a place to sleep, etc. (United Nations AIDS Inter-Agency Task Team on Gender & HIV/AIDS, 2008).

Therefore, in the United States, as is the case internationally, CSEC includes the sexual exploitation of children in the form of child pornography, prostitution, and child sex tourism, in which something of value is exchanged to anyone.

■ NATURE AND SCOPE OF CSEC

Coming to an acceptable definition of CSEC is not merely an academic enterprise. It then leads to a discussion of what behaviors do and do not constitute CSEC, which has critical implications for the crafting of social, legal, and clinical responses to child victims. The broad local and international acceptance of such a comprehensive definition of CSEC means that many behaviors and many actors fall within it.

A discussion of the nature and scope of CSEC reveals the parasitic relationship between the two concepts. On the one hand, it may seem logical to first examine the numbers (i.e., the scope) of those victimized through CSEC. This is a challenge, however, due to the secretive nature of the crime, the characteristics of the victims, as well as the many forms of the abuse. Examining the nature of CSEC first leads to so many qualifications that the numbers seem almost meaningless.

Scope

With this understanding, many trends come to light about the current forms of CSEC. As a threshold matter it is critical to note that little, if any, sound scientific research exists to understand the scope of CSEC (Stransky & Finkelhor, 2008). This is due in large part to the underground nature of the crime, the psychological dynamics between victims and offenders, as well as characteristics of involved children who, by virtue of their developmental status and vulnerabilities, are easily silenced. Indeed, one research group reports that the most common incident location for human trafficking is a residence, which speaks to the hidden nature of the crime (DOJ, 2012). Further, only recently have social scientists explicitly conceptualized juvenile prostitution as a form of child maltreatment and abuse as opposed to delinquency (Mitchell, Finkelhor, & Wolak, 2010). Related confusion exists among law enforcement as to whether prostituted youth are seen as victims or delinquents (Halter, 2010), and these tensions continue in the legal system (Adelson, 2008; Birkhead, 2011). Thus, the lack of reliable scientific data on the true prevalence of prostituted children in the United States may reflect these larger tensions around how youth are perceived and treated within and across the systems charged with their protection.

Exact statistics about child sex trafficking or prostituted children remain unknown in part because research is lacking (Finklea, Fernandes-Alcantara, & Siskin, 2011). An often miscited statistic claims that between 244,000 and 325,000 American children are involved in prostitution annually (Estes & Weiner, 2001). However, this report by Estes and Weiner (2001, p. 10) actually concluded that these numbers reflect the number of youth who are *at risk* each year of being a victim of CSEC due to their status as "runaways, throwaways, victims of physical or sexual abuse, users of psychotropic drugs, members of sexual minority groups, illegally trafficked children, children who cross international borders in search of cheap drugs and sex, and other illicit fare." While this estimate reflects the number of vulnerable children in the United States, and the circumstances discussed are highly relevant risk factors for CSEC, the authors themselves expressly warned the number is not to be considered a measure of children involved in CSEC. They continue to call for further research to determine an accurate figure. It is difficult, if not quixotic, to accurately assess the number of children in prostitution (DOJ, 2007; National Institute of Justice [NIJ], 2012; Stransky & Finkelhor, 2008.)

While reliable epidemiologic data are elusive, trends can be observed. Most women over age 18 involved in prostitution began when they were adolescents

(Abramovich, 2005; Silbert & Pines, 1981, 1982). DOJ research places the average age of entry between 12 and 16 (NIJ, 2012; DOJ, 2007). Indeed over half of the human trafficking cases examined in one study involved minor victims, concluding not only that minors are involved in human trafficking at a high rate, but also that they are involved in a higher percentage of sex trafficking cases than any other type of human trafficking (DOJ, 2012). Another national survey of over 13,000 American children concluded that nearly 4 percent of children in grades 7 to 12 have exchanged sex for drugs or money (Edwards, Iritani, & Hallfors, 2006). The authors extrapolate from this figure that over 650,000 children have engaged in commercial sex. Although arrests are not a reliable source for accurate numbers, of CSEC events, one study found that 79 percent of sex trafficking victims were between 16 and 20 and 24 percent were under 16 (DOJ, 2012). This same study found the average age of an offender was 33, and a third of the offenders were women.

The scope of child pornography is equally drastic. A similar pattern can be seen when examining the growth of child abuse images through recent decades. As will be discussed, the Internet affords the offender access to child abuse images, the mass distribution makes the images affordable if not free between collectors, and offenders can do so anonymously. Similarly, offenders can, through the use of peer-to-peer groups, share their common interest and receive validation from networks.

While precisely determining the amount of images traded or the number of offenders is impossible (DOJ, 2010), some statistics confirm the trend of an increase in both the production and trade of child abuse images. The Protect Our Children Act (2007) mandates that various federal government agencies study the child exploitation industry, develop a research-based national strategy, and report to Congress every two years on the state of child exploitation and the advancement of the strategy. According to their initial report in 2010, a majority of experts conclude that "child pornography is growing exponentially or there is an overwhelming increase in the volume of child pornography images available" (DOJ, 2010, p. 11). This increase is measured back to the 1990s (U.S. Government Accountability Office, 2011, p. 11) Although it is impossible to quantify the number of images with precision, many indicators confirm this conclusion about the growth of the industry since the advent of the Internet.

One measure includes complaints and tips from the public who come across such material. Prior to the Internet, the chances of an accidental encounter with child sexual abuse images were significantly less than today. Now, with the ability to produce the images cheaply through digital technology, massively distribute them, and access them through the Internet, the public can encounter them at a much greater rate. The Internet Crimes Against Children (ICAC) task forces are over 50 federal, state, and local partnerships throughout the country that focus exclusively on responding to such exploitive crimes against children. From 2006 to 2010, these task forces estimated an increase of more than 80 percent in the number of complaints from the public regarding child pornography; this has led to an increase in arrests of approximately 150 percent over the same time period (U.S. Government Accountability Office, 2011).

The National Center for Missing and Exploited Children (NCMEC) receives reports from the public regarding child exploitation observed on the Internet through its CyberTipline and forwards the information to the appropriate investigating agency or ICAC task force. NCMEC reports similar trends. Not only are reports of child pornography increasing exponentially, but also federal agencies are deeming within their jurisdiction over 100 percent more referrals from the CyberTipline, and referrals to ICAC task forces have similarly increased by approximately 70 percent in two years (U.S. Government Accountability Office, 2011, pp. 24–25).

NCMEC is also the warehouse for images recovered by law enforcement. It operates a Crime Victim Identification System, which receives child abuse images from law enforcement and electronically reviews them to locate any children within the images. NCMEC reports that submissions of recovered child abuse images from law enforcement increased by over 400 percent between 2005 and 2009 (DOJ, 2010).

Not only reports but also arrests and prosecutions have increased as well. ICAC task forces, the FBI, United States Immigration and Customs Enforcement (ICE), and the Secret Service have all reported increased arrest rates for child sexual abuse image cases (U.S. Government Accountability Office, 2011, p. 11). Importantly, however, the U.S. Postal Service has reported a 54 percent decline in cases arising from the use of the U.S. Mail (U.S. Government Accountability Office, 2011, p. 11), which officials believe is in part due to the increased availability of child pornography through the Internet rather than the mail.

Nature of CSEC

As understood today, CSEC involves much more than what has traditionally been considered "child prostitution" in which a child has sexual contact with an adult in exchange for money. It arguably also includes more forms of exploitation than sexual abuse as well as any time that a child is "sexually objectified" in exchange for remuneration of any kind. Sexual objectification occurs when one is "made into a thing for others' sexual use…and/or sexuality is inappropriately imposed upon a person" (American Psychological Association [APA], 2007, p. 1). Although youth in prostitution "are by definition sexualized— objectified and treated as sexual commodities" (p. 16), such objectification may occur in other circumstances as well.

For example, CSEC also encompasses so-called "survival sex." This is when a child engages in a sexual act in exchange not necessarily for money but for a safe place to sleep, food, shelter, etc. (DOJ, 2012). This can occur both within the family and outside the home. Within the home, often a family member may demand sexual acts or the child will lose access to food and shelter. Outside the home, many children who ultimately become prostituted are runaway or throwaway children fleeing an abusive or neglectful home. Childhood abuse occurs in situations of neglect and/or compromised attachments to adult caretakers, and such a history, in addition to limiting economic opportunities, renders youth highly vulnerable to the attachment that a pimp or other exploiter may initially offer. In this chapter, the authors define "pimp" as "a person who solicits customers for a prostitute, usually in return for a share of the prostitute's earnings" (Garner, 2009). Pimps target youth from vulnerable backgrounds and may offer prolonged periods of "romance" where the child receives monetary goods (e.g., shelter, clothes) and psychological ones (e.g., companionship, romance, the promise of safety and protection, self-esteem from the attention and interest afforded her). Maltreated, neglected, and abused youth are extremely vulnerable to such tactics. This process may resemble "grooming," a process more widely understood as associated with other forms of childhood sexual abuse. This process serves ultimately to gain control over the victim, which the pimp may leverage against the victim through violence, substance abuse, intimidation, or the threat of terminating the food, shelter, protection, and seeming companionship that a pimp provides. In either circumstance, the victim is totally dependent on an abuser to meet her basic needs, and such is sufficient to establish the remuneration element of CSEC.

CSEC can also include the situation when a child is induced into participating in a sexually explicit image (i.e., is part of a production of child pornography, or is induced to send an image to an individual) if the other elements are met. Similarly, it includes when a child is induced to engage in a sexual performance, although no sexual contact occurs. As long as there is an exchange of some form of remuneration, it is CSEC. The remuneration need not be to the child and need not be money. Therefore, if a pimp, parent, or guardian received anything of value in exchange for making the child even available for such exploitation, that is CSEC. In short, offenders are not limited to the stereotypical pimp on the street corner: "Individuals, families, and networks of individuals buy and sell human beings primarily for sexual services and domestic services" (Crane & Moreno, 2011, p. 3). Relatives have always played a significant role in exploiting children; more recently, gangs have played an increasing role (Foley, 2011).

Whatever the form of the exploitation, it is clear that the victims share vulnerabilities that offenders exploit. The broadening understanding of CSEC necessarily leads to a broadened understanding of the actors involved in the exploitation of a child. Thus far, the chapter has used the word "pimp" to refer to the individual who controls the exploited victim and profits from her victimization (Davis, 2013). Although originally a vernacular term, the word is accepted terminology in research on exploitation and often denotes one who utilizes sexual seduction, coercion and physical abuse to control the exploited person (Davis, 2013; Frug, 1992). The term includes those who control the victim's exploitation, inside and outside the family, and it has often been used interchangeably with "human trafficker," as the latter is defined under federal law as one who recruits, entices, harbors, transports, provides, receives, or obtains a person for a commercial sex act (18 U.S.C. §1591(a)(i). As such, trafficking could technically also apply to a purchaser (*US v. Jungers*, 702 F. 3d 1066 (8th Cir. 2013)).

While "trafficker" can apply to both a purchaser and seller of a child, each plays distinct roles. As such, the term "offender" could refer to both kinds of exploiters throughout this chapter. This role can be distinct from the person who purchases the child for sexual exploitation. This buyer of the child is obviously also an exploiter and could fall within the definition of "offender."

■ COMMONALITIES AMONG VICTIMS

No matter the form of CSEC, victims possess one or several vulnerabilities that "conspire to keep them" in prostitution (NIJ, 2012). Indeed, prostitution has been described as a process of victimization across the life cycle (Brannigan & Gibbs Van Brunschot, 1997), which neglect and abuse in one's family of origin may initiate. An NIJ-funded study found the most common characteristics of victims of CSEC to include economic need, trauma suffered from sexual abuse, physical abuse, or neglect, running away or being thrown out from home due to abuse-related dynamics, high levels of truancy, and poor employment skills (NIJ, 2012). This study further reported that running away from home and homelessness are among the most important predictors of prostitution. Indeed, those most at risk are runaways, homeless children, or youth leaving foster care (Crane & Moreno, 2011).

Although many studies have linked sexual abuse with later entry into prostitution (Nixon et al., 2002, Silbert & Pines, 1981, 1982; Van Brunschot & Brannigan, 2002), more research is needed on what moderates this relationship, since a majority of abused children will not be prostituted. Wilson and Widom (2010) suggested the importance of understanding the complex ways in which developmental factors interact to shape child outcomes such as involvement in prostitution. These researchers used a prospective cohort design to examine possible mediators of the relationship between childhood abuse/neglect and prostitution in young adulthood. Structural equation modeling evaluated the pathways between several problem behaviors during childhood (e.g., sexual initiation prior to age 15, running away, juvenile crime involvement, school problems) among a cohort of abused and nonabused matched controls. Although victims of childhood abuse/neglect were at increased risk for all problem behaviors except drug use, only early sexual initiation significantly predicted of entry into prostitution in the final model. Findings were consistent across forms of maltreatment examined (physical and sexual abuse as well as neglect). Additional research of this kind may help identify those risk factors most related to involvement in CSEC in order to more effectively tailor prevention, identification, and rehabilitation efforts.

Although empirical research is limited, at least one study suggests that children affected by sexual exploitation with a commercial aspect may be a subgroup of victims at particularly high risk compared with children whose sexual exploitation lacks a commercial element. For example, a nationally representative longitudinal study of approximately 2,600 local, state, country, and federal law enforcement agencies across the United States surveyed arrests in 2006 for Internet-related sex crimes against minors (National Juvenile Online Victimization Study; Mitchell et al., 2011). This study reported few demographic differences between commercially versus noncommercially sexually exploited victims. When researchers compared victims of CSEC to sexually exploited children where no commercial element was present, CSEC victims were more likely to be involved with the production of sexual abuse images, offered or given illegal drugs or alcohol, and physically assaulted (the majority of both victim groups experienced sexual assault). Further, more victims of CSEC had a history of failing grades in school, running away from home, and some form of criminal conduct compared with noncommercially sexually exploited youth (Mitchell et al., 2011).

With respect to offenders in this same study, those profiting from the commercial sexual exploitation of children were more likely to have prior arrests for both sexual and nonsexual offenses, were more prone to violence, and were more likely to work with other offenders and to involve female offenders (Mitchell et al., 2011). Black offenders were overrepresented among CSEC profiteers; the authors suggested that this finding required additional study since in general Internet sex crimes are disproportionately committed by white men. This research suggests that even if child sexual exploitation with a commercial element is less prevalent than sexual exploitation without a commercial aspect, CSEC may be associated with more risk for involved children due to aggravating aspects of the crime and the particular offenders involved (Mitchell et al., 2011).

Based on these results, Mitchell and colleagues (2011) argue that CSEC must be understood to include Internet-facilitated commercial sexual exploitation, given the migration of sex crimes to this environment. The fact that scarce empirical data exist about these issues suggests the importance of professionals understanding what is known—and unknown—about the role of technology in CSEC, which is considered next.

■ TECHNOLOGY AND CSEC

It is axiomatic to observe that "technology changes everything," and this is equally true in the realm of CSEC. Here, it is important to subdivide CSEC into child pornography and other forms of CSEC because the effect of technology is far more direct in child sexual abuse images; technology and the Internet fundamentally changed the production, possession, and distribution of child abuse images, transforming it to a global enterprise. Thus, the effect of technology on this form of CSEC merits a separate discussion.

Technology and Child Sexual Abuse Images

Cooper (1998) coined the term the "Triple A Engine" to describe three aspects of the Internet that could facilitate problematic online sexual behavior: affordability, anonymity, and accessibility. Prior to the advent of the Internet, child pornography was created by either video or still image (Lanning, 2010). It was traded primarily through the mail or through purchase in an "adult bookstore" (*New York v. Ferber*, 1982). There was, therefore, an element of risk involved in distributing or obtaining this material. Furthermore, because the material is clearly illegal, and an interest in it socially unacceptable in mainstream society, there was no easy way to locate other like-minded individuals. This posed challenges to connecting the producers to distributors, and distributors to purchasers. Similarly, the production aspect of child abuse images was also more challenging. Although most child sexual abuse is committed by a person known to the victim or family (Finkelhor et al., 2005) unless the producer of child pornography lives with the victim, he still needs access to children to produce the material. As such, whether an offender is commercially producing the images or producing them as part of a larger child sexual abuse strategy, there was a higher level of risk in locating potential victims and engaging in the grooming process (DOJ, 1994) or outright abduction in order to produce the child abuse images.

However, just as it claims, the Internet "brings people together." As Cooper (1998) observed, it provides accessibility: access to victims by producers, access to child abuse images by potential purchasers, access to like-minded individuals who can validate a sexual interest in children not found in mainstream society. Furthermore, much of this can occur anonymously or at least under the cover of another identity. The risk once associated with approaching and grooming a victim, locating the illegal material or potential consumer, conducting the transaction, or identifying like-minded individuals who can direct offenders to other sources of child abuse images is all facilitated by the Internet and done with relatively little risk. All uses of the Internet facilitate connection among the parties, as suggested by recent cases across a range of online modalities: chat rooms (e.g., *United States v. Bowser*, 2008; *United States v. Rowe*, 2005), social networking sites (*United States v. Strom*, 2012), and online advertising services such as Craigslist (*United States v. Nestor*, 2009). Peer-to-peer file-sharing organizations such as Gnuttella (*United States v. C.R.*, 2011) allow people to share child abuse images. More sophisticated underground networks allow for rings of child abuse image trading (Frieden, 2011; McKim, 2012).

Similarly, the Internet has made obtain child sexual abuse images affordable. Testimony by Ernie Allen, then the president and CEO of NCMEC, delivered to the Institute of Medicine Committee on Commercial Sexual Exploitation and Sex Trafficking of Minors in the U.S., described how one can join a website that offers such images to offenders for a monthly fee (Allen, 2012). Moreover, the very business model of child sexual abuse images has been altered. Prior to the Internet, case law reflected material commercially produced, albeit often crudely (*New York v. Ferber*, 1982). The Internet, digital cameras, relatively inexpensive high-quality filming equipment, and computers with massively increased memory as well as alternative storage ability with relatively little space has allowed for a flood of images to the market. As described in 2012 testimony by Michelle Collins to the U.S. Commission on Sentencing, "Technology such as smartphones and thumb drives and cloud computing have made it easier for offenders to collect and store their child pornography" (United States Sentencing Commission Public Hearing on Federal Child Pornography Crimes, 2012). As Ernie Allen discussed, prior to the advent of the Internet, the problem of child abuse images had been reduced to a relatively negligible size, but the Internet led to a resurgence of child abuse images to unimaginable levels. As of August 2010, NCMEC received 753,390 tips to its CyberTipline (in contrast to the 4,560 received in 1998); acting on those tips, NCMEC reviewed more than 28.5 million child pornography images and videos that were used to identify victims (DOJ, 2012). Peer-reviewed research converges with these data, with the University of New Hampshire's Crimes Against Children Research Center reporting threefold increases in arrests for technology-facilitated child exploitation cases of all types between 2000 and 2006 (Wolak et al., 2003; Wolak et al., 2004; Wolak, Finkelhor & Mitchell, 2009).

The affordability of the technology has altered the available material not only quantitatively but also qualitatively. Many of the child abuse images today are not commercially made, but homemade (Lanning, 2010). Child abusers now record their abuse for a number of reasons, including the desire to keep and relive the abuse as part of the sexual offending cycle (Lanning, 2010). However, this material is now currency within the child abuse community that has been facilitated on the Internet. Collectors of child abuse images are constantly looking for new images. Research has shown the ways in which users of pornography require more extreme images to obtain the same level of sexual stimulation (Wortley & Smallbone, 2012); as such, child sexual abuse images have become more sadistic and violent (DOJ, 2010). Therefore, many file-sharing groups require members to provide new images in exchange for gaining access to the informal network (Frieden, 2011). The result is that offenders are creating their own images, and today offenders create the vast majority of images of child sexual abuse (Lanning, 2010).

Technology and Prostituted Children

The use of social media to facilitate juvenile prostitution has been discussed in popular-press editorials (Kristof, 2012a, 2012b) and stories about FBI raids of prostitution rings (Kuo, 2012). In 2010 there was a highly publicized outcry among advocates, politicians, and law enforcement about Craiglist's purported role in facilitating the sexual exploitation of minors via its Adult Services section (Abrams, 2010; Latonero et al., 2011). Despite the visibility of this issue in the popular media, peer-reviewed research on the role of technology and prostitution of U.S. minors is in its "infancy" (Latonero et al., 2011; Latonero et al., 2012, p. 8). Experts nevertheless assert that based on available data, trends observed in law enforcement, and recent case law, technology has facilitated the growth and changing case dynamics of juvenile prostitution in the U.S. (Hughes, 2002; Latonero et al., 2011, 2012; Mitchell, Jones, Finkelhor, & Wolak, 2011). Shared Hope International (2012, p. 15) found technology to be "the single greatest facilitator of the commercial sex trade" in nearly all the countries it studied. The adult entertainment industry is a notorious early adopter of novel technology to facilitate its business model, and this is also true of the commercial sex industry (Hughes, 2002). For example, one of the early uses of videoconferencing technology was to facilitate the live transmission of girls being sexually abused to prospective buyers (Hughes, 2000). If one examines CSEC through a business model, technology clearly plays a role in this criminal enterprise just as it does within legitimate businesses.

Thus, the increasingly networked sociality of life in general is now apparent in the dynamics of CSEC: "Just as individuals are leading ever more 'mobile and networked' lives...trafficked minors and traffickers are too, but with varying degrees of technological fluency" (Latonero et al., 2012, p. 28). Technology has led to efficiency and innovation in legitimate businesses and has also led to more efficient CSEC. A recent report highlighted the centrality of mobile phones in the crime's ecosystem and described technology in CSEC as increasingly diffuse and extending beyond specific online platforms such as classified ad sites (Latonero et al., 2012). Diffusion here refers to blurred boundaries between recruitment and advertisement and online social networks, which facilitate a "multidimensional, participatory, networked realm for minors, traffickers and johns to communicate with each other" (Latonero et al., 2012, p. 28). Mobile phone technology may aid exploiters in reaching a larger client base and schedule more episodes of sexual exploitation per child (DOJ, 2010). Exploiters and traffickers can directly market to buyers, the transaction can occur in private with significantly decreased risk, and traffickers can have greater control over the victims. Thus prostitution grows as a potentially rich source of criminal activity and criminal enterprises are drawn to it away from other criminal work, which may be associated with greater risk (Cramer, 2008).

Cooper's Triple A Engine (1998) (*accessibility, affordability, anonymity*) also helps describe the effects of technology on youth in prostitution. This includes enhanced access to victims both in terms of recruitment and ways to sharpen the crime's commercial element (e.g., arranging meetings between prostituted children and buyers of sex, exploiters' use of technology to control and monitor sexually exploited youth). Technology provides access to victims, access between prostituted children and buyers of sex, and the ability to make the connection between purchaser and victim with decreased risk. Similar to child sexual abuse images, children must be groomed, recruited, coerced or forcibly abducted into prostitution. Whichever method is used, the exploiter must have access to potential victims who may be vulnerable to recruitment (e.g., abuse/neglect, compromised parental attachment, truancy/running away, few financial alternatives). It is well documented in case law that traffickers and exploiters use social networking sites to recruit victims (e.g., *United States v. Strom*, 2012) in addition to the traditionally recognized in-person recruitment. This use of technology enlarges the pool of potential victims both quantitatively and qualitatively: use of social networking sites provides an exploiter with access to a larger pool of victims as well as access to a broader pool. No longer must exploiters recruit children who are homeless, runaways, or otherwise obviously vulnerable; they may now reach children who are settled at home, attend school, and lead seemingly acceptable lives.

Although there are limited, if any, studies that empirically describe youth who are most vulnerable to recruitment into prostitution via online technology, the authors suggest a judicious extrapolation from research on youth vulnerable to other forms of high-risk behavior online. For example, maladjusted youth (e.g., depressive symptoms, strained parent–child relationships, history of abuse/neglect) are most vulnerable to interacting with unknown adults online and discussing sex with strangers, both of which are associated with offline victimization (Wolak et al., 2008; Ybarra, Alexander, & Mitchell, 2005). Case law describes the ways in which, via digital technology, exploiters can begin manipulating the child before he or she even leaves the household (*United States v. Buculei*, 2001; *United States v. Carmona*, 2002, *United States v. Crain*, 2009; *United States v. LoFlin*, 2007).

A recent case involving youth in northern Virginia showed the ways that pimps may involve young victims in recruiting other adolescents via social networking sites (*United States v. Strom*, 2012). This case also suggested ways in which the Internet may foster the crime's migration to youth who have been historically less affected. An affidavit quotes Facebook chats between a 17-year-old female victim (referred to as M.W.) and another 17-year-old (Victim 2) who attended the same high school. M.W. had run away from home and been recruited into prostitution by Justin Strom, and M.W. recruited other girls into Strom's enterprise on his behalf via social media and in person at school. A 2011 Facebook exchange that occurred between M.W. and Victim 2 read in part:

M.W.: Lol u tryna make sum money n shyt?
Victim 2: howww
M.W.: Trickin. Like u get 50 percent n u get all da drugs n shyt uwwant basically.
Victim 2: escorting type shit? As long as I don't have to sleep with them, but ill
        go out and shit just hit me up with the details
M.W.: Leme give u mi mans number hit him up tlk to him n shyt.

                (Aff. *United States v. Strom*, 2012, p. 8)

In addition to a means of recruitment, digital access to victims becomes an instrument of control. Pimps can keep track of the location of victims through GPS devices stored in an adolescent's cellphone or smartphone. By demanding photos from the victim at any time to confirm his or her location, pimps establish tight psychological control over victims. The use of disposable mobile phones facilitates conversation between a pimp and victim and makes tracing the phone back to the exploiter difficult to impossible. Often pimps have the child participate in the production of sexually explicit images, which may then serve as tools for extortion and control over victims (Farley, 2013). Exploiters may, for example, threaten to disclose the images to the victims' friends, family, school, etc. if they do not participate in expected sexual acts (*United States v. Buculei*, 2001).

Another facet of the Triple A Engine is anonymity, and this aspect of technology has facilitated juvenile prostitution. Case law and research document that "Prostitution is moving off the street and into cyberspace" (Kendall, 2011, p. 273). A nationally representative study of arrests involving Internet-facilitated CSEC in 2006 found that online advertising via social networking sites was the most common role the Internet played in this crime (Mitchell et al., 2011). This shift from street corners to private residences and hotels results in the reduced visibility of involved youth, which prevents detection by law enforcement and may limit social awareness about the issue. Prior to the advent of websites, social networking, and other online spaces that host juvenile prostitution, the ultimate connection between the sex purchaser and victim necessarily occurred in public. This required a known meeting place and the eluding of law enforcement, which posed a risk for the buyer of sex as well as the victim. Now, many pimps are using the Internet to advertise for victims (Kirk, 2011). Buyers can search for child victims online through Craigslist or Backpage.com (or another similar source), locate a victim, and arrange for the meeting and payment, all before leaving their home. This allows a level of anonymity previously unavailable. In the context of child sex tourism, purchasers of children can locate ads for destinations where they can purchase sex from children, preorder children, and arrange the entire trip as they would an ordinary legal vacation, without risk (Song, 2011). Streamlined access and anonymity arguably facilitate CSEC. Offenders who may have been deterred from engaging in this exploitation because the risk of capture was too significant may no longer be deterred.

Pimps/exploiters as well as purchasers may communicate covertly through the Internet about illicit activities, which may contribute to the crime's relative anonymity. As summarized by boyd and colleagues (2012), pimps and exploiters use coded language to advertise minors (e.g., "new girl in town"), repurpose technology such as gaming (e.g., Xbox Live) to communicate "in game," and use Skype and other video products that are more difficult to trace than mobile phones to coordinate online. An analysis of Craigslist advertisements suggested that although children are not explicitly advertised as children or girls, adult services advertising implies as much, with taglines such as "cute little Barbie doll" and "I look young but I'm over 18" (i.e., Craigslist 2009, in Farley 2013). Advertisers may furthermore use the Internet as a site where prostituted adolescents are promoted alongside adults (Farley, 2013; Mitchell et al., 2011). Online pornography advertisements, therefore, blur the line between adults who appear childlike and images that represent the sexual abuse of children who are trafficked online. This online blurring is consistent with the "childification" of adult women in mainstream adult pornography in print and visual media (Dines, 2009). This confusion over age (and therefore legal status) has obvious ramifications for law enforcement efforts but also for the lived experience of sexual development among adolescents (the authors return to this important point in the conclusion).

Even in the absence of extensive research, trends apparent in clinical and anecdotal reports as well as case law suggest that technology has substantially changed juvenile prostitution in the manner it has for sexual images of children. A recent study that compared Internet-facilitated juvenile prostitution and non-Internet cases of juvenile prostitution reported differences between the two groups (Wells, Mitchell, & Ji, 2012). Internet cases were significantly more likely to involve younger child victims (i.e., younger than 15) and to involve a family member or acquaintance as an exploiter. Police were more likely to treat juveniles as victims than offenders in Internet-based cases, which suggests the intriguing possibility that law enforcement may be more likely to perceive involved youth as victims when third-party exploiters advertise a minor online (Wells et al., 2012).

■ CONCLUSIONS: PSYCHOLOGICAL PERSPECTIVES AND PRACTICE IMPLICATIONS

Addressing the commercial sexual exploitation of children and adolescents in the United States requires collaboration among multiple disciplines. As this chapter has reviewed, a consensus definition of CSEC is difficult to reach, and there is little scientifically credible information about the problem's true scope and prevalence. In the meantime, mediated technologies such as social networking sites, online classifieds, and mobile phone applications suggest a rapidly changing, multi-platform, digital crime ecosystem (Latonero et al., 2012). Technology-related changes include increased access to victims, the potential for better identification of exploiters by law enforcement, and the location of the crime itself ("from the streets to cyberspace"). The effects of technology on CSEC therefore significantly alter aspects of the crime, and detailed information about these effects is needed to address the problem.

The authors encourage research that generates empirically derived information about the role of technology in CSEC and support the innovative use of technology to combat the problem. One promising model to guide this process is a working framework that boyd and colleagues (2012) produced for Microsoft Research and the Microsoft Digital Crimes Unit as well as the recent work of Latonero and colleagues (2012). These models outline how technology is used in CSEC and how it may also be leveraged to combat trafficking in the United States and other forms of CSEC. As boyd and colleagues (2012) note, although technology may sharpen the criminal element of exploiters and pimps, it may also be used creatively in law enforcement, rehabilitation, and prosecutorial efforts to aid child victims. boyd and colleagues urge reflection on how technology "reconfigures what is known and what is unknown [about CSEC]. Fears and anxieties emerge out of concern that things will get worse as a result of technology. Yet, new opportunities also present themselves" (boyd et al., 2012, p. 3).

To conclude, the authors highlight two aspects of CSEC that complicate all levels of discourse about the topic as well as the clinical and legal responses to child victims and suggest the ways that technology may affect both matters. First, the crime of CSEC presents the unique situation where youth tend not to self-identify readily as victims, particularly in the case of prostituted juveniles. The authors discuss the psychological reasons youth may not self-identify and how information about technology may help address but also potentially complicate this challenging dynamic. Second, the authors consider how CSEC may be one way in which sexualization is normalized for contemporary adolescents, how prostitution may represent an extreme example of such dynamics, and how mainstream adolescents' use of technology has affected this process.

When Victims Do Not Self-Identify

A majority of juveniles in prostitution may not self-identify as victims when law enforcement, attorneys, clinicians, and advocates/mentors initially encounter them. This aspect of CSEC impedes victim identification, frustrates service providers and attorneys, and may obscure the harm associated with the crime. Importantly, a child's refusal to identify as a victim or assertion of loyalty to her exploiter expresses a traumatic bond and an attempt to salvage self-efficacy rather than serving as evidence that no harm has occurred (Reid & Jones, 2011). As one researcher on prostitution has suggested, "If [observers] do not see a teenaged girl being trafficked at gunpoint from one country to another, if what they see is a streetwise teenager who says, 'I like this job, and I'm making a lot of money,' then they don't see the harm" (Farley, 2003, p. 248). This misperception may be even greater for girls of color due to stereotypes of hypersexuality among black girls (Kittling, 2006; Ward et al., 2013) and the structural relationship between social inequalities and prostitution (Farley, 2003, 2013; MacKinnon 2011; Nelson, 1993).

From a psychological perspective, however, an adolescent's reluctance to self-identify as a victim may be self-protective and reflect, among other things, adaptation to trauma and a way to survive psychological captivity (Herman, 1992; Reid & Jones, 2011). A child affected by CSEC may, for example, show a range of perplexing behaviors such as identifying with the pimp's perspective, denying the extent of violence and harm the pimp is capable of and hypervigilance to her exploiter's needs, all of which are psychological adapations to trauma (Briere, 2002). The literature on adult prostitution has identified similarities between pimp control and the dynamics of interpersonal violence, as both represent a system of power and coercive control (Leidholdt, 2003; Stark & Hodgson, 2003; Williamson & Cluse-Tolar, 2002). In the case of juvenile prostitution, coercive control may include an exploiter's isolation of child victims from family and friends; vilification of outside support networks as untrustworthy, hostile, and judgmental; economic control; sexual abuse; and rape and physical violence. Although no research exists on this topic, the effects of coercion and control may have even stronger effects on prostituted youth due to developmental differences that render children and teens more vulnerable (e.g., immature neurodevelopment, limited coping due to prior abuse, greater dependence on adult caretakers, fewer resources to exit).

In addition to psychological factors, the legal response of criminalization and social stigma may also influence children's reluctance to self-identify as victims (Adelson, 2008; Birkhead, 2011). As one advocate for youth affected by CSEC has argued, "It's difficult to view yourself as a victim, no matter what happens to you, when your pimp, the men who buy you, and even those who are supposed to protect you see you as incapable of being victimized" (Lloyd, 2011, p. 126). There are therefore psychological as well as sociolegal factors that help explain why youth affected by CSEC are reluctant to self-disclose or may not readily identify their experiences as exploitative.

Children involved in the production of sexual abuse images are also often reluctant to disclose their experiences due to guilt, self-blame, and complex feelings toward the offender, particularly in cases of abuse by a family member (Cooper, 2009). Researchers in the United Kingdom asked child victims who were pictured in pornographic images why they did not tell anyone about this aspect of their sexual abuse (Palmer, 2004). Results suggested that children were reluctant to tell because they believed that they appeared to allow the abuse to happen, since they cooperated and/or were made to smile during the abuse. Other reasons included children's guilt at helping recruit other children who were ultimately photographed, an abuser's threats that family members would be shown the images if victims did not cooperate, and victims' participation in masturbation and sexual encounters with other children as they were instructed to do (Palmer, 2004).

Given the ways in which psychological and sociolegal factors may inhibit disclosure and self-identification, CSEC victims may typically initially rebuff the help extended by clinicians, attorneys, law enforcement, and advocates/mentors. For example, M.W., the 17-year-old victim cited earlier in the chapter, told a staff person at her high school that she was spending time with a pimp (i.e., Justin Strom) who gave her money for the sexual favors she provided to others and that she did not know what to do. When this staff person reported the matter to law enforcement and an investigator questioned M.W. the following day, she told investigators, per the affidavit, "she does not need help, was not in danger, and is living the life she chose" (Aff. *United States v. Strom*, 2012, p. 5). Clinical experience suggests that this pattern of disclosure and recanting is very common among victims of CSEC and exemplifies the complex internal dialectic that most child victims of sexual abuse experience. Feelings of guilt and self-blame, attachment to one's exploiter, and culpability typically alternate in the minds of exploited youth and make self-identification as a victim a complicated, often lengthy, process.

Victims' reluctance to self-disclose is therefore an important feature of CSEC and one that each stakeholding group must address in its own way. The authors suggest, however, that the effects of technology on CSEC may render this process even more complicated for child victims. Similar to the ways in which images of child sexual abuse inhibit a victim's self-disclosure and increase children's feelings of culpability (Cooper, 2009; Palmer, 2004), these dynamics may also affect prostituted juveniles. For example, online advertisements and the use of social media to recruit/advertise youth may obscure the fact of children's victimization through text and imagery, or even falsely imply a child's willing participation in her own exploitation.

For example, to cite again a recent case that involved the recruitment of juveniles via social networking and the advertisement of victims through online classifieds (*United States v. Strom*, 2012), law enforcement found advertisements on the laptop of a 17-year-old victim that depicted "scantily clad women" and postings on Cragslist.com and Backpages.com. These advertisements of minor victims stated, among other things, "I'm fun, sexy n down to have a good time... I love what I do and so will you" (Aff. *United States v. Strom*, 2012, p. 5). Although such digital traces may be an "evidentiary goldmine" (Latonero et al., 2012, p. 29) for prosecutors of exploiters, this same text ("sexy n down to have a good time... I love what I do") may be misconstrued as evidence of a child's willing participation in prostitution. These kinds of tensions are offered as examples of how the proliferation of technology in CSEC may affect the already complicated process of victim identification and self-disclosure, including the response of various systems to child victims.

In terms of practical implications, professionals working with CSEC-affected youth must inquire about the role of technology and exchange information with other professionals where appropriate to do so. Importantly, this may introduce unchartered professional and ethical dilemmas with respect to how professionals use information obtained online, not to mention the potential validity of such evidentiary material. With respect to the mental health community, for example, clinicians and forensic evaluators may access the Facebook profile of a child with suspected involvement in prostitution to aid law enforcement in the child's safe return or attempt to corroborate a child's involvement. No professional consensus exists about the ethics of so-called "patient-targeted Googling" (Clinton, Silverman, & Brendel, 2010; DiLillo & Gale, 2011), let alone the implications of clinicians or forensic evaluators consulting online sources in their work with child victims. Thus, professionals should anticipate unresolved ethical dilemmas in the use of technology, refer to ethical codes and the current literature, and anticipate that uses of technology will likely outpace the revision of professional guidelines (see Chapter 14).

Adolescent Sexual Exploration, Sexualization, and Technology

Involvement in CSEC is an outcome of cumulative risk factors in the child and his or her adult caretakers and major social inequalities. In addition, theorists have proposed that CSEC may be understood as an extreme form of a process known as sexualization, which exists on a continuum among children and adolescents today.

Sexualization is distinguished from healthy sexuality, which is characterized by "intimacy, bonding, and shared pleasure... [involving] mutual respect between consenting partners" (Roberts & Zurbriggen, 2013, p. 4). In contrast, sexualization occurs when any one of the following are present: "A person's value comes only from his or her sexual appeal or behavior; a person is held to a standard that equates physical attractiveness (narrowly defined) with being sexy; a person is sexually objectified—that is, made into thing for others' sexual use, rather than seen as a person with the capacity for independent action and decision making, and/or sexuality is inappropriately imposed on a person" (APA, 2007, p. 1). Clinicians may note that certain aspects of sexualization resemble Finkelhor and Browne's (1985) classic description of traumatic sexualization, one dynamic by which child sexual abuse causes harm. Sexualization as defined here refers to a broader set of influences that are not confined to an abusive context but may still be associated with intrapsychic and social consequences for girls, women, men, and boys (Tolman, 2013).

Public and professional concern about the sexualization of young girls led the APA to establish a Task Force on the Sexualization of Girls in 2005. The task force's report (APA, 2007) synthesized over a decade of research on the negative effects of sexualization across emotional, cognitive, and behavioral domains (e.g., diminished performance on administered exams; less critical attitudes toward gendered violence; greater body dissatisfaction and preoccupation with appearance; for a review see APA, 2007). This corpus of research brings an empirical, data-driven perspective to bear on the controversial and often polemical topics such as child and adolescent sexuality and representations of girls and women in the media. Empirical findings about sexualization led the task force authors to opine that sexualization may relate to the phenomena of prostitution and trafficking. The definition of sexualization itself clearly invokes the situation of CSEC: where a child is "made into a tool for others' sexual use and pleasure rather than treated as a person with the capacity for independent action and decision making" for commercial reasons (APA, 2007, p. 1).

One researcher, also a member of the task force, takes this supposition a step further and asserts, "Much of what has been termed the *sexualization of girls* is the promotion of prostitution-like activities for children (and for young women)" (Farley, 2013, p. 166). Farley therefore argued that juvenile prostitution is an extreme form of girls' sexualization. She and other theorists have called attention to the role of technology on this dynamic since in online spaces, "Boundaries between normal adolescent sexual exploration and prostitution-like activity have disappeared" (Farley, 2013, p. 182). Examples of such blurred boundaries include the advertising of prostitution and adult and child pornography on sites that youth frequent, such as MySpace, Yahoo, Facebook, Flickr, and individual websites such as Stickam, a website where teens post live sexual activity by webcam (Farley, 2013; Stone, 2007). Manning (2010) has similarly observed, "Although pornography is nothing new, the proximity of the sex industry to the public and private squares is new" (p. 70), which may also result in the kind of blurring Farley described.

Seen in this way, CSEC may be considered relative to its broader sociocultural context and at the extreme end of a continuum of sexualizing influences for contemporary youth, a process that itself has online and offline dimensions. Technology such as social networking therefore may play a role in recruiting child victims and in producing psychosocial norms about sexuality that influence a far broader population of youth than are involved in CSEC per se. Although future research is required to evaluate this claim, we can draw from longitudinal research on the effects of early exposure to online sexually explicit materials in concluding that these media are not inert. Prospective longitudinal research shows that exposure to sexually explicit content may powerfully affect sexual behavior among certain youth (e.g., earlier initiation of sexual activity for females; more sexual harassment behaviors and less progressive gender role attitudes for males) (Brown & L'Engle, 2009; L'Engle, Ladin, Brown, & Kenneavy, 2006).

Thus, although CSEC may at present affect a relatively small portion of youth (Mitchell et al., 2011), representations of adolescent sexuality that emphasize voyeurism and performance for and servicing of boys and men (for which CSEC is the extreme form) are far more widespread (Farley, 2013; Manning, 2010). Importantly, youth are not merely passive recipients of such influences but are active shapers of online spaces and innovators of novel technology (Subramanyam & Šmahel, 2011). In the realm of sexual development, this will inevitably give rise to a range of complicated phenomena (e.g., youth-produced sexual images, self-exploitation) that press the boundaries of sexual behavior and legal responses. That is not to say that if a behavior becomes prevalent, it is by definition either normative or healthy.

Despite cogent theoretical claims about a possible relationship between sexualizing influences and CSEC, research is needed to evaluate these topics. Further, some researchers and theorists have criticized the APA's task force report for misconstruing the effects of media on youth outcomes and omitting an emphasis on developmental factors (e.g., Else-Quest & Hyde, 2009; Gill, 2012). There are at present no studies that directly link exposure to sexualizing material with aggressive behavior toward girls and women, although numerous studies link exposure to material that sexualizes women with attitudes associated with sexual aggression (for a review, see Purcell & Zurbriggen, 2013). It is also worth noting that child prostitution has historically thrived without a hypersexualized girl culture (Birkhead, 2011; Gilfoyle, 1994). What is different today is the ways in which adolescents' action via mediated technologies may usurp developmental readiness for certain behaviors in part due to the disembodied, disinhibited nature of such communications (Subramanyam & Šmahel, 2011). Additional differences include the mainstream nature of representations of sexuality that are based on a nonrelational sexuality and influences of the commercial sex industry (Farley, 2013; Manning, 2010; Nikunen, Paasonen, & Saarenmaa, 2008).

▪ SUMMARY

This volume has explored ways in which the digital revolution affects child and adolescent sexual development and the legal dilemmas that may result. Although certain aspects of online spaces may facilitate adolescent sexual development (see Chapter 4), the effects of technology on CSEC are perhaps the most problematic confluence of these issues.

Examined overall, the effects of technology on CSEC create a paradox: on the one hand technology may foster the underground, criminal, and invisible aspects of the crime, while in other ways technology may render certain elements more visible. *Invisibility*, for example, includes clandestine online communities that validate sexual criminal acts against children and facilitate networking among pimps, pedophiles, and child pornographers (Holt, Blevins, & Burkert, 2010), the migration of street-based crime to remote locations (e.g., hotels, residences), the misrepresentation of victims' age and identities via coded language in online classifieds, and the use of technology to conceal exploiters' digital traces (boyd et al., 2012). Technology may in this way foster what has been described as prostitution's social invisibility (Farley, 2003) and therefore collude to keep the associated psychological and social damages unseen, marginalized, and misperceived. Because the defensive minimization of danger and identifying with one's perpetrator are known aspects of coping with trauma, aspects of technology that render CSEC invisible may collude with victims' own dissociative coping as well as the issue's social marginalization.

On the other hand, technology also makes certain aspects of CSEC more *visible*. This may be a double-edged sword. As is seen by the mainstreaming of pornography or "pornification" (Nikunen, Paasonen, & Saarenmaa, 2008), the movement of exploitation more into the public view could have the collateral effect of suggesting a social endorsement. Minors in particular could process the exposure to such material as within acceptable limits due to their neurodevelopmental immaturity and limited impulse control, judgment, and risk assessment (Giedd, 2012); therefore, the visibility of CSEC could facilitate victimization or its normalization. In addition, the increased visibility of some aspects of CSEC also makes the crime more traceable when interactions occur through mediated technologies and digital evidence is produced (boyd et al., 2012). Indeed, online undercover operations where law enforcement officers target exploiters and use computer forensics to apprehend those who produce, distribute, and consume child sexual abuse images capitalize on such digital traces (DOJ, 2010b; Grocki & Nguyen, 2006; McKim, 2012). Furthermore, as findings by Wells and colleagues (2012) suggest, exploiters' use of online advertising may literally illustrate to law enforcement the coerced nature of minors' involvement in prostitution and therefore underscore their status as victims rather than criminals or delinquents. The evidentiary role of technology in aiding law enforcement and prosecution may be particularly useful given the tendency among youth affected by CSEC not to self-identify as victims.

■ DISCLOSURES

Abigail M. Judge and Mary Graw Leary have no conflicts to disclose.

■ REFERENCES

Abramovich, E. (2005). Childhood sexual abuse as a risk factor for subsequent involvement in sex work: A review of empirical findings. *Journal of Psychology and Human Sexuality*, *17*(1/2), 131–146.

Abrams, J. (2010, September 25) Craigslist tells Congress its adult services section is gone for good. *The Huffington Post*. Retrieved from http://www.huffingtonpost.com/2010/09/15/craigslist-adult-services-shutdown-congress_n_718803.html

Adelson, W. J. (2008). Child prostitute or victim of trafficking? *University of St. Thomas Law Journal*, *6*(96), 1–37.

Aff. United States v. Strom (2012). Case No. 1:12mj172 at 8

Allen, E. (2012, Jan. 4). Testimony to the Institute of Medicine Committee on Commercial Sexual Exploitation and Sex Trafficking of Minors in the U.S. Retrieved from http://www.missingkids.com/missingkids/servlet/NewsEventServlet?LanguageCountry=en_US&PageId=4632

American Humane Association (2012). Retrieved from http://www.americanhumane.org/about-us/who-we-are/history/.

American Psychological Association, Task Force on the Sexualization of Girls (2007). *Report of the APA Task Force on the Sexualization of Girls*. Washington, DC: American Psychological Association. Retrieved from www.apa.org/pi/wpo/sexualization.html

Birkhead, T. R. (2011). The "youngest profession": Consent, autonomy and prostituted children. *Washington University Law Review*, *88*(5), 1055–1115.

boyd, d., Casteel, H., Thakor, M., & Johnson, R. (2012). Human trafficking and technology: A framework for understanding the role of technology in the commercial sexual exploitation of children in the U.S. Retrieved from http://research.microsoft.com/en-us/collaboration/focus/education/human-trafficking-rfp.aspx.

Brannigan, A., & Gibbs Van Brunschot, E. (1997). Youthful prostitution and child sexual trauma. *International Journal of Law and Psychiatry*, *20*(3), 337–354.

Briere, J. (2002). In J. E. B. Myers, L. Berliner, J. Briere, C. T. Hendrix, T. Reid, & C. Jenny (Eds.), *The APSAC handbook on child maltreatment* (2nd ed., pp. 1–26). Newbury Park, CA: Sage Publications.

Brown, J., & L'Engle, K. (2009). X-rated: Sexual attitudes and behaviors associated with U.S. early adolescents' exposure to sexually explicit media. *Communications Research*, *36*, 129–151.

Clinton, B. K., Silverman, B. C., & Brendel, D. H. (2010). Patient-targeted Googling: The ethics of searching online for patient information. *Harvard Review of Psychiatry*, *18*, 103–112.

Cooper, A. (1998). Sexuality and the Internet: Surfing into the new millennium. *CyberPsychology and Behavior*, *1*, 181–187.

Cooper, A., et al. (1999). Sexuality and the Internet: The next sexual revolution. In F. Muscarella & L.T. Szuchman (Eds.), *The psychological science of sexuality: A research-based approach* (pp. 519–545). New York: Wiley.

Cooper, S. W. (2009). The sexual exploitation of children and youth: Redefining victimization. In S. Olfman (Ed.), *The sexualization of childhood*. Westport, CT: Praeger.

Council of Europe, Convention on the Protection of Children Against Sexual Exploitation and Sexual Abuse (2007). CETS No. 201.

Craigslist (2009, Aug. 20). "cute little Barbie doll" Adult Services, Las Vegas. Retrieved from http:lasvegas.craigslist.org

Cramer, M. (2008, Oct. 26). Targeted, some drug dealers turn to prostitution. *The Boston Globe*. Retrieved from http://www.boston.com/news/local/articles/2008/10/26/targeted_some_drug_dealers_switch_to_prostitution/?page=full

Crane, P., & Moreno, M. (2011). Human trafficking: What is the role of the healthcare provider? *Journal of Applied Research on Children*, *2*(1), 1–27.

Davis, H. (2013). Defining pimp: Working towards a definition in social research. *Sociological Research Online*, *18*(i). Retrieved from http://www.socresonline.org.uk/18/1/11.html

DiLillo, D., & Gale, E. B. (2011). To Google or not to Google: Graduate students' use of the Internet to access personal information about clients. *Training and Education in Professional Psychology*, *5*(3), 160–166.

Dines, G. (2009). Childified women: How the mainstream porn industry sells child pornography to men. In S. Olfman (Ed.), *The sexualization of childhood* (pp. 121–142). Westport, CT: Praeger.

ECPAT (2008). *Questions and Answers About the Commercial Sexual Exploitation of Children*. http://www.ecpat.net/ei/Publications/About_CSEC/FAQ_ENG_2008.pdf

Edwards, J. M., Iritani, B. J., & Hallfors, D. D. (2006). Prevalence and correlates of exchanged sex for drugs or money among adolescents in the United States. *Sexually Transmitted Infections*, *82*(5), 354–358.

Else-Quest, N. M., & Hyde, J. (2009). The missing discourse of development: Commentary on Lerum and Dworkin. *Journal of Sex Research*, *46*(4), 264–267.

Estes, R. J., & Weiner, N. A. (2001). *The commercial sexual exploitation of children in the United States, Canada, and Mexico. Executive Summary*. Retrieved from http://www.sp2.upenn.edu/restes/CSEC_Files/Exec_Sum_020220.pdf

Farley, M. (2003). Prostitution and the invisibility of harm. *Women & Therapy*, *26*, 3–4, 247–280.

Farley, M. (2013). Prostitution: An extreme form of girls' sexualization. In E. L. Zurbriggen & T. Roberts (Eds.), *The sexualization of girls and girlhood: Causes, consequences and resistance* (pp. 166–194). New York: Oxford University Press.

Finkelhor, D., & Browne, A. (1985). The traumatic impact of child sexual abuse: A conceptualization. *American Journal of Orthopsychiatry*, *55*(4), 530–541.

Finkelhor, D., et al., (2005). Victimization of children and youth: A comprehensive, national survey. *Child Maltreatment, 10*(1), 5–25.

Finklea, K. M.,Fernandes-Alcantara, A. L., & Siskin, A. (2011). *Sex trafficking of children in the United States: Overview and issues for Congress*, Congressional Research Services. Retrieved from http://www.fas.org/sgp/crs/misc/R41878.pdf

Foley, K. (2011).*Voices From the Field*. Connections, Washington Coalition of Sexual Assault Programs (XVIII). Retrieved from http://ccasa.org/wp-content/themes/skeleton/documents/CommericalSexualExploitationofYouth2011.pdf

Frieden, T. (2011, August 3). 72 charged in online global child porn ring. *CNN*. Retrieved from http://www.cnn.com/2011/CRIME/08/03/us.child.porn.ring/index.html?eref=mrss_igoogle_cnn

Frug, M. (1992). A postmodern feminist legal manifesto. *Harvard Law Review, 105*, 1045–1075.

Garner, B. A. (2004). *Blacks Law Dictionary* (8th ed.).

Garner, B. A. (2009). *Black's Law Dictionary* (9th ed.).

Giedd, J. N. (2012). The digital revolution and adolescent brain evolution. *Journal of Adolescent Health, 51*, 101–105.

Gilfoyle, T. J. (1994). *City of Eros: New York City, prostitution and the commercialization of sex, 1790-1920*. New York: W.W. Norton & Co.

Gill, R. (2012). Media, empowerment and the "sexualization of culture" debates. *Sex Roles, 66*, 736–745.

Graham v. Florida, 130 S. Ct. 2011, (2010), as modified (July 6, 2010).

Grocki, S. J., & Nguyen, L. D. (2006). How computer forensics can dramatically improve a case. *United States Attorneys' Bulletin, 54*(7), 24–30.

Halter, S. (2010). Factors that influence police conceptualizations of girls involved in prostitution in six U.S. cities: Child sexual exploitation victims or delinquents? *Child Maltreatment, 15*, 152–160.

Herman, J. L. (1992). *Trauma and recovery*. New York: Basic Books.

Herman, J. L. (2003). Introduction: Hidden in plain sight: clinical observations on prostitution. In M. Farley (Ed.), *Prostitution, trafficking and traumatic stress* (pp. 1–16). New York: Haworth Maltreatment & Trauma Press.

Holt, T. J., Blevins, K. R., & Burkert, N. (2010). Considering the pedophile subculture online. *Sexual abuse: A journal of research and treatment, 22*(1), 3–24.

Hotaling, N., Burris, A., Johnson, B. J., Bird, Y. W., & Melbye, K. A. (2003). "Been there done that": SAGE, a peer leadership model among prostitution survivors. In M. Farley (Ed.), *Prostitution, trafficking and traumatic stress* (pp. 255–265). New York: Haworth Maltreatment & Trauma Press.

Hotaling, N., Miller, K., & Trudeau, E. (2006). Sex for sale: The commercial sexual exploitation of women and girls: A survivor service provider's perspective. *Yale Journal of Law and Feminism, 18*(1), 181–190.

Hughes, D. M. (2000). Welcome to the rape camp: Sexual exploitation and the Internet in Cambodia. *Journal of Sexual Aggression, 6*, 1–23.

Hughes, D. M. (2002). The use of new communication and information technologies for the sexual exploitation of women and children. *Hastings Women's Law Journal, 13*(1), 129–148.

International Labour Organization (ILO), Convention Concerning the Prohibition and Immediate Action for the Elimination of the Worst Forms of Child Labour, art. 3, adopted June 17, 1999, 38 I.L.M. 1207.

Kendall, T. (2011). Prostitution 2.0: The changing face of sex work. *Journal of Urban Economics, 69,* 273–287.

Kirk, M. (2011, March 6). National Association of Attorneys General (available at http://www.kirk.senate.gov/?p=blog&id=434)

Kittling, N. (2006). God bless the child: The United States' response to domestic juvenile prostitution. *Nevada Law Journal, 6,* 913–926.

Kristof, N. D. (2012a, Jan. 25). How pimps use the Web to sell girls. *The New York Times.* Retrieved from http://www.nytimes.com/2012/01/26/opinion/how-pimps-use-the-web-to-sell-girls.html?_r=0

Kristof, N. D. (2012b, March 17). Where pimps peddle their goods. *The New York Times.* Retrieved from http://www.nytimes.com/2012/03/18/opinion/sunday/kristof-where-pimps-peddle-their-goods.html.

Kuo, L. (2012, June 25). Teen prostitutes rescued, pimps held, in FBI sweep. *Reuters Online.* http://mobile.reuters.com/article/idUSBRE85O19H20120625?irpc=932.

Lanning, K. V. (2010). *Child molesters: A behavioral analysis for professionals investigating the sexual exploitation of children.* National Center for Missing and Exploited Children.

Latonero, M., Berhane, G., Hernandez, A., Mohebi, T., & Movius, L. (2011). Human trafficking online: The role of social networking sites and online classifieds. USC Annenberg, School for Communication and Journalism, Center on Communication Leadership & Policy. Retrieved from http://technologyandtrafficking.usc.edu/report/

Latonero, M., Musto, J., Boyd, Z., Boyle, E., Bissel, A., Gibson, K., & Kim, J. (2012). *The rise of mobile and the diffusion of technology-facilitated trafficking.* USC Annenberg, School for Communication and Journalism, Center on Communication Leadership & Policy. Retrieved from https://technologyandtrafficking.usc.edu/2012-report/#.UYbQeL89p0o

Leidholdt, D. A. (2003). Prostitution and trafficking in women: An intimate relationship. In M. Farley (Ed.), *Prostitution, trafficking and traumatic stress* (pp. 167–183). New York: Haworth Maltreatment & Trauma Press.

L'Engle, K. L., Brown, J., & Kenneavy, K. (2006). The mass media are an important context for adolescents' sexual behavior. *Journal of Adolescent Health, 38*(4), 186–192.

Lloyd, R. (2011). *Girls like us: Fighting for a world where girls are not for sale.* New York: Harper Collins.

MacKinnon, C. A. (2011). Trafficking, prostitution, and inequality. *Harvard Civil Rights-Civil Liberties Law Journal, 46,* 271–277.

Manning, J. C. (2010). The impact of pornography on women: Social science findings and clinical observations. In J. R. Stoner & D. M. Hughes (Eds.), *The social costs of pornography: A collection of papers* (pp. 69–87). Princeton, NJ: The Witherspoon Institute, Inc.

McKim, J. B. (2012, July 29). Child pornography investigation uncovers a web of evil. *The Boston Globe.* Retrieved from http://www.bostonglobe.com/business/2012/07/28/led-innocent-into-web-evil/Sk9VoLSnM9uQqZQAggmQJL/story.html.

Melrose, M. (2002). Labour pains: some considerations on the difficulties of researching juvenile prostitution. *International Journal of Social Research Methodology, 5*(4), 333–351.

Miller v. Alabama, 132 S. Ct. 2455 (2012).

Mitchell, K., Finkelor, D., & Wolak, J. (2010). Conceptualizing juvenile prostitution as child maltreatment: Findings from the National Juvenile Prostitution Study. *Child Maltreatment, 15,* 18–36.

Mitchell, K., Jones, Finkelhor, D., & Wolak, J. (2011). Internet-facilitated commercial sexual exploitation of children: Findings from a nationally representative sample of law enforcement agencies in the United States. *Sexual Abuse: A Journal of Research and Treatment, 23*(1), 43–71.

National Institute of Justice (2007). *Commercial sexual exploitation of children: What do we know and what do we do about it.* Washington, DC: U.S. Government Printing Office.

National Institute of Justice (2012). National Overview of Demand Decrease Efforts. *New York v. Ferber,* 458 U.S. 747, 759–760 (1982).

Nelson, V. (1993). Prostitution: Where racism and sexism intersect. *Michigan Journal of Gender & Law, 1,* 81–89.

Nikunen, K., Paasonen, S. & Saarenmaa, L. (2008). *Pornification: Sex and sexuality in media culture.* Berg Publishers.

Nixon, K., Tutty, L., Downe, P., Gorkoff, K., & Ursel, J. (2002). The everyday occurrence. *Violence Against Women, 8,* 1016–1043.

Optional Protocol to the Convention on the Rights of the Child on the Sale of Children, Child Prostitution and Child Pornography (2000). G.A. Res. 54/263, U.N. Doc. A/RES/54/263.

Palermo Protocol, United Nations Convention Against Transnational Organized Crime, Protocol to Prevent, Suppress and Punish Trafficking in Persons, Especially Women and Children (2003), T.I.A.S. No. 13127, 2225 U.N.T.S. 209.

Palmer, R. (2004). *Just a click.* UK: Barnado's Children's Charity.

Polaris Project (2012). *Majority of states passing laws to combat human trafficking.* Retrieved from http://www.polarisproject.org/media-center/press-releases/634-majority-of-states-actively-passing-laws-to-combat-human-trafficking

Prensky, M. (2001). Digital natives, digital immigrants. *On the Horizon, 9*(5), 1–11.

Protect Our Children Act (2007).

Purcell, N. J., & Zurbriggen, E. L. (2013). The sexualization of girls and gendered violence: Mapping the connections. In E. L. Zurbriggen & T. Roberts (Eds.), *The sexualization of girls and girlhood: Causes, consequences and resistance* (pp. 149–165). New York: Oxford University Press.

Reid, J. A., & Jones, S. (2011). Exploited vulnerability: Legal and psychological perspectives on child sex trafficking victims. *Victims and Offenders, 6,* 207–231.

Rio de Janeiro Declaration and Call for Action To Prevent and Stop Sexual Exploitation of Children and Adolescents 3 (2008). World Congress Against Sexual Exploitation of Children and Adolescents III.

Roberts, T. A., & Zurbriggen, E. L. (2013). The problem of sexualization: What it is and how does it happen?" In E. L. Zurbriggen & T. Roberts (Eds.), *The sexualization of girls and girlhood: Causes, consequences and resistance* (pp. 3–21). New York: Oxford University Press.

Shared Hope International (2006). *Report from the Mid-Year Review on the Commercial Sexual Exploitation of Children and Adolescents in America.* Retrieved from http://sharedhope.org/wp-content/uploads/PIC/US_MTR_of_CSEC.pdf

Shared Hope International. (2012). *Executive Summary.* Retrieved from http://www.sharedhope.org/Portals/0/Documents/demand_exec_summary.pdf

Silbert, M. H., & Pines A. M. (1981). Sexual abuse as an antecedent to prostitution. *Child Abuse & Neglect, 5,* 407–411.

Silbert, M. H., & Pines, A. M. (1982). Entrance into prostitution. *Youth & Society*, *13*, 471–500.

Song, S. (2011). *Children as tourist attractions*. Retrieved from http://www.yapi.org/rpchild-sextourism.pdf.

Stark, C., & Hodgson, C. (2003). Sister oppressions: A comparison of wife battering and prostitution. In M. Farley (Ed.), *Prostitution, trafficking and traumatic stress* (pp. 17–32). New York: Haworth Maltreatment & Trauma Press.

Stone, B. (2007, Jan. 2). Using web cams but few inhibitions, the young turn to risky social sites. *The New York Times*. Retrieved from http:www/nytimes.com/2007/01/02/technology/02net.html?_r=1&ref=business&oref=slogin.

Stransky, M., & Finkelhor, D. (2008). *How many juveniles are involved in prostitution in the U.S.?* Retrieved from http://www.unh.edu/ccrc/prostitution/Juvenile_Prostitution_fact-sheet.pdf

Subrahmanyam, K., & Šmahel, D. (2011). *Digital youth: The role of media in development.* Advancing Responsible Adolescent Development series. New York: Springer Publishing.

Testimony of Michelle Collins to U.S. Sentencing Commission (2012, Feb. 15). *Federal child pornography offenses.* Available at http://www.missingkids.com/missingkids/servlet/NewsEventServlet?LanguageCountry=en_US&PageId=4628

Tolman, D. (2013). It's bad for us too: How the sexualization of girls impacts the sexuality of boys, men and women. In E. L. Zurbriggen & T. Roberts (Eds.), *The sexualization of girls and girlhood: Causes, consequences and resistance* (pp. 84–106). New York: Oxford University Press.

Turkle, S. (1997). *Life on the screen: Identity in the age of the internet (1st ed.).* New York: Touchstone.

United Nations AIDS Inter-Agency Task Team on Gender & HIV/AIDS (2008). Fact Sheet: HIV/AIDS, Gender and Sex Work. Retrieved from www.unfpa.org/hiv/docs/factsheet_genderwork.pdf

United Nations Blog (2012). Most-ratified international treaties. Retrieved from http://blogs.un.org/blog/2012/09/24/most-ratified-international-treaties/#sthash.WhtAYB4B.dpbs.

United Nations Convention of the Rights of the Child (1989). G.A. Res. 44/25, U.N. GAOR, 44th Sess., U.N. Doc. A/Res/44/25.

United Nations Treaty Collection (2013). Status, Chapter IV, 11. Convention on the Rights of the Child. Retrieved from http://treaties.un.org/pages/ViewDetails.aspx?src=TREATY&mtdsg_no=IV-11&chapter=4&lang=en.

U.S. Department of Health and Human Services (2012). Administration for Children and Families. Retrieved from http://www.acf.hhs.gov/

U.S. Department of Health and Human Services, Office of Refugee Resettlement (2012). Fact Sheet Sex Trafficking. Retrieved from http://www.acf.hhs.gov/trafficking/about/fact_sex.html

U.S. Department of Justice (1994, June 26). Half of women raped in 1998 were younger than 18 years old [press release]. Retrieved from http://bjs.ojp.usdoj.gov/content/pub/press/crv92.pr.

U.S. Department of Justice (2007). *Domestic sex trafficking of minors.*

U.S. Department of Justice (2010). *The national strategy for child exploitation and inter-diction: A report to Congress.* Retrieved from http://www.justice.gov/psc/docs/natstrat-egyreport.pdf

U.S. Department of Justice (2012). *Identifying challenges to improve the investigation and prosecution of state and local human trafficking cases.* Retrieved from http://www.mass.gov/ago/docs/ihttf/prosecutor-briefing-sheet.pdf

U.S. Department of Justice, Office of Public Affairs (2010). *Final U.S. defendant to face charges related to international child pornography conspiracy case.* Retrieved from http://www.justice.gov/opa/pr/2010/May/10-crm-619.html

U.S. Government Accountability Office (2011). *Combating child pornography.* GAO-11-334.

28 USC §533 (2010).

18 U.S.C. §§2251, 2251A (2010).

18 USC §2421.

18 U.S.C. §1591(e) (2010).

22 USC §7101(b)(2) (2010).

United States Sentencing Commission Public Hearing on Federal Child Pornography Crimes (2012), Summaries of the Testimony of the Witnesses, Washington, D.C. Retrieved from http://www.ussc.gov/Legislative_and_Public_Affairs/Congressional_Testimony_and_Reports/Sex_Offense_Topics/201212_Federal_Child_Pornography_Offenses/Appendix_D.pdf

United States v. Bowser, 317 F. App'x 525, 526 (7th Cir. 2008).

United States v. Buculei, 262 F.3d 322 (2001).

United States v. C.R., 792 F. Supp. 2d 343, 348 (E.D.N.Y. 2011).

United States v. Carmona, 38 F. App'x 875 (2002).

United States v. Crain, 321 F. App'x 320 (2009).

United States v. LoFlin, 240 Fed. App'x. 574 (2007).

United States v. Nestor, 574 F.3d 159, 160 (3d Cir. 2009).

United States v. Rowe, 414 F.3d 271, 273 (2d Cir. 2005).

United States v. Strom, Justin Aff. ¶ 21 (2012) Case No 1:12mj172.

Van Brunschot, E. G., & Brannigan, A. (2002). Childhood maltreatment and subsequent conduct disorders: The case of female street prostitution. *International Journal of Law and Psychiatry, 25*, 219–234.

Ward, L. M., Rivadeneyra, R., Thomas, K., Day, K., & Epstein, M. (2013). A woman's worth: Analyzing the sexual objectification of black women in music videos. In E. L. Zurbriggen & T. Roberts (Eds.), *The sexualization of girls and girlhood: Causes, consequences and resistance* (pp. 39–62). New York: Oxford University Press.

Wells, M., Mitchell, K. J., & Ji, K. (2012). Exploring the role of internet in juvenile prostitution cases coming to the attention of law enforcement. *Journal of Child Sexual Abuse, 21*, 327–342.

Williamson, C., & Cluse-Tolar, T. (2002). Pimp-controlled prostitution. *Violence Against Women, 8*(9), 1074–1092.

William Wilberforce Trafficking Victims Protection Reauthorization Act (2008). Washington, DC: U.S. Department of Justice. Retrieved from www.usdoj.gov/olp/pdf/wilberforce-act.pdf.

Wilson, H. W., & Widom, C. S. (2010). The role of youth problem behaviors in the path from child abuse and neglect to prostitution: A prospective examination. *Journal of Research on Adolescence, 20*(1), 210–236.

Wolak, J., Finkelhor, D., & Mitchell, K. J. (2009). *Law enforcement responses to online child exploitation crimes: The National Juvenile Online Victimization Study, 2000 and 2006.* Retrieved from cola.unh.edu/ccrc/internet

Wolak, J., Finkelhor, D., Mitchell, K. J., & Ybarra, M. (2004). Internet-initiated sex crimes against minors: Implications for prevention based on findings from a national study. *Journal of Adolescent Health, 12,* 545–548.

Wolak, J., Mitchell, K. J., & Finkelhor, D. (2003). *Internet sex crimes against minors: The response of law enforcement* (No. 10-03-022). Alexandria, VA: National Center for M&E C.

Wortley, R., & Smallbone, S. (2012). *Child pornography on the Internet.* U.S. Department of Justice & Community Oriented Policing Services.

Ybarra, M. L., Alexander, C. A., & Mitchell, K. J. (2005). Depressive symptomatology, youth Internet use, and online interactions: a national survey. *Journal of Adolescent Health, 36,* 9–18.

10 Legal and Clinical Issues in Interpreting Child Pornography on the Internet

■ LISA MURPHY, REBEKAH RANGER, AND J. PAUL FEDOROFF

The legal term *child pornography* is one of the terms most commonly used to describe media depicting sexual exploitation of children. Other terms, such as *child sexual abuse images* or *child sexual abuse material*, have been proposed as more appropriate since they avoid confusion with pornographic materials that are both legal and socially acceptable (Sinclair & Sugar, 2005; Taylor & Quayle, 2003). A problem with any single term is that people with persistent sexual interests in prepubescent children and young adolescents (clinically referred to as pedophilia) use a variety of materials for sexual stimulation, including ones that do not meet conventional legal definitions of child pornography. For instance, while children's programs like *Sesame Street* are clearly not pornographic, they can be used by people with pedophilia to facilitate sexual fantasy. These materials interest people with pedophilia because they are sexually arousing to them. Legal definitions of child pornography do not cover all the materials that an individual with a persistent sexual interest in children may consider sexual (Fedoroff, 2012; Lanning, 2001; Taylor & Quayle, 2003). Aside from more explicit material that would be legally deemed child pornography, materials collected and viewed by people with a sexual interest in children can include legal pictures of children in department-store catalogs, children's television and movies, stories, cartoons, and pictures. It also includes media produced by parents with innocent intent (such as photos of their children in the bath) but misused by people with a sexual interest in children. Although such materials would not legally be considered child pornography, they can be used for sexual purposes by individuals with a persistent sexual interest in children (Fedoroff, 2012; Lanning, 2001; Taylor & Quayle, 2003). In contrast, materials involving sexual exploitation of children may at times be collected by people intrigued by "forbidden" materials but who have no pedophilic interests whatsoever (for example, people with obsessive collecting interests or some people with Asperger's syndrome) (Fedoroff, 2012).

Since legal definitions of child pornography vary throughout jurisdictions, more general definitions are used by forensic clinicians, researchers, and prevention and advocacy workers. In this chapter the term *child pornography* is used to refer to any media record of sexual activity involving prepubescent children and/ or young adolescents (Wortley & Smallbone, 2012).

Child pornography preceded both computers and creation of the Internet. However, during the 1980s and 1990s the Internet quickly became the most versatile and accessible medium for accessing and transmitting both legal and illegal pornographic materials. Computers with Internet connectivity are an ideal means for people who have sexual interests in children to connect with like-minded individuals and groups, since the Internet provides an anonymous method to create, view, store, and distribute child pornography (Edwards, 1994; Taylor, 1999). While the Internet has made child pornography more widely and easily accessible, it has also simultaneously provided a method for police to identify and arrest people who access child pornography, and as such, these arrests are increasing (Wolak, Finkelhor, & Mitchell, 2011). Most new investigations involve first-time offenders with no previous criminal or psychiatric history (Babchishin, Hanson, & Hermann, 2011; Finkelhor & Ormrod, 2004; Young, 2000).

Although sexual victimization of children has been recognized as a major social problem for decades, the emergence of Internet-facilitated sex crimes has created new challenges and opportunities for law enforcement officials, clinicians, and researchers (Wells, Finkelhor, Wolak, & Mitchell, 2007). The increased availability of child pornography raises several still unresolved issues:

1. Does the prevalence of child pornography on the Internet reflect increased sexual interest in children?
2. Does the prevalence of child pornography on the Internet mirror the prevalence of clinically diagnosed pedophilia?
3. Are some incidents of child pornography possession worse than others?
4. How should incidents where children or adolescents are in possession of child pornography be dealt with?
5. Are people who access child pornography online more or less likely to commit a "hands-on" sexual offense?

Consideration of these questions has been complicated by problems defining child pornography and its significance within specific contexts. These challenges are based on the nature of the materials and actions depicted, the different professional perspectives (i.e., legal vs. clinical), and variation in legislation between international jurisdictions. The aim of this chapter is to review the literature concerning definitional issues of child pornography, interjurisdictional issues, and differences between legal and clinical conceptions of child pornography used by those with a sexual interest in children.

■ UNDERSTANDING THE BREADTH OF THE ISSUE

During the Victorian era, sexualized images of children were commonly displayed in art galleries of private collectors and in the newly invented art form known as photography (Gillespie, 2011; Ost, 2009; Wortley & Smallbone, 2012). Famous writers of children's books, such as Lewis Carroll (known for *Alice in Wonderland*) and J. M. Barrie (known for *Peter Pan*), over time have been subject to scrutiny regarding the questionably sexual depictions of children in their work and the nature of their real-world interactions with children (Jewkes, 2012; Wortley & Smallbone, 2012).

From a contemporary perspective, the increased ease of access and the sheer quantity of child pornography on the Internet can be linked to the popularity of the Internet and World Wide Web (WWW) beginning during the early 1990s (Bryant, 2011). Investigators, clinicians, and researchers now agree that the Internet has played a significant role in increasing the accessibility, production, and sharing of child pornography (Adler, 2008; Finkelhor, Mitchell, & Wolak, 2000; Palmer, 2004; Taylor & Quayle, 2003). Individuals seeking child pornography prior to the inception of the Internet would either produce it themselves or identify a covert (underground) distributor or local collector interested in trading or selling child pornography (Gillespie, 2011; Taylor & Quayle, 2003). In the past, obtaining child pornography required risk and physical exposure because collectors had to visit specialized sex shops or have mail-ordered material sent to their homes (Carr, 2001; Wortley & Smallbone, 2012).

Currently, affordable and sophisticated computers and the rise in popularity of the Internet throughout the 1980s and onward have created a channel for anonymous information gathering (Wortley & Smallbone, 2012). One view is that this increased use of the Internet did not create an interest in child pornography, nor did it create a new demand for child pornography that did not previously exist (Ferraro & McGrath, 2005; Wortley & Smallbone, 2012). According to this view, the Internet simply provided a new medium by which people could anonymously access vast quantities of child pornography within minutes, from the comfort of their own homes. Individuals with a persistent sexual interest in children and child pornography collectors were able to go from trading hard copies in local underground networks to using a medium by which they could anonymously gain instant access to large quantities of digital materials from all over the world (Gillespie, 2011; Jenkins, 2001; Ost, 2009; Wortley & Smallbone, 2012).

Some claim that both the legal and illegal pornography industries have flourished with increased global access to the Internet (Gillespie, 2011; Wortley & Smallbone, 2012). One popular American child pornography magazine was estimated to sell 800 copies in 1980; by 2000, one online company providing access to child pornography was found to have over 250,000 subscribers worldwide (Wortley & Smallbone, 2012). Child pornography can be found embedded in adult pornography sites or in websites specifically designated for material depicting children. Due to the illegal nature of child pornography, it is difficult for researchers to estimate the number of websites that provide access to child pornography and the quantity of images or videos that can be accessed from each site. One reason for this is because sites are frequently shut down and reinstated under different domain names to avoid detection by law enforcement. Websites often involve temporary hosting locations where images rotate automatically among a number of host sites. In other cases, website redirects and zipped files with the password noted in another location are used (Benzeluk, 2009; Wortley & Smallbone, 2012).

With the emergence of Internet child pornography a number of criminal justice officials and researches have attempted to produce figures that reflect the magnitude of the issue. In many of these cases the rates reported are purely conjecture based on an individual's estimate or best guess. A series of figures have been re-reported in a number of publications and subsequently are regarded as being authentic (Wortley & Smallbone, 2012). Although often dated and questionably reliable, the following are some frequently cited statistics on the prevalence and characteristics of Internet child pornography. It is important to regard these rates with caution.

In 2008 it was reported that every second, 28,258 online users were accessing adult pornographic material and in that second $3,075.64 was being spent on online pornography (Internet Watch Foundation, 2008). In the same year there were approximately 116,000 daily Internet searchers for "child pornography" (Internet Watch Foundation, 2008).

Between 1997 and 2009 the number of available child pornography materials is believed to have increased by 1500 percent, and more than 200 new images of children were posted daily (Berkowitz, 2009). When examining the prevalence of child pornography in relation to adult pornography, some sites have claimed that approximately 20 percent of all Internet pornography depicts children (Enough is Enough, 2008). In 2010, the Internet Watch Foundation identified 17,000 different websites hosted in 41 different countries that contained material suspected to be child pornography (Internet Watch Foundation, 2010).

Since the Internet has become the largest and most affordable source for legal and illegal pornographic materials, the child pornography industry is said to have become increasingly lucrative. It has been reported that child pornography generates an annual profit of approximately $3 billion (Enough is Enough, 2008). A review of commercial and freely accessible child pornography websites revealed that internationally approximately 12.6 percent of all child pornography websites required payment to access the material. The survey noted that the rate of required payment seems to depend on the host location. For many countries there is no commercial component, while 80 percent of child pornography websites hosted in Poland were commercial. Child pornography websites hosted in the United States require payment only 13.3 percent of the time; the figure for Canada is 8.2 percent (Benzeluk, 2009). However, given the fact that even individuals with intellectual disability, minimal computer knowledge, and no financial resources can find child pornography, estimates based on commercial transactions leading to conviction certainly underestimate the true prevalence of the problem.

One well-publicized and frequently cited example of the potential for funds to be obtained through the sale of child pornography via the Internet occurred in November 2001. During that month the Federal Bureau of Investigation (FBI) took down a website hosted by Landslide Productions that provided access to several sites offering child pornography and other legal pornography. Hosted in Fort Worth, Texas, the site was reported to have had over 250,000 subscribers from 60 different countries, and the host site was said to have grossed up to $1.4 million monthly. The production consisted of 5,700 computers worldwide, many hosted in Russia and Indonesia (Sher, 2007; Wortley & Smallbone, 2012). This case is frequently cited as one of the largest child pornography sites (Wortley & Smallbone, 2012). However, most child pornography is created by "amateurs" and distributed to like-minded offenders. "Payment" typically involves an invitation to child pornography websites or chat rooms. This fact is known to law enforcement, and undercover officers are faced with the dilemma of convincing offenders they can be trusted while not engaging in child pornography distribution themselves. Despite the Landslide case, often cited to highlight the potentially lucrative industry of online child pornography, most sites hosting such material can be accessed free of charge (Fedoroff, 2012; Lanning, 2001).

In the past 10 years, the Royal's Sexual Behaviours Clinic, which assesses over 100 sex offenders per year, has had only one offender who has reported accessing child pornography commercially. This case involved a man who purchased *hentai* legally from a major seller of mainstream books and media in the world, including Japan. *Hentai* is a form of animated pornography, often involving childlike characters and animals. While *hentai* is legal in the United States, he was arrested when he traveled to Canada, where these materials are illegal. He readily admitted he planned to continue to use *hentai* in the United States, where it is legal.

If child pornography is becoming increasingly financially profitable, it is defying the trend in adult pornography. For example, one of the largest adult pornography distribution companies, New Frontier Media, has seen the value of its stocks drop to penny stock status, having fallen 300 percent in the last five years (New Frontier Media Inc., 2012).

While child sexual abuse is an international phenomenon, research on the extent and nature of child pornography has largely focused on Western societies, possibly because these areas have played a more active role in the production and consumption of such materials (Healy, 2004; Wortley & Smallbone, 2012). It has been suggested that the United States is the largest consumer and producer of child pornography, accounting for 54 percent of all child pornography (Enough is Enough, 2008; Sinclair & Sugar, 2005). Based on research by Cybertip.ca, Canada's national tip line, the top five countries hosting child pornography websites in 2009 were the United States (49.2 percent), Russia (20.4 percent), Canada (9 percent), Japan (4.3 percent), and South Korea (3.6 percent) (Benzeluk, 2009). It is difficult to be certain about the exact statistics, not only because child pornography production is illegal but also because most is produced by nonprofessionals in private locations. These productions are then distributed through decentralized routes, making tracking even more difficult. For example, investigators may arrest a child pornography offender in the United States for possession and distribution of images that were initially created in Eastern Europe or Asia.

■ GENERAL THEMES IN CHILD PORNOGRAPHY

Some investigators and researchers claim there is an increasing demand for more violent and sadistic forms of child pornography (Benzeluk, 2009; Davidson, 2011; Hughes, 2001; Internet Watch Foundation, 2007, 2008). In addition to this, investigators and researchers have reported trends in child pornography depicting younger victims (Bunzeluk, 2009; Davidson, 2011; Internet Watch Foundation, 2007, 2008; Quayle & Sinclair, 2012; Sinclair & Sugar, 2005; Taylor & Quayle, 2003).

The mandate of Cybertip is to accept and assess tips from citizens pertaining to online sexual exploitation and to liaise with law enforcement about potential investigations. One review of Cybertip files indicated that 93 percent of reports of confirmed child pornography depicted children under the age of 8 years (Cybertip, 2008). Similar data were presented by the Internet Watch Foundation (2010), based in the United Kingdom, which noted that 73 percent of victims of child pornography were under the age of 10 and two thirds of material depicts penetrative acts. A more extreme example of child pornography depicting younger victims includes a recent trend in accessing medical ultrasound photos of fetuses with other forms of child pornography (Jonsson & Svedin, 2012). The extreme nature of this material illustrates that for some individuals, accessing child pornography is not motivated by sexual purposes but rather in collecting unusual or extreme materials. The difficulty lies in distinguishing images accessed for sexual purposes and images accessed for nonsexual purposes, as illustrated by the ultrasound example (Jonsson & Svedin, 2012).

Consumers and collectors seek a range of online material, including single still photos or photos that are part of a broader series of the same victim over time. In addition to photographs, videos, animations, and written stories describing abuse of children are also highly sought after. Webcams have also become popular so that people can interact via live video-feeds in real time. Inevitably this has led to live sexual interactions via webcam, including ones involving children. Most are likely amateur sites, but some commercial webcam child pornography sites have been described (Hughes, 2002; Klain, Davies, & Hicks, 2001; Sinclair & Sugar, 2005; Wortley & Smallbone, 2012).

Quayle and Jones (2011) conducted research on the victim characteristics in child pornography based on materials seized in police investigations throughout the United Kingdom. Although a range of ethnicities was represented in the material, Caucasian children outnumbered nonwhite children ten to one. Asian children were the second most frequent victim ethnicity. Girls outnumbered boys by four to one. The most common age group of children depicted in the material was prepubescent (designated in this study as children under age 10). The authors noted a comparative absence of African or African-American children in the child pornography they reviewed. This surprising finding argues against the widely held myth that children in child pornography are more likely to come from disadvantaged or Third World backgrounds.

The most common collections among child pornography offenders in the United Kingdom consisted of Caucasian girls under the age of 10. These findings are consistent with other studies of child pornography victim characteristics (Baartz, 2008; Benzeluk, 2009, Carr, 2004; Sinclair & Sugar, 2005; Wolak, Finkelhor, & Mitchell, 2005). Anecdotal information obtained through interviews with child pornography collectors indicates that their preferences focus on thin children with fair skin who have no secondary sexual characteristics and have their genitalia clearly visible in the material (Taylor & Quayle, 2003). Of course, this finding is not surprising since child pornography is legally defined as depicting children with those developmental characteristics because these interests are common in men with pedophilia.

■ DETERMINING THE DEFINITIONAL CRITERIA FOR CHILD PORNOGRAPHY

Despite universal social condemnation of child pornography as morally reprehensible, legislative responses vary significantly. Even the question of what constitutes child pornography is disputed. One reason for this lack of consensus is that domestic laws and the rationale for legal enforcement on which they are based do not easily translate into internationally accepted standards and regulations (Gillespie, 2010, 2011). In addition, standards and tolerance can change over time and between jurisdictions depending on different moral, cultural, social, political, legal, or religious factors (Grant et al., 1997; Healy, 2004; O'Donnell & Milner, 2007).

While it may seem impossible to create a single universally accepted legal definition, attempts to identify areas and characteristics of consensus will provide greater clarity to the breadth of the problem and promote international cooperation (Gillespie, 2011; O'Donnell & Milner, 2007). To understand the parameters in defining child pornography, it is helpful to examine some of the definitional properties. When examining the international variation in the definition of child pornography it is important to begin by examining the definition of what constitutes a "child".

Age of a "Child"

In some cultures the transition to adulthood is marked not by chronological age but by rites of passage. Such rituals may include puberty, marriage, or death of the head of the family. Other cultures rely on the legal concept of adulthood as determined in jurisdictional legislature, usually on the basis of chronological age (Sinclair & Sugar, 2005).

In Western cultures, concerns have arisen regarding whether the definition of a "child" should be based on chronological age or on degree of physical or social maturity (Gillespie, 2011). In Canada the current age of consent for sexual activity is 16. The age of consent to participate in the production of pornography is 18. Because it is not always known how old a person in a pornographic image is, some jurisdictions use legislation that is based on the *apparent* age of the child depicted in images as opposed to the *actual* age (Gillespie, 2011; Grant et al., 1997). However, issues arise concerning the difference between pornography that uses 18-year-old women who are selected and presented to appear as age 13, and pornography that uses 13-year-old girls selected and presented to appear 18. One solution, which some jurisdictions have adopted, is to define children in pornography as people who are either under age 18 or appear to be under age 18.

A primary international legislative ruling on this issue is the Optional Protocol to the United Nations Convention on the Rights of the Child. This legislation defines a child as a human being under the age of 18 years (unless under local jurisdictional law a child is defined as younger) (Akdeniz, 2008; Gillespie, 2010). While some commentators argue that 18 is an arbitrary age cutoff for the purposes of child pornography, it remains the current consensus among most North American and European countries (Gillespie, 2010; Jenkins, 2001).

In Europe, distinctions in child pornography classification are often made depending upon the chronological age of the child depicted. While European countries broadly define children as being under the age of 18, sexualized depictions of children under 14 are classified as "child pornography" and sexualized depictions of children 15 to 17 are described as "juvenile pornography" (Cattaneo et al., 2012). In Australia, legislation defines a child as an individual who is (or is depicted to be) under the age of 16 (Krone, 2004). Having clear parameters of the age cutoff for child pornography is critical because it determines the legality of the material (Grant et al., 1997; Sinclair & Sugar, 2005).

The determination of the age of a child is also difficult in countries that have different age distinctions for consent to sexual activity and for consent to participate in pornography. Even within a country, different legal jurisdictions can have varying ages of consent for sexual activity. Canada, for example, has a federal age of 16 to consent to vaginal sex but age 18 to consent to anal sex; in the United States, the age of consent for vaginal sex is determined by state legislation and ranges from 14 to 18. Larger variation in the age of consent exists internationally[1] (AVERT, 2011). For example, boys in Namibia are able to consent to sexual activity at age 7, girls at age 12. In other locations, such as Austria or Turkey, there is no specific stipulation on the age of consent (O'Donnell & Milner, 2007).

The varying definitions of a child in reference to pornography and the legal cutoff ages for consent to sexual activity complicate the situation (Carr & Hilton, 2011; Gillespie, 2011; Sinclair & Sugar, 2005). For example, in some U.S. jurisdictions, a 15-year-old is deemed legally able to consent to sexual relations with an adult. However, the adult could be prosecuted for the creation of child pornography if he or she creates a permanent recording (such as videos or pictures) of the activities because the person is under the age of 18 and is therefore deemed unable to consent to being photographed or videotaped.

From an investigative standpoint, one problem that police experience is the ability to accurately determine whether or not the individual being depicted in confiscated material is indeed a child. When the victim is prepubescent, determining that the victim meets the age criteria for a child is quite obvious. However, for postpubescent children (for example, 13 to 17 years old), reliably and accurately determining age becomes more challenging (Jonsson & Svedin, 2012; Taylor & Quayle, 2003).

Victim identification investigators have noted that how the child is positioned and which body parts are exposed can have a significant impact on accurate determination of the child's true age. Many children depicted in child pornography are never identified; subsequently, physical characteristics become the only way to estimate their age (Wells, Finkelhor, Wolak, & Mitchell, 2007). Wolak, Mitchell, and Finkelhor (2003) found that images of pubescent children are much less likely to result in legal charges and convictions than images of prepubescent children.

Defining "Child Pornography"

Given the challenges involved in establishing consensus on the definition of a child, no universal standard currently exists upon which to judge the legality of the material. While global information sharing allows for immense benefits, the dangers associated with largely unrestricted exchange of certain materials has created a new set of problems for law enforcement agencies and customs agents on an international scale (Gillespie, 2011; Healy, 2004; Wortley & Smallbone, 2012). Not only has policing the content shared over the Internet become increasingly difficult, but there is not always a consensus regarding whether the material meets the legal requirements to constitute child pornography between different jurisdictions.

Jurisdictional issues become especially problematic when an offender is found possessing child pornography in one country and it is determined that the images were created by an unknown offender in another country with a different legal definition of child pornography. Under international law, the state that holds jurisdiction is the location where the offense itself was actually committed (Arnaldo, 2001). Given the international scope of child pornography and ease with which it can be traded online, identifying the location where the material was created can be difficult (Gillespie, 2011).

Despite legislative variation, some international bodies have been able to reach a consensus on common definitions of child pornography. Such legislation focuses on visual depictions rather than written material (Gillespie, 2011; Healy, 2004; Sinclair & Sugar, 2005). One example is the International Criminal Police Organization (Interpol) working group, which defines child pornography as "the visual depiction of the sexual exploitation of a child, focusing on the child's sexual behavior or genitals" (Interpol Recommendations on Offenses against Minors, as cited in Healy, 2004, p. 1). As of 2010, Interpol's definition now also includes written and audio material (Carr & Hilton, 2011; Gillespie, 2010).

Whether for international, national, or state legislative definitions, certain overarching factors are considered when determining key components in the definition of child pornography. Once the determination has been made about what constitutes a child, definitional properties that are examined include the behaviors depicted in the material, whether the material depicts real or simulated behaviors, and the intended effect of the material (Carr & Hilton, 2011; Gillespie, 2011; Grant et al., 1997).

The type of behavior depicted in the images affects how narrow or broad the definitions are. For example, legislation that seeks to establish a narrow legal definition for child pornography would only include depictions of children who are engaging in sexually explicit activities. Conversely, other countries may have broader definitions of what constitutes child pornography that include more "erotic" types of images and do not require sexually explicit activity to meet the criteria (Gillespie, 2011; Grant et al., 1997).

A primary argument against the use of child pornography is the victimization of the child depicted in the material. Critics have highlighted the importance of identifying whether definitions include only "real" behaviors or if imagined or simulated behavior should be included within the definition. "Pseudo" child pornography refers to virtually or digitally created images that are "morphed" or blended images of nude children or of adults and children sexually engaged (Gillespie, 2011). Given current technological options readily available to anyone with access to a computer, it is possible to create material that would be arousing to a person with a sexual interest in children that does not actually require a child's involvement.

Programs can create "pseudo" images by digitally altering or enhancing photographs in a manner that creates the appearance of sexualized images of children (Carr & Hilton, 2011; Gillespie, 2011). One example may be a nonsexualized image of a fully clothed child that has been digitally altered by cutting the photographed head of the child from one photo and superimposing it onto another photo of a nude child's body. Another example may include a photo of a man and a child, both fully clothed, that has been altered so it appears that the child has his or her hand on the groin of the adult. Some of the images can be altered so successfully that it is difficult to determine if the product is real or digitally created (Grant et al., 1997; Sinclair & Sugar, 2005).

A similar concept arises concerning the possession of *anime* or *hentai*. These are Japanese comics or animations depicting childlike characters with exaggerated sexual characteristics. They often behave in a sexually suggestive manner or are depicted as engaged in sexual activity (Gillespie, 2011; Ito, 2005; McNicol, 2004; Poitras, 2010). *Anime* may have scenes that illustrate sexual situations and depict nudity, even though the materials are intended for child audiences. *Hentai*, however, refers specifically to more "perverse" material that can become explicit enough to be considered pornographic. Such material often portrays characters that appear prepubescent and includes sex involving animals (McLelland, 2005). A Canadian analysis of cartoons and drawings determined to meet the legal criteria for child pornography indicated that 75.2 percent of the material depicted sexual assaults against children. Ninety-three percent of the images depicted children who appeared to be less than 12 years of age; 69.2 percent were girls and 21.8 percent were boys (Benzeluk, 2009).

Some argue that obscene fictional images that portray children as sexual objects reinforces deviant sexual interest in children and may contribute to in-person sexual offenses against children (Gillespie, 2011; McLelland, 2005). In Japan these materials are not illegal to create or possess even if they include drawings depicting sexually explicit images of children. Japanese authors make these materials readily available in comic book shops throughout the country and they can easily be purchased on the Internet (Purdy, 2005). Of interest is the fact that the rates of sex crimes in Japan dropped when these materials were legalized (Diamond & Uchiyama, 1999).

New Zealand, the United Kingdom, Austria, Sweden, Canada, and the Netherlands are examples of countries that have made *hentai* material illegal (Camero & Yambot, 2009). In these countries, since these images depict the sexual activity of a child, they have been deemed to fit the definition of child pornography.

Another consideration in determining the legal criteria for child pornography pertains to the intended effect of the material. In some instances mildly erotic depictions of children have appeared in artwork or advertisements (Grant et al., 1997). It has been argued that few individuals would find explicit child abuse material tasteful; however, some materials depicting nude or seminude children can be considered to have artistic merit. Since what is regarded as erotic is subjective depending on the context, an image that is judged as sexually immoral and victimizing in nature in one context can be seen by another as a tasteful expression of art (Gillespie, 2011). This issue is still considered in some jurisdictions.

A recent example of this issue involves a 2008 exhibit by an acclaimed Australian photographer, Bill Henson. The invitation to Henson's gallery opening in Sydney reportedly featured a photo of a young male "bare-chested and glistening with sweat, looking pensively away from the camera" (Taylor, 2012). Henson's show included several photographs of young models in various stages of undress. The police responded to complaints from the public and the press regarding the legality of his materials. His artwork was seized in a police raid just prior to the show's opening. In 2010, following this controversy, the New South Wales government adapted its child pornography legislation to remove the potential defense of "artistic purpose" (Taylor, 2012).

◼ LEGISLATIVE APPROACHES TO CHILD PORNOGRAPHY

Law enforcement agencies worldwide are presented with unique challenges in combating the issue of child pornography. Such obstacles include the cross-jurisdictional nature of child pornography on the Internet, inadequate and inconsistent application of legislation, constantly evolving technology, and the vast number of users and material on the Internet (Carr & Hilton, 2011; Wortley & Smallbone, 2012). Most countries have enacted legislation prohibiting the use of child pornography. Despite considerable thought into how to define the age of a child and child pornography, individual cases do not necessarily conform to the circumstances anticipated by the lawmakers. Therefore, legislation has evolved as significant cases in Canada and the United States have required modifications, amendments, and new legislation.

American Legislative Approaches

Beginning in 1978, the United States introduced several legislative amendments aimed to censor both legal pornography and child pornography. The evolution of child pornography legislation in the United States is summarized in Table 10.1. This section will provide a more comprehensive overview of two influential pieces of legislation: the Child Pornography Protection Act and the PROTECT Act.

The Child Pornography Protection Act (CPPA) (1996) was the first law in the United States that prohibited virtual depictions of child pornography. It was enacted to keep up with changing technology and the increased availability of Internet child pornography. The CPPA was also the first act in the United States to introduce mandatory prison sentences of 15 years for production of child pornography and five years for possession of child pornography. It included the provision that computer-generated images warranted prohibition, even if no real children were used. Harm done to children was no longer the sole focal point; instead, it became the assertion that child pornography is "obscene" or "immoral," thus justifying the prohibition of virtual images without child contact (Akdeniz, 2008; Bird, 2011; Gillespie, 2011).

Not long after the enactment of the CPPA, it was challenged by the American Civil Liberties Union (ACLU) because of concerns about the criminalization of child pornography produced without the involvement of a real child. The ACLU argued that the CPPA went beyond protecting real children by including materials that depicted "pseudo," digital, or illustrated children, and therefore it was unconstitutional. The ACLU's argument was rejected on the grounds that digital images could be used to entice children into abuse.

Echoing the ACLU's concerns, the Free Speech Coalition (FSC) also argued that the legislation was unconstitutional. The FSC's primary concern was that the

TABLE 10.1. *Significant American Legislation in Addressing Child Pornography*

Year	Name of Legislation	Significant Amendments	Landmark Cases
1970	President's Commission on Obscenity and Pornography	Legalization of all pornography on the basis of research	Defeated by Senate
1978	Protection of Children against Sexual Exploitation Act	Age cutoff for a child changed to 16 years	*Miller v. California* (1973) Ruling established that material can be judged obscene if, taken as a whole and judged by community standards, it appeals to the "prurient interest" in sex, depicts sexual conduct in a patently offensive manner, and lacks serious literary, artistic, political, and scientific value. The decision reiterated that obscenity was not protected by the First Amendment and established the *Miller* test for determining what constituted obscene material. *New York v. Ferber* (1982) Ruling upheld the constitutionality of a state statute that prohibited anyone from knowingly producing, promoting, directing, exhibiting, or selling any material showing a "sexual performance" by a child under the age of 16. It found that images of children need not meet the legal definition of obscenity to be prohibited as the state's interest in protecting children trumps the First Amendment.
1984	Amended 1978 Act	Age cutoff for a child changed to 18 years; mandatory minimum sentences increased; child pornography legality no longer subject to obscenity standards	*United States v. Jacobson* (1992) Ruling pertained to issue of entrapment by government. A narrowly divided court overturned the conviction for receiving child pornography through the mail, ruling that postal inspectors had implanted a desire to do so through repeated written entreaties.
1986	Child Sexual Abuse and Pornography Act	Prohibition of transporting minors for the purposes of pornography and the production of child pornography for advertisements	*United States v. Osborne* (1991) Supreme Court ruling held that prohibiting the possession of child pornography, even in the privacy of one's home, "passes muster under the First Amendment." Furthermore, the ruling held that "undercover operations provide a means by which participants in the clandestine child pornography industry can be detected." *Osborne v. Ohio* (1990) The intent of the law was to protect victims of child pornography by attempting to destroy the market. The Court held that it was "reasonable for the State to conclude that it will decrease the production of child pornography if it penalizes those who possess and view the product, thereby decreasing demand." Extended legislation for the mere possession of child pornography.

(continued)

TABLE 10.1. *Continued*

Year	Name of Legislation	Significant Amendments	Landmark Cases
1988	Child Protection and Obscenity Enforcement Act	Introduction of computer prohibition for possession and distribution of child pornography; mandated that all those overseeing any artistic materials (films, art, or otherwise) keep records of all ages of models involved in the production; new prohibition against the sale and purchase of children for the purposes of child pornography	*American Library Association v. Thornburgh* (1989)The American Library Association challenged the Act on the grounds that recordkeeping of all models was too tedious for those who had no direct input in the production of any materials and was not effective in preventing child pornography. Ruling held that recordkeeping would only be enforced to those directly involved in the process of photographing models, and only to underage models.
1996	Telecommunications Act	Federal prosecution for obscenity over the Internet; overturned in 1997	*United States v. Maxwell* (1995) Privacy of Internet content once it has been sent to another user was a major focus of this case. Under the Fourth Amendment, a person can expect privacy until his or her online content is transmitted to another individual. In a legal sense, the more open materials are, the less private they become.
1996	Child Pornography Protection Act (CPPA)	Child pornography now includes any visual depictions of a minor engaged in sexual conduct, or materials that allude to depictions of sexual conduct with a child.	*ACLUFree Speech Coalition v. Reno* (1999) Ruling held that the CPPA was unconstitutional to the extent that it proscribed computer images that do not involve the use of real children in their production or dissemination. *Ashcroft v. Free Speech Coalition* (2002) Ruling overturned the CPPA due to overbroad provisions because they abridged "the freedom to engage in a substantial amount of lawful speech."
2008	PROTECT Act (previously briefly referred to as the Child Obscenity and Pornography Prevention Bill)	Law to incorporate more than child pornography and to address all amendments and legal concerns	*United States v. Williams* (2008) Ruled that one component of the PROTECT Act, the "pandering provision," violated the First Amendment. It further held that the law was unconstitutionally vague in that it did not adequately and specifically describe what sort of speech was criminally actionable. The Supreme Court reversed the Eleventh Circuit Court's ruling in May 2008 and upheld this portion of the act. *United States v. Irving* (2006) The case took place after the recent legislative challenges related to constitutionality, and it was misunderstood that the burden of proof was on the prosecution to prove that real children were harmed in the production of the material. On appeal, ruling held that the defendant was guilty of possession of cartoon images of child pornography. *United States v. Whorley* (2005) It was argued that since no real children were involved in *anime*, no harm was done to children. The judge upheld the guilty verdict on the grounds that the material met the criteria for obscenity.

act was a violation of the First Amendment freedom of speech because the language used to define the legislation was too broad and ambiguous and therefore could potentially censor material with artistic merit or scientific value (Akdeniz, 2008; Bird, 2011; Davidson, 2011; Gillespie, 2011). *Free Speech Coalition v. Reno* ruled that the language used in the legislation was not too vague as to confuse artistic merit or scientific value, and that the legislation allowed for differentiation of these cases from child pornography. However, when appealed to the Ninth Circuit, the FSC's concerns were held to be legitimate and the CPPA was found to be an invalid piece of legislation (Akdeniz, 2008; Bird, 2011; Wastler, 2010). The case was brought before the U.S. Supreme Court by Attorney-General John Ashcroft. In *Ashcroft v. Free Speech Coalition*, it was ruled again that the government did not show a link between child pornography and harm to actual children and that the ambiguity of the legislation's wording created problems in identifying which material is considered illegal (Akdeniz, 2008).

While this ruling had many opponents, including Mr. Ashcroft himself, it was the impetus for the next piece of legislation (Bird, 2011; Davidson, 2011; Gillespie, 2010; Kimpel, 2010; Wastler, 2010): the 2002 Child Obscenity and Pornography Prevention Bill (COPP). This bill aimed at refining the definition of child pornography to avoid controversy over virtual images. A goal was to encourage prosecution of offenders regardless of whether the images they accessed were of virtual or real children (Akdeniz, 2008; Bird, 2011; Davidson, 2011).

Another aspect of online child pornography that had largely been overlooked in previous legislation concerned those offenders who had intentions to sell or offer children online. COPP emphasized prosecution for these offenders regardless of whether the selling or offering actually took place, downplaying the importance of intent. It also added a provision to encourage voluntary reporting of suspected child pornography cases. Lastly, it created an FBI database intended to identify victims depicted in child pornography (Akdeniz, 2008). COPP was not initially passed by the Senate but was reintroduced with amendments in 2003 as the PROTECT Act (Prosecutorial Remedies and Other Tools to end the Exploitation of Children Today) (Akdeniz, 2008; Bird, 2011; Schell et al., 2007).

The PROTECT Act of 2003 included the reintroduction of the Miller test as a valid tool to determine if the material met legal criteria for obscenity in child pornography cases (Berkowitz, 2009; Bird, 2011; Kimpel, 2010). Material that is deemed obscene using the Miller test is not protected under the First Amendment. It must meet all three of the following criteria:

1. Would the average person, applying contemporary community standards, find the work, taken as a whole, appealing to prurient interests?
2. Does the work depict/describe, in a patently offensive way, sexual conduct or excretory functions, specially defined by applicable state law?
3. Does the work, take as a whole, lack serious literary, artistic, political, or scientific value? (SLAPS test) (Berkowitz, 2009)

The problem inherent in the Miller test is its subjectivity, as the determination of obscenity will depend on the jurisdiction in which the case is heard (Berkowitz, 2009). The use of the Miller test was exempted under the previous CPPA legislation, as it was deemed unnecessary due to the ruling that child pornography automatically met the definition of "obscene" by virtue of the content (Berkowitz, 2009; Bird, 2011; Kimpel, 2010).

While it could be argued that the reintroduction of the Miller test could create more confusion than was necessary, the PROTECT Act did seek to clarify previous legislative problems with the definition of child pornography. Table 10.2 summarizes major amendments to the 2002 COPP, defined as the PROTECT Act. This material has been more comprehensively reviewed elsewhere (Akdeniz, 2008; Berkowitz, 2009; Bird, 2011).

Since 2003, several cases have been brought forth challenging the amendments made by the PROTECT Act. One such case is *United States v. Williams*. Williams was charged with pandering under the 2003 legislation. He had been accused of trading pictures with an individual online for the purposes of chatting, but one of the pictures showed him and his daughter, fully clothed. The Court ruled that while the government's intentions are to protect children, the pandering provisions were bordering on infringement of Williams' freedom of speech. Williams' pandering conviction was overturned (Akdeniz, 2008).

Several issues arose as a result of Williams' affirmative defense amendment. One such case was *United States v. Irving* (2006), in which the defendant was convicted of possession of 76 video files of child pornography as well as other sexual abuse charges. On appeal, it was argued that since the controversy surrounding the FSC's challenges of unconstitutionality against the CPPA, it was the responsibility of the prosecution to prove that the images depicted actual child abuse by offering additional evidence as proof. This argument was rejected by the Second Circuit Court following the assertion that while it may be difficult to differentiate real from virtual images, the government is not obligated to offer any specific type of proof as evidence for or against real images. In this case, without proof of evidence, the conviction was upheld (Bird, 2011).

The case of *United States v. Whorley* (2005) further illustrates the difficulties the government faces when prosecuting individuals based on virtual images of child pornography. Whorley was found guilty of possession of 20 Japanese *anime* comics that included drawings of children engaged in sexual acts, as well as sending and receiving emails detailing fantasies about child molestation. On appeal, the defendant argued that the legislation under which he was charged (the PROTECT Act) was unconstitutional because it included cartoon images as illegal materials. The Fourth Circuit Court ruled that even though the law did not require the depiction of a real child, the inclusion of the obscene provision, reintroduced since its abolishment in the CPPA of 1996, constituted an exception. The inclusion of the obscene provision was enough to make the act constitutional, as the statute operates under the premise of prohibiting obscene speech, and not just prohibiting child pornography. One Circuit judge believed Whorley had a valid argument

TABLE 10.2. *PROTECT Act Amendments from the COPP Bill*

Defining child pornography	The definition of sexually explicit conduct was changed to include computer-generated images. Visual depictions were changed to include underdeveloped films and videotapes and digital images that are indistinguishable. This category also included two new paragraphs that defined "graphic" and "indistinguishable" in the context of child pornography.
Child pornography offenses	Certain activities relating to material constituting or containing child pornography including mailing, shipping, reproducing, and distributing were added as acceptable actions for which to charge and prosecute a defendant.
Pandering offenses	Pandering offenses were added, meaning that an individual who knowingly advertises, promotes, presents, distributes, or solicits through the mail could be subject to charges and prosecution.
Selling, distribution, and possession offenses	Longer prison terms were added for these offenses; however, shorter prison terms remained practical, depending upon the defendant's level of involvement in the offense.
Distribution of child pornography to minors	A provision was added that any individual who knowingly distributes child pornography to minors could be subject to charges and prosecution.
Affirmative defenses	A provision was added stipulating that the burden of proof must be shifted to the defendant to prove the person depicted in the material was not a minor.
Obscene visual representation of sexual abuse of children	A provision that a person who knowingly depicts, creates, distributes, draws, paints, or sculpts a child engaged in sexual explicit conduct and is obscene and lacks serious or artistic merit should be subject to charges and prosecution.

and challenged the obscenity provision on its inability to consider the issue of freedom of speech by the individual. Despite this, Whorley was convicted on all counts of possession and of sending and receiving child pornography materials. He appealed to the U.S. Supreme Court in 2010, but it was denied (Bird, 2011).

Since *United States v. Whorley*, other cases have raised similar constitutional concerns. In *United States v. Ryan*, it was argued that since virtual children are not real children, possession of this type of material is a victimless crime. Similarly, in *United States v. Mees*, it was argued that drawings of children have no age, and therefore age could not be determined on a nonexistent child. In both cases, the obscenity provision was upheld and was instrumental in ascertaining the constitutionality of the legislation (Bird, 2011). Many cases are currently before the courts with issues similar to those described in *United States v. Irving, United States v. Whorley, United States v. Ryan*, and *United States v. Mees* (Bird, 2011). It is apparent that U.S. lawmakers are trying to balance the commonly challenged arguments concerning freedom of speech, harm to children, and society's views of child pornography as "morally reprehensible."

Canadian Legislative Approaches

In contrast to early U.S. approaches, the first significant Canadian legislation specifically addressing the problem of child pornography was not enacted until

1993. Prior to 1993, legal concerns about child pornography were sparse, while the level of obscenity in sexualized materials was the subject of frequent discussion. It was not until 1985 that child pornography offenses were first expanded in the Criminal Code (Casavant & Robertson, 2007; Gillespie, 2011). The progression of child pornography legislation within Canada is summarized in Table 10.3.

The three most influential pieces of legislation to date are Bill C-128, Bill C-15a, and Bill C-2. It wasn't until Bill C-128: An Act to amend the Criminal Code and the Customs Tariff (child pornography and corrupting morals), under section 163.1 of the Canadian Criminal Code (CCC), that Canadian law specifically targeted child pornography offenses. It sought to prevent harm to children by prohibiting all forms of child pornography, including both written and visual materials (Akdeniz, 2008; Casavant & Robertson, 2007; Gillespie, 2011).

At the time of its enactment, this was the only legislation in Canada that used the term "pornography"; all previous legislation concerning sexualized material used the term "obscene" under the CCC obscenity standards. This legislative focus on obscenity is similar to the American Miller test (Casavant & Robertson, 2007). Section 163 of the CCC outlines the definition of obscene since *Regina v. Butler*, by which sexualized material is evaluated:

> [B]y its nature the conduct at issue cases harm or presents a significant risk of harm to individuals or society in a way that undermines or threatens to undermine a value reflected in and thus formally endorsed through the Constitution or similar fundamental laws by (a) confronting members of the public with conduct that significantly interferes with their autonomy and liberty, (b) predisposing others to anti-social behavior, or (c) physically or psychologically harming persons involved in the conduct.
>
> (S. 163 CCC as referenced in Casavant & Robertson, 2007)

One of the most controversial cases that arose directly after the inception of Bill C-128 was *Regina v. Langer*. Langer was a Toronto-based artist charged in 1993 for displaying artwork depicting children engaged in various sexual acts at his gallery. The charges were dropped the following year, but a forfeiture order was sought for the destruction of Langer's art. In response to the forfeiture order, Langer's art was ruled legal because the judge ruled the materials had "artistic merit" despite being "shocking and disturbing." The prosecutor also failed to convince the judge that the material in question posed a "reasonable risk of harm to children," which was the major focus of Bill C-128. This case highlighted the problems associated with determining the artistic merit of art that could be considered child pornography (Casavant & Robertson, 2007; Gillespie, 2011; Schell et al., 2007).

Although Bill C-128 was crafted primarily to protect children, the 1999 landmark case of *Regina v. Sharpe* identified key problems with enforcement. Sharpe was charged with two counts of illegal possession and two counts of possession

TABLE 10.3. *Significant Canadian Legislation in Addressing Child Pornography*

Year	Name of Legislation or Committee	Significant Amendments	Landmark Cases
1983	Fraser Committee	Formation of committee for the legal discussion on pornography and prostitution	
1984	Committee on Sexual Offenses against Children and Youth (Bagdley Committee)	Recommendations were made by the Bagdley Committee for new child pornography offenses prohibiting production and sale of such materials.	
1985	Royal Assent of Bill C-38: An Act to amend the Criminal Code and the Customs Tariff (child pornography and corrupting morals)	Inclusion of obscenity standards for evaluation of pornographic materials; recommendation of pornography law reform by the Fraser Committee	*Regina v. Butler* (1992) Ruling upheld constitutionality of obscenity standards in legislation, regardless of freedom of speech concerns.
1993	Royal Assent of Bill C-128: An Act to amend the Criminal Code and the Customs Tariff (and corrupting morals)	New child pornography laws; addition of "artistic merit" defense	*Regina v. Langer* (1995) Langer was acquitted of charges due to "artistic merit." *Regina v. Sharpe* (2001) This case involved the creation of child pornography materials for personal use and obtaining child pornography materials for sale and distribution. The case was brought to the Supreme Court of Canada and Sharpe was found guilty of sale and possession of the materials; however, he was acquitted of the production of written materials.
2002	Royal Assent of Bill C-15A: An Act to amend the Criminal Code and other Acts	New amendments included adding provisions to include prohibition of online child pornography and Internet luring and making it an offense to "knowingly" access child pornography.	
2005	Royal Assent of Bill C-2: An Act to amend the Criminal Code (Protection of Children and other Vulnerable Persons) and the Canadian Evidence Act	New legislation incorporating previously failed laws (Bill C-20 and Bill C-12) with special focus on protecting children and vulnerable persons; legislation replaced "artistic merit" with "legitimate purpose" in child pornography cases; new category of offense "voyeurism," prohibiting secretly videotaping a minor for sexual purposes; inclusion of advertising for child pornography as an offense; increase of mandatory minimum sentences for child pornography offenses.	*Regina v. Beattie* (2005) Ruling held that a case of material describing sexual activity between child and adults did not encourage sexual abuse of children nor did it advocate for it to be pursued. There was no evidence to suggest the material was distributed, and the case was dismissed.

for the purposes of distribution and sale. The material in question involved self-created photographs and written material. The ruling, heard by the British Columbia Supreme Court, was found to be unconstitutional. It was argued that since the law was in place to protect children, Sharpe should not have been charged, since there was no evidence to suggest he had actually harmed a child (Akdeniz, 2008; Casavant & Robertson, 2007; Doyle & Lacombe, 2000; Persky & Dixon, 2001; Schell et al., 2007). Controversy arose about the invasiveness necessary to prove guilt in cases where the defendant had not directly harmed a child. Further, it was questioned whether the Supreme Court of Canada needed proof that the depictions harmed children when the creator was using them only for personal use (Akdeniz, 2008; Casavant & Robertson, 2007; Doyle & Lacombe, 2000; Persky & Dixon, 2001; Schell et al., 2007).

The charges against Sharpe for possession were dismissed on the rationale that the invasiveness necessary to prove guilt was unconstitutional; however, the charges for possession for the purposes of distribution and sale were upheld. The defense argued that strict possession in the absence of performing any other actions with the material was not a criminal act in a free democratic society. The Crown argued that accessing and possessing child pornography is itself an incentive to the "market" of such materials, and concerns regarding invasiveness necessary to prove guilt should not be an excuse. The Supreme Court ruling outlined several associations between possession of child pornography and harm to children: it promotes sexual fantasies of children, it encourages cognitive distortions by those in possession of it, it is used in victim grooming, and children are sexually abused in the production of such material (Akdeniz, 2008; Casavant & Robertson, 2007; Doyle & Lacombe, 2000; Persky & Dixon, 2001; Schell et al., 2007).

During the retrial, the defense argued that Sharpe's written material had artistic merit and did not encourage the commission of sex crimes against children. Sharpe was found not guilty of possession of the written material due to "artistic merit," and he was found guilty only of possession of the photographs, since there was no evidence to suggest that he did not distribute the material (Akdeniz, 2008; Casavant & Robertson, 2007).

As a result of the findings in the Sharpe case, Bill C-15A: Child Pornography and Luring Children over the Internet was introduced as an act to amend the CCC. It was given Royal Assent in June 2002. This bill introduced offenses such as accessing child pornography and "communicating with a child for sexual purposes via a computer." There were also amendments to the CCC making any child pornography-related charges an automatically indictable offense with prison terms from five to 10 years (Akdeniz, 2008; Casavant & Robertson, 2007; Doyle & Lacombe, 2000; Persky & Dixon, 2001). Bill C-15A emphasized the concept of "intent" as critical for prosecution. For example, if a defendant accidentally came across child pornography material while browsing the Internet, it could not be assumed that he had intent to search for that material (Akdeniz, 2008; Casavant & Robertson, 2007; Mackay, 2005).

In 2005 Bill C-2: An Act to Amend the Criminal Code (Protection of Children and Other Vulnerable Persons) was introduced to remedy the perceived deficiencies of Bill C-15A. This amendment was enacted in response to confusion in child pornography laws after the Sharpe case. The revision clarified the definition of *materials* to include any written material, visual representation, or audio recording. Mandatory minimum sentences for those convicted of child pornography charges were also added to Bill C-2. These changes mark the first time that Canada ratified the United Nations Protocol on the Rights of the Child by endorsing and agreeing upon their definition of child pornography. The concept of intent was kept in Bill C-2 and added as an aggravating factor to child pornography charges (Akdeniz, 2008; Carr & Hilton, 2011; Casavant & Robertson, 2007; Gillespie, 2011; Mackay, 2005). Although Bill C-2 abolished the "merit of art" defense, which was controversial in previous legislation, the defense could still technically be used in cases where the material was instrumental in the administration of natural sciences or social justice. This includes any material depicting nude children for non-sexual purposes. Further, the defense could be used if no risk to individuals under the age of 18 could be identified (Akdeniz, 2008; Casavant & Robertson, 2007; Mackay, 2005).

Commonalities between the U.S. and Canada's child pornography legislation have focused on identifying what material type and characteristics constitute child pornography. Both countries have faced questions about the criminalization of personal written material and the extent to which such material is harmful to children. Indeed, most prosecutions for child pornography charges in Canada, the United Kingdom, and the United States are based on photos or videos depicting nude children or sexual acts with children; prosecutions based strictly on personal written material remain relatively rare (Akdeniz, 2008; Gillespie, 2011).

■ EXAMINING MATERIAL THROUGH A CLINICAL LENS

The primary difference in the clinical as compared to the legal conceptualization of child pornography is a focus on the capacity to invoke sexualized feelings or fantasies. Determining criteria using this perspective can be difficult in legal contexts where an objective definition is preferred. The range of materials that can be arousing to an individual with a sexual interest in children can be extensive. Such materials can include visual depictions (i.e., family photo albums or children's clothing catalogs), written literature (i.e., sexualized or erotic stories involving children), or even physical materials (i.e., articles of children's clothing or a toy). Such material may not meet legislative definitions of child pornography but may still play a significant role in eliciting sexual feelings toward children.

Research conducted by Lanning (1992) made a significant early contribution to understanding the clinical role with the distinction between child pornography and "child erotica." He argued that separate from the sexual explicitness of child pornography, child erotica refers more broadly to any child-related material that serves a sexual purpose for the individual possessing it. The importance of this distinction is to highlight potential sexual meaning in a wider range of materials, not all of which exhibit the sexual explicitness seen in child pornography. When looking at materials found in child pornography offenders' collections, typically a range of materials may include clothed children, nudity, erotic posing, and explicit materials of the sexual assault of a child.

Such materials can be placed on a continuum of deliberate and explicit sexual harm to the child. Materials in a collection can fall anywhere on this continuum. Collections may include seemingly innocent, nonsexualized material, such as a scrapbook of pictures from the children's pajama section of a department-store catalog, to materials depicting explicit and sexually aggressive assaults on a child. Even if an individual's collection does not necessarily meet the legal definition of child pornography, it may still be problematic from a clinical perspective as it may reinforce his deviant sexual desires and fantasies. In some cases it has been predicted that the sexualized use of such materials may facilitate a contact sexual offense (Healy, 2004; Lanning, 2001; Sinclair & Sugar, 2005; Wells et al., 2007; Wortley & Smallbone, 2012).

By examining collections on this continuum, the approach provides information on the legality of the materials in the collection while also providing a broader clinical understanding of the preferred material type and specific child characteristics of interest to the collector (Taylor & Quayle, 2003; Wells et al., 2007; Wortley & Smallbone, 2012). This emphasizes a psychological approach to understanding the range of materials that are attractive or arousing to an adult with a sexual interest in children, many of which would not meet the legal criteria for child pornography.

Such a continuum permits the construction of a graded system by which to understand the range of materials that people with a sexual interest in children may possess. Research conducted by a team from the COPINE (Combating Pedophile Information Networks in Europe) Project set forth a grading system of materials found in collections of individuals with a sexual interest in children (Taylor, Holland, & Quayle, 2001). This 10-point scale is still used and referred to throughout Europe and North America.

Within the COPINE classification system, *Indicative* material, at the first level of the scale, includes nonerotic, nonsexualized images depicting children in their underwear or bathing suits. Typically this material comes from commercial sources or family photo albums. Although such images on their own do not elicit concern, the context or organization of the material may indicate problematic interests. *Nudist* and *Erotica* are COPINE categories that include images of nude or seminude children in legitimate settings or play areas seen by many as a safe environment (i.e., a child in a bathtub).

The COPINE posing categories (*Erotic Posing, Explicit Posing,* and *Explicit Erotic Posing*) include deliberately posed images that range from being suggestive of sexuality to a pose emphasizing the genital area. *Explicit Sexual Activity* includes images of a child or children (in the absence of an adult) participating in self-touching, mutual masturbation, and oral and penetrative sex. *Assault* includes images of children being subject to sexual assault through digital touching by an adult. *Gross Assault* refers to more obscene images of sexual assault on a child by an adult that includes mutual masturbation, oral sex, and penetrative sex. *Sadistic/Bestiality* images include children being tied, bound, or beaten and animals involved in sexual behavior with children. Sadistic images can occur with or without acts of bestiality (Benzeluk, 2009; Taylor et al., 2001).

The COPINE categorization attempts to combine materials that would meet legal definitions of child pornography with materials that may be clinically significant. Some of the materials in these categorizations would not in and of themselves be indicative of inappropriate sexual interest; rather, it is the context in which these materials are organized and stored that may lead to concern about their use for sexual stimulation. The intention of child pornography legislation is not to penalize nonabusive parents who simply have photos of their children in the bath or playing in the nude, but to criminalize the production and possession of materials depicting sexual abuse or nude photos of children in which the possessor would have no legitimate reason for possessing such materials (Taylor & Quayle, 2003; Wortley & Smallbone, 2012). A problem with this approach is that most sex offenders against children are well known to the victim and may have an excuse for possessing the images, such as being the child's parent (Benzeluk, 2009; Freeman-Longo, 1996; Greenfield, 1997; Wortley & Smallbone, 2012).

In most jurisdictions materials that would fall into *Nudist, Erotica,* or *Erotic Posing* categories would not meet legal criteria for the definition of child pornography. However, they may be considered by clinicians to be significant or problematic in nature (Taylor et al., 2001). Investigators should be trained to include borderline material in their considerations (Benzeluk, 2009; Lanning, 1992, 2001). For example, if the only photos found are pictures in a family photo album of a child in a bathtub that is known to everyone in the family, there is less cause for concern. However, if the same photos are located in a neighbor's home, stored in a location with other child pornography, or as part of a homemade collage of children from department-store flyer photos, this would raise concerns about the intended purpose and use of such materials. Materials suggestive of a sexual interest in children that do not meet the legal criteria for child pornography are often used as corroborating evidence during a trial (Healy, 2004).

"Pedophilia" is a clinical term that refers to an individual with a persistent sexual interest in children. The following are the criteria for pedophilia as set out in the American Psychiatric Association's proposed *Diagnostic and Statistical Manual of Mental Disorders* (DSM-V):

A. Over a period of at least 6 months, recurrent, intense sexually arousing fantasies, sexual urges, or behaviors involving sexual activity with a prepubescent child or children (generally age 13 years or younger).

B. The individual has acted on these sexual urges, or the sexual urges or fantasies cause marked distress or interpersonal difficulty.

C. The individual is at least age 16 years and at least 5 years older than the child or children in Criterion A. (APA, 2013)

Materials depicting nude children or children involved in overt sexual acts, legally identified as child pornography, have also been suggested to play a vital role in sexual fantasy and can be used for sexual gratification by men or women with pedophilia (Benzeluk, 2009; Gillespie, 2011; Lanning, 1992, 2001; Seto, Maric, & Barbaree, 2001; Wortley & Smallbone, 2012). Seto, Cantor, and Blanchard (2006) investigated whether the use of child pornography is a valid indicator of pedophilia by assessing the child pornography interests of a group of sexual offenders. The sample included a group of child pornography offenders, a group of men charged with sex offenses against children (with no known child pornography offenses), a group of men charged with sex offenses against adults, and "general sexology patients." Participants underwent penile tumescence testing to determine arousal patterns across a normal–pathological spectrum based on a series of images and/or audiotapes. Results were interpreted as showing that child pornography offenders were more likely to show a pedophilic pattern of sexual arousal than were all other groups. In this study, men with child pornography offenses were almost three times more likely to be identified as pedophilic based on their phallometric responses than sexual offenders with child victims but no child pornography offenses. The authors of this study concluded that a history of child pornography offending is a valid indicator of pedophilia. The same authors offered an explanation for their results by pointing out the risk of relying on in-person child sexual abuse, since not all those who offend against children meet the clinical criteria for a diagnosis of pedophilia. Conversely, when men choose the type of pornography they are going to view, it is usually consistent with their sexual interests. Therefore, child pornography offenders would be expected to have a higher phallometric pedophile index than men who only have a history of sexual offenses against children. This reasoning is supported by research by Quayle and Taylor (2002) that included interviews with 13 child pornography offenders. Participants acknowledged that the material they downloaded was consistent with the content in their sexual fantasies and that the pornography was obtained to enhance sexual arousal.

■ CONCLUSIONS

The Internet and technological advances have created a new and anonymous way for offenders to produce, view, store, and distribute child pornography. The number of criminal investigations into online child sexual exploitation has exploded over the past two decades. The increasing number of individuals who possess and distribute child pornography has raised concern regarding the use of the Internet by individuals who have a sexual interest in children and the law enforcement challenges associated with combating these offenses.

In this chapter we have shown the need to pay careful attention to the definition of child pornography, the definition of a "child," and the context in which the questions are considered. There are difficulties surrounding the legal definition of child pornography compared to material that would be deemed clinically significant. Many of the problems with defining child pornography are rooted within cross-jurisdictional enforcement, determination of what constitutes a "child," and the separation between age of consent for sexual activity versus participation in the production of child pornography.

One positive aspect of the increasing popularity of child pornography is that child pornography arrests appear to bring men and women with pedophilia to attention at a stage when they are fantasizing about sexual interactions with children but perhaps before they have acted on their fantasies. A second positive aspect is that child pornography may provide a substitute to hands-on offending. While neither possibility excuses the production of child pornography, both suggest important areas for investigation and future research.

■ DISCLOSURES

Lisa Murphy and Rebekah Ranger have no conflicts of interest to disclose.

J. Paul Fedoroff confirms he has no conflicts of interest. He has received funding from Janssen Pharmaceuticals for two consultant workshops; the University of Ottawa Medical Research Fund; and the American Academy of Psychiatry and the Law Research Foundation.

■ NOTE

1. For a list of worldwide ages of consent, see http://www.avert.org/age-of-consent.htm

■ REFERENCES

Adler, A. (2008). All porn all the time. *N.Y.U. Review of Law and Social Change, 31*(695), 1–16.
Akdeniz, Y. (2008). *Internet child pornography and the law: National and international responses.* Hampshire, England: Ashgate Publishing Limited.
American Library Association v. Thornburgh, 713 F. Supp. 469 (1989).
American Psychiatric Association (2013). *Diagnostic and Statistical Manual of Mental Disorders,* 5th ed. Washington, DC: American Psychiatric Association.
Arnaldo, C. A. (2001). *Child abuse on the Internet: Ending the silence.* United Nations Educational, Scientific and Cultural Organization (UNESCO) & Bergahahn Books.
Ashcroft v. Free Speech Coalition, 535 U.S. 234 (2002).
AVERT: Averting AIDS and HIV (2011). *Worldwide ages of consent.* Retrieved from http://www.avert.org/age-of-consent.htm

Baartz, D. (2008). *Australians, the Internet and technology-enabled child sex abuse: A statistical profile*. Canberra: Australian Federal Police.

Babchishin, K., Hanson, K., & Hermann, C. (2011). The characteristics of online sex offenders: a meta-analysis. *Sexual Abuse: A Journal of Research and Treatment, 23*(1), 92–123.

Benzeluk, K. (2009). *Child sexual abuse images: An analysis of websites by Cybertip.ca.* Premier Printing, Winnipeg, Manitoba: Canadian Centre for Child Protection.

Berkowitz, C. (2009). Child pornography: Legal and medical considerations. *Advances in Pediatrics, 56*, 203–218.

Bird, P. (2011). Virtual child pornography laws and the constraints imposed by the First Amendment. *Barry Law Review, 16*, 161–178.

Bryant, M. (2011, August 6). *20 years ago today, the World Wide Web opened to the public.* Insider: Part of the Next Web Family. Retrieved from: http://thenextweb.com/insider/2 011/08/06/20-years-ago-today-the-world-wide-web-opened-to-the-public/

Bunzeluk, K. (2009). *Child sexual abuse images*. Winnipeg, Manitoba: Canadian Centre for Child Protection.

Camero, J., & Yambot, I. (2009). *House wants to ban pornographic cartoon*. House of Representatives of the Republic of the Philippines. Retrieved from: http://www.congress.gov.ph/press/details.php?pressid=3253

Canadian Criminal Code, R.S.C. 1985.

Carr, A. (2004). *Internet traders of child pornography and other censorship offenders in New Zealand*. Wellington, New Zealand: Department of Internal Affairs.

Carr, J. (2001). *Proceedings from the 2nd World Congress on Commercial Sexual Exploitation of Children*. ECPAT International, Theme Paper on Child Pornography. Bangkok, Thailand.

Carr, J., & Hilton, Z. (2011). Combating child abuse images on the Internet: International perspectives. In J. Davidson & P. Gottschalk (Eds.), *Internet child abuse: Current research and policy* (pp. 52–78). New York: Routledge.

Casavant, L., & Robertson, J. (2007). *The evolution of pornography law in Canada.* (Publication No. CIR 84-3E). Law and Government Division, Government of Canada.

Cattaneo, C., Obertova Z., Ratnayake, M., Marasciuolo, L., Tutkuviene, J., Poppa, P., Gibelli, D., Gabriel, P., & Ritz-Timme, S. (2012). Can facial proportions taken from images be of use for ageing in cases of suspected child pornography? A pilot study. *International Legal Medicine, 126*, 139–144.

Cybertip (2008). *Cybertip.ca: Canada's National Tip-line for Reporting Online Sexual Exploitation of Children*. Retrieved from: www.cybertip.ca

Davidson, J. (2011). Legislation and policy: Protecting young people, sentencing and managing Internet sex offenders. In J. Davidson & P. Gottschalk (Eds.), *Internet child abuse: Current research and policy* (pp. 8–26). New York: Routledge.

Diamond, M., & Uchiyama, A. (1999). Pornography, rape and sex crimes in Japan. *International Journal of Law and Psychiatry, 22*(1), 1–22.

Doyle, K., & Lacombe, D. (2000). Scapegoat in risk society: The case of pedophile/child pornographer Robin Sharpe. *Studies in Law, Politics and Society, 20*, 184–194.

Edwards, S. (1994). Pretty babies: Art, erotica or kiddie porn. *History of Photography, 18*(1), 34–36.

Enough is Enough (2008). *Making the Internet safer for children and families: Statistics.* Retrieved from: http://www.enough.org/inside.php?id=3K03RC4L00

Fedoroff, J. P. (2012). *Sex crimes and the World Wide Web*. Panel presentation at American Academy of Psychiatry and the Law 2012 Annual Meeting, Montreal, Quebec.

Ferraro, M. M. & McGrath, M. (2005). *Investigating child exploitation and pornography: The Internet, the law and forensic science*. Burlington, MA: Elsevier Academic Press.

Finkelhor, D., Mitchell, K. J., & Wolak, J. (2000). *Online victimization: A report on the nation's youth.* Alexandria, VA: The National Centre for Missing & Exploited Children. Retrieved from: http://www.missingkids.com/en_US/publications/NC62.pdf

Finkelhor, D., & Ormrod, R. (2004). *Child pornography: Patterns from NIBRS.* Washington, DC: U.S. Department of Justice Office of Justice Programs, Office of Juvenile Justice and Delinquency Prevention.

Freeman-Longo, R. (1996). Feel good legislation: Prevention or calamity. *Journal of Child Abuse & Neglect, 20*(2), 95–101.

Free Speech Coalition v. Reno, U.S. 9th Circuit Court of Appeals, 97-16536 (1999).

Gillespie, A. (2010). Legal definitions of child pornography. *Journal of Sexual Aggression, 16*(1), 19–31.

Gillespie, A. (2011). *Child pornography: law and policy.* New York: Routledge.

Grant, A., David, F., & Grabosky, P. (1997). Child pornography in the digital age. *Transnational Organized Crime, 3*(4), 171–188.

Greenfield, L. (1997). *Sex offenses and offenders: An analysis of data on rape and sexual assault* (pp. 1–39). Washington, DC: U.S. Department of Justice.

Healy, M. (2004, Aug. 2). *Child pornography: An international perspective.* Computer Crime Research Center. Retrieved from: http://www.crime-research.org/articles/536/

Hughes, D. M. (2001). *Recent statistics on Internet dangers.* Retrieved from: http://www.protectkids.com/dangers/stats.htm

Hughes, D. M. (2002). The use of new communications and information technologies for sexual exploitation of women and children. *Hastings Women's Law Journal, 13*(1), 129–148.

Internet Watch Foundation (2007). *Internet and charity report.* http://www.iwf.org.uk/accountability/annual-reports/2007-annual-report

Internet Watch Foundation (2008). *Annual report.* http://www.iwf.org.uk/accountability/annual-reports/2008-annual-report

Internet Watch Foundation (2010). *Internet and charity report* http://www.iwf.org.uk/assets/media/annual-reports/Internet%20Watch%20Foundation%20Annual%20Report%202010%20web.pdf

Ito, K. (2005). A history of manga in the context of Japanese culture and society. *Journal of Popular Culture, 38*(3), 456–475.

Jenkins, P. (2001). *Beyond tolerance: Child pornography on the Internet.* New York: New York University Press.

Jewkes, Y. (2012). Online child pornography, pedophilia and the sexualized child: Mediated myths and moral panics. In E. Quayle & K. Ribisl (Eds.), *Understanding and preventing online sexual exploitation of children* (pp. 116–132). New York: Routledge.

Jonsson, L., & Svedin, C.G. (2012). Children within the images. In E. Quayle & K. Ribisl (Eds.), *Understanding and preventing online sexual exploitation of children.* (pp. 23–43). New York: Routledge.

Kimpel, A. (2010). Using laws designed to protect as a weapon: Prosecuting minors under child pornography laws. *NYU Review of Law and Social Change, 34,* 299–337.

Klain, E., Davies, H., & Hicks, M. (2001). *Child pornography: The criminal justice system response.* National Center for Missing & Exploited Children, U.S. Department of Justice.

Krone, T. (2004). A typology of online child pornography offending. *Trends and Issues in Crime and Criminal Justice, Australian Institute of Criminology, 279.*

Lanning, K. V. (1992). *Child molesters: A behavioral analysis.* Washington, DC: National Centre for Missing and Exploited Children.

Lanning, K. V. (2001). *Child molesters: A behavioral analysis.* Washington, DC: National Centre for Missing and Exploited Children

MacKay, R. (2005). *Bill C-2: An Act to amend the Criminal Code (Protection of Children and Other Vulnerable Persons and the Canada Evidence Act).* (Publication No. LS-480E), Law and Government Division, Government of Canada.

McLelland, M. (2005). *A short history of "hentai."* Retrieved from: http://intersections.anu.edu.au/issue12/mclelland.html

McNicol, T. (2004). Does comic relief hurt kids? Is the eroticization of children in Japanese anime a serious social problem or just a form of rebellion? *The Japanese Times.* Retrieved from: http://ecpat.net/eng/Echild pornographyAT_news/japantime.htm

Miller v. California, 413 U.S. 15 (1973).

New Frontier Media Inc. (2012, Oct 7). Interactive stock chart for New Media Frontier, Inc. Retrieved from http://www.bloomberg.com/quote/NFM:GR/chart

New York v. Ferber, 458 U.S. 747 (1982).

O'Donnell, I., & Milner, C. (2007). *Child pornography: Crime, computers and society.* Willan Publishing, U.K.

Osborne v. Ohio, 495 U.S. 103 (1990).

Ost, S. (2009). *Child pornography and sexual grooming: Legal and societal responses.* Cambridge University Press.

Palmer, T. (2004, Feb. 4). Just one click from abuse. *The Guardian.* Retrieved from: http://society.guardian.co.uk/children/comment/0,1144430,00.html

Persky, S., & Dixon, J. (2001). *On kiddie porn: Sexual representation, free speech and the Robin Sharpe case.* Vancouver: New Star Books.

Poitras, G. (2010, April 20). *The teacher's companion to the Anime Companion.* Retrieved from: http://www.koyagi.com/teachers.html

Prentky, R., Dowdell, E., Fedoroff, P., Burgess, A., Malamuth, N., & Schuler, A. (2010). *A multi-prong approach to strengthening Internet safety.* U.S. Office of Juvenile Justice and Delinquency Prevention.

Purdy, C. (2005, November 20). Fire case of child-porn cartoons. *Edmonton Journal.* Retrieved from: http://www.make-it-safe.net/eng/news_archives/2005_10_20_01.asp,.

Quayle, E., & Jones, T. (2011). Sexualized images of children on the Internet. *Sexual Abuse: A Journal of Research and Treatment, 23*(1), 7–21.

Quayle, E., & Sinclair, R. (2012). An introduction to the problem. In E. Quayle & K. Ribisl (Eds.), *Understanding and preventing online sexual exploitation of children* (pp. 3–22). New York: Routledge.

Quayle, E., & Taylor, M. (2002). Paedophiles, pornography and the Internet: Assessment issues, *British Journal of Social Work, 32*, 863–875.

Regina v. Beattie (2005) 75 O.R. (3d) 117.

Regina v. Butler (1992) 70 C.C.C. (3d) 129.

Regina v. Langer (1995) 97 C.C.C. (3d) 290.

Regina v. Sharpe (2001) SCC 2. File No. 237376, 26 January 2001.

Schell, B., Martin, M., Hung, P., & Rueda, L. (2007). Cyber child pornography: A review of the social and legal issues and remedies—and a proposed technological solution. *Aggression and Violent Behavior, 12*, 45–63.

Seto, M., Cantor, J., & Blanchard, R. (2006). Child pornography offenders are a valid diagnostic indictor of pedophilia. *Journal of Abnormal Psychology, 115*(3), 610–615.

Seto, M., Maric, A. & Barbaree, H.E. (2001). The role of pornography in the etiology of sexual aggression. *Aggression and Violent Behavior, 6*, 35–53.

Sher, J. (2007). *One child at a time: The global fight to rescue children from online predators.* Random House Canada.

Sinclair, R., & Sugar, D. (2005). *International based sexual exploitation of children and youth: Environmental scan.* The National Child Exploitation Coordination Centre, Research and Development. Ottawa, Ontario.

Taylor, A. (2012, Sept. 13). Henson delivers a fresh body blow in latest show. *Gippsland Times & Maffra Spectator.* Retrieved from: http://www.gippslandtimes.com.au/story/327772/henson-delivers-a-fresh-body-blow-in-latest-show/

Taylor, M. (1999). Proceedings from the International Conference "Combating Child Pornography on the Internet": The Nature and Dynamics of Child Pornography on the Internet. Vienna, Austria.

Taylor, M., Holland, G. & Quayle, E. (2001). Typology of pedophile picture collections. *The Police Journal, 74*(2), 97–107.

Taylor, M., & Quayle, E. (2003). *Child pornography: An Internet crime.* Hove: Brunner-Routledge.

United States v. Irving, 452 F.3d 110 (24th Cir. 2006).

United.States. v. Jacobson 503 U.S. 540 (1992)

United States v. Maxwell, 42 M.J. 568, 574 (A.F.C.C.A. 1995).

United States v. Osborne, 935 F.2d 32, 37 (4th Cir. 1991).

United States v. Whorley, 386 F. Supp. 2d 692 (2005) affirmed, 550 F.3d 326 (2008).

United States v. Williams, 553 U.S. 285 (2008).

Wastler, S. (2010). The harm in "sexting"? Analyzing the constitutionality of child pornography statutes that prohibit the voluntary production, possession, and dissemination of sexually explicit images by teenagers. *Harvard Journal of Law and Gender, 33,* 687.

Wells, M., Finkelhor, D., Wolak, J., & Mitchell, K. (2007). Defining child pornography: Law enforcement dilemmas in investigations of Internet child pornography possession. *Police Practice and Research, 8*(3), 269–282.

Wolak, J., Finkelhor, D., & Mitchell, K. J. (2005). *Child pornography possessors arrested in Internet-related crimes: Findings from the National Juvenile Online Victimization Study* (Publication No. NCMEC 06–05–023). Alexandria, VA: National Center for Missing & Exploited Children.

Wolak, J., Finkelhor, D., & Mitchell, K (2011). Child pornography possessors: Trends in offender and case characteristics. *Sexual Abuse: A Journal of Research and Treatment, 23*(1), 22–42.

Wolak, J., Mitchell, K. J., & Finkelhor, D. (2003). *Internet sex crimes against minors: The response of law enforcement.* Washington, DC: National Center for Missing and Exploited Children.

Wortley, R., & Smallbone, S. (2012). *Internet child pornography: Causes, investigation and prevention.* Santa Barbara, CA.

Young, K. (2000). Proceedings from the 108th Annual Meeting of the American Psychological Association: Profiling cybersex addiction and true online pedophilia among virtual sex. Washington, DC.

PART THREE

Implications and Considerations for Professionals

11 Parenting Through the Digital Revolution

■ ANDREW B. CLARK

Effective parenting of preteens and teenagers has never been easy, and the advent of the digital age presents parents with a novel set of challenges. The current generation of children has grown up with a great deal of their social lives, exploration of the world, and developing sexuality played out on the Internet, and many parents struggle to maintain an authoritative presence in what is often a unfamiliar and rapidly changing domain. As parents attempt to strike the often-delicate balance between protecting and guiding their children on the one hand, and allowing appropriate freedom and autonomy on the other, they need tools and skills to extend their sphere of influence into their children's digital lives.

Parents' worries in regard to the Internet are not different in kind from those worries that preceded the digital age, but the unique aspects of the Internet do heighten certain risks. In addition, children's relative comfort and facility with navigating the online world can make it easier for them to engage in poorly supervised behaviors, beyond the oversight of responsible adults. For many parents, trying to navigate the Internet will always feel a bit like speaking a foreign language badly, and they may end up feeling disempowered in the face of their children's native ease with the medium. The recent rapid rise of mobile devices such as smartphones and tablets means that Internet access for youth is no longer restricted to the family's home computer but rather can occur wherever the child happens to be.

Given these challenges, this chapter will consider a range of dilemmas parents may face as they seek to understand, advise, and supervise their adolescent children within the current digital age. This includes an overview of the sexually related online behaviors in which teens engage, the importance of parents' developing a basic digital literacy, the merits and limitations of monitoring software, and the research base on fostering healthy communication with adolescents about sex and sexuality, both online and offline. The chapter emphasizes the ongoing central role of certain basic parenting strategies in the digital age—for example, being aware of and knowledgeable about their children's activities, protecting them from risk, and communicating guidance and family values.

■ INTERNET-RELATED SEXUAL RISK

The Internet-related risks that parents worry about can be divided into three categories: inappropriate exposure to pornographic material, inappropriate online sexual communication with peers (including sexual harassment and bullying), and vulnerability to predators.

With the advent of the Internet, many of the practical impediments protecting teenagers and children from exposure to pornographic images have disappeared—an individual is no longer required to physically go into a store or order material through the mail to access pornographic images. It can be exceptionally easy for a curious adolescent to access a wide range of sexually violent or sadistic pornographic images over the Internet, and disturbingly common for children of any age to inadvertently stumble upon pornography during innocent Internet browsing. In a large survey of youth ages 10 to 17, about one third reported having had an unwanted exposure to Internet pornography within the past year (Wolak, Mitchell, & Finkelhor, 2007). There is concern that such exposure, whether inadvertent or deliberate, may be psychologically harmful to children and teenagers of any age, and some evidence that exposure to sexual content in the media as a whole can influence sexual attitudes and speed up the initiation of sexual behavior for some adolescents (Brown, L'Engle, Pardun, Guo, Kenneavy, & Jackson, 2006; Villani, 2001).

The technology available to teenagers with mobile phones makes it possible for them to easily create and publish a sexualized digital image of themselves. What many teens do not appreciate is that even though the image may have been produced in the context of a close personal relationship, or in the privacy of one's own bedroom, it can then be widely disseminated and can never be fully erased. Many teens may not understand that such images usually violate legal statutes around child pornography, and they may not have the judgment to anticipate the potential impact of the misuse of such images. Clay Calvert discusses this matter from a legal perspective in greater detail in Chapter 5.

The Internet has, for some teenagers, become a forum for teasing, mocking, and bullying of others, sometimes with a sexualized dimension. It is possible that the illusion of anonymity that the Internet provides, and the youth's experience of a lack of adult oversight, acts to foster such maladaptive behaviors.

As children and teenagers have come to spend more and more time online, child predators have followed them, using social networking as a medium through which to pose themselves, develop emotionally engaged online relationships, and then seek to obtain pornographic images or arrange real-world encounters. The dangers of predatory pedophiles have received a great deal of media attention over the past several years, arousing deep fears for many families. At the same time, researchers in the field point out that there is no systematic evidence that children are at an increased risk of danger through Internet-related contacts than they had been previously, and that the great majority of pedophilic exploitation overall is committed by individuals who are well known to the family. In regards to the youth who are involved, the Harvard University Berkman Center Safety and Technical Task Force (2008) concluded, after a comprehensive literature review, that most cases of sexual solicitation of minors over the Internet involved postpubescent youth who were aware that they were meeting an adult male for the purpose of engaging in sexual activity. Nevertheless, the Internet does provide predatory adults with new opportunities for seeking out vulnerable children (see, for example, Chapter 9), along with new opportunities for teenagers to exercise poor judgment around their sexual behaviors.

■ **HEALTHY ASPECTS OF INTERNET SEXUALITY**

As children's lives and social interactions have moved online to a significant degree, the Internet has become a major medium for teenagers to express and explore their sexuality in a normative manner. Chatting and flirting with opposite-sex peers, communicating perceptions, opinions, and experiences about peers, and seeking information from peers around sexual matters are all time-honored early-teen activities that have moved in recent years, to some extent, from the square dance to the mall to the chat rooms.

The Internet is a broad and deep (and sometimes unreliable) ocean of information, and many children and teenagers turn to it for education regarding sexual matters. For many teenagers it provides a stigma-free opportunity to ask potentially embarrassing questions about sexual topics, perhaps especially in situations where teens feel uncomfortable speaking openly with their parents. Parents can play an important role in helping their children become critical consumers of information, discerning authoritative and trustworthy sources of information.

For older teens, Internet-based dating has become an increasingly common method of meeting individuals for potential romantic partners, and Internet-based friendships can develop romantic dimensions even in the absence of significant real-world interactions. Teenagers who are somewhat unconventional, whether through appearance or affliction or sexual orientation, may find the Internet a much more hospitable and welcoming forum to explore their romantic interests than, say, their high-school cafeteria.

For some parents, the child's exposure to certain sexualized images or material online can be seen as part of normal psychosexual development. Teenage boys in particular use the Internet to view sexually explicit images; in one large study 38 percent of 16- and 17-year-old boys, but only 8 percent of same-age girls, had used the Internet for this purpose over the past year (Wolak et al., 2007). For many parents of older teens, especially those who are close to moving out of the house, blanket restrictions on online viewing come to seem less useful (and perhaps less possible) than tolerating limited access in the context of a discussion of the family's values and sensibilities.

Although the dangers posed by the Internet to children are novel and unique in certain ways, the fundamental strategies for parents in helping to keep their children safe remain unchanged. Educate yourself regarding your children's lives and activities online; protect your children by setting appropriate limits; monitor your child's Internet activity; and communicate with your child about what occurs.

■ TALKING TO CHILDREN ABOUT OFFLINE SEXUAL ACTIVITY

Conversations with children and teenagers about Internet-based sexual behaviors are embedded in, and very much a part of, the larger conversations that parents have with their children about sex. In families where such broader conversations are fraught, sparse, or nonexistent, it may be difficult to create satisfying communication regarding the more unfamiliar world of Internet sexuality.

The experience of talking to their children about sexuality has been awkward and difficult for many parents, even before the development of the Internet. Indeed, the caricature of the anxious, clumsy parent having the "Big Talk" with their often-perplexed child has become a comedic staple and captures some of the difficulty parents have in initiating a genuine dialog with their child about such a potentially charged topic. The development of the Internet, adding another (often unfamiliar) dimension in which children seek to explore and express their sexuality, may be seen as a further challenge to parents who may already feel mystified and somewhat helpless about how to communicate and influence their child's burgeoning sexuality. Parents who struggle around discussing real-world sexuality with their children are unlikely to find their conversations about Internet-based sexual matters to be significantly more satisfying or effective.

A growing body of research suggests that parental communication with children about sexual matters can have a significant impact on the choices they make, such as early sexual activity, high-risk sexual behaviors, multiple sexual partners, and condom use (Parkes, Henderson, Wright, & Nixon; 2011; Weinman, Small, Buzi, & Smith 2008). Indeed, in a national survey of teenagers, parents were overwhelmingly identified as having the most influence over their decisions about sex, compared with peers and the media (Albert, 2012). A majority of teenage boys, and a substantial majority of teenage girls, wish they had waited longer before having sex; at the same time, 87 percent of teenagers said it would be easier for them to delay sex if they could have more open conversations with their parents about the topic.

There is good reason to fear that many teenagers are not receiving adequate guidance from their parents about sexual matters. In national surveys of adolescents, only one in ten reported having discussed sex with their parents before engaging in sexual behaviors. Asked to grade their parents on their "understanding of teen sex," only a third of teenagers gave them grades of average or better, and about 30 percent of older teenagers report never having had a conversation with a parent about sexual matters (Albert, 2012).

Research indicates that the most effective conversations between parent and child about sexual matters occur early and often (Martino, Elliot, Corona, Kanouse, & Schuster, 2008). For younger children, this may involve discussions about their bodies, gender differences, and zones of privacy, as well as the topic of appropriate and inappropriate touching. The birth of a new child or pet can provide natural opportunities for age-appropriate discussions of reproductive matters. Parents can begin discussing, in age-appropriate ways, issues related to relationships, intimacy, and commitment with even very young children.

For school-age children, who may be receiving a great deal of both information and misinformation from peers and the media, parents can began to address more overtly sexual matters and can continue to reinforce family values dealing with healthy and responsible relationships and sexual behaviors. School-age children are often confused and sometimes distressed by the sexual information to which they are exposed and are prone to making erroneous and sometimes bizarre interpretations of the fragmentary pieces of information they have at hand. Parents who broach sexual topics with their children at this stage, and who develop expectations of openness and frankness in their discussions, lay the groundwork for a more mutually satisfying mode of communication when the storms and silences of adolescence begin to appear.

For many parents, their children's rapidly developing sexuality takes them unawares, and they underestimate the amount of sexual knowledge that their child has accumulated, as well as the possibility that their child has begun to engage in some form of sexual activity. National surveys of teenagers conducted by the Centers for Disease Control and Prevention indicate that about one third of ninth-grade children and two thirds of twelfth-graders had had sexual intercourse, with about one third of high-school students being sexually active at any given time (National Campaign to Prevent Teen and Unplanned Pregnancy, Fast Facts, 2012). For parents of preteens, the challenge is not simply to accurately discern where they are at in regards to sexuality, but to anticipate where they will soon be, so that the parents can help in some ways to equip their children when they are faced with novel and often-bewildering sexual opportunities (Beckett, Elliot, Martino, Corona, Klein, & Schuster 2009). Parents can engage in "anticipatory guidance" with their preteens, helping them to envision and think through expectable challenging scenarios.

Parents are sometimes concerned that frank discussions of sexuality may offer an implicit message of approval to their child, and that the sexually aware teen is more likely to become the sexually active teen. There are few research data to support this concern; on the contrary, teenagers who have good communication with their parents about sexual matters are actually less likely to engage in early sexual activity (Levine, 2011). There is an active debate around abstinence-only sexual education versus a more comprehensive reproductive education approach, but in both cases the scope of concern encompasses a broad range of topics that go far beyond the mechanics of sex, and provide rich opportunities for parents to communicate foundational family values dealing with relationships, intimacy, and trust.

While parents are generally good at talking to teenagers about factual aspects of sexual behaviors, such as the risk of sexually transmitted diseases or the need for contraception, there is a range of more delicate and potentially awkward topics that often prove more challenging—these include masturbation, orgasms, proper condom use, and the parents' own sexual experiences as teenagers. Perhaps surprisingly, an overwhelming majority of teenagers indicate in surveys that they would like to talk to their parents more about relationships rather than simply being told about risks and contraceptive techniques. While the prospect of discussing a topic such as masturbation with one's child may seem daunting or even terrifying to many parents, it may be much easier to do if it is just one of a long series of sexually frank discussions that have been ongoing for years, rather than a *de novo* introduction of a previously avoided topic.

Skillful parenting often involves knowing when to delegate responsibilities, and many couples find that one or the other has more facility or standing to engage in conversations about sex with their children. Parents sometimes lean on trusted others in the family circle, such as a favorite uncle or godparent, to help provide their child with knowledge, resources, and useful relationships about sexual matters.

Recurrent conversations between parents and teenagers are likely to help parents overcome the awkwardness of "the Big Talk," allow opportunities for a range of topics and questions to be addressed, and demonstrate the parent's interest and commitment. (Martino et al., 2008) Although most parents feel awkward at some point in talking with their child about sex, recurrent conversations allow for that discomfort to dissipate and help in developing more relaxed and bilateral communication. While there may be a certain amount of specific information that the parent wishes to communicate to the child, these conversations are also opportunities for the parent to learn from the child about the things that worry or puzzle him or her, and about the child's struggles in developing and navigating intimate relationships.

■ PARENT EDUCATION AND DIGITAL LITERACY

For many parents, the digital world will always feel like something of a foreign place, and their children's facility and familiarity with digital activities and resources create a barrier to the parents' ability to understand and influence the child's Internet activities. Therefore, parents must achieve some basic level of digital literacy in the service of helping to guide and protect their children online.

Parents can access a wide array of trustworthy Internet-based resources to help them learn more about Internet-based activities, and Internet safety in particular. These include parent resource or Internet safety sites from the American Library Association (2008), the Federal Communications Commission (2013) the Federal Bureau of Investigation (U.S. Department of Justice, 2012) and the nonprofit groups GetNetWise and Common Sense Media. As might be expected, these sites often represent groups with a range of perspectives and perceived sense of Internet danger. In addition, many school districts provide information about

Internet safety for children, either on their own websites or through local discussion groups and talks.

Professionals who are involved in helping parents develop their Internet supervisory skills can enhance their own effectiveness by becoming familiar with a few parent education sites, viewing the sites together with the parent in the room, and then providing the parent with the link to that site. Such facilitated guidance is likely to be more effective for many parents than simply providing them a listing of resources.

Another approach to enhancing digital literacy is for a parent to become an active participant in Internet-based social activities, such as by creating his or her own profile on social networking sites. Many parents ask their children to "friend" them on Facebook, or otherwise allow them the same degree of access as their peers, so they can intermittently monitor the child's online activity. As in the real world, however, the prudent parent may not choose to comment aloud on all that he or she hears or sees.

In a similar vein, asking children to take a parent on a tour of their favorite Internet sites can be an opportunity for parents to learn both some of the nuts and bolts of digital literacy and a great deal about their child's experiences online. With the child in the role of expert, and a parent's attitude of curiosity and engaged interest, a "guided tour" of the child's digital world can be an exceptionally rich opportunity for a parent to learn about the child's life online.

■ RESTRICTING CHILDREN'S ONLINE ACTIVITIES

Parents may be well advised to develop the habit of placing time restrictions on their child's Internet use and overall media exposure from an early age. In addition, many children find that being online just before bedtime interferes with their ability to fall asleep. Allowing children to have a computer in their own bedroom or, increasingly, allowing a child to have an Internet-enabled phone, allows them a significantly greater degree of autonomy in their Internet explorations; these transition points provide opportunities for parents to discuss, educate, and set limits with their children.

For younger children who are interested in the Internet, there are a range of Web browsers geared to children of specific ages that limit access to all but age-appropriate material. Acting much like a digital fenced-in playground, these services offer a significant degree of protection against both sexually inappropriate material and rampant commercialism.

Most social media sites such as Facebook and MySpace have set 13 years as the minimum age for teenagers to set up an account, mirroring the restrictions set by Congress in the Children's Online Privacy Protection Act (COPPA). Studies indicate that many younger children have social networking accounts, but this requires them to dissemble about their actual age when signing up.

There are many social media sites for preadolescent and younger children, such as Club Penguin and Disney, that have more restrictive privacy protection and that require parental permission to join. However, parents should carefully assess the level of commercialism their children will be exposed to on these for-profit sites. The American Academy of Pediatrics recommends that the minimum age requirement for social networking sites be respected, due to both safety concerns for younger children on these sites and the message communicated by parents who allow their child to falsify their online information (American Academy of Pediatrics, 2011b).

When setting up a social networking account such as Facebook, a child has an opportunity to choose privacy settings that place meaningful restrictions on how much information he or she reveals. Parents can negotiate with their children over this question and in doing so help to minimize the associated risk. Privacy settings address the question of who is allowed access to online postings (friends only vs. the general public, for example) and whether a child's location can be posted (probably never a good idea), as well as allowing notification whenever a child is "tagged" on someone else's page.

■ MONITORING AS A FORM OF PARENTAL ACTIVITY

A large body of research shows an association between parental knowledge of children's activities and a lower incidence of behavior problems (Dishion & McMahon, 1998). It had long been thought that parents obtained this information from high levels of active monitoring, and on this basis parents have been encouraged to exercise active surveillance of their child's activities (Liau, Khoo, & Ang, 2008). However, more recent research has called this conclusion into question, suggesting that parents gain the most knowledge of their children from child disclosure, and that a parenting style that encourages children to share openly with their parents is the most effective method (Kerr & Statin, 2000; Racz & McMahon, 2011).

Parental Monitoring of Media

Research on parents' attempts to protect children from harmful media exposure (such as television and movies) has focused on several strategies commonly used by families. For younger children, in particular, the strategy of *cocooning* (also known as restrictive mediation) explicitly limits exposure to certain objectionable material. The strategy of *prearming* (also known as active mediation) involves parent–child discussions regarding exposure to questionable content, with a goal of both communicating family values and helping the child become a critical thinker when it comes to the media. Finally, parents of older teenagers often use a degree of *deference* (deliberately choosing not to intervene) in an active attempt to demonstrate trust in their adolescents (Padilla-Walker & Coyne, 2011). Parents who use cocooning (i.e., restriction) as a primary mode of control for older adolescents have been found to be less connected to their children, more likely to engender resentment from their children, and less successful in the long run (Nathanson, 2002). However, parents who use a combination of cocooning (often for younger children) and prearming (as children become teenagers) find it to be a generally successful strategy and feel more connected to their children.

Much of the research on parental monitoring has been done on the medium of children's viewing of television and movies, which is an inherently passive experience. Early research into children's use of the Internet has begun to emphasize the opportunities for children's participatory learning, and for parents to learn from and engage with their children and teens online, making parental monitoring a less hierarchical and more interactive experience for parents (Clark, 2011).

In a study of parental monitoring approaches and website restriction, Lwin, Stanaland, and Miyazaki (2008) found that older teenagers whose parents employed restriction as a primary mode of monitoring had a rebellious "boomerang" response to website-based restrictions, expressing the intent to circumvent them in some ways. Teens whose parents were more active and collaborative in their mediation strategies disclosed the least amount of personal information online in those studies (Lwin et al., 2008). Similarly, in looking at a group of children ages 10 to 16, Byrne and Lee (2011) found that the children's openness to parental restrictions on Internet use was enhanced in situations when the children felt they could talk openly with their parents about difficulties that they encountered online.

A recent survey from the Kaiser Family Foundation (2010) found a substantial increase in the amount of time youth spend in entertainment media, up to a remarkable 53 hours a week (much of which time is spent multitasking). Most of this increase was attributed to the rapid rise in ownership rates of cellphones and other mobile devices. Although only 30 percent of youth said they had rules at home limiting their media use, those who did noted a markedly decreased number of hours spent each day consuming media of whatever sort, affirming the powerful effect parents can have on their children's media use.

Monitoring Children's Online Activities

Many families, especially those with younger children, choose to establish a family computer that remains in a shared area of the house in order to provide a degree of "over the shoulder" monitoring. However, the increasingly popularity of cellphones and personal tablets, and children's ready access to peers' Internet-enabled devices, limits the efficacy of this approach for many older children.

Given the substantial interest of families in effectively monitoring their children's Internet activities, there are a number of popular, mainstream, and user-friendly services that can be very effective (but never infallible) in blocking access to certain sites, monitoring children's activities, calculating total time online, and alerting parents to violations. These include, among others, Norton Online Family, Net Nanny, Microsoft Live Family Safety, and Apple Parental Controls. Installing this sort of software and determining the restrictions to be applied offer opportunities for parents to discuss with children their expectations and standards for Internet use.

Family safety software can be largely effective in reducing the risk that a child will be inadvertently exposed to pornographic images and can monitor and enforce limits on the amount of time a child spends online. It can also provide a parent with a complete history of the child's Internet activities—all computers have this capacity, but surveys show that many teenagers erase their history on a regular basis. After choosing a family safety service, parents need to educate themselves about its functional capabilities, choose the limits to set, discuss expectations with their children, and then monitor the service on a regular basis. As their children grow, the parents and child will likely wish to renegotiate the terms of their understanding in regard to these services.

A recent survey by the National Center for Missing and Exploited Children found that only about 20 percent of families used parental control on Internet-enabled devices, although a majority of parents monitor their children's online activities in some ways. The Pew Internet and American Life Project (2011) found, however, that about 60 percent of parents used some form of parental control. Most parents in the Pew survey favored frank discussions with their children over technical tools as the most effective approach to monitoring Internet activities. Research regarding parental monitoring of teenagers' Internet activities suggests similarly that simple surveillance may be somewhat ineffectual, but that children who communicated to their parents about disturbing Internet experiences were less likely to engage in high-risk Internet behavior (Liau et al., 2008).

In recent years, with the explosion of handheld and portable Internet-enabled devices, more and more parents have begun using monitoring software for their children's cellphones. These applications can monitor children's text messages (and even translate "teen-speak" abbreviations for parents), scour popular social media sites, and scan for inappropriate language. For teenagers who drive and who own a cellular phone, it is possible for a parent to be alerted whenever the teen is texting while driving or is speeding.

For many parents, establishing their own profile on social media sites is the most effective way to come to understand the technology (and gives an opportunity to allow their children to be the experts). Some parents insist that their children "friend" them so they can actively monitor the children's activities online. Before allowing a child or teenager to register on a social networking site, a parent may wish to explore the site in some depth, looking at the nature of the profiles posted and the social norms that seem to be present.

Parents of older teens often choose to actively monitor the child's online activities but try to strike a balance between allowing them an appropriate degree of latitude and privacy and remaining alert to possible dangerous situations. Parents of older teens often realize that their child is likely to be leaving home shortly, so their goal is not so much to provide a blanket protection from possible harm as to prepare the child to become a reasonably responsible young adult.

In monitoring children's Internet behaviors, the technological tools available to parents are, no matter how sophisticated, secondary in importance to the attention, communication, and guidance provided by the parents in regard to these concerns. Ideally, family safety software can serve as a vehicle for meaningful discussions between parent and child about Internet safety and norms.

■ EDUCATING AND COMMUNICATING WITH CHILDREN

Providing a child with an Internet-enabled device is akin in some ways to providing a teenager with a car—it allows for unparalleled opportunities for experience and exploration but brings with it significant risks. Both instances call for a substantial degree of orientation, education, and practice, and in both situations it is likely that mistakes will be made.

In educating their children about the risks of the Internet, parents seek to provide the information necessary for their children to be forewarned and forearmed, and to establish mutual lines of communication on these topics. As noted above, children who feel comfortable talking to their parents about sexual matters in general are the most likely to be willing to speak to their parents about any Internet-related sexual concerns.

Just as children are warned about "stranger danger" in the real world, they need to be informed about the risks of predators and imposters on line. Often these individuals take the time to gradually develop online relationships with their potential victims before introducing any sexual component into the interaction (Wolak, Finklehor, Mitchell, & Ybarra, 2008). Teens can be instructed that such individuals tend to prey on teenagers' interest in romance, risk taking, and adventure, using flattery and sympathy as tools to engage their interest. In talking with children and teenagers about the risk of sexual solicitation, it may be useful to point out that while about one in seven youth have received unwanted sexual solicitation, the great majority of the initiators of such unwanted contact were other teenagers. Helping teenagers think through how best to respond to their peers and acquaintances is therefore an essential element of online safety.

Teenagers who are willing to talk about sex online with people they do not know (or do not know well), teens who post sexually provocative material on their sites, and teens who are alienated from their parents are at significantly increased risk (Mitchell, Finkelhor, & Wolak, 2007). Teenagers can be informed that the risk of sexual exploitation rises dramatically when the online contact move offline, either via telephone, regular mail, or actual personal contact. Teenagers may benefit from education about the definitions and criminal consequences of sending or possessing child pornography. Finally, children and teenagers should be encouraged to report to responsible adults any unwanted sexualized solicitation and to save the interaction for possible investigation.

Wolak and colleagues (2008) point out that most Internet-related sexual crimes fit a model of statutory rape, in which the adult offender develops an intimate relationship with and then openly seduces an underage teenager. In these cases parental restrictions on Internet use may have limited impact, and the youth who are most vulnerable may be those who are least open to influence from their parents. Youth thought to be at high risk include those with a pattern of risky online behavior, and they may benefit from interventions that focus on their interactive patterns online and the nature of their online relationships. May such teens do not regard their online activities as problematic, and for them parents and clinicians may need to combine actual restrictions and encouragement of more positive peer interactions with a more patient "stages of change" model of skill development.

The American Academy of Child and Adolescent Psychiatry, along with the American Academy of Pediatrics, recommend that parents have explicit discussions with their children about the public and enduring nature of information sent out over the Internet. For younger children this may involve emphasizing the need to keep identifying information such as full name and address, date of birth, or social security number to themselves.

Children of all ages need to hear from their parents about the inappropriateness of receiving sexual messages, and the dangers in sending such messages, as well as the illegal nature of such activity.

Older adolescents and even young adults need to be reminded that their Internet persona is open for scrutiny by potential employers and schools (American Academy of Child and Adolescent Psychiatry, 2012; American Academy of Pediatrics, 2011a). In all cases parents must attempt to disabuse the child of the illusion of privacy that the Internet sometimes creates.

■ SIGNS OF CONCERN

The Berkman Center report (2008) points out that the online risks faced by children and teens have more to do with their own psychosocial makeup and family dynamics than the specific media or technology itself. Teenagers who lack emotionally secure relationships with peers or other adults, who have a history of high-risk behaviors, or who are struggling in other aspects of their lives are all at an increased risk of engaging in risky or inappropriate Internet behaviors. Having a group of healthy friends is a powerful protective factor, and parents can actively try to support and facilitate such friendships. Similarly, having close relationships with stable adults, such as coaches, ministers, or extended family, offers a degree of protection from a child being drawn into inappropriate Internet activities.

■ RESOURCES FOR FAMILIES

Before the Internet, many parents learned to leverage their influence by actively collaborating with other parents in the community, particularly the parents of their children's friends. This teamwork helped parents both to share valuable information (often to verify what they may have heard from their own child) and to establish shared social norms such as curfews. Parents who collaborate can reap myriad benefits in regards to their children's digital lives as well, such as establishing shared norms for Internet use times, the kinds of sites on which their children are allowed, and expectations about the use of digital devices during homework times. In addition, parents can agree to jointly oversee the online behavior of their children's friends and report back to the parent if such behavior becomes problematic (Willard, 2007).

■ ENHANCING PROFESSIONAL COMPETENCE

Professional organization such as the American Academy of Pediatrics encourage their members to increase their knowledge of digital technology so they can serve as better-educated references, can provide more informed anticipatory guidance, and can better discern and diagnosis Internet-related issues as they arise. Given the prominent role that the online world plays in the lives of children and teens, professionals who work with young people need to become familiar with Internet-related issues and technology as an essential component of continuing professional education.

■ SUMMARY

As the world of our children and teenagers has shifted increasingly to the digital realm, the challenges facing parents have become more complex and daunting. Extending parental oversight and authority into the online world requires a meaningful degree of digital literacy and an awareness of tools and resources adapted to the rapidly shifting technologies available. At the same time, familiar principles of effective parenting such as learning to engage in substantive conversations about sex, restricting and monitoring children's behaviors, allowing an appropriate degree of freedom and privacy, and talking about difficult subjects continue to serve as basic organizing themes of effective parenting in this regard.

■ **DISCLOSURES**

Andrew B. Clark has no conflicts to disclose.

■ **REFERENCES**

Albert, B. (2012, Aug. 28). Teens (still) say parents most influence their decisions about sex. Retrieved from http://www.thenationalcampaign.org/parents/default.aspx

American Academy of Child and Adolescent Psychiatry (2012). *Facts for families: Children online.* Retrieved from http://www.aacap.org/cs/root/facts_for_families/children_online

American Academy of Pediatrics (2011a). *Talking to kids and teens about social media and sexting.* Retrieved from http://www.aap.org/en-us/about-the-aap/aap-press-room/news-features-and-safety-tips/pages/Talking-to-Kids-and-Teens-About-Social-Media-and-Sexting.aspx

American Academy of Pediatrics (2011b). Clinical report—The impact of social media on children, adolescents, and families. *Pediatrics, 127*(4), 800–804.

American Library Association (2008). *Navigating the 'Net With Your Kids.* Retrieved from http:www.ala.org

Beckett, M. K., Elliot, M. N., Martino, S., Corona, R., Klein, D. J., & Schuster, M. A. (2009). Timing of parent and child communications about sexuality relative to children's sexual behaviors. *Pediatrics, 125*(34), 34–42.

Berkman Center for Internet and Society at Harvard University (2008). *Enhancing child safety and online technologies: Final report of the Internet Safety Technical Task Force to the Multi-State Working Group on Social Networking of State Attorneys General of the United States.* Retrieved from www.cyber.law.harvard.edu/pubrelease/isttf/.

Brown, J. D., L'Engle, K., Pardun, C. J., Guo, G., Kenneavy, K., & Jackson, C. (2006). Sexy media matter: Exposure to sexual content in music, movies, television and magazines predicts black and white adolescents' sexual behavior. *Pediatrics, 117*, 1018–1027.

Byrne, S., & Lee, T. (2011). Toward predicting youth resistance to Internet risk prevention strategies. *Journal of Broadcasting and Electronic Media, 55*(1), 90–113.

Clark, L. S. (2011). Parental mediation theory for the digital age. *Communication Theory, 21*, 323–343.

Dishion, T. J., & McMahon, R. J. (1998). Parental monitoring and the prevention of child and adolescent problem behavior. A conceptual and empirical formulation. *Clinical Child and Family Review, 1*, 61–75.

Federal Bureau of Investigation (2012). *A Parents' Guide to Internet Safety.* Retrieved from http://www.fbi.gov/stats-services/publications/parent-guide.

Federal Communications Commision (2013),TV and Parental Controls, retieved from http://reboot.fcc.gov/parents/tv-and-parental-controls.

Kaiser Family Foundation (2010). *Daily media use among children and teens up dramatically from five years ago.* Retrieved from www.kff.org/entmedia/entmedia012010nr.cfm

Kerr, M., & Statin, H. (2000). What parents know, how they know it, and several forms of adolescent adjustment: Further support for a reinterpretation of monitoring. *Developmental Psychology, 36*, 366–380.

Levine, S. B. (2011). Facilitating parent–child communication about sexuality. *Pediatrics in Review, 32*(3), 129–130.

Liau, A. K., Khoo, A., & Ang, P. H. (2008). Parental awareness of monitoring of adolescent Internet use. *Current Psychology, 27*, 217–233.

Lwin, M. O., Stanaland, A. J. S., & Miyazaki, A. D. (2008). Protecting children's privacy online: How parental mediation strategies affect website safeguard effectiveness. *Journal of Retailing, 84*(2), 205–217.

Martino, S. C., Elliot, M. N., Corona, R., Kanouse, D. E., & Schuster, M. A. (2008). Beyond the "big talk": The roles of breadth and repetition in parent-adolescent communication about sexual topics. *Pediatrics, 121*, e612–e618.

Mitchell, K., Finkelhor, D., & Wolak, J. (2007). Youth internet users at risk for the most serious online sexual solicitations. *American Journal of Preventive Medicine, 32*(6), 532–537.

Nathanson, A. I. (2002). The unintended effects of parental mediation of television on adolescents. *Media Psychology, 4*, 207–230.

National Campaign to Prevent Teen and Unplanned Pregnancy (2012). Fast facts: Teen sexual behavior and contraceptive use: Date from the Youth Risk Behavior Survey 2011. Retrieved from http://www.thenationalcampaign.org/national-data/teen-pregnancy-birth-rates.aspx

National Center for Missing and Exploited Children (2011). *Keeping kids safer on the Internet: Tips for parents and guardians.* Retrieved from http://www.missingkids.com/missingkids/servlet/PageServlet?LanguageCountry=en_US&PageId=3601

Padilla-Walker, L., & Coyne, S.M. (2011). "Turn that thing off!" Parent and adolescent predictors of proactive media monitoring. *Journal of Adolescence, 34*, 705–715.

Parkes, A., Henderson, M., Wright, D., & Nixon, C. (2011). Is parenting associated with teenagers' early sexual risk-taking, autonomy and relationship with sexual partners? *Perspectives on Sexual and Reproductive Health, 43*(1), 30–40.

Pew Internet and American Life Project (2011). *Teens, kindness and cruelty on social network sites.* Retrieved from www.pewinternet.org/Reports/2011/Teens-and-social-media.aspx

Racz, S. J., & McMahon, R. J. (2011). The relationship between parental knowledge and monitoring and child and adolescent conduct problems: A 10-year update. *Clinical Child Family Review, 14*, 377–398.

U.S. Department of Justice, Federal Bureau of Investigation. *A parents' guide to Internet safety.* Retrieved from www.fbi.gov/stats-services/publications/parent-guide.

Villani, S. (2001). Impact of media on children and adolescents: A 10-year review of the research. *Journal of the American Academy of Child and Adolescent Psychiatry, 40*(4), 392–401.

Weinman, M. L., Small, E., Buzi, R. S., & Smith, P. B. (2008). Risk factors, parental communication, self and peer's beliefs as predictors of condom use among female adolescents attending family planning clinics. *Child and Adolescent Social Work Journal, 25*(3), 157–170.

Willard, N. E. (2007). *Cyber-safe kids, cyber-savvy teens.* San Francisco: John Wiley & Sons.

Wolak, J., Finkelhor, D., Mitchell, K. J., & Ybarra, M. L. (2008). Online predators and their victims: Myths, reality and implications for prevention and treatment. *American Psychologist, 63*, 111–128.

Wolak, J., Mitchell, K., & Finkelhor, D. (2007). Unwanted and wanted exposure to online pornography in a national sample of youth Internet users. *Pediatrics, 119*(2), 247–257.

12 Teens, Sex, and Technology: Implications for Educational Systems and Practice

■ ANDREW J. HARRIS
AND JUDITH DAVIDSON

In recent years, policymakers and practitioners have grappled with mounting concerns related to teenagers' self-production and distribution of sexually explicit visual content via cellphone, online social media, and other digital communication technology—a diverse group of behaviors commonly referred to as "sexting." While concern over teen sexting has been particularly pronounced in the United States, growing attention to the issue has emerged in many other countries, suggesting an increasingly global phenomenon (Agustina & Gómez-Durán, 2012).

As schools, juvenile justice systems, and state legislatures have sought to develop appropriate responses, surveys of youth have begun to shed light on the prevalence, nature, and correlates of these behaviors. This research has provided a useful context for understanding the scope of the policy and practice challenges but has not fully elicited youths' perspectives on the sexting issue or examined it in the context of youths' social and developmental experience. Further, little is known about the attitudes and beliefs of parents, educators, and other concerned adults regarding these issues and how those attitudes and beliefs align with those of youth. Gaining such a comparative perspective may help to highlight communication barriers and inform the development of viable interventions to improve youth safety.

This chapter draws from the results from a multistate, mixed-method study investigating youths' and adults' perspectives on teen sexting behavior, its motivations and consequences, and the parameters of effective responses. Over a period of approximately 18 months, our research team collected and analyzed focus group data gathered from youth, parents, and school-based professionals in three states—one in New England, one in the Midwest, and one in the Southeast. The youth focus groups encompassed 123 youth representing nine high schools; the parent groups included 92 caregivers representing the same nine schools; and the school personnel included a diverse group of 110 educational administrators, teachers, guidance counselors, school resource officers, school health professionals, and others. Following data analysis, the research team convened a multisite stakeholder forum—consisting of educational and justice practitioners, policymakers, and youth—to discuss the results and generate policy and practice recommendations.

We begin the chapter with a brief overview of the literature to date concerning the prevalence and correlates of youth sexting behaviors and place those findings into the context of adolescent development in the digital age. Following a discussion of the study's sampling, data collection, and analysis process, we present the dominant themes emerging from our research. We conclude with a discussion of how these results may be placed into the broader context of educational practice, drawing from the stakeholder forum conducted during the latter stage of the study.

■ BACKGROUND: EMERGENCE OF THE "TEEN SEXTING PROBLEM"

Concern over teen "sexting" is a fairly recent phenomenon. Although the legal and policy issues surrounding "self-produced child pornography" had begun to surface among legal scholars as early as 2007 (Leary, 2010), attention to teen sexting in the United States may be largely traced to the December 2008 release of a survey by the National Campaign to Prevent Teen and Unplanned Pregnancy (NCPTUP). This survey, which received widespread media coverage throughout 2009, indicated that approximately 20 percent of teens reported transmitting or receiving sexually explicit images of themselves or peers via their cellphones (National Campaign to Prevent Teen and Unplanned Pregnancy, 2008). The survey's confluence with national news stories such as the July 2008 suicide of an Ohio teen following the dissemination of compromising pictures she had sent to a former boyfriend (Kranz, 2009) and the child pornography prosecution of six teenagers in Pennsylvania (Brunker, 2009) prompted a surge in sexting-related stories and commentary on television, newspaper editorial pages, talk radio, blogs, and Internet message boards.

Amidst this expanded media attention, some commentators questioned the significance and extent of the "sexting problem." Some asserted that survey data collected via Internet surveys or cellphone interviews may have overestimated the magnitude of the behavior by "self-selecting" technology-focused youth (Bialik, 2009). Others suggested that the media's response to the NCPTUP survey results was misguided and that alternative assessments had failed to identify sexting as a widespread practice (Berton, 2009). In evaluating political responses to the issue, some commentators suggested that concerns over sexting were largely driven by generalized adult alarm over the changing modes and norms of teen sexual expression in the information age (Levine, 2009; Lithwick, 2009).

■ EMERGING RESEARCH ON TEEN SEXTING

While much of the initial discourse surrounding teen sexting was based primarily on speculation and limited data, recent years have produced expanded empirical investigation of the phenomenon, leading to a greater understanding of sexting behaviors' scope, dynamics, and correlates. During 2009, additional survey-generated data concerning the incidence, prevalence, and correlates of teen sexting behavior were released by several organizations, including the Pew Research Center (Lenhart, 2009), Cox Communications (2009), and MTV in conjunction with the Associated Press (2009). Throughout 2010 to 2012, several studies began to emerge in peer-reviewed research journals, including analyses of sexting cases coming to the attention of law enforcement (Wolak, Finkelhor, & Mitchell, 2012) and several surveys assessing the prevalence and/or correlates of sexting behaviors among teens and young adults (Mitchell, Finkelhor, Jones, & Wolak, 2012; Dake, Price, Maziarz, & Ward, 2012; Dowdell, Burgess, & Flores, 2011; Strassberg et al., 2012; Temple et al., 2012)).

Definitional and Measurement Issues

Before exploring the prevalence and correlates of teen sexting behavior, it is important to first place these results in context.

The first point of note is that the "sexting" label has been applied to a broad range of behaviors and contexts, not only within popular discourse, but also within the growing body of survey research. The 2009 Pew study, for example, asked respondents to describe scenarios and comment on why teens might engage in these behaviors. Descriptions included the exchange of sexually suggestive text messages, images sent as part of "joking around," images sent in the context of flirting and courtship, and cases that involved clear harassment or intent to embarrass or harm. This broad range of behaviors—typically conflated in the context of media accounts—suggest that the "sexting" label may have limited practical utility and that it is generally more useful to discuss this phenomenon in terms of specific behaviors and motivations.

The diversity of behaviors commonly assigned the "sexting" label is underscored by an analysis of approximately 500 sexting cases that had come to the attention of law enforcement (Wolak, Finkelhor, & Mitchell, 2012). In developing a typology stemming from these findings, Wolak and colleagues distinguished between "aggravated" cases and those they deemed "experimental" cases. Within the aggravated category, they included cases that involved adults, as well as those where there was either an explicit intent to harm or reckless behaviors. Among experimental cases, which encompassed a majority of the cases in their sample, Wolak and colleagues described a wide range of circumstances consistent with developmentally normal, albeit often irresponsible, adolescent behaviors (Wolak, Finkelhor, & Mitchell, 2012).

While this study represented a unique sample consisting of cases severe enough to warrant police involvement, the diversity of circumstances under which sexting behaviors may occur has been supported by the survey literature. The Pew survey data suggest that youth who had engaged in these behaviors reported a wide range of motivations, including gaining the attention of a romantic interest and joking around. These and similar findings suggest that interpretation of any sexting prevalence figures must carefully account for the manner in which the behaviors are commonly framed by in the context of media reports, policy discourse, and research.

Beyond the variety of diversity of covered behaviors, comparing prevalence estimates must also account for differences in survey sampling frames and methods. Many surveys have included non-minor teens and in some cases young adults within their samples, or may have oversampled minor youth at the higher end of the age spectrum (16 and 17 years old). Based on what we know about the effect of age on the likelihood of engaging in these and other sexual behaviors, it should be noted that such a sampling strategy is likely to obscure important distinctions within the teen population. Additionally, the various surveys have been administered through a variety of means, including Internet surveys, phone surveys, and school-based surveys. Each of these approaches is likely to produce its own form of methodological limitations and concerns. While it would be erroneous to assume that one approach is superior to another, awareness of these differences in sampling and potential response bias does help to explain some of the varying results.

Prevalence and Incidence Estimates

Given this definitional ambiguity and methodological variation, it is not surprising that estimates of teen engagement in sexting behaviors have varied considerably. Here, we briefly summarize the research to date regarding the prevalence of these behaviors and attempt to place these results into some general context. To do so, we include separate assessments of the prevalence statistics concerning three sets of activities commonly associated with sexting—producing and sending images of oneself, receiving such images, and transmitting or sharing these images with others.

Creating and sending images—The original 2009 NCPTUP survey reported that 20 percent of teens had sent or posted nude or partially nude images of themselves via Internet or cellphone. Studies from school-based samples confined to specific jurisdictions have produced somewhat higher estimates. A survey of 948 Texas high-school students suggested that 28 percent had engaged in the behavior (Temple et al., 2012), and another school-based study in Utah placed the figure at 18 percent (Strassberg, McKinnon, Sustaíta, & Rullo, 2012). Neither of these studies found statistically significant differences between boys and girls engaging in the behavior, although within both samples the rates for boys were slightly higher. Studies using national samples have generally produced significantly lower estimates—the Pew study from 2009, based on a phone-based sample of 800 youth, indicated that 4 percent of teens aged 12 to 17 reported sending nude or partially nude sexually suggestive pictures; and Mitchell and colleagues, in a 2011 study of 1,560 Internet users aged 10 to 17, suggested that the prevalence of these behaviors may be somewhat lower than that indicated by other surveys, estimating that 2.5 percent of teens indicated that they had appeared in and/or created an image, 1.8 percent had self-produced the image, and 1.3 percent had appeared in or created "images showing breasts, genitals, or someone's bottom" (Mitchell, Finkelhor, Jones, & Wolak, 2012). In reconciling these varying results, it should be noted that the Texas and Utah high-school surveys primarily consisted of youth aged 15 and older, while the two national surveys also included younger youths.

Receiving images—Compared to the numbers of youth who have reported creating and/or appearing in digital sexual images of themselves, the proportion reporting having received such images is two to four times higher. The Pew study suggested that 15 percent reported receiving such an image (compared to 4 percent who had reported creating and sending); the Cox Communication survey reported that 17 percent had received sexts (vs. 9 percent creating/sending); the school surveys out of Utah reported that nearly 50 percent of all boys and 31 percent of girls had been receivers; and the study by Mitchell and colleagues indicated that 7.1 percent (5.9 percent with nudity) reported receiving a sexual image, compared to the 2.5 percent (1.8 percent with nudity) who reported creating or appearing in such an image (Mitchell et al., 2012).

Being asked to send an image—Among the surveys that have evaluated teen sexting behavior, only a limited number have asked youth about their experiences of being asked to send an image of themselves. These experiences, however, may represent salient dimensions of the dynamics of sexting, particularly related to subtly coercive gender dynamics that may be associated with these activities. This experience seems to be far more common among girls than boys—the study by Temple and colleagues, evaluating the experiences of Texas high school students, suggested that more than two thirds (68 percent) of girls and 42 percent of boys had been asked to send a sexting image—a statistically significant difference. Further, 27 percent of girls reported being bothered by receiving such a request, compared to only 3 percent of boys. Beyond gender effects, the study also found that Hispanic and African-American youth were more likely than white youth to send an image upon receiving a request (Temple et al., 2012).

Forwarding and sharing images—Although initial image creation may be thought of as the most troubling within the spectrum of sexting behaviors, the activity of forwarding or sharing may be viewed as the least socially condoned and potentially the most harmful. Whereas sending and receiving activity may often occur within the confines of one-on-one relationships, forwarding and sharing implicitly involves one or more third parties and may typically occur without the consent or knowledge of the image's original sender. This not only suggests a nexus between sexting and bullying behavior but also feeds into potential legal issues surrounding the distribution of illegal pornographic material. In terms of reported prevalence, forwarding behavior seems to occupy a middle ground between creating/sending and receiving. The Utah high school study, for example, indicated that 27 percent of boys and 21 percent of girls have forwarded pictures to others (Strassberg et al., 2012).

Correlates and Risk Factors

While much media and policy discourse tends to focus on the overall incidence and prevalence of sexting behaviors, focusing on such aggregate measures may obscure important sources of variation in these behaviors across the teen population. Notably, data have shown that the probability and nature of sexting involvement varies considerably among teens and is associated with a range of demographic and psychosocial characteristics. Understanding these types of interactions represents a vital link in generating effective responses and solutions.

Age effects—Studies have fairly consistently established a positive correlation between age and various forms of sexting experience, with older teens more likely to have engaged in these behaviors than younger teens (Mitchell et al., 2012; Strassberg et al., 2012; Temple et al., 2012). While it is therefore likely that sexting activity increases with age, these results should be cautiously interpreted for two main reasons. First, surveys have generally framed their questions in terms of lifetime prevalence (e.g., "Have you ever.....") rather than period-based measures (e.g., "During the past month/year, have you..."). Accordingly, it is not surprising that the cumulative experiences of older teens will yield higher numbers than those for younger ones. Although the age effects are significant enough to warrant attention, it remains possible that these effects may not be as pronounced as shown in the data. Secondly, as discussed in our interview data that will be presented in the next section, the motivational and behavioral dynamics for sexting behaviors among younger teens seem to differ significantly from those observed within older teen populations.

Gender differences—Studies have been mixed in their assessment of the differences between genders in terms of overall engagement in sexting behaviors. Examining rates of creating and sending images, some studies have shown significantly higher proportions of girls engaging in the behavior (Cox Communications, 2009, Englander, 2012), while others have shown no significant gender differences (Strassberg et al., 2012; Temple et al., 2012). Studies have been fairly consistent, however, in establishing that certain important gender differences exist in terms of underlying motivations, social conditions, and attitudes toward the behavior. For example, the study by Temple and colleagues found that girls were significantly more likely than boys to have been asked to send an image of themselves, and moreover, that they were nine times more likely to be bothered by such a request. Hence, while the overall rates of engaging in certain types of sexting behavior may ultimately be similar for males and females, it is reasonable to assume that the dynamics of these behaviors are likely to be substantially different across genders— a theme that will be explored in the next section's presentation of interview data.

Risky behaviors—Even prior to the emergence of sexting as a distinct issue of concern, a substantial body of literature examining technology-facilitated risky teen behaviors suggested a strong association between "online" risks and behaviors and "offline" risks and behaviors (Palfrey, 2008). Consistent with this, research conducted to date has been fairly consistent in establishing that youth who engage in sexting behaviors are more likely to be sexually active and more likely to show indications of depression, suicidality, substance abuse, and general mental health symptoms.

A survey of teens in several school districts in a Midwestern state found connections between reported sexting and sexually risky behaviors (i.e., unprotected sex, anal intercourse), mental health symptoms such as depression and suicidality, substance use and abuse, and academic difficulties (Dake & Price, 2012). These findings are consistent with other survey research on teens and young adults that has identified correlations between sexting and mental health symptoms (AP/MTV, 2009) and between sexting and general sexual activity (Rice et al., 2012; Temple et al., 2012). Several studies have shown a relationship between sexting and rates of sexual activity and sexually risky behaviors, particularly among girls (Baumgartner, Sumter, Peter, & Valkenburg, 2012; Temple et al., 2012). Additionally, a study of California teens found that knowing someone who had engaged in sexting behaviors was strongly associated with the individual's own behavior, consistent with broader public health literature showing that behavior among adolescents is strongly tied to perceptions of normative behavior among peers (Rice et al., 2012).

■ SEXTING IN A DEVELOPMENTAL RISK FRAMEWORK

A critical reading of the survey literature suggests that sexting may often occur within the bounds of normative adolescent social relationships and, for some youth, may reflect developmental immaturity in which immediate gratification is prioritized over concerns about long-term consequences. From a social vantage, it is also important to view these behaviors as embedded within a broader framework of youth norms and culture, including differing generational views of privacy and the manner in which teens view communication technology as an integral part of their social lives (Lenhart, Ling, Campbell, & Purcell, 2010; Marwick, Murgia-Diaz, & Palfrey, 2010).

Yet while much of the "sexting problem" may be attributable to these types of social and developmental factors, certain aspects of the issue command the attention of practitioners and policymakers. Notably, those who work directly with youth in educational and juvenile justice settings recognize the behaviors' potential linkages to various forms of peer-based aggression such as cyber-bullying, dating violence, coercion, and sexual exploitation. This is consistent with research cited above suggesting that the potential for risky online behaviors is not equally distributed among teens, and the "psychosocial makeup of and family dynamics surrounding particular minors are better predictors of risk than the use of specific media or technologies" (Palfrey, 2008).

■ FOCUS OF CURRENT STUDY

The growing number of youth surveys that have been conducted since the original NCPTUP report have thus provided an emerging picture of the general prevalence of certain behaviors, the distribution of these behaviors across age and gender, common sexting scenarios, and general motivations. The survey research has also yielded useful data concerning teen knowledge, attitudes, and beliefs about sexting and its consequences. Yet these studies have been limited in their ability to fully capture and reflect the "youth voice" that is vital to understanding sexting behaviors and to framing attempts to effectively address sexting within appropriate social, behavioral, attitudinal, and subcultural contexts. Additionally, none of the research studies has gathered the views of parents, educators, and other concerned adults and compared those views to those of youth—a vital point of comparison for purposes of crafting effective responses.

To address this gap in the research, a multidisciplinary team from the fields of criminal justice, psychology, public policy, and educational research—including the current authors—collected questionnaire data and conducted focus groups with 123 youth (55 boys and 68 girls), 92 parents, and 110 educators and other school-based professionals across three states and a range of communities between March 2011 and March 2012. The project was designed to understand and compare youth and adult perspectives on sexting and related issues and to inform the development of effective, proportional, and properly targeted responses.

The project's primary goal was to develop recommendations that can inform law and policy, system responses to sexting incidents, and prevention initiatives involving youth, schools, communities, and families. As part of this process, the research team convened a policy and practice integration forum in fall 2012 to enlist a select group of youth, parents, policymakers, and practitioners to help translate the study findings into actionable guidelines and recommendations.

The following findings stem from the analysis and synthesis of the focus group data from all three phases of data collection. The findings presented here aim to depict the general themes that emerged from the three phases of data collection, with an emphasis on comparing the views of the main stakeholder groups—youth, parents, and school-based professionals. Following the presentation of these findings, the final section of this chapter draws upon the outcomes of the 2012 forum to summarize the challenges involved in addressing this issue and to present a series of principles for balanced and informed responses.

■ SEXTING: TEEN, PARENT, AND PRACTITIONER PERSPECTIVES

Role of Technology in the Lives of Youths

All three groups of participants—youths, parents, and practitioners—recognized the pervasive role of technology in the social lives of young people. The groups, however, diverged in their attitudes toward this trend. Understandably, discussion of problems related to youths' use of technology was framed by each group's experiences, concerns, and worldviews. The youths spoke mostly in positive terms, viewing technology as a social facilitator and a necessity. In the words of two teens:

> "It's really important to me. I remember one time, I had to go without a phone for like…it felt, forever, and it was just like the worst time of my life…"

> "Every time I think about it, [I]…kind of die a little bit inside…It's like, oh, I got a text message…I get, like, withdrawal from not having my cell phone all the time. And then if [I don't] have it, I feel my leg vibrate."

Parents and practitioners were mixed in their views about technology and voiced more negative opinions than the youths about technology itself and its effect on teens' lives and communication. One parent stated:

> "[these are] just the social norms established right now. So they'll be at the dinner table texting. They'll be at a function texting. I mean, they just don't have the self-control to put it away and kind of manage that."

These general sentiments about the centrality of technology in teens' lives were echoed in many comments by school practitioners, including this one:

> "I have worked at a school where the policy was if you're caught with a cell phone or some type of technology, you either get suspended for two days, or the technology device has to be confiscated for two days. And probably more often than not, way more than 50 percent, the students were willing to take the two-day suspension and keep their device."

Some practitioners suggested (and many youth anecdotes confirmed) the idea that technology may serve to magnify the intensity of certain social interactions, leading to certain problems such as cyber-bullying. For example:

> "what I found really interesting is the fighting over the cell phone…their level of communication that's needed in relationships to get through any conflict is not there because now they're using the technology to argue with each other, and to fight. A student will say 'he was yelling at me.' How did you know he was yelling at you? [laughter] You know? So they already know, you know the tone in the text…So now their conflict resolution is all done via texting, they would rather text than confront the person face to face."

Defining "Sexting" and Patterns of Behavior

Consistent with the definitional issues explored in the prior section, all three sets of participants in our focus groups—youth, parents, and practitioners—struggled to describe exactly what "sexting" is. As one teen put it,

> "Sexting...I don't know...it's kind of vague to me...I've heard a lot about it on TV and news and stuff. It kind of went through a trend for a while...everybody was talking about all these charges...I guess I don't really have a definition. I don't really know. Inappropriate things being texted or sent via text message?"

These sentiments were echoed by our adult groups:

> *Parent:* "when I sent out information about this [focus group], there were people saying, what is that? And I'd have to go into the details...I ended up including a blurb, because I had people saying, what's sexting? And I'd say, you know, think of sex and texting...there were people who didn't know about it, who learned from me what it was."

> *School Practitioner:* "I think for me the obvious examples are easy to find...the pictures...Where I fall down a little bit is appropriate versus inappropriate...exactly what is that definition? Does it go down to certain words? Does that cover flirting and what is over the line with flirting? So it gets a little bit confusing in those areas for me."

In terms of specific patterns of behavior, teen participants spoke of a wide range of scenarios, including those involving sending, receiving, and forwarding pictures within a wide range of contexts, including experimentation, joking around, romance and courtship, and (less frequently) aggression/intent to harm. Youth in our groups also commonly raised the transmission of sexually explicit text messages, with some suggesting that such messages may often be more disturbing and problematic than the transmission of pictures. In general, parents and practitioners spoke of a narrower spectrum of behaviors than those cited by youth, generally those involving negative consequences.

How Common Is It?

As a cluster of behaviors, both youths and practitioners appeared to agree that sexting is an emerging part of teens' social landscape. These quotations provide a lens into these sentiments:

> *Youth Participant:* "I think it's a lot more common than people think. Because I hear about it a lot...but I don't know, it's just not frowned upon. It's weird because it's not like shocking when you hear that any more. That's what I'm realizing right now. I'm not judging anyone...I'm not weirded out, I don't feel uncomfortable. I'm kind of freaked out because it's not frowned upon."

Practitioner 1: "As a middle-school counselor, I think 50 percent of the kids might've been exposed to it, but it's probably frequent for about 25 percent, 20 percent of the kids are getting it all the time."

Practitioner 2: "I think that it's out there. I think it's happening. But I don't think it's as much as people think is happening."

Practitioners felt that sexting behaviors were "common" but seemed primarily focused on the cases that have come to their attention, which typically involved particularly problematic behaviors or situations.

Parents were less certain about the prevalence of sexting behaviors, and their opinions were more based on what they had heard through the media and other second-hand sources than on first-hand knowledge and personal experiences. Notably, parents in our groups varied in their level of attunement to their teens' possible exposure to the behavior. These two quotations, taken from the same focus group in the same community, represent the differing senses that parents have about how common the behavior is:

Parent 1: "When I got the thing to come here, I thought, I don't have any input for this, because I've never, ever heard of this happening, other than an instance in the paper and an instance with an administrator at the school. But I do wonder how prevalent that is. I have not heard of it going on at all."

Parent 2: "I have daughters in high school, so I have a junior and I have a freshman, and we have a lot of kids that come around. It's actually amazing—you guys would really be shocked at how many people and how many kids are doing this. These kids are very readily talking about it … [a]s parents, you've got to talk to each other. Because when one of the kids said, `Oh, I did this,' … I'm immediately on the phone with my friends, saying, `Yeah, you need to stop this now.' We as parents actually talk without the kids knowing. Because if they know that we're talking, then they won't open up. So we actually back door, literally, to each other, very secretively. I hate to say that, but we really do. We'll meet somewhere for lunch or whatever, and we all literally catch up on what's happening. The moms kind of collectively know what's going on, but I am shocked at how often this is happening in the kids."

Motivators and Reasons for Sexting

Consistent with the diverse spectrum of behaviors that may be subsumed under the "sexting" label, participants in our focus groups cited a broad range of motivational factors. In the process of coding and analyzing data in this area, we identified several motivational categories:

- **Social motivators**, including peer group dynamics, gender roles and expectations, courtship and dating rituals
- **Cognitive and/or emotional motivators**, including those related to self-image, need for attention, risk-seeking personality traits, and mental health

- **Developmental motivators**, highlighting adolescent traits such as experimentation, feelings of invulnerability, or impulsivity
- **Environmental motivators**, including influences of family and community, the media, and popular culture.

The varying emphasis that each of our participant groups—youth, parents, and practitioners—placed upon each of these motivational categories provides a critical lens through which to view the diversity of perspectives on the sexting issue.

Youth Perspectives

Among these factors, youths tended to focus primarily on social and cognitive/emotional motivators and to a lesser extent on environmental influences, including media and popular culture. To the extent that developmental factors were indeed referenced, they were typically raised in the context of older teens talking about the relative impulsivity and poor judgment of younger teens.

Evaluating the various motivators of sexting behavior, the research team spent considerable time seeking a viable and meaningful typology to explain teens' motivational influences. Based on this assessment, our data suggest that youths' descriptions of the motivations for sexting may be placed along a spectrum consisting of three general categories, illustrated in Figure 12.1.

At one end of the spectrum is the category we refer to as "mutual interest." In these scenarios, teens spoke of the private exchange of messages or images within the context of a trusting relationship. Considering that teenagers are engaged in active exploration of intimacy and intimate connection, behavior in this category may be framed as a convergence of normal teenage exploration of intimacy and the emergence of digital technology.

At the other end of the spectrum is the category designated as "intent to harm," representing scenarios in which teens spoke of behaviors that were deliberately

Figure 12.1 Motivational Continuum of Sexting Behaviors.

and overtly manipulative and harmful, including transmitting or sharing images with the specific purpose of inflicting harm on another person.

Between these two extremes was a category of behaviors that seemed occupy a prominent place in the world of teens. This involved scenarios that occupy the "gray area" of being neither overtly harmful nor carried out in the context of unequivocal trust and privacy. This encompassed a range of motivators for sexting behavior, such as gaining status among the peer group, attracting attention, or seeking to take a relationship to another level. While these motivators and scenarios varied considerably, it seemed that the common thread linking them together was the phenomenon of self-interest. In some way, all of these scenarios involved engaging in the various forms of sexting behaviors (i.e., sending, receiving, forwarding, or sharing) in pursuit of some instrumental purpose related to one's individual needs.

Of note, the boundaries between these categories tend to be quite porous. For example, one party in a relationship may attribute behavior to mutual interest and trust, while the other party is acting purely out of self-interest. Similarly, youth may often act in harmful ways without being fully aware of the consequences of their behaviors on others.

To the extent that youth recognize developmental factors, they do so by differentiating between the motivators of sexting for younger (middle-school) teens (e.g., experimentation, an alternative to sex, and immature and "stupid" behavior) and the motivators for older teens, which are more often discussed in terms of dating, courtship, intimacy, and adjuncts to sexual relationships (e.g., "a 'gift' for my boyfriend" or a way to quickly identify willing sexual partners). In this way, older teens often describe these behaviors as part of their transition out of childhood and into young adulthood.

Parent Perspectives

As a group, parents we spoke to tended to focus less on social motivators and more on cognitive/emotional (with an emphasis on negative pathological traits), developmental factors, and popular culture. This sequence of quotations from parents reflects these general themes:

"It's a hormonal thing."

"They don't really think things through."

"They don't see the consequences of their acts because once it is out, they really freak out."

"A sense of invulnerability"

As reflected in these quotes, parents tended to attribute the behavior to immaturity and generally did not view teen behavior as a mature form of intimate expression. However, some parents—albeit a minority—recognized that sexting might just be a new way of engaging in typical teen courtship/sexuality. These quotes from two fathers reflect this general sentiment:

"I would agree with number two that I think they think it's no big deal. It's just another way of communicating. Just as we may have, as youth, explored sexuality in very different ways, it's just another medium to that, no big deal."

"If two kids want to send a picture of themselves to each other, you know, it's not something I would encourage, it's not something I think they should do, but if they're going to do that, how is that different than two kids in the backseat of a '57 Chevrolet? You know, or in the back of a buggy out behind the barn, you know, in 1899. You know, it's been around for a long time. If the real issue comes from the potential long-term harm of it, and that's what other people—the bullying of it with a sexual context—is the problem that a lot of people have alluded to, and that—and/or the people making money in the child pornography kind of stuff where it gets forwarded on. And so again, you know, doing it is not as big an issue as—I don't want to say profiting off of doing it, but manipulating or continuing or, again, forwarding it. And that's where the problem is."

Practitioner Perspectives

Practitioners shared a similar range of concerns regarding motivations with parents (and as mentioned earlier, practitioners were in many cases also parents themselves), but in their professional roles they focused more on social and environmental issues than did parents. Practitioners also seemed somewhat more inclined than parents to place sexting into the context of teen psychosexual development. As one educator stated, "They are sexual beings."

As practitioners discussed behaviors that were closer to the continuum area of "intent to harm," these kinds of comments arose: "It's easy, it's attention getting, they're bored, it's a way to bully, and I think some of them have low self-esteem and they don't know any other way to communicate." One practitioner spoke of teens "luring people in a way to punish them or get back to them. They think they can lure someone into the situation, and then use that to humiliate them publicly."

Finally, this comment by a practitioner sums up the concerns both parents and practitioners shared about the environmental pressures teens face in our society: "I think it's just society in general, the sexualization of kids."

Gender Issues

Whether exploring behaviors, motivators, or consequences, both youth and adult participants discussed sexting as a highly gendered phenomenon. There was a striking level of uniformity across the sample that for the most part:

- Boys gain status through sexting whereas girls lose status through sexting (even while thinking that they may gain status).

- Boys are more often considered to be "forwarders" and "requesters" whereas girls are more often seen as "senders" and "instigators."
- Boys engage in these behaviors to brag and gain status; girls engage in these behaviors to gain attention, build trust, and enhance a relationship.

Members of all three groups held similar views about how males and females experienced the impact of sexting. (Our sample did not to our knowledge contain gay, lesbian, bisexual, or transgendered individuals, and almost no mention was made of this group by participants.) The consensus was that boys were tolerated for engaging in this behavior, but girls stood to lose status that could be unredeemable if they were caught engaging in this behavior. The quotations in Table 12.1 are representative of the views participants expressed about the gendered differences facing males and females when sexting.

Despite these shared gendered characterizations of sexting behaviors, our participants noted several exceptions to the "traditional" rules of gender dynamics. For example, youth shared scenarios involving "role reversals"—for instance, boys expressing concerns with their body image, girls asking boys to send them pictures, and girls sharing boys' pictures with their female friends. One girl stated:

" I feel like it might make the girl feel more confident, because when she sends it, and they're like, oh, you look nice, or whatever, then that, like, makes her self-esteem

TABLE 12.1. *Perspectives on Gender Differences*

Teens	*Teen 1 (female):* "And people might call you names, like in the hallways. When they see you, they call you `slut' or whatever. And they'll just yell it, like right in your face."
	Teen 2 (female): "if you're a guy...you do this...and you was the man. You getting backed up and all of this good stuff."
	Teen 3 (female): "Guys are usually more comfortable with themselves, so they would usually just send one to send them...guys usually have to ask girls to send them one...Guys usually just send it and they don't really think about who will this go to. The girls actually think about like, `oh, who else will see this picture if I send it to this person?'"
	Teen (male): "Yeah, they [girls] get called a lot of mean names. Like, there are just reputations around school, and there have been, like, trash...if it were a guy, it would be a little bit more, `Oh, that's, like, you're a stud or you're a player.'"
Parents	*Parent 1:* "For boys it's more like sex, booty-wise. So, you know, it's more girls, there's a competition."
	Parent 2: "I think...too the girls today throw themselves more at the boys, and chase them."
	Parent 3: "I see the girls as being the one who maybe starts it, but the boys are the ones who pass it around."
Practitioners	*Practitioner 1:* "I would say it's not specific to a gender. I think both genders engage in sexting."
	Practitioner 2: "There seemed to be a double standard, that it was acceptable for the boys to ask for these and receive them. But the minute the word got out about the girls sending them, they were complete social pariahs. I mean, they were looked down upon for being `hos,' and slutty, and how could they do this? Even though it wasn't frequent, but it wasn't infrequent."

go up or whatever, and like, saying how girls are, like, more self-conscious and whatever, that makes, like, that probably helps it out."

In the words of another girl:

"Well, and if you hear about it, like if you're a guy, like, and a group of guys, and, like, a guy got a picture from a girl, like, every guy wants to see it. Like, oh my God, like, I love girls. [laughter] But then, like, if you're in a group of girls, and, like, a guy sends a picture, everyone's like, `ew, that's disgusting.' [laughter] Like, `ew, like, no one wants to see that.' Like, I don't know, it's just, like, different views. Like, even the girl getting the picture from a guy, it's, like, I didn't want that. Like, it's gross. But then guys get it, and they're, like, oh my God, yeah. [laughter] So, like, it's just different. Like, girls don't want to see guys, but guys want to see girls. I mean some girls may want to see guys, whatever. But, I mean, every person, like, from every, like, thing I've seen, I know, like, girls are kind of, like, grossed out by getting guys' pictures, and they never really ask for them. They just get them, it's weird. [laughter]"

Parents and practitioners both expressed the sentiment that gender roles have changed from when they were young, with girls behaving more assertively (some said "aggressively") than in prior generations, particularly in the context of flirting and courtship. In the words of one mother from our parent groups:

"The one thing that amazes me about sexting is that the teenagers do not have any modesty, whether they're walking around with their pants hanging down, or the girls, you know, pushed up and out everywhere, so to send a picture like that, it doesn't faze them that there's anything wrong with that. I mean things that were so taboo when I was their age, there's no boundaries anymore. I mean, they feel that it's no big deal they have pictures like that out there, and circumstance I just saw a few weeks ago, when I was a teenager, if someone got pregnant, that was bad. On Facebook, in here, is this young girl, in full display, proud of her pregnancy, with the pictures, with the father, and her sisters, and it's like it's out there for teachers to see, the world to see. I mean, she has very little, and I just don't understand that, yeah, where's the parent, and there's just no sense of modesty anymore. It's not a big deal to be totally exposed, and it's not frowned upon anymore."

Comparing Teen and Adult Attitudes About Sexting

Young people suggested that sexting can be problematic under certain circumstances but expressed the sentiment that adults do not understand and often overreact. Teens also expressed strong views of the negative opinions they believe adults hold of youth. Many of the young people we spoke with complained that adults do not "get" this generation, are incredulous of teen behavior, and have totally forgotten what it was like to be young. These three quotations illustrate these general youth sentiments:

Teen 1: "I think they look down on it. Because they didn't have that, back growing up…They don't understand what it is like…It wasn't [as] easy for them to do that than it is for us to do…so they don't understand."

Teen 2: "I think parents are going to be real judgmental. Like right away, off the bat…but we're like, whatever, like we're their age, we understand…But parents, they're just, like, oh my gosh, like, why'd they do that…and they might judge their parents…or not let you hang out with their kid."

Teen 3: "I just think once you become an adult, when you look back at all of that and, like, hear about, like, a freshman, like, sexting or something like that, you'll just be, like, 'oh, that's immature.'"

While some teens expressed strong negative attitudes toward sexting (e.g., it's dumb, wrong, no one should be doing it, etc.), there was not an overwhelmingly disapproving response from the majority of teens with whom we spoke. Based on our data, it would appear that youth accept sexting as a given in their digital world.

Adults, on the other hand, expressed a more nuanced attitude toward sexting behaviors. Parental attitudes were expressed in fairly negative terms—for instance, "it's just wrong," "it is porn," "it's inappropriate," "weird," "creepy," and "something you don't want to hear about." A smaller number of parents took a more middle-of-the-road position, wondering about how sexting might compare to other behaviors that existed before digital phones.

As a whole, school personnel also spoke of sexting in mostly negative terms, expressing similar sentiments (and using similar language) as the parents. Many, however, expressed a more ambivalent attitude, attempting to explain the behavior in the context of adolescent development.

These two quotations illustrate the ambivalent attitudes adults shared:

Parent: "Sometimes I wonder if a child knows, for instance, if they were sent something for them to forward it on. Like, if they didn't initiate it, you know, kind of, would they consider that sexting?…I mean, to me, you're spreading the rumor, or the message…I mean, who's responsible, I mean, aware, do you take responsibility to stop it?…but I wonder if the kids really think, 'OK, if I got this, I didn't start it, but, oh, wait a minute, like you said, isn't this funny.' Boys think, for instance, things are funny, or even the girls, and they just send it on to somebody else. You know, they didn't initiate it, but they can spread it. And I do consider that sexting."

Practitioner: "I think that as adults, I think our views are very different than that kid's. And I think everybody in here has made a good point that we understand the lasting impact that when you write something down, you know, what's the old adage, if you don't write it down, it didn't happen. So if you write it down, it happened…I think it goes back to, my views on sexuality are probably different from my children, and the children that I work with, simply because I wasn't as sexualized at that age."

In these statements made by adults, one can see the complexity with which adults view the issue of sexting, as compared to the youth perspective. They are aware that the world in which they grew up may differ considerably from that of their child, their children's friends, or the young people with whom they work.

Many of the differences in teen and adult attitudes toward sexting may be viewed and understood in the context of the "here and now" orientation of youth and the "future-oriented" views held by adults. When asked about the differences between teen and adult attitudes toward sexting, parents and practitioners spoke of how teens lack a sense of consequences and accountability; that they think it is no big deal; and that teens think they are invincible.

Communication About Sexting

Youths indicated that they generally do not discuss sexting per se with their peers but rather talk in terms of specific normative behaviors (forwarding, sharing). They indicated that they rarely mention these things to adults.

Parents expressed concern that teens were not likely to approach school personnel with a problem like sexting, as illustrated by these remarks:

Parent 1: "They aren't going to their teachers, because…they think…the teacher's going to tell the next person…I think it'll be all around the school and get back to a parent, and I will be real upset, real upset."

Parent 2: "I don't think that the adult figures at school are seen as a go-to person anymore. I think that the kids are too busy, the adults are too busy, and there's not an open line of communication on things that really matter, much less private aspects of their life."

In contrast, practitioners (in this case school personnel) believed youth would be more likely to speak with them about an issue like sexting than they were to speak with their parents. These two quotations express this perspective:

Practitioner 1: "I think that even if they have a really good relationship with their parents…I don't think that they would talk about this. I think they'd go through a counselor…or to a teacher that they have a really tight relationship with."

Practitioner 2: "It's kind of sad…I don't think they're talking to their parents at all, but I run a lot of open discussion groups…and they bring up sex all the time…and they tell me, they tell me. So they want to talk about it."

Teens' opinions differed remarkably from those of adults—they said they were not likely to speak to either parents or school personnel. Here are some quotations that are representative of this divide between teen and adult:

Teen 1 (communication with parents): "if any kid's parents found out about it, they would, like, kill them, so I don't understand why they would even ever bring it up to them. Like, I don't think I've ever had that conversation with my parents."

Teen 2 (communication with school personnel): "first, you have to be able to trust the teacher and make sure that…it's a respected relationship, and then second, you're going to want to make sure that the teacher's cool, pretty laid-back…they are scared if the school found out what you were doing…that's why they don't want to talk to teachers."

Teen 3 (communication with school personnel): "I mean, teachers try to get all close to me. I mean, it's nice for a teacher to act like they care, and it's nice and all of that good stuff, but, I mean, 'uh-uh' [laughter]."

Teen 4 (communication with parents or school personnel): "if you slip up and say the wrong thing to a guidance counselor or somebody, they'll tell either your parents or the police officer, when it's not that big of a deal."

Perceived Consequences

Youth and adults are both strongly aware that sexting can have negative consequences that will put youth in danger, but the orientations expressed by youth and adults differed considerably. Teens spoke mostly of near-term social impacts such as the effects sexting might have on their reputation, peer relationships, and social standing. In this sense, the youth view reflected the "here and now" orientation that we consider to be part of the developmental stage in which teens can be found. Adults, on the other hand, spoke more of long-term life impacts. Their perspective reflected their future orientation more appropriate to a more mature and experienced viewpoint.

Teen 1 (personal consequences): "[i]t's just embarrassing…the embarrassment you would go through would be awful…you don't think about all the people that could potentially receive this picture…you have to constantly wonder, has this person seen you before? Like, have they seen that picture? It just has to be really stressful and really embarrassing for you."

Teen 2 (legal consequences): "[i]t definitely ruins your life because you have to put it on job applications and college. So that's sort of legal…you're a registered sex offender and that probably means that you can't move to certain places because if you're a sex offender you can't live across from a school."

From the personal perspective, teens fear embarrassment. From the legal perspective, teens project a range of problems they might encounter if they were caught sexting. In keeping with their developmental perspective, they view the legal consequences from a highly personal stance, imagining the problems identification might cause with daily living and future plans.

Not surprisingly, adults' views of the consequences teens will face from sexting are more complex. This parent speaks to the personal and legal issues that teens might encounter if they are caught sexting:

"So you would think that a teenage child would understand that there are consequences to this, but most girls don't even understand that you ain't ready for sex until you're at least 21. So their mind does not mature, because once you get that, you can't take it back. So a lot of things that we think the kids understand, especially about laws, and the wrongness of whatever, a lot of teens don't understand and you'd think they would, but they don't. They don't. Just like they don't understand the consequences. All they know is, if I have sex, I'll get pregnant, but they don't understand that once I have sex with this person, and he don't like me again in the morning, that's going to hurt me worse than getting pregnant."

In this statement, the parent describes how the youth view cannot yet encompass what an adult can understand of the complexity of desire versus reality and the ways emotions can cloud or lead one astray. As this parent points out, the act of sex carries much more with it than the teen can yet comprehend.

Like parents, practitioners were aware of the divide that separated their views of consequences from those of youth. This practitioner expresses a developmental perspective in discussing the youth view of consequences to sexting:

"I think that teenagers have always felt invincible. You know, 'nothing's going to happen to me. I'm not going to get caught, it's OK for me.' It's developmental. I don't think they've reached the age where they realize there are serious consequences down the road. You know, it's their freedom. 'It's my choice. It's my business.'"

Indeed, we did hear teens who insisted that they should be free to conduct their business as they wished and that they were able to make these decisions on their own. Their words sounded much as this practitioner stated.

Practitioners, however, do see young people in the daily light of school, where they frequently talk with them about civics and social life. Their conversations and experiences with teens have taught them that youth may have difficulty making sense of how legally damaging it could be to engage in sexting.

"Just had a conversation with kids the other day, and it seems like time after time after time, no matter how many times you seem to, I don't know, talking to different kids every semester, but no matter how many times you bring out the legal ramifications, you get shocked looks in a classroom. You assume they know, because they're seniors and talking about it in the school system for four years. But somehow it seems to be the shock factor every single time. So my answer is, for some reason, they don't know, many of them don't know."

Members of all groups mentioned legal impacts such as possible prosecution for creating or distributing child pornography and possible sex offender registration status, but far fewer discussed other common types of juvenile justice interventions (e.g., diversion programs). Beliefs, understanding, and assumptions surrounding these areas varied considerably—for youth and parents, much of what they believe seems driven by media accounts rather than primary knowledge. For practitioners, understanding seems more refined and informed in part by direct experience. Given the lack of uniformity regarding legal responses to sexting, it is not surprising that none of the groups demonstrated a firm understanding of possible legal ramifications.

Policy and Practice Responses to Sexting

"I feel as though our textbooks and curriculums are almost moving too slow for the daily pace of life."

This statement from one of the teens participating in our focus groups struck to the core of the divide between youth and schooling, a divide that permeated all discussions. Youth, digital natives, lead rich and complex lives outside of school in which cellphones and texting, the Internet, social media, and many other forms of technology support them to find information, connect with friends, attend to family members, and interact with civic issues, to name just a few of the things they do with digital technology. For many teens, however, entering school is similar to entering the halls of some quaint monastic center, where technology and communication are restricted and carefully guarded. Many chafe at the digital restrictions, which in their mind are pervasive and far-reaching. Sexting seems like only one component of those restrictions that adults (digital immigrants) impose upon them as they struggle to control what they fear and do not understand.

That is not to say that teens want the danger, embarrassment, and legal problems sexting could bring. Indeed, they want to be safe and stay safe, and they know they need parents and other adults to help them to maintain good boundaries and ward off unexpected danger from the outside world. However, they want this safety to be delivered through respectful messages that accompany open conversation about the issue of sexting and with an attitude of trust toward young people. As one teen put it succinctly, "what a parent could do is be more open, talk to us more, try to see what is going on...don't be so quick to judge, don't be so quick to jump on our throat if you see half a thing go bad."

Adults participating in our parent and practitioner focus groups, despite their differing perspectives on certain issues, generally agreed on several key principles regarding responses to teen sexting. First, both groups agreed that schools are limited in their capacity to effectively respond to the sexting issue in the absence of effective parental engagement.

Practitioner: "I'd say...it's the primary role of the parent to parent. The role of the school is to educate. So I think they have a valuable voice in all of that, but at the end of the day, it's the parent's job to raise your kid, and to...create consequences that outweigh the reward and get them to a place where they're, "OK, the risk of this is not worth the consequence that I will face in my home if it comes to light.'"

Parent: "I think, you know, you have to assume responsibility, you have to assume an educational role, you have to be willing to perhaps do things that your kid isn't going to like, you know, as a parent."

Second, parents and practitioners agreed in their concerns about the limits of legal responses. Adults who are parents or who work with youth in a professional capacity are deeply worried about the best ways to shape legal responses to the issue of sexting.

> *Parent*: "But I don't think legislation will change the behavior, personally. I think it's culture. The cultural force is far too big for legislation to stop that train, in my opinion."
> *Practitioner*: "I think one area that needs to be looked at is the law itself. I think that the legislature needs to take another look at it. What it was intended for originally, child pornography, is that what they really meant with kids in high school and junior high sending to each other? And I don't think it should be legalized, but I think maybe there's another alternative that can bring a different charge in that at least still people will bring it forward maybe more, gets to the court level, but it can be dealt with a little differently than a felony level that's gonna be on someone's record for the rest of their life, the way it is right now. So that's something they need to kind of relook at it, that area."

Finally, in discussing the best ways to address the sexting issue, adults in all of our focus groups consistently referenced the need for a multipronged approach. As one parent stated, "You've got to hit it from every angle, where you think you might get to them." One school-based practitioner summed up these general sentiments, stating:

> "I don't think there's the silver bullet, it's got to be...a combination of corporations, school districts, and government entities that get the word out there. And then as educators, the better we equip our kids to make good decisions, no matter what those decisions are, I mean, the kids, you know, ultimately are going to make their own decisions."

■ IMPLICATIONS FOR EDUCATIONAL POLICY AND PRACTICE

So where does this leave us? This final section of our chapter aims to set forth a series of considerations that can help guide educational system responses to growing concern over teen sexting—considerations guided by our research, the research of others, and the input of a wide range of stakeholders participating in our 2012 roundtables. Our discussion consists of two parts, the first framing some of the complex challenges that should be addressed as part of any comprehensive solution and the second setting forth some basic principles that might be employed in responding to those challenges.

Challenge #1—Establishing Narrative Clarity and Consistency

Our research findings, as well as the exchanges that took place in our stakeholder roundtables, suggest that both teens and adults hold diverse views of what the "sexting problem" really is. Beyond the definitional ambiguity discussed earlier in the chapter—the fact that the "sexting" label has tended to homogenize a rather diverse array of behaviors and circumstances—stakeholders differ considerably in their views of exactly why these behaviors are a problem. Common narratives include generalized panic over teen expressions of their sexuality, concern over legal consequences, potential effects on a teen's future life prospects, linkages to bullying and teen dating violence, and reputational impacts stemming from the potentially viral nature of sexts that are transmitted beyond their intended recipients.

Related to this, there is wide divergence among professionals who deal with youth regarding the appropriate messages that should be sent to young people about the consequences of these behaviors. In some respects, one's choice of narrative represents a classic example of the adage "where you stand depends on where you sit." For example, justice system actors such as prosecutors and school resource officers tend to stress messages to youth that emphasize legal ramifications of the behavior; school guidance professionals and health educators may favor approaches that emphasize future prospects or social dynamics; and school administrators may think in terms of implications for school discipline, incident response, and limiting liability.

Discourse surrounding the legal ramifications of sexting presents a particular set of challenges, with messages to youth in this area presenting somewhat of a double-edged sword. Although most agree that use of the legal system should be limited to the most egregious cases and should be used sparingly, it remains common for messages directed at youth to highlight the risks of justice involvement. This divergence between actual practice (i.e., diverting youth from justice system involvement whenever possible) and the implicit message (i.e., serious legal repercussions await if you engage in this behavior) carries great potential for creating a "credibility gap" that could ultimately undermine efforts to address the problem.

Challenge #2—Engaging Families

There is little question that the efficacy of school-based interventions depends in part on the consistency of those interventions with messages received at home and in the community. A major challenge cited by educational practitioners in our focus groups and our subsequent stakeholder forum concerned the challenges of engaging families in response to the sexting issue.

How does one engage families with differing levels of commitment, time availability, geographic constraints, communication preferences, or value systems? No matter how homogeneous the educational setting might seem, there will always be divergence in family views about such fundamental issues such as adolescence, technology, and sexuality. These views may be influenced by a range of factors, including socioeconomics, cultural values, choice of parenting styles, and beliefs about adolescence and the role of schools. Added to this is the paradox that families of youths who are typically at the greatest risk of harm related to sexting behaviors may often be among those that are the most difficult for institutions to engage.

Ironically, in an age where new technologies are in the fore, schools may not have the access to or be as up to speed with technology as some younger parents. Thus, parents are texting but schools are emailing (a form many younger people have given up). Parents may live their lives on Facebook (like their teens), but schools, by administrative policy, may not be allowed to have a Facebook page to communicate critical information with them. It behooves educators to be bold and experimental when it comes to finding the best ways to communicate with the caregivers of today's youth.

Educators are front-line experts in the communities in which they work and must draw upon this expertise to develop appropriate ways to connect with the families with whom they work. There is no one-size-fits-all approach. Most families, regardless of their cultural differences, appreciate authenticity and sensitivity when they find it in their educational system. Hence, while a topic such as sexting may appear to be a difficult one to broach, most caregivers appreciate hearing from those in schools whom they know to be concerned about the safety and well-being of their teens.

Challenge #3—Coordinating Responses

As we learned from our many conversations with the different groups in our study, policy and practice responses to the issue of teen sexting contains many moving parts. Legislative frameworks, school technology policies, incidence response protocols, juvenile justice processes and interventions, primary prevention initiatives, and community norms and values are just some of the many factors that feed into our response. While successful responses depend largely on how these systems and processes are prioritized, and on how effectively they are aligned with one another, each of these areas involves a different set of stakeholders with varying perspectives and concerns. In such an environment, unfounded fears and myths may easily assume a prominent position in guiding our responses.

What seems to be essential in sorting through issues related to policies, laws, and community expectations is distinguishing between the reactive mode that is endemic to responding to sexting incidents and the proactive mode that forms the basis for effective prevention and harm-reduction strategies. While there are undoubtedly points at which these two modes converge—for example, the use of catalyst events as opportunities for preventive interventions or taking action to mitigate the harm caused by an unfolding incident—it remains vital to remain focused on the paramount concern, which is to ensure the safety and well-being of youth.

Challenge #4—Finding the Bandwidth

Another prominent theme emerging from our dialogs with school professionals involves the growing constraints on time and resources, often in response to legislative and regulatory mandates. Schools are increasingly mandated to address a wide spectrum of issues related to curriculum, school safety, and discipline. They are also being asked to address issues such as bullying, teen dating violence, school discipline, bloodborne pathogens, and a multitude of other important concerns affecting the well-being of youth. Sexting is not the only item on the minds of educators. In truth, they have a lot of other things to deal with in the normal school day—instruction, curriculum, assessment—and all of these take time, too. So many asked us, When do you do it all? How does one add this in?

Certainly, if each of these social concerns was dealt with separately, there will be no way to prioritize and address any of them adequately. However, many of the social concerns that schools deal with are grounded in adolescent development and its many facets. Thus, a developmental approach that focuses on integrating attention to problems from the view of healthy adolescent growth will allow for conversations that are complementary rather than exclusive. The values and information from discussions of bullying will have great resonance with discussions of sexting; discussions of intimacy and relationships can have connection to sexting and healthy sexual behavior.

Challenge #5—Defining Roles and Boundaries

In seeking understanding among the parties concerned with sexting, it is important to try to define roles and set boundaries for those involved. What roles must belong to families and caregivers? How do the roles and responsibilities of caretakers differ from those of schools—teachers, administrators, and counselors? When should the justice system become involved? How should police and courts be engaged? What is appropriate and inappropriate for their participation?

Sexting is still in its infancy, so to speak, and is a problem with which we have limited experience. For that reason clarifying roles and defining boundaries for those concerned with it is a work in progress. Roles and boundaries are being questioned, challenged, and reworked. Unfortunately, this period of uncertainty can give rise to finger pointing and blame shifting. Parents wonder why teachers don't do something about it, while teachers complain about parents who don't keep a tighter hold on their young people. Police and legal authorities demand that the law be obeyed—but which law is not always clear.

Defining roles and boundaries is an issue that must be debated at local levels and at higher jurisdictional levels. It is not a conversation that should be avoided or allowed to take its own course.

Principles for Effective Policy and Practice

Think Broadly About the "Sexting Problem" and Our Responses

Returning to the definitional challenges presented earlier, a central tenet of our responses should be a recognition of the fact that sexting is neither a clearly defined nor an isolated set of behaviors. First and foremost, this requires attunement to the wide diversity of behaviors, circumstances, and motivations that may be associated with the "sexting" label.

The sexting typology emerging from our research represents one of several possible ways of thinking about the problem and solutions. By distinguishing between cases involving mutual trust, those involving self-interest, and those involving intent to harm, and by framing these distinctions across a continuum, we have aimed to focus attention on the diverse range of interpersonal dynamics that may be in play. Other typologies, including those related to case characteristics (Wolak, Finkelhor, & Mitchell, 2012) and the content of sexting messages (Mitchell et al., 2012), present alternative lenses through which to view the diversity of activities commonly subsumed under the "sexting" label. While the categorical boundaries of these typologies (ours and those of others) are at times porous and relative to one's perspective, we believe that they provide a helpful means of parsing out cases for purposes of devising effective means of prevention and incident response.

Thinking broadly also means considering sexting behavior within its appropriate developmental, social, and cultural context. Sexting is not an isolated behavior. In some cases, it may be thought of as a manifestation of normal teen developmental processes and inclinations, including normative risk taking, identity development, and experimentation with boundaries and notions of intimacy. Certainly, the apparent prevalence of the behavior among adult populations suggests that labeling sexting as the primary domain of "impulsive teens" may be somewhat alarmist and misguided.

At the same time, there is reason to believe that engaging in sexting behaviors under certain contexts (e.g., repetitiveness, recklessness, extreme sexually explicitness, wanton disregard for others) suggests the presence of generalized behavioral risk factors, including anxiety, depression, family dysfunction, delinquency, and problematic peer relations. These types of correlations, which have been well supported by survey research, suggest that sexting is just one of many possible outlets for risk-taking behaviors and that our attention should be focused on addressing these underlying risk factors rather than simply responding to the behavior.

A key to responding to sexting in all its manifestations is, as we have indicated before, maintaining a focus on healthy social and emotional health for young people. It is easy in the flurry of the moment to become focused on rules and negative repercussions. Better responses, however, will be those that are responsive to what will be in the best interests of young people's social and emotional health—that is, responses that are grounded in a thorough understanding of adolescent development.

Related to this is the tendency among many to over-focus on the technology as the root of the "sexting problem." While there is little doubt that mobile phones and social media present a particular array of challenges, an over-focus on technology may lead educators to create overly negative or restrictive technology policies that constrict a learning environment in which technology is also key to instruction and curriculum.

Develop Credible and Meaningful Messages

Lacking narrative clarity, communities struggle to present young people and their families with a clear and consistent message about the consequences of sexting. Confused about the legal enforcement (which law and how to use it), young people may quickly realize that the message is not credible and the consequences can be all over the map in terms of the severity of the penalty. Unsure of the consequences or punishments that will be applied, adults worry about what to say and what to do in the face of a sexting incident. This is a scenario for chaos.

The message needs to be credible, and it needs to be backed up by meaningful consequences. By "meaningful" we mean that where harm has been perpetrated, there will be a clear and effective path of action to follow.

Limit Reliance on Legal Remedies

During our 2012 practitioner forums, some of the liveliest discussion concerned the role of the justice system in responding to sexting incidents. As expected, those who were charged with upholding the law, including prosecutors and school resource officers, tended to underscore and focus on the existing statutory landscape, under which minors could be subject to prosecution for engaging in these behaviors. Perhaps more surprisingly, however, these sentiments were echoed by some school officials, with many citing mandatory reporting laws that guided many of their internal disciplinary procedures.

In our view, this is a troubling scenario. Certainly, laws must be calibrated in a manner that protects youth from harm and holds accountable those who engage in intentionally harmful or deliberately reckless behaviors that cause such harm. Moreover, school officials should not be faulted for taking actions that are mandated by existing law, particularly when failing to do so might present risks or liabilities. At the same time, however, those charged with serving the needs of youth should be vocal advocates for ensuring that laws ostensibly designed to protect children do not also serve to criminalize adolescence.

Turn the "Problem" into the Solution

Our roundtable discussions yielded significant ideas on how to more effectively engage youth on their own terms. Suggestions fell into two broad categories: leveraging peer dynamics and leveraging technology.

Leveraging peer dynamics, in this context, means encouraging and promoting normative change among youth related to harmful or potentially harmful sexting behaviors. This, in turn, requires shifting from a mode of edicts and threats to one of guidance and empowerment. In such a culture, teens would teach other teens through their behavior and words what was acceptable and what was not. Teens were vocal in telling us that teens would be willing to listen to teens when they were not open to listening to adults. Part and parcel to peer-based strategies, emphasis should be placed on empowering youth to talk about sexting and its related issues. Ultimately, the aim is to promote a normative shift among youth toward attitudes that emphasize respect, positive relationship development, and empowerment of bystanders.

Another way to safeguard teens from sexting's more harmful manifestations is to leverage the technology itself. For better or worse, the lives and interactions of millennial youth are profoundly shaped by digital interactions. Schools have increasingly recognized this, as reflected in the tremendous growth and investment in technology-mediated teaching and learning strategies and infrastructure. The proliferation of school-based technology has created certain challenges for educational systems in terms of defining appropriate rules and boundaries, with issues such as sexting and online bullying serving as particular flashpoints and areas of concern. At the same time, however, the increased availability of technology within educational settings, along with the expansion of tools that empower young people to create and express themselves within the digital arena, creates tremendous opportunities to promote communication, engagement, and dialog about these issues of concern.

Address the Issue on Multiple Fronts

Particularly given the range of mandates and competing priorities facing the majority of school systems today, we must develop comprehensive solutions that draw upon existing curricular and student wellness and safety initiatives. A common error that those seeking to address the problem of sexting make is that they assign one area the task of solving the problem. This means that sexting is addressed by the health class, or perhaps the school technologists, when actually the issues of sexting are the issues of digital technologies that span all areas of school responsibility.

A better approach is to task a broad area of school specialists with delivering the message on sexting and supporting a comprehensive approach, one that is grounded in adolescent development and recognizes the expanded role of social media in our society. By doing this, young people have the opportunity to think about the issue of sexting from a variety of vantage points. In health and wellness classes they encounter it as part of discussions about relationships, social skills, boundaries, emotional health, sexuality, and intimacy. In the various places where the school discusses technology issues, they encounter concerns about sexting as part of talk about digital citizenship and technological awareness. Finally, guidance counselors and school nurses can serve as points of prevention and intervention. In this way, the school multiplies its capacity to address the problem and to ensure that young people will be kept safe from harmful sexting incidents.

Focus on Transitions

Finally, a critical strategy that emerged from all of our focus group participants, youth and adult, was the importance of acknowledging the developmental transitions that are taking place as young people enter, move through, and exit adolescence. In other words, how a middle-school student understands or engages in sexting will be different than a high-school student or a young college student. Each stage has its own perspectives that should be attended to in developing strategies to address sexting incidents. Developmentally targeted interventions will be an important means of increasing the impact of the message adults want to deliver to young people.

■ DISCLOSURES

Andrew J. Harris and Judith Davidson have no conflicts to disclose. The research described in this chapter was supported by Grant No. 2010-MC-CX-0001 awarded by the Office of Juvenile Justice and Delinquency Prevention, Office of Justice Programs, U.S. Department of Justice. Points of view or opinions in this chapter are those of the authors and do not necessarily represent the official position or policies of the U.S. Department of Justice.

■ REFERENCES

Agustina, J. R., & Gómez-Durán, E. L. (2012). Sexting: research criteria of a globalized social phenomenon. *Archives of sexual behavior*, 41(6), 1325–1328. doi:10.1007/s10508-012-0038-0

Associated Press & MTV. (2009). 2009 AP-MTV Digital Abuse Survey. Associated Press & MTV. Retrieved from http://www.athinline.org/MTVAP_Digital_Abuse_Study_Executive_Summary.pdf

Baumgartner, S. E., Sumter, S. R., Peter, J., & Valkenburg, P. M. (2012). Identifying teens at risk: Developmental pathways of online and offline sexual risk behavior. *Pediatrics*, *130*(6), e1489–1496. doi:10.1542/peds.2012-0842

Berton, J. (2009). "Are Lots of Teens 'Sexting'?" Experts Doubt it. The San Francisco Chronicle, March 21, 2009.

Bialik, C. (2009). Which is Epidemic—Sexting or Worry about it. *Wall Street Journal*, April 8, 2009, at A9.

Brunker, M. (2009). 'Sexting' surprise: Teens face child porn charges, 6 Pa. high school students busted after sharing nude photos via cell phones. Retrieved from http://www.msnbc.msn.com/id/28679588/

Cox Communications & National Center for Missing and Exploited Children. (2009). Teen online & wireless safety survey: cyberbullying, sexting, and parental controls. Cox Communications Teen Online & Wireless Safety Survey, in Partnership with the National Center for Missing & Exploited Children (NCMEC).

Dake, J., Price, J., Maziarz, L., & Ward, B. (2012). Prevalence and Correlates of Sexting Behavior in Adolescents. American Journal of Sexuality Education. Retrieved from http://www.tandfonline.com/doi/abs/10.1080/15546128.2012.650959

Dowdell, E. B., Burgess, A. W. & Flores, J. R. (2011). Online social networking patterns among adolescents, young adults, and sexual offenders. *American Journal of Nursing*, *111*(7):28–36.

Englander, E. (2012). Low risk associated with most teenage sexting: a study of 617 18-year-olds. In Marc Research Reports. Paper 6. Retrieved from http://vc.bridgew.edu/marc_reports/6.

Kranz, C. (2009). Nude photo led to suicide. Retrieved from http://news.cincinnati.com/article/20090322/NEWS01/903220312/Nude-photo-led-suicide

Leary, Mary G. (2010). Sexting or self-produced child pornography? The dialogue continues—structured prosecutorial discretion within a multidisciplinary response. *Virgina Journal of Social Policy and the Law*, 486.

Lenhart, A. (2009). Teens and Sexting. Pew Internet and American Life Project. Washington DC: Pew Research Center.

Lenhart, A., Ling, R., Campbell, S., & Purcell, K. (2010). Teens and mobile phones. Pew Internet and American Life Project. Retrieved from http://pewinternet.org/Reports/2010/Teens-and-Mobile-Phones.aspx

Levine, J. (2009). What's the Matter with Teen Sexting? The American Prospect. Retrieved from http://www.prospect.org/cs/articles?article=whats_the_matter_with_teen_sexting.

Lithwick, D. (2009). Teens, Nude Photos and the Law, NEWSWEEK Feb. 23, 2009, Retrieved from http://www.newsweek.com/2009/02/13/teens-nude-photos-and-the-law.html.

Mitchell, K. J., Finkelhor, D., Jones, L. M., & Wolak, J. (2012). Prevalence and characteristics of youth sexting: a national study. *Pediatrics*, *129*(1), 13–20. doi:10.1542/peds.2011-1730

National Campaign to Prevent Teen and Unplanned Pregnancy. (2008). Sex and tech: results from a survey of teens and young adults. Cosmogirl.com. http://www.thenationalcampaign.org/sextech/pdf/sextech_summary.pdf

Palfrey, J. (2008). Enhancing child safety & online technologies. Retrieved from http://www.cap-press.com/pdf/1997.pdf

Rice, E., Rhoades, H., Winetrobe, H., Sanchez, M., Montoya, J., Plant, A., & Kordic, T. (2012). Sexually explicit cell phone messaging associated with sexual risk among adolescents. *Pediatrics, 130*(4), 667–673. doi:10.1542/peds.2012-0021

Strassberg, D. S., McKinnon, R. K., Sustaíta, M. a, & Rullo, J. (2012). Sexting by high school students: An exploratory and descriptive study. *Archives of Sexual Behavior* [E-pub before print, June 7]. doi:10.1007/s10508-012-9969-8

Temple, J. R., Paul, J.A., Van den Berg, P., Le, V. D., McElhany, A., & Temple, B. W. (2012). Teen sexting and its association with sexual behaviors. *Archives of Pediatrics & Adolescent Medicine, 166*(9), 828–833.

Wolak, J., Finkelhor, D., & Mitchell, K. J. (2012). How often are teens arrested for sexting? Data from a national sample of police cases. *Pediatrics, 129*(1), 4–12. doi:10.1542/peds.2011-2242

13 Problematic Internet Behaviors: Diagnostic and Treatment Implications for Clinicians

■ LIWEI L. HUA, SCOTT YAPO,
AMY YULE, AND TRISTAN GORRINDO

■ INTRODUCTION

The pervasive use of social media and texting has greatly influenced child and adolescent development today. Although insight and judgment develop throughout adolescence, this period of development is also characterized by an increase in novelty seeking, risk taking, and separation from parents (Johnson et al., 2009). With recent advances in technology, children and adolescents have expanded their ability to interact with the world and others around them. And while there are benefits and risks to this new avenue of social, emotional, and moral exploration, the opportunity for developmental missteps using technology carries added risk for adolescents.

■ OVERVIEW OF TECHNOLOGY USE

A survey conducted by Common Sense Media of 1,384 parents of children ages zero to eight years (May to June 2011) found that this group of children spends an average of about three hours a day on media, which for the purposes of this study included screen time, reading/being read to, and listening to music. Screen time ranged from a little less than an hour for children under two years old (although the recommended screen time for this age group is zero hours per the Council on Communications and Media) to a little more than two hours for children ages two to four years and almost three hours for children ages four to eight years. Most of this screen time consists of television: about 65 percent of children ages zero to eight years watch TV at least once a day, while only about 58 percent read or are read to at least once a day.

This same survey showed that among these children zero to eight years old, 98 percent have at least one TV set in the home, 72 percent have a computer, and 67 percent have a video game player. A shocking 42 percent of these children have a television set in their rooms, 29 percent have a DVD/VCR player, 11 percent have a video game console player, and 4 percent have a computer. Twenty-nine percent have their own educational gaming device, 24 percent own a handheld gaming device, 7 percent possess an iPod, and 2 percent have a cellphone. Use of computers begins at a young age: approximately 53 percent of children two to four years old have used a computer, and about 90 percent of children four to eight years old have used a computer at some point. On average, zero- to eight-year-olds use the computer 17 minutes a day: eight minutes are spent playing video games; three minutes are spent watching videos; three minutes are spent on educational programs; two minutes are spent doing homework; and one minute is spent on other computer activities. Interestingly, 5 percent of children in this age range have visited social networking sites such as Facebook or MySpace, despite the minimum age requirement of 13.

In the 2010 Youth Pulse Study, an online study conducted by the Kauffman Foundation, 5,077 children/young adults from ages eight to 24 were interviewed. Of the 1,600 eight- to 12-year-olds interviewed, 79 percent are on the Internet at least an hour a day (average 1.9 hours daily). Eight- to 12-year-olds report an average of 2.4 hours of TV watching daily, and 59 percent report having a TV set in their rooms. About 78 percent of eight- to 12-year-olds report playing online games. Of 13- to 17-year-olds, 88 percent spend at least an hour a day on the Internet (average of 3.5 hours), 65 percent visit social networking sites, and 52 percent play online games. About a quarter of eight- to 12-year-olds say they use Facebook (despite the minimum age requirement of 13), while about 71 percent of 13- to 17-year-olds visit the site (Pieters, 2010).

Common Sense Media conducted an online poll of 1,030 13- to 17-year-olds in February and March 2012 and found that 90 percent of teens use social media, 75 percent have a profile on a social networking site, and 51 percent log on to a social networking site at least once daily. A 2009 Common Sense Media poll reported that 50 percent of teens log on to social networking sites more than once a day and 22 percent of teens 13 to 17 years old log on more than 10 times a day. At least 75 percent of teens have their own cellphones, 54 percent use them to text, and 25 percent use them for social media.

According to the Teens and Digital Citizenship Survey sponsored by the Pew Research Center's Internet and American Life Project (polling 799 teenagers aged 12 to 17), texting among teens has risen from about 50 text messages sent daily in 2009 to 60 messages sent daily in 2011 (Lenhart, 2012). This same poll also found that 95 percent of teens use the Internet, and 80 percent of these teens are on social networking sites. About 77 percent of teens own cellphones (23 percent own smartphones, while 54 percent own regular cellphones); most teens state that they got their first cellphone when they were 12 or 13 years old. Of these teens, 74 percent have a desktop or a laptop computer. Daily means of communication preferred by teens are text (63 percent), voice (39 percent), in-person socialization outside of school (35 percent), social networking sites (29 percent), instant messaging (22 percent), landlines (19 percent), and email (6 percent). Of online teens, 80 percent use social networking sites; of these

80 percent, 93 percent have a Facebook account, and 24 percent have an account on MySpace. The majority of teens who use social media (69 percent) say that peers are mostly kind to each other on social networking sites, while 20 percent say that most peers are not kind; however, 88 percent of these teens who use social media say they have witnessed peers being cruel to others on social networking sites (15 percent say they themselves have been victims of "online meanness").

In the 2009 Cox Communications Teen Online and Wireless Safety Survey (655 teens aged 13 to 18 polled), 91 percent of teens reported having their own email addresses, 72 percent reported having a social networking profile, and 22 percent reported having or using a webcam. Although rates vary according to survey, anywhere from 2 to 20 percent of teens have sent sext messages (Lenhart, 2012; Mitchell et al., 2012), and 4 to 30 percent have received them, with older teens being more likely to send/receive than younger teens and more teens in general receiving than sending such messages (Cox Communications, 2009; Delmonico & Griffin, 2008; Lenhart, 2009; Lounsbury et al., 2011; Mitchell et al., 2012; National Campaign to Prevent Teen and Unplanned Pregnancy & Cosmogirl.com, 2009). A 2005 survey showed that 42 percent of youth Internet users had been exposed to online pornography in the past year, with 66 percent describing the exposure as "unwanted" (Wolak et al., 2007a).

The results from these surveys clearly demonstrate recent increased use of media in children and adolescents, as well as increased access to cellphones, computers, and gaming consoles/handheld games.

▪ BENEFITS AND RISKS

Benefits for children/teens include increased means of maintaining relationships with friends and family near and far. They can also broaden their friendship base by either nurturing relationships with people they have met only once or twice or by forming new relationships with people they have never met in person but who have similar interests. Activities such as blogging and use of social networking sites can afford an opportunity to express thoughts and feelings and enhance creativity (with blogs, podcasts, videos) that children and adolescents may be reluctant to express otherwise. Additionally, use of the Internet can also be a powerful educational tool, allowing access to health resources, such as information on medical illnesses, sexually transmitted infections, signs of mental illness, and effects of drug use. A recent Pew survey (Lenhart, 2009) found that 31 percent of online teens search for health, dieting, and physical fitness information, while 17 percent search for drug use and sexual health information.

In contrast, risks of using the Internet and cellphones include exposure to sexts, pornography, and sexual predators; cyber-bullying; problematic Internet use/Internet addiction; and health issues, such as obesity and sleep deficit. Problematic Internet use, or "Internet addiction," can be defined as excessive use of the Internet leading to a compulsion to use, withdrawal symptoms when unable to use the Internet, and negative social, psychological, and academic/occupational consequences

(Lee & Stapinski, 2012). Problematic online gaming, also a relatively new term, is defined as spending more time playing video games online than intended, resulting in negative consequences on school/work and social relationships and withdrawal symptoms when not able to game (Demetrovics et al., 2008). Spending hours in front of a computer, whether in isolation or engaging in online interactive gaming, can lead to physical health consequences associated with a sedentary lifestyle, such as obesity, as well as sleep deprivation. Grades, work quality, and personal relationships can also be negatively affected. Although the literature about how the use of this technology can affect mental health is still nascent, some studies suggest that excessive/problematic use of the Internet and cellphones correlates with mental health disorders, such as depression, anxiety, and substance use (Carli et al., 2012; Lee & Stapinski, 2012; Young & Rodgers, 1998). It is important to stress that available research is largely correlational; thus, determining causality is unclear.

Although there has been much outcry about how technology is abused and the dangerous repercussions of this abuse, there are also benefits to the use of technology by children and adolescents, especially when used in moderation and with appropriate guidance by parents/guardians.

■ IDENTIFICATION OF PROBLEMATIC INTERNET BEHAVIORS USING RATING SCALES

A plethora of psychometric instruments have been developed to screen for problematic Internet use. The instruments differ in their length, focus, conceptual framework, the population in which they have been validated, and whether they are designed for online or offline use. To date, no consensus has emerged on which instruments to use for any given purpose, leaving researchers and clinicians with a veritable alphabet soup of rating scales to choose from, including the following:

- Chinese (or Chen) Internet Addiction Scale (CIAS) (S. Chen et al., 2003)
- Compulsive Internet Use Scale (CIUS) (Meerkerk et al., 2009)
- Generalized Problematic Internet Use Scale (GPIUS) (Caplan, 2002)
- Internet Addiction Scale (IAS) (Nichols & Nicki, 2004)
- Internet Addiction Test (IAT) (Young, 1998)
- Internet-Related Addictive Behavior Inventory (IRABI) (Brenner, 1997)
- Internet Related Problem Scale (IRPS) (Armstrong et al., 2000)
- Online Cognition Scale (OCS) (Davis et al., 2002)
- Pathological Internet Use Scale (PIUS) (Morahan-Martin & Schumacher, 2000)
- Problematic Internet Use Questionnaire (PIUQ) (Demetrovics et al., 2008)
- Use, Abuse and Dependence on Internet (UADI) (Gnisci et al., 2011)

There are also scales focusing on specific types of Internet use, for example the Problematic Online Game Use (POGU) scale (Kim & Kim, 2010).

The Internet Addiction Test, developed by Dr. Kimberly Young, was one of the first validated and reliable measures of addictive Internet use and is one of the most commonly used today. It is a 20-item questionnaire with "How often do you..." scales related to various online behaviors. Each item is scored from 0 (does not apply) to 5 (always). The total is then used to divide participants into three groups: average online users, individuals who experience occasional or frequent problems secondary to frequent Internet use, and individuals whose use causes significant problems.

Despite an abundance of instruments, their use in practice appears to be limited to research on problematic Internet use in adolescents. One issue is that there is no standard definition for "Internet addiction" for adolescents and controversy as to whether the nomenclature of addiction appropriately describes these behaviors. Unlike in adults, where Internet addiction includes personal distress secondary to excessive online use, it is not completely applicable to the adolescent population, where high media use is egosyntonic and normative to peers (Gorrindo et al., 2012). Moreno and colleagues (2011) conducted a literature survey of studies of Internet addiction in youth. They included all "English-language studies that (1) involved a US population, (2) focused on adolescents or college student participants, and (3) assessed Internet addiction symptoms empirically through the use of a scale or set criteria" published through July 2010 (Moreno et al., 2011, p. 3). Of the 18 studies that met their criteria, only one used an existing rating scale for a purpose other than introducing or validating it: the remaining studies either adapted or modified a scale or used questions based on the DSM-IV criteria for substance abuse (Moreno et al., 2011).

Clinicians need to be aware of the potential weaknesses of these instruments: they are self-reported measures that may be susceptible to lying or underreporting; many have been validated only on small, nonrepresentative samples; some patients may not understand all of the questions; different cutoffs are sometimes used to identify problematic behavior for the same scale; and some of the questions become out of date over time (Beard, 2005; Meerkerk et al., 2009; Widyanto et al., 2011). Most of these scales highlight frequency of Internet use rather than intensity of Internet use, even though the latter has been shown to be more correlated with adolescents and their likelihood of major depression symptoms (Ybarra et al., 2005). Not all the screens are validated by uniform measures, and there is still no consensus on which measures are "gold standards" for determining problematic use of the Internet/cellphones (although part of the problem is the lack of a consensus on the definition of problematic Internet use).

■ COMORBIDITIES ASSOCIATED WITH PROBLEMATIC INTERNET BEHAVIORS

A meta-analysis of published studies on patients with problematic Internet use reveals a high comorbidity of other psychiatric conditions (Aboujaoude, 2010).

However, none of the studies was designed to comment on the association between problematic Internet use and psychiatric comorbidities. In a general population study of adults, 41.4 percent of adults with problematic Internet use reported feelings of depression in the year prior to the study versus 15.8 percent of the nonproblematic users. The study also noted that the problematic users had increased sleep disturbances, anxiety, and substance abuse compared to their counterparts (Aboujaoude, 2010). In adolescents, numerous studies have suggested an association between heavy Internet use and negative health consequences such as depression, ADHD, and increased alcohol use (Ko et al., 2009; Lam et al., 2009). Other studies have linked excessive Internet use with truancy and academic troubles in young adults (Chen & Tzeng, 2010).

Given the levels of consumption of digital and online media among contemporary adolescents, adolescents can run into a number of problematic Internet behaviors that may harm their psychosocial well-being. Two dominant problems include cyber-bullying and sexting.

Cyber-bullying

There is no universally accepted definition of "cyber-bullying." Studies have employed a variety of approaches to identify cyber-bullying and related forms of online harassment. These approaches have included a range of behaviors from bothering someone online to threatening him or her to posting text or images intended to harm or embarrass him or her (Finkelhor et al., 2000; Moessner, 2007; Patchin & Hinduja, 2006). Studies using data from the Youth Internet Safety Survey have defined "online harassment" or "online bullying" as "an affirmative response to at least one of the following two questions: (a) 'In the past year, did you ever feel worried or threatened because someone was bothering or harassing you online?' (yes/no) and (b) 'In the past year, did anyone ever use the Internet to threaten or embarrass you by posting or sending messages about you for other people to see?' (yes/no)" (Mitchell et al., 2007; Wolak et al., 2007b, p. 3).

These definitions distinguish cyber-bullying from "offline" bullying in important respects. Bullying research typically requires three elements for bullying: "(1) aggressive acts, verbal included, made with harmful intent, (2) repetition, and (3) an imbalance of power between the perpetrator and target" (Wolak et al., 2007b). Importantly, in many studies the definition of cyber-bullying lacks the intent and repetition that are understood to be a key part of traditional bullying. To capture these important criteria, others have suggested that cyber-bullying should be defined as willful, repetitive behavior occurring over electronic devices that causes harm to the target (Dooley et al., 2009). A study that attempted to identify repetitive online harassment inflicting harm estimated that between one fifth and one quarter of online harassment reported by youth could be considered cyber-bullying using this stricter definition (Wolak et al., 2007b). The Youth

Internet Safety Survey found that 55 percent of victims reported multiple incidents of harassment within the previous year, although each incident may have had a different perpetrator.

Studies of adolescent bullying have found significant overlap between online and offline bullies and bullying. The majority of victims of cyber-bullying report being bullied offline, and similarly, most youths who admit to bullying others online admit to offline bullying as well (Raskauskas & Stoltz, 2007; Schneider, O'Donnell, Stueve, & Coulter, 2012). There may be differences in the actions of bullies and the effect on their victims. Unlike traditional bullying, cyber-bullying has the potential to be anonymous, to be experienced at any time and location, and to be instantly and easily shared with a large number of people. Also, material posted online can live "forever," which can therefore prolong its consequences.

Surveys conducted in the United States, Europe, and Australia demonstrated that between 10 and 35 percent of teenagers report having been cyberbullied (Donnerstein, 2012). The wide range in these estimates arises from how cyberbullying was defined and how the questions were asked. Surveys that asked more broadly about Internet harassment tended to yield higher percentages compared to surveys with more specific questions or narrower definitions of cyber-bullying. Data from the three Youth Internet Safety Surveys, conducted in the United States in 1999/2000, 2005, and 2010, indicate that rates of online harassment almost doubled from 2000 to 2010 from 6 to 11 percent (Jones, Mitchell, & Finkelhor, 2012).

Not surprisingly, adolescents engaging in more online activity are more likely to be victims of cyber-bullying (Wolak et al., 2007b; Ybarra, 2004). Adolescents who have social network accounts are also more likely to be victims of online harassment (Lenhart, 2007). Cyber-bullying victimization is correlated with a variety of demographic characteristics: adolescents are more likely to be bullied online if they are female, younger, or identify as non-heterosexual (Schneider et al., 2012). This is generally consistent with the patterns observed in traditional bullying, although gender has not been found to be correlated with being bullied. Of note, the reported rate of cyber-bullying does not decline with age as quickly as in traditional bullying (Schneider et al., 2012).

In one study, almost one third of adolescents reported being a cyberbully (Ybarra, Diener-West, & Leaf, 2007). Victims of cyber-bullying appear to be more likely to report bullying others online than non-victims, although it is unclear whether this relationship is driven by the intensity of Internet use (Wolak et al., 2007b). Males and females appear equally likely to be cyberbullies (Wolak et al., 2007b; Ybarra, 2004). Youth cyberbullies are more likely than non-bullies to report behavioral problems, such as rule-breaking and aggression, and physical and sexual abuse (Mitchell et al., 2007; Ybarra et al., 2007).

Like traditional bullying, cyber-bullying and online harassment are associated with a variety of psychopathology and problematic behaviors, including low self-esteem, depression, suicidal ideation, delinquency, and substance use (Mitchell et al., 2007; Prinstein et al., 2001).

With respect to problematic behaviors, an online study conducted in 2004 and 2005 of over 1,000 mostly American youths found that victims of cyber-bullying were more likely to report substance abuse, truancy, cheating, aggression, and shoplifting (Hinduja & Patchin, 2007). A study of data from the first Youth Internet Safety Survey, conducted in 1999 and 2000, found that online harassment is correlated with delinquency and substance use, but showed that these correlations are largely explained by demographics (e.g., sex, age, and household income) and measures of "life adversity" (death of a family member, moving to a new home, parental divorce or separation, and parental unemployment) (Mitchell et al., 2007).

Studies have consistently shown significant correlations between cyber-bullying and psychopathology varying from low self-esteem to depressive symptoms to suicidal ideation and even suicide attempts. The results are generally consistent with research on traditional bullying. Both perpetrators and victims of cyber-bullying have been shown to have significantly lower self-esteem than non-perpetrators and victims (Patchin & Hinduja, 2010). Adolescent victims of online harassment are about three times more likely to report depressive symptoms than non-victims (Ybarra, 2004). The relationship between depressive symptoms and Internet harassment appears to be stronger for males than females, with evidence that depressed males, but not females, are more likely to be the target of online harassment (Ybarra, 2004).

A 2007 survey of almost 2,000 middle-school students in a single large U.S. school district found online harassment to be significantly correlated with suicidal ideation (Patchin & Hinduja, 2010). This is consistent with the extensive literature linking traditional bullying to increased suicidal ideation. The study found that victims of cyber-bullying were about twice as likely to have attempted suicide as students who were neither perpetrators nor victims of cyber-bullies. This is similar to the increased rate of attempted suicide among victims of traditional bullying (Hinduja & Patchin, 2010).

Comparing across studies, there is evidence that the psychological impact of cyber-bullying may increase with age. A 2008 census of more than 20,000 Massachusetts high-school students found that victims of both cyber-bullying and traditional bullying demonstrated an increased likelihood of depressive symptoms, suicidal ideation, self-injury, and suicide attempts (Schneider et al., 2012). In contrast to the finding by Hinduja and Patchin of a doubling of suicide risk among middle-school cyber-bullying victims, the authors of this study of high-school students reported that "compared with nonvictims, victims of both cyber and school bullying were more than 4 times as likely to report depressive symptoms, suicidal ideation, and self-injury, and more than 5 times as likely to report a suicide attempt and a suicide attempt requiring medical treatment" (Schneider et al., 2012, p. 4).

There are many challenges to interpreting these reported correlations. For example, the relationship between reported rates of online harassment and depression are complicated by potential differences in how youth with depressive symptoms experience online interactions: they may be more likely to interpret interactions negatively. In support of this hypothesis, Finkelhor and colleagues (2000) reported that youth with depressive symptoms are about 50 percent more likely to report emotional distress from Internet harassment. Additionally, as noted above, existing studies of Internet activities and psychosocial problems are almost all cross-sectional, making causal interpretations of the observed correlations speculative. Further confounding interpretation is the extent to which reported correlations can be explained by demographics and related behaviors or outcomes. For example, there is evidence in at least one study that no significant correlation between depressive symptoms and online harassment exists once demographics, life adversity, and offline victimization rates (including but not limited to traditional bullying) are controlled for (Mitchell et al., 2007). The topic of cybersexual harassment is discussed in more detail in Chapter 7.

Although a formal definition of cyber-bullying has yet to be determined, there are clear consequences of both being bothered/threatened/humiliated online and bothering/threatening/humiliating, including resulting psychopathology that may include depression and/or suicidal behavior. However, again, the data presented so far demonstrate correlation and not causality.

Sexting

Sexting, a combination of "sex" and "texting," has been defined straightforwardly as "the practice of electronically sending sexually explicit images or messages from one person to another" (Temple et al., 2012). Researchers have also proposed the term "youth-produced sexual images" (Wolak & Finkelhor, 2011, p. 1) since the term "sexting," derived from the popular press, lacks specificity and may include sexual images sent by or to adults, a situation associated with different case dynamics. For practical reasons, it may be important in some situations to distinguish between the degree of explicitness (e.g., sexually suggestive clothed photos vs. photos showing genitalia) and the source of the image or message (e.g., sending commercial photos vs. photos of oneself).

As with other Internet behaviors, sexting may be viewed as the modern presentation of longstanding behaviors such as a sexually explicit love letter or a nude Polaroid. Adolescence is a period of heightened interest in one's own developing sexuality. During this stage of their development, it is typical for adolescents to demonstrate a proclivity toward impulsivity, grandiosity, and risk-taking and to place increasing emphasis on peer relationships. This combination creates the potential for some very dangerous situations for today's youth (Sadhu, 2012). Clinicians have yet to reach consensus as to whether sexting is part of typical sexual development in a new Internet era or if it is a more deviant type of behavior.

The difference is that in this digital era, every adolescent with a cellphone is now a potential producer and distributor of child pornography, and the repercussions of this dangerous activity can have lasting effects as teens transition into adulthood. Calvert explicates the legal dimensions of youth-produced sexual images in Chapter 5.

Advances in technology have made it easier to copy material and widely distribute it on the Internet and have expanded the availability of this content online. This is problematic because not only can sexting be detrimental to a youth's psychological well-being, it can have serious legal consequences as well. In many states, individuals who send or receive nude photographs of minors (including themselves) run the risk of legal charges such as possession or distribution of child pornography (Lewin, 2010). These crimes often carry severe penalties, which include registering as a sex offender.

Reported rates of sexting have varied greatly across recent studies of U.S. adolescents. The National Campaign to Prevent Teen and Unplanned Pregnancy was one of the first organizations to conduct a study on youth and sexting, although it was not peer-reviewed. Using an online survey of 653 teens (ages 13 to 19), they found that 22 percent of girls and 18 percent of boys admitted to having sent or posted online a nude or seminude picture or video of themselves, and 31 percent reported having such a picture or video from someone else (National Campaign to Prevent Teen and Unplanned Pregnancy, 2008). It is noteworthy that this survey included young adults aged 18 and 19. In a longitudinal study of seven high schools in Texas with a larger sample, Temple and colleagues (2012) found that 28 percent of participants reported having sent a nude photograph of themselves via text or email.

However, other studies have shown sexting to be less common. A study by the Pew Research Center found that only 15 percent of adolescents age 12 to 17 years reported ever receiving a sext and only 4 percent reported having sent one (Lenhart, 2009). In a recent national study where sexting was defined as sharing naked images, researchers found that only 1.3 percent of youths age 10 to 17 years had created or were the subject of a sext and only 5.9 percent had received one (Mitchell et al., 2012). These differences may be due to differences in the adolescents sampled or the questions asked, for example whether non-naked images were considered sexts.

Motivations associated with sexting vary, including whether it occurs within an existing or hoped-for relationship (Lenhart, 2009). Studies generally find that the incidence of sexting increases with age, perhaps due at least in part to increased access to cellphones (Rice et al., 2012; Strassberg et al., 2013). There appears to be little correlation between sex, race, and propensity to sext. The most significant predictor of sexting appears to be knowing someone else who does so (Rice et al., 2012). Adolescents with parents who had a high-school education or less were more likely to have requested a sext (Temple et al., 2012).

Unlike cyber-bullying, there is little research on the correlation between sexting and psychopathology or problematic behavior. There have been some high-profile cases in the media about the alleged involvement of sexting in the suicides of a number of teens, but this is not a common occurrence (Meyer, 2009). There has been no published research studying the amount of sexting done by patients with depression. Although sexting is not indicative of a major mood disorder, it may be secondary to underlying depressive symptoms (Sadhu, 2012). A study of data from the third Youth Internet Safety Survey found that between 20 and 25 percent of senders and receivers of sexts reported "feeling very or extremely upset, embarrassed, or afraid as a result" (Mitchell et al., 2012). This study also found that 28 percent of senders and receivers of texts "either reported incidents to an authority or an authority found out some way." Another potential risk for adolescents who engage in sexting is cyber-bullying, because receivers of the material can blackmail the original senders.

Not surprisingly, sexting is highly correlated with being sexually active. In a study of U.S. high-school students, researchers demonstrated that "participants who had sent sexually explicit cell phone messages or photos were statistically significantly more likely to have ever engaged in sexual intercourse and exhibited a trend toward unprotected sex during their last sexual encounter" (Rice et al., 2012, p. 5). A study of seven high schools in Texas similarly found that participants who had engaged in sexting were statistically significantly more likely to have started dating and having sexual intercourse than their peers who did not sext (Temple et al., 2012). This study also found that for adolescent girls, sexting was associated with risky sexual behaviors such as having multiple sexual partners and using alcohol and drugs before having sexual activity. This association was not present for adolescent boys.

The existing studies of sexting are cross-sectional, making it difficult to determine how sexting affects sexual behaviors. There is a concern that sexting might have important implications for how adolescents think about sex and what behaviors they consider normal. It has been hypothesized that repeated exposure to sexts may lead adolescents to view sex as "glamorous" and to underestimate the associated risks (Moreno et al., 2009). Teens who are exposed to images of sexual practices, even if they do not appear directly harmed by viewing them, may nevertheless be more inclined to participate in similar activities themselves (Brown et al., 2009). When adolescents repeatedly post sexual messages or images of themselves, they may begin to engage in a form of self-objectification, thinking of their bodies as an object of others' desires (Rice et al., 2012). At a minimum, a significant correlation between sexting and risky sexual practices would suggest that sexting could be a valuable indicator for clinicians and parents of other sexual behaviors in adolescents.

As stated above, opinion remains unclear at this time whether sexting has become part of normative developing sexual behavior in adolescents. It is also unclear what the true prevalence of this behavior is, which also makes this question difficult to answer. What is clear is that there can be very serious and dangerous consequences to sexting, including victimization; there are also correlations with increased sexual/sexualized behavior and psychopathology.

Rebecca

Rebecca is a 17-year-old junior who presents with her mother for psychiatric evaluation. She reports a happy childhood with no significant worries until she began struggling with low self-esteem in middle school. She felt isolated and reports having no friends throughout the eighth grade. During ninth grade she began receiving attention from a boy, Jake, primarily via text messaging. During one of their interactions she sent an image of her whole naked body. She reports initially regretting sending the pictures but for the most part had no concerns about the incident since no one else knew about them at the time. Later, she began sending similar naked photos of herself to Jake and his male friends. One of these male friends soon began blackmailing Rebecca with threats that if she did not do tasks for him, such as completing his homework, he would either distribute the photos to their peers or would tell the school administration about them. Rebecca then told her guidance counselor at her school about the situation. Her counselor was supportive, had the boy delete the pictures from his phone, and told her parents about the incident.

Rebecca's parents were concerned about her behavior and switched her to a different school in tenth grade. After switching schools, Rebecca reports that she missed the boys and started sending naked photos of herself to them again, this time with increased frequency. She reports that she knew it was wrong at the time but was unable to resist sending them because she worried that they would be upset with her if she stopped. Over time, the boys began calling her names and treating her cruelly over the content of the photos.

Throughout the fall of tenth grade Rebecca began to feel increasingly sad and depressed. She felt like she was unable to express her sadness to her family and began superficially cutting herself. She also had difficulty falling asleep, decreased energy, feelings of guilt, and anhedonia but denies having had changes in appetite or suicidal ideation. In the winter of that year, her parents found out about her self-injurious behavior and continued sexting habits after one of Rebecca's friends expressed concern to her parents. Subsequently, Rebecca began working with a therapist and reports that her mood improved during that time, she stopped sexting images of herself, and her self-injurious behavior decreased.

As the following school year concluded, Rebecca ended her therapy and went away with her family for summer break. She reports that her feelings of persistent sadness and anhedonia returned. She had minimal contact with her friends and began having increased difficulty falling asleep, feelings of guilt, and decreased energy. She soon began to have feelings of not wanting to be alive but denied any suicide plans. While feeling upset she again began sending nude pictures of herself to the boys she had been in contact with previously. Her parents soon found out and followed up by denying her access to all her digital devices. She reports that she knows sexting is wrong but struggles to say "no" to boys when they request pictures because she fears upsetting them. She denies a history of sexual activity. She continues to report worsening mood and passive suicidal ideation.

This case is an example of an adolescent who struggles with problematic use of electronic media in the form of sexting. For Rebecca, the act of sending nude images of herself electronically could be categorized as an impulsive behavior and/or a maladaptive attempt to recruit attention/soothing from male peers. Her case highlights the association of depressive symptoms in adolescents who engage in sexting and also the ways in which the misuse of social media can suggest offline developmental vulnerabilities too (see Chapter 4). However, it is unclear whether her mood disorder motivated her to seek unhealthy attention from her male peers or whether her symptoms were a result of her sexting. It also demonstrates the opportunity for bullying to occur when a private picture is made available to others. Once Rebecca's parents identified her problem, they limited her access to cellular devices to help prevent future incidents.

Dan

Dan is a 14-year-old freshman with a history of ADHD (inattentive type) and depression who reports for an urgent check-in to the clinic after a rumor began circulating that he was going to take a gun to school. It is unclear who started the rumor, but it spread to the community via a text that was posted on Twitter and subsequently re-tweeted over the course of a few hours. Eventually his school's administration became aware of the rumor and contacted Dan's parents and the police. The police investigated the situation and felt the allegation was inaccurate and cleared Dan of any wrongdoing.

Dan's parents report that he was very upset and angry about the incident. They report that later that evening he was irritable and tearful, subsequently engaging in self-injurious behavior by superficially cutting his forearm. He reports that he had been experiencing a cycle of shame, worry, embarrassment, and anger. He was fixated on trying to understand why this had happened to him and what he had done wrong. For a brief period of time, Dan considered overdosing on his mother's medication in hopes of "ending all of this." In time, Dan began to cope with his emotions by playing basketball and drawing while his parents concurrently restricted his electronic media use. Dan is able to calmly discuss the situation and voices understanding of both his parents' and the school's perspectives.

Dan's case highlights how cyber-bullying can be more intrusive and devastating than traditional bullying in that it can take place at any time of the day, occur off school grounds, be anonymous, and be communicated to a wide audience. Dan already had a history of depressive symptoms, but it can be concluded that cyber-bullying contributed to his decompensation. This case also highlights how important it is for schools to monitor for cyber-bullying and educate their students about its consequences.

Psychoeducation

Whether cyber-bullying, sexting, and other problematic Internet behaviors are deemed "pathological" or peer-normative, whether they are due to Internet addiction or a manifestation of an underlying psychiatric disorder, or whether they result from a combination of all these things, psychoeducation for both adolescents and parents is critical (Hua, 2012). Treatment providers must keep up to date with the ever-changing trends of technology use so they can provide a better understanding to children/adolescents and their caretakers of what is peer-normative. However, in addition to being able to normalize/reassure parents about use, mental health providers must also assess the functioning of the child/adolescent because these "normal trends" are only guidelines; not every child does well with the same exposure to this technology. Complete abstinence from use of social media and cellphones is unfeasible. Parents/guardians must be counseled on the fact that the more parents are open to discussing use of technology, the more likely their children will be to approach their parents with questions/concerns and to let their parents know about potentially dangerous situations as they occur (e.g., cyber-bullying, receiving sext messages, predation by strangers, and pornography). Children and adolescents should also realize that being able to use the computer and cellphone is a privilege that is earned with a trusting relationship between them and their parents.

In addition, mental health providers should be able to provide guidance on how to set reasonable limits for use of the Internet/cellphones: keep the computer in a public part of the home, use programs to restrict access to dangerous/questionable websites (especially for younger children), check privacy settings on social networking sites, be aware of what is being posted to online profiles, "friend" their children on social networking websites, and adhere to age restrictions of these websites (usually 13). Also important are setting appropriate time limits on the computer, limiting cellphone text plans to a certain number of texts per month (possibly also restricting the people to whom the child may text), and having the child/adolescent "turn in" phones/laptops at a reasonable bedtime for charging in a separate room.

Discussing the risks and consequences of posting too much information on the Internet or revealing sext messages or photos is also important to discuss with both the child and the parent. Adolescents may not realize that once posted/sent, these messages/pictures/blogs remain in cyberspace forever and can be searched (and found), affecting potential college/job placements (McBride, 2011; O'Keeffe et al., 2011). Sext messages and other inappropriate or bullying texts can easily be retrieved from wireless carriers and shown to school principals; they can also be easily forwarded to peers, unintentionally or with the purpose of ridiculing/bullying the original sender. It is very important for children and parents to know that child pornography charges can result from sending pictures of naked/seminaked children or adolescents under 18 via cellphone or Internet, even if the images are of oneself. Such a legal consequence can have far-reaching effects on the child's self-esteem and future.

Due to the anonymity that the Internet often allows, children and adolescents may write or post messages that they might not be as tempted to offline. Therefore, they should be reminded of the people at the receiving end of their messages/posts and strongly encouraged to practice the same respectful behavior on the Internet and over the phone as they would in person (referred to online as good "netiquette"). Education on empathy and mindfulness is strongly recommended here. In addition, teens should be reminded that email/text messages can often be misconstrued due to a lack of context and the necessary brevity of messages; therefore, meaning must be clarified before offense is taken. In children who have difficulty reading/understanding social cues, this is especially important.

There has been some evidence in the literature that psychoeducation can be helpful in decreasing risky behavior on the Internet. A recent randomized controlled pilot intervention trial found that a single email message addressing the consequences of posting too much information on the Internet (of a sexual nature or about substance use) delivered on the social networking site MySpace was enough to significantly decrease the number of inappropriate sexual posts by young adults (Moreno et al., 2009). Although this pilot study was performed in young adults and this is still a burgeoning field of research, the finding is encouraging in demonstrating how a generic piece of psychoeducation can be effective in decreasing sexually provocative posts on social media. Of course, further research should be conducted to determine if such intervention would also be effective in children and adolescents.

Parent Contracts

There are many sample contracts between parents and their children that can be helpful in starting a discussion about safe and acceptable use of the computer and cellphone, as well as expectations for appropriate behavior. Common Sense Media (www.commonsensemedia.org) offers such media contracts, which they refer to as "Family Media Agreements." These contracts promote safety and strive to provide children with a healthy balance of technology, since complete abstinence is a rather unrealistic expectation in today's digitally driven world. They are helpful in keeping communication lines open and holding children accountable for their actions. To ensure target behaviors appropriate for each developmental stage, contracts are available for elementary-school, middle-school, and high-school children. They contain different sections that focus on key principles such as safety, mindfulness, and guidelines for proper Internet etiquette that help to safeguard children from problematic Internet behaviors. In exchange for following such rules, parents in return pledge to respect their children's needs for digital media.

It is not uncommon for parents to lack knowledge about how to monitor or control their children's access to digital media. Common Sense Media also provides educational handouts with various computer tips, such as enabling Internet filters, creating strong Internet passwords, and setting parental controls, which intercept inappropriate content from coming in contact with children. Parents who are more digitally inclined should set appropriate examples with media for their children to model.

Psychotherapies

Although there are few empirical data about the use of psychotherapy to help adolescents with problematic Internet behavior, the basic tenets of good care are likely to be helpful. Therapists who can maintain a curious, observational stance with patients are likely to help nurture insight. Lines of inquiry that help adolescents explore the sequence of decisions and events that led up to a sext, for example, may afford the adolescent an opportunity to consider places for intervention should a similar circumstance arise in the future. Basic skills related to mindfulness and dialectical behavioral therapy may also be helpful (Pridgen, 2010).

Pharmacotherapy

There is limited evidence on the efficacy of pharmacological treatment of problematic Internet use (Aboujaoude, 2010). There are case reports of successful treatment, including the use of naltrexone to treat adult Internet sex addiction (Bostwick & Bucci, 2008), as well as a published report of the successful treatment of problematic Internet use in a 24-year-old with quetiapine and citalopram (Atmaca, 2007).

At least two small trials looking at the treatment of problematic Internet behaviors have been undertaken. One studied escitalopram for treating "impulsive-compulsive Internet usage disorder" in 19 adults (Dell'Osso et al., 2008). Study participants reduced their Internet use significantly over the 19-week trial, but it was unclear how much of the effect was due to the treatment. The other trial studied the use of methylphenidate to treat 63 children with ADHD who played Internet video games (Han et al., 2009). Over the eight weeks of the study, there was a significant reduction in Internet use, measured Internet addiction (using a Korean version of Young's Internet Addiction Test Scale), and ADHD symptoms.

While these case studies and preliminary trials provide evidence of the possibility of pharmacotherapy for problematic Internet behavior, larger and better-controlled studies are needed to establish the efficacy of drugs in treating these disorders. Additionally, consistent definitions of problematic Internet use and Internet addiction are needed to allow for comparison of treatment results across studies.

Psychopharmacology may be particularly helpful when comorbidities—with clear pharmacological indications—are present.

Motivational Interviewing

Adolescents with problematic Internet behaviors frequently lack motivation to change. Problematic Internet behaviors can cause significant conflict within families, and parents are often very concerned about their child's maladaptive behavior. One treatment intervention that may be effective in helping parents motivate children with problematic Internet behavior to engage in treatment is the Community Reinforcement and Family Training (CRAFT) intervention (Meyers et al., 1998; Waldron et al., 2007). CRAFT is an intervention designed to motivate adolescents and adults with substance use disorders to engage in treatment. The intervention is targeted to parents and concerned significant others. Goals of the intervention include improving the parent's emotional functioning, teaching principles of contingency management to help reinforce behavioral change, and helping build skills such as communication and problem solving. A key component of contingency management is having rewards for positive behavioral change in addition to clear consequences for continued problematic behavior. Some families find it helpful to use a written contract explicitly stating terms of the behavioral agreement with the specific incentives and consequences included.

■ CONCLUSION

The availability and use of technology today have risen dramatically, with far-reaching implications for children and adolescents. Children are able to multitask with their computers, laptops, or cellphones for purposes of communication and education (or both) for several hours a day. Although the use of this technology is beneficial in many ways, it does carry risks, including those of sexting and cyber-bullying, as well as contributing to and/or exacerbating psychopathology. It can also affect children's perception of what is appropriate for social etiquette and sexual practices. Surveys of use of technology among children and adolescents abound, but there is still no clear consensus of how much technology use is peer-normative and appropriate. Although there are several diagnostic questionnaires circulating, many of them have not been validated in specific, non-generalizable populations; many ask about frequency of use rather than intensity, limiting the ability to fully assess whether use is excessive/pathological.

There is some evidence for treatment options, including psychotherapy (such as cognitive-behavioral therapy and dialectical behavioral therapy), motivational interviewing techniques, and pharmacotherapy; these therapies should be targeted not only toward the problematic behavior itself but also toward any underlying psychopathology that may coexist. However, preventive measures, such as psychoeducation for children and adolescents, as well as their parents/guardians, are important for establishing safe practices on the Internet and with cellphones before problems arise. It is imperative to educate children and adolescents (and their parents/guardians) that what is engaged in and posted to the Internet can be very difficult to erase and often remains online "forever." All must recognize that the content they post online can affect how their peers, including friends and sexual partners, view and treat them. Future relationships, as well as future educational and career opportunities, may also be affected by inappropriate use of this technology.

Ideas for future directions include agreement on universal definitions (such as of "problematic Internet behavior" and "cyber-bullying") as well as validated diagnostic tools that are appropriate for more than specific populations. In addition, appropriate and peer-normative use of this technology should be further defined. A consensus on algorithms for evaluation and treatment of these children and adolescents would also be extremely helpful. Although surveys of children and adolescents have demonstrated that the prevalence of technology use is ever-increasing, how and whether use correlates with psychopathology continues to be of great interest and needs more research. More evidence-based treatment for this behavior is also important, as problematic Internet behaviors continue to rise among youths.

■ DISCLOSURES

Liwei L. Hua, Scott Yapo, Amy Yule, and Tristan Gorrindo have no conflicts to disclose. Dr. Yule received research funding through the American Academy of Child and Adolescent Psychiatry Pilot Research Award for Junior Faculty supported by Lilly USA, LLC in 2012. Dr. Gorrindo receives partial salary support from a United States Department of Education grant.

■ REFERENCES

Aboujaoude, E. (2010). Problematic Internet use: an overview. *World Psychiatry*, 9(2), 85–90.

Armstrong, L., Phillips, J., & Saling, L. (2000). Potential determinants of heavier Internet usage. *International Journal of Human Computer Studies*, 53, 537–550.

Atmaca, M. (2007). A case of problematic Internet use successfully treated with an SSRI–antipsychotic combination. *Progress in Neuropsychopharmacology & Biological Psychiatry*, 31(4), 961–962.

Beard, K. W. (2005). Internet addiction: a review of current assessment techniques and potential assessment questions. *Cyberpsychology & Behavior*, 8(1), 7–14.

Bostwick, J. M., & Bucci, J. A. (2008). Internet sex addiction treated with naltrexone. *Mayo Clin Proceedings*, 83(2), 226–230.

Brenner, V. (1997). Psychology of computer use: XLVII. Parameters of Internet use, abuse and addiction: the first 90 days of the Internet Usage Survey. *Psychological Reports*, 80(3 Pt 1), 879–882.

Brown, J., Keller, S., & Susannah, S. (2009). Sex, sexuality, sexting, and sex ed: Adolescents and the media. *The Prevention Researcher*, 16(4).

Carli, V., Durkee, T., Wasserman, D., Hadlaczky, G., Despalins, R., Kramarz, E., Wasserman, C., & Sarchiapone, M. (2012). The association between pathological internet use and comorbid psychopathology. *Psychopathology, 46*(1), 1–13.

Caplan, S. (2002). Problematic Internet use and psychosocial well-being: development of a theory-based cognitive-behavioral measurement instrument. *Computers in Human Behavior, 18*(5), 553–575.

Chen, S., Weng, L., Su, Y., Wu, H., & Yang, P. (2003). Development of Chinese Internet Addiction Scale and its psychometric study. *Chinese Journal of Psychology, 45*, 279–294.

Chen, S. Y., & Tzeng, J. Y. (2010). College female and male heavy Internet users' profiles of practices and their academic grades and psychosocial adjustment. *Cyberpsychology, Behavior & Society Networking, 13*(3), 257–262.

Cox Communications, in partnership with the National Center for Missing and Exploited Children and John Walsh (2009). *Teen online & wireless safety survey.* Retrieved from http://www.cox.cox/takecharge/safe_teens_2009/mediat/2009_teen_survey_internet_and_wireless_safety.pdf

Davis, R. A., Flett, G. L., & Besser, A. (2002). Validation of a new scale for measuring problematic internet use: implications for pre-employment screening. *Cyberpsychology & Behavior, 5*(4), 331–345.

Dell'Osso, B., Hadley, S., Allen, A., Baker, B., Chaplin, W. F., & Hollander, E. (2008). Escitalopram in the treatment of impulsive-compulsive internet usage disorder: an open-label trial followed by a double-blind discontinuation phase. *Journal of Clinical Psychiatry, 69*(3), 452–456.

Delmonico, D. L., & Griffin, E. J. (2008). Cybersex and the E-teen: what marriage and family therapists should know. *Journal of Marital & Family Therapy, 34*(4), 431–444.

Demetrovics, Z., Szeredi, B., & Rozsa, S. (2008). The three-factor model of Internet addiction: the development of the Problematic Internet Use Questionnaire. *Behavioral Research Methods, 40*(2), 563–574.

Donnerstein, E. (2012). Internet bullying. *Pediatric Clinics of North America, 59*(3), 623–633, viii.

Dooley, J., Pyzalski, J., & Cross, D. (2009). Cyberbullying versus face-to-face bullying. *Journal of Psychology, 217*(4).

Finkelhor, D., Mitchell, K. J., & Wolak, J. (Producer) (2000). *Online victimization: A report on the nation's youth.*

Gnisci, A., Perugini, M., RnPedone, & Conza, A. D. (2011). Construct validation of the Use, Abuse and Dependence on the Internet inventory. *Computers in Human Behavior, 27*(1), 240–247.

Gorrindo, T., Fishel, A., & Beresin, E. (2012). Understanding technology use throughout development: What Erik Erikson would say about toddler tweets and Facebook friends. *Journal of Lifelong Learning in Psychiatry, X*(3).

Han, D. H., Lee, Y. S., Na, C., Ahn, J. Y., Chung, U. S., Daniels, M. A., et al. (2009). The effect of methylphenidate on Internet video game play in children with attention-deficit/hyperactivity disorder. *Comprehensive Psychiatry, 50*(3), 251–256.

Hinduja, S., & Patchin, J. W. (2007). Offline consequences of online victimization: School violence and delinquency. *Journal of School Violence, 6*(3).

Hinduja, S., & Patchin, J. W. (2010). Bullying, cyberbullying, and suicide. *Archives of Suicide Res, 14*(3), 206–221.

Hua, L. L. (2012). Technology and sexually risky behavior in adolescents. *Adolescent Psychiatry, 2*(3), 221–228.

Johnson, S. B., Blum, R. W., & Giedd, J. N. (2009). Adolescent maturity and the brain: the promise and pitfalls of neuroscience research in adolescent health policy. *Journal of Adolescent Health, 45*(3), 216–221.

Jones, L. M., Mitchell, K. J., & Finkelhor, D. (2012). Trends in youth Internet victimization: findings from three Youth Internet Safety Surveys 2000–2010. *Journal of Adolescent Health, 50*(2), 179–186.

Kim, M., & Kim, J. (2010). Cross-validation of reliability, convergent and discriminant validity for the problematic online game use scale. *Computers in Human Behavior, 26*(3), 389–398.

Ko, C. H., Yen, J. Y., Chen, C. S., Yeh, Y. C., & Yen, C. F. (2009). Predictive values of psychiatric symptoms for Internet addiction in adolescents: a 2-year prospective study. *Archives of Pediatric & Adolescent Medicine, 163*(10), 937–943.

Lam, L. T., Peng, Z., Mai, J., & Jing, J. (2009). The association between Internet addiction and self-injurious behaviour among adolescents. *Injury Prevention, 15*(6), 403–408.

Lee, B. W., & Stapinski, L. A. (2012). Seeking safety on the Internet: relationship between social anxiety and problematic Internet use. *Journal of Anxiety Disorders, 26*(1), 197–205.

Lenhart, A. (2007). *Cyberbullying and online teens.* Washington, DC: Youth Online Safety Working Group, Pew Internet & American Life Project, PEW Research Center.

Lenhart, A. (2009). Teens and sexting. Washington, DC: Millenials: A Portrait of Generation Next, Pew Internet & American Life Project, PEW Research Center.

Lenhart, A. (2012). *Teens, smartphones, & texting.* Pew Internet & American Life Project. Retrieved from http://pewinternet.org/~/media//Files/Reports/2012/PIP_Teens_Smartphones_and_Texting.pdf

Lewin, T. (2010, March 20). Rethinking sex offender laws for youth texting. *New York Times.* Retrieved from http://www.nytimes.com

Lounsbury, K., Mitchell, K., & Finkelhor, D. (2011). The true prevalence of "sexting". Retrieved from http://www.unh.edu/ccrc/pdf/Sexting%20Fact%20Sheet%204_29_11.pdf

McBride, D. L. (2011). Risks and benefits of social media for children and adolescents. *Journal of Pediatric Nursing, 26*(5), 498–499.

Meerkerk, G. J., Van Den Eijnden, R. J., Vermulst, A. A., & Garretsen, H. F. (2009). The Compulsive Internet Use Scale (CIUS): some psychometric properties. *Cyberpsychology & Behavior, 12*(1), 1–6.

Meyer, E. (2009). "Sexting" and suicide. Retrieved from http://www.psychologytoday.com

Meyers, R. J., Miller, W. R., Hill, D. E., & Tonigan, J. S. (1998). Community Reinforcement And Family Training (CRAFT): engaging unmotivated drug users in treatment. *Journal of Substance Abuse, 10*(3), 291–308.

Mitchell, K. J., Finkelhor, D., Jones, L. M., & Wolak, J. (2012). Prevalence and characteristics of youth sexting: a national study. *Pediatrics, 129*(1), 13–20.

Mitchell, K. J., Ybarra, M., & Finkelhor, D. (2007). The relative importance of online victimization in understanding depression, delinquency, and substance use. *Child Maltreatment, 12*(4), 314–324.

Moessner, C. (2007). Cyberbullying. *Harris Interactive's Trends and Tudes*, (6), 1–4

Morahan-Martin, J., & Schumacher, P. (2000). Incidence and correlates of pathological Internet use among college students. *Computers in Human Behavior, 16*(1), 13–29.

Moreno, M. A., Jelenchick, L., Cox, E., Young, H., & Christakis, D. A. (2011). Problematic Internet use among US youth: a systematic review. *Archives of Pediatric & Adolescent Medicine, 165*(9), 797–805.

Moreno, M. A., Parks, M. R., Zimmerman, F. J., Brito, T. E., & Christakis, D. A. (2009). Display of health risk behaviors on MySpace by adolescents: prevalence and associations. *Archives of Pediatric & Adolescent Medicine, 163*(1), 27–34.

National Campaign to Prevent Teen and Unplanned Pregnancy & Cosmogirl.com (2008). *Sex and Tech: Results from a survey of teens and young adults.* Available at http://www.thenationalcampaign.org/sextech/pdf/sextech_summary.pdf

Nichols, L. A., & Nicki, R. (2004). Development of a psychometrically sound Internet addiction scale: a preliminary step. *Psychology of Addictive Behavior, 18*(4), 381–384.

O'Keeffe, G. S., Clarke-Pearson, K., Council, on, C., & Media (2011). The impact of social media on children, adolescents, and families. *Pediatrics, 127*(4), 800–804.

Patchin, J. W., & Hinduja, S. (2006). Bullies move beyond the schoolyard: A preliminary look at cyberbullying. *Youth Violence and Juvenile Justice, 4*(2), 148–169.

Patchin, J. W., & Hinduja, S. (2010). Cyberbullying and self-esteem. *Journal of School Health, 80*(12), 614–621.

Pieters, A. (2010). Editorial: Our Take on It. *Harris Interactive's Trends and Tudes*, (9), 1–4.

Pridgen, B. (2010). Navigating the Internet safely: recommendations for residential programs targeting at-risk adolescents. *Harvard Review of Psychiatry, 18*(2), 131–138.

Prinstein, M. J., Boergers, J., & Vernberg, E. M. (2001). Overt and relational aggression in adolescents: social-psychological adjustment of aggressors and victims. *Journal of Clinical Child Psychology, 30*(4), 479–491.

Raskauskas, J., & Stoltz, A. D. (2007). Involvement in traditional and electronic bullying among adolescents. *Developmental Psychology, 43*(3), 564–575.

Rice, E., Rhoades, H., Winetrobe, H., Sanchez, M., Montoya, J., Plant, A., et al. (2012). Sexually explicit cell phone messaging associated with sexual risk among adolescents. *Pediatrics, 130*(4), 667–673.

Sadhu, J. M. (2012). Sexting: the impact of a cultural phenomenon on psychiatric practice. *Academic Psychiatry, 36*(1), 76–81.

Schneider, S. K., O'Donnell, L., Stueve, A., & Coulter, R. W. (2012). Cyberbullying, school bullying, and psychological distress: a regional census of high school students. *American Journal of Public Health, 102*(1), 171–177.

Strassberg, D. S., McKinnon, R. K., Sustaita, M. A., & Rullo, J. (2013). Sexting by high school students: an exploratory and descriptive study. *Archives of Sexual Behavior, 42*(1), 15–21.

Temple, J. R., Paul, J. A., van den Berg, P., Le, V. D., McElhany, A., & Temple, B. W. (2012). Teen sexting and its association with sexual behaviors. *Archives of Pediatric & Adolescent Medicine, 166*(9), 828–833.

Waldron, H. B., Kern-Jones, S., Turner, C. W., Peterson, T. R., & Ozechowski, T. J. (2007). Engaging resistant adolescents in drug abuse treatment. *Journal of Substance Abuse Treatment, 32*(2), 133–142.

Widyanto, L., Griffiths, M. D., & Brunsden, V. (2011). A psychometric comparison of the Internet Addiction Test, the Internet-Related Problem Scale, and self-diagnosis. *Cyberpsychology, Behavior & Social Networking, 14*(3), 141–149.

Wolak, J. & Finkelhor, D. (2011). *Sexting: A Typology.* University of New Hampshire Crimes Against Children Research Center, 1–10.

Wolak, J., Mitchell, K., & Finkelhor, D. (2007a). Unwanted and wanted exposure to online pornography in a national sample of youth Internet users. *Pediatrics, 119*(2), 247–257.

Wolak, J., Mitchell, K. J., & Finkelhor, D. (2007b). Does online harassment constitute bullying? An exploration of online harassment by known peers and online-only contacts. *Journal of Adolescent Health, 41*(6 Suppl 1), S51–S58.

Ybarra, M. L. (2004). Linkages between depressive symptomatology and Internet harassment among young regular Internet users. *Cyberpsychology & Behavior, 7*(2), 247–257.

Ybarra, M. L., Alexander, C., & Mitchell, K. J. (2005). Depressive symptomatology, youth Internet use, and online interactions: A national survey. *Journal of Adolescent Health, 36*(1), 9–18.

Ybarra, M. L., Diener-West, M., & Leaf, P. J. (2007). Examining the overlap in Internet harassment and school bullying: implications for school intervention. *Journal of Adolescent Health, 41*(6 Suppl 1), S42–S50.

Young, K. (1998). *Caught in the Net: How to recognize the signs of Internet addiction—and a winning strategy for recovery*. New York: John Wiley & Sons.

Young, K., & Rodgers R. (1998). The relationship between depression and Internet addiction. *Cyberpsychology & Behavior, 1*(1), 25–28.

14 Ethical and Legal Considerations for Psychiatry Regarding Adolescents and Technology Use

■ ARIEL SEROUSSI, DANIEL BONNICI,
GREGORY B. LEONG, AND
ROBERT WEINSTOCK

■ INTRODUCTION

As highly social animals, human beings create rules and standards for interacting with each other, to preserve groups and benefit their collective members. These rules and standards take many forms, among them laws, morals, and informal agreements. The advancement of science and its related technologies has greatly influenced such regulations of human interaction, and today continues to influence the ethical framework by which societies operate.

In the past two hundred years, we have witnessed rapid scientific and technological advances by which information can be disseminated. Resulting from the harnessing of electricity, the telegraph, telephone, and radio transmissions allowed for personal information to be transmitted nearly instantaneously, at great distances. Within the past four decades, advances in computer technology and the rise of the Internet have greatly affected the flow of information between people. For practical purposes, anyone with a computer or computer-related derivatives (i.e., smartphones, tablet personal computers) can access, disseminate, or receive instantaneous, real-time information. Information and communication appear in various forms, such as instant messaging, text messaging, online chat rooms and electronic bulletin boards, blogs, listservs, and social networking sites. Even face-to-face communication can occur, via real-time video chatting for personal or professional purposes. Communication can increasingly be performed from anywhere, at any time, and is ever more instantaneous.

These computer-driven electronic advances have created new challenges to confidentiality and privacy, and continue to test the ethical frameworks by which society operates. The medical field has encountered a unique set of such challenges, where patient care and confidentiality must be prioritized due to the sensitivity of medical interactions and information in the face of increased access to information. The challenges posed by technology are magnified in the field of psychiatry, where emotions and relationships are the subject of clinical decision making. So central has this subject become that psychiatry residents are increasingly being formally educated regarding professionalism and use of technology such as the Internet. In 2010, the President of the American Association of Directors of Psychiatric Residency Training (AADPRT) established a Taskforce on Professionalism and the Internet to this aim (DeJong et al., 2012).

Furthermore, ethically difficult situations gain yet more complexity in the context of treating children and adolescents. In the field of child and adolescent psychiatry, legal, developmental, behavioral, and cultural factors all combine to test clinicians' commitment to patient care and morally responsible behavior. In today's day and age, adolescents outpace adults in their use of computers and smartphones to access the Internet to send emails, or send text messages at a breakneck pace. They use sites such as Facebook and Twitter, social networking platforms where one can affiliate with other users as their "friend" or follow their posts, can communicate privately or publicly with other users, and can share personal information and photos. Psychiatrists who treat adolescents will increasingly need to develop skills in addressing this technological behavior. They will need to be mindful of professional boundaries in order to behave ethically, yet appreciate the integral role that technology plays in the lives of most teenagers.

Many questions will arise that test these requirements to provide ethically sound clinical care. For instance, what should psychiatrists do when an adolescent patient asks to be their "friend" on Facebook? How should they react to a patient or a parent who has been scouring the Internet for information about them, and when might they themselves use search engines to find out more about a troubled teenager? How does one approach communication by email when patients begin to use this method to discuss their symptoms, send files such as pictures or videos, email while the clinician is out of town, or express emergent concerns such as suicidal ideation in the middle of the night via email rather than telephone?

Those practitioners most knowledgeable about the uses of the Internet and social networking sites are generally the younger members of the profession, as opposed to older but more clinically experienced practitioners. As a result, these areas may be best addressed by those at both ends of the age and experience spectrum (as reflected in this chapter's authors), and we will attempt to combine these perspectives through our present discussion.

This chapter will focus on the ethical and legal considerations regarding technology and the Internet, as they relate to adolescents and the psychiatrists who treat them. We will survey the historical and present approaches to biomedical ethics that inform our approaches to treating psychiatric patients, and specifically children and adolescents. A discussion of legal precedents regarding adolescents and mental health will follow, along with a primer on scientific research regarding the nature of adolescent brain and behavioral development. Finally, we will describe specific areas of ethical relevance where technology and the doctor–patient relationship intersect, with particular attention to psychiatrists treating adolescents. Among these areas are ethical dilemmas related to the use of social networking sites, search engines, and email communication, which have received significant attention in academic literature and popular culture. This chapter may serve to elucidate situations that deserve heightened attention from clinicians, suggest ethical facts that should be consider in clinical scenarios, and outline different approaches to clinical and ethical decision making.

▪ ETHICAL APPROACHES TO TECHNOLOGY AND ADOLESCENTS

Ethics is a branch of philosophy that involves systematizing, analyzing, defending, and recommending concepts of right and wrong behavior (Fieser, 2009). Often referred to as moral philosophy, the field of ethics is most commonly divided into three subfields by philosophers: meta-ethics, normative ethics, and applied ethics. Meta-ethics seeks to examine the fundamental nature of ethical properties and evaluations, asking questions such as "What *is* morality?" It delves into the meaning of moral language, and the metaphysics of moral facts. In contrast, normative ethics is a more practical endeavor devoted to examining standards for right or wrong conduct. It seeks to answer such questions as "*How* should one behave morally (or ethically)?" Finally, the subfield of applied ethics seeks to address specific, controversial issues. Examples include environmental ethics, business ethics, or the disciplines of bioethics and forensic psychiatric ethics being addressed in this chapter.

Some have tried to make distinctions between ethics and morality. Although one or the other word tends to be used in certain contexts, both have been used interchangeably in philosophy (Foot, 1990). When discussing professionalism, the usual term is "ethics," while in religion the usual term is "morals." But in describing personal behavior, both "ethical" and "moral" are used interchangeably. So the use of one or the other term does not help solve dilemmas. Organizations can establish ethical guidelines and ethical (or moral) practitioners will usually follow them, with rare exceptions due to difficult ethical guidelines or situations. Because this area is so new, ethical guidelines still are being developed.

Bioethics can be defined as an area of applied ethics that seeks to address issues related to the life sciences surrounding human beings, animals, and nature (Gordon, 2012). As all areas of applied ethics, it draws from both meta-ethical and normative ethical approaches. Medical or biomedical ethics is a yet another subfield of this discipline devoted to issues arising in the clinical setting, and has evolved over several millennia. Edicts on the role of a physician can be traced to antiquity, in such guidelines as the Hippocratic Oath from the fifth century B.C. written by Hippocrates, widely regarded as the father of Western medicine (Edelstein, 1996). "First do no harm" is not part of the Oath, but is part of the Hippocratic corpus of ethics described later by the Romans. There can be differences in current practice with regard to prioritizing patient and societal welfare in clinical and forensic settings, and as such application of the Hippocratic corpus of ethics may vary in today's day and age (Weinstock et al., 1990).

The field developed in subsequent centuries in the Middle Ages through writing by noted scholars and philosophers in the Muslim and Jewish traditions, with Christian medical ethics developing later. The term "medical ethics" would ultimately be coined by Thomas Percival, an English physician who published his influential *Code of Medical Ethics* in 1803 (American Medical Association, 2006). When the American Medical Association held its inaugural meeting in 1847, it adopted its first *Code of Ethics* based largely on Percival's original text. Biomedical ethics would again be transformed by the Doctors' Trial in the Nuremberg trials after World War II. Subsequently, the Tuskegee syphilis experiment in the middle of the twentieth century raised serious ethical concerns about abuse of medicine even in the United States. These infamous events generated awareness of informed consent as an essential moral practice, which has informed practices in human subject research, and physicians' obtaining patient consent for treatment including medications or procedures.

Modern biomedical ethics has been greatly influenced by the *Principles of Biomedical Ethics*, published by Beauchamp and Childress in 1979. This work formalized the field significantly and espouses ethical tenets that, like the Hippocratic Oath, are taught in medical schools worldwide. Prior to this work, K. Danner Clouser called the field a "mixture of religion, whimsy, exhortation, legal precedents, various traditions, philosophies of life, miscellaneous moral rules and epithets" (Clouser, 1993; Rauprich & Vollmann, 2011). Beauchamp and Childress set out explicitly to "bring some order and coherence to the discussion" by means of a "systematic analysis of the moral principles that should apply to biomedicine." Their work outlined four clusters of moral principles that have become a cornerstone of biomedical ethics (Beauchamp, 2009):

1. Autonomy: an acknowledgment that patients are free to make decisions
2. Nonmaleficence: the fundamental principle of avoiding the potential for harm
3. Beneficence: a consideration of the equation of weighing benefits versus risks
4. Justice: fairness in how burdens and benefits are distributed

Beauchamp and Childress have published several updated editions to their seminal work from 1979, refining an approach that has been labeled "principlism." They have argued that their framework is globally applicable, as a consequence of the above moral (or ethical) principles being norms that form part of a "common morality." The common morality has been understood as "a collection of very general norms adhered to by everybody, everywhere, who is authentically committed to morality" (Herissone-Kelly, 2011, p. 584). A responding criticism holds that we can empirically demonstrate that there is not one universal morality but rather many, varied systems of morality. As the *Principles of Biomedical Ethics* has been revised, Beauchamp and Childress have sought to disprove this criticism, arguing that particular moralities are applications of the common morality.

A practical element of Beauchamp and Childress' principlist approach is specification, which can be defined as a "way of bringing general moral norms to bear on concrete cases and issues by adding context-specific and action-guiding content" (Rauprich, 2011, p. 592). Specification was formalized by Henry Richardson and adopted by Beauchamp and Childress in the fourth edition of their book (Richardson, 1990). By this method of applied ethics, one first determines the essential morally relevant features of a case or issue, and then determines their relation to the general norms of morality being applied in an explicit and systematic fashion. At the end of this chain of reasoning, one may reach a decision based on an action's alignment with these norms. Beauchamp and Childress acknowledge that specification operates under limitations—equally informed, impartial, and rational persons may come to different judgments about the moral features of a case, and how moral norms apply to these facts. Rauprich (2011, p. 593) has noted that we "cannot deal with the diversity and complexity of real-life moral problems in a simple, uniform way." Nevertheless, specification involves explicitly listing morally relevant facts of a case in a way that physicians might emulate, making their ethical decision making more systematic than haphazard. Specification is thus a meticulous method in academic ethics that is relevant to normative considerations by physicians, but may not feasibly be expected to guide decision making on its own.

Ethical principles alone cannot resolve dilemmas in part because they can often conflict in complex situations, without a meta-ethical rule to establish priorities. As Hundert (1990) has described, such situations require the physician to balance conflicting duties. It has been described that psychiatrists in particular are taking on increasingly complex roles in different contexts, having to reconcile competing duties with a robust requirement for professionalism (Candilis & Layde, 2007). Frameworks such as Beauchamp and Childress' principles do not assist in determining which principle should have priority when they lead to different courses of action. An academic discussion and even best formal training might be helpful on the subject of ethics in mental health, as psychiatrists will have to draw on several ethical approaches and considerations beyond a clear-cut set of rules. However, thinking out ethical dilemmas in practical situations can and should be attempted by every conscientious practitioner.

A relevant normative ethical theory is that of care ethics, inspired by feminist philosophy and often attributed to the works of psychologist Carol Gilligan and philosopher Nel Noddings in the mid-1980s (Sander-Staudt, 2011). Their work suggests that moral thinking displays a degree of dimorphism in humans, such that males and females approach ethical dilemmas in reliably different patterns. Gilligan, Noddings, and other feminist theorists have noted previous moral systems to have a male bias toward justice and abstract obligations. They advocated for the alternative consideration of themes associated with a more female bias, including empathy and compassion. The resulting theory of care ethics identifies a moral significance in the fundamental elements of relationships and dependencies among human beings. It emphasizes that one's degree of moral consideration should correspond to the vulnerability of the person being affected by one's actions in any given situation. Furthermore, it calls for the careful consideration of the specific, contextual details of every situation in order to preserve the interests of those involved. Beauchamp and Childress have cited this in addressing limitations to the use of universal principles, noting, "We can produce rough generalizations about how caring physicians and nurses respond to patients, for example, but these generalizations will not be subtle enough to give helpful guidance for the next patient. Each situation calls for a set of responses outside any generalization" (Beauchamp & Childress, 2001, p. 373).

Care ethics has substantial implications for biomedical ethics, given that medicine is a field where the physician explicitly sets out to care for the patient. Beauchamp and Childress again validate the relevance of care ethics when describing the unique nature of the health-care field. They have suggested that "the care perspective is especially meaningful for roles such as parent, friend, physician, and nurse, in which contextual response, attentiveness to subtle clues, and the deepening of special relationships are likely to be more momentous morally than impartial treatment" (Beauchamp & Childress, 2001, p. 372). The role for care ethics is particularly important in psychiatry, the medical field where attentiveness to clues and context, and the formation of a doctor–patient relationship, may be of most therapeutic importance. Although the caring approach originated in the context of feminist ethics, psychiatrists of either sex should consider the central tenets of care ethics in determining the most ethical (or moral) thing to do. In the discussion that follows, we will address the even further importance of care ethics when treating adolescents.

We have described that care ethics and applied principlism involve processing ethically relevant facts of each clinical scenario before deciding how to act. Both ethical theories acknowledge the lack of a purely abstract and formulaic system for determining ethical practice. After thoroughly examining a clinical scenario, the physician will have to be flexible and use judgment and reason to behave as ethically as possible. In this process, psychiatrists in particular may be well served to meld widely established norms such as Beauchamp and Childress' four principles with a consideration of their relationship with the patient, the patient's emotional state and predisposition, and the effects their actions may have on the patient. Using this approach, principles of care ethics may critically inform a psychiatrist's application of principles such as beneficence and nonmaleficence.

Taking such an inclusive, contextually oriented, and compassionate approach may be particularly germane to challenging clinical situations where the law or professional ethical codes may not clearly inform the most ethical course of action. The psychiatrist should always consider the ethical codes and recommendations of professional organizations such as the American Medical Association and the American Psychiatric Association. It always is ethically permissible to follow the law and regulations, so it is necessary to consider federal and state law and medical board requirements. They do not determine ethics, but there are potential consequences for not following them. Scenarios may arise commonly where these references do not provide the psychiatrist adequate clarity in directing ethical behavior. Furthermore, there may be situations where the law and formalized ethical codes may not coincide with the most ethical course of action. The American Medical Association has acknowledged this explicitly in its Code of Ethics:

> Ethical values and legal principles are usually closely related, but ethical obligations typically exceed legal duties. In some cases, the law mandates unethical conduct. In general, when physicians believe a law is unjust, they should work to change the law. In exceptional circumstances of unjust laws, ethical responsibilities should supersede legal obligations (American Medical Association, 1994).

The American Psychiatric Association has echoed these sentiments, stating, "While no committee or board could offer prior assurance that any illegal activity would not be considered unethical, it is conceivable that an individual could violate a law without being guilty of professionally unethical behavior" (American Psychiatric Association, 2009). A number of examples of this arise in psychiatry. For instance, in certain cases a psychiatrist may exhaust the legally prescribed period of involuntary detention for danger to self on patients who still continue to endorse suicidal ideation. Such instances might lead to many practitioners "stretching" the legal criteria to get patients needed treatment in clinical as opposed to forensic practice. Other examples of conflict between legal and ethical action that could involve breaking the law may arise in cases of mandated reporting for child abuse or HIV, where the psychiatrist may assess that the report will ultimately cause more harm than withholding information. Similar consideration may apply to patients who disclose a past history of illegal activity but are currently assessed to represent a low risk of repeating such actions. In these instances, the requirements for confidentiality likely outweigh reporting them absent a current or likely future danger. The law likely would support such a decision as well in most cases where there is not mandated reporting. However, violating the law can have serious legal consequences, including incarceration, even absent any ethical sanctions. As such it should be very unusual and extremely rare that a practitioner should elect not to follow the law when there are legal requirements. The issue should be of sufficient importance to warrant facing possible legal punishment. Also, it is always to our knowledge considered ethically acceptable by professional organizations to follow the law even in something that otherwise would be unethical. So there is room for different practitioners to make different decisions.

In the above cases the psychiatrist may appeal to the aspirational nature rather than the strictly regulatory nature of ethics, making normative decisions on how to act when explicit and predetermined rules either do not exist, exist but are inadequate, or exist and are inconsistent with the most moral or ethical course of action. This is particularly relevant to our present discussion, as technological advances most often outpace the capacity of formal legal and ethical regulation. Guidelines are evolving and developing as well. We will outline specific examples regarding social networking sites, search engines, and email communication, where strictly regulatory ethics has yet to provide comprehensive guidance to clinicians. With the advent of future novel technologies beyond those mentioned in this text, clinicians will be called upon to continue to make decisions affecting the lives of patients in an ethically uncertain landscape.

Definitions in Biomedical Ethics

It will be useful to define terms that are cited frequently in literature on biomedical ethics and professionalism, and are often associated with the Internet and technology. Among these are the term "boundary crossing," defined as a transient, non-exploitative deviation from the standard of care, which is minor and at times may actually be beneficial in treatment (Gutheil, 2005). Examples include providing a patient with limited personal information, assisting a civilian or patient who has fallen outside of the treatment office or hospital, or doing a home visit for a patient. A "boundary violation," on the other hand, may be defined as a deviation from the standard of care that is exploitative and harmful to the patient, such as entering into a sexual relationship with him or her. Another concept often cited in discussion on the interaction between patient and physician on the Internet is that of "dual relationships," defined as the existence of several, separate relationships with the same individual (Endacott et al., 2006). An example might be going into business with a patient. Finally, the term "double effect" refers to the two distinct consequences that may be produced by a single action. In biomedical ethics, this often involves the combined effect of an action that challenges the tenets of both beneficence and nonmaleficence to achieve some other desirable result.

Biomedical Ethics Concerning Adolescents

The influence of mainstream biomedical ethics, such Beauchamp and Childress' principles, extends into the treatment of minors in the medical field. Within medicine psychiatry is no exception, as the American Academy of Child and Adolescent Psychiatry (AACAP) has its own code of ethics that is largely based on the previously described, principlist approach to biomedical ethics (AACAP, 2009). This code is molded, however, to the set of challenges unique to treating children and adolescents, highlighted in the code's preamble. As such it provides useful guidance for our present discussion of ethical issues related to adolescents. The code notes, for instance, that since the services of an adolescent psychiatrist are often sought by a patient's parent(s) or guardian(s), "The practitioner has obligations to both the individual patient and the youngster's guardians" (AACAP, 2009, p. 2). Furthermore, the preamble reiterates the present consideration of the child and adolescent's developmental capacities (AACAP, 2009, p. 2):

> The child and adolescent psychiatrist is responsible for assessing and providing treatment recommendations for young individuals who, owing to their cognitive, emotional, behavioral, and/or physical immaturities, typically lack adult developmental capacities and are legally considered minors...Assent, consent, confidentiality, and, separately, professional responsibility, authority, and behavior, must be viewed within the framework of ongoing child development. The rights and interests of the child or adolescent, and the professional's behaviors toward the child or adolescent, demand considerations of maturational factors.

With these formal recommendations in mind, we can see how the aforementioned ethical theories will have specific applications to scenarios with adolescent patients. For instance, the principle of autonomy will apply not only to the particularly immature adolescent patient, but also to his or her parent or legal guardian. Moreover, the care ethics model may also be highly relevant to cases involving adolescent patients where the fiduciary responsibilities of the therapist to the adolescent can be especially strong. Fiduciary responsibilities are legal ones. The psychiatrically ill adolescent may be considered particularly vulnerable and may be uniquely affected by the actions of a clinician as compared to an adult. As such, adolescent patients may warrant greater attention to the principles of care ethics, including a clinician's attentiveness to the patient's unique circumstances and emotional state and the clinician–patient relationship.

Ethical considerations relating to psychiatric patients and technology use are undoubtedly complex, across all age ranges. Many of the dilemmas encountered by today's psychiatrist are novel given the rapid changes in the past several decades, and an ethical literature and set of practical guidelines that are yet catching up with such changes. Practitioners treating adolescent psychiatric patients will thus be charged with a uniquely difficult task. Not only must they make difficult ethical decisions based on a limited amount of established ethical and legal precedent, they must also incorporate the developmental considerations unique to the field of adolescent psychiatry. Also, in complex situations duties and guidelines sometimes conflict, necessitating an ethical analysis with differing conclusions among practitioners, since guidelines rarely explicate how to balance conflicting duties. Through a discussion of legal precedent regarding minors, their parents, and mental health professionals, we will provide further background before proceeding to discuss recent scientific research relevant to the ethics of treating adolescent patients.

■ PARENTS, MINORS, GOVERNMENT, AND MENTAL HEALTH PROVIDERS IN THE INTERNET AGE

Parents, government, and mental health professionals have distinct, intersecting roles in the context of providing mental health care to children and adolescents. Under the default paradigm, parents retain control over individual children and adolescents. However, the advancement of technology into the home has brought together multiple parties in an intricate network that implicates the police and other regulatory powers of the state, health-care providers, and individual families.

First, parents are charged with protecting their children's interests, and also with protecting others from their children's behaviors. Parents' interests, presumably, generally align with their children's interests and the parent–child relationship is afforded sanctity, with deference given to parental decision making. Constitutionally, parents have a liberty interest and right to "establish a home and bring up children," protected under the Fourteenth Amendment Due Process Clause (*Meyer v. Nebraska*, 1923). The U.S. Supreme Court observed in *Troxel v. Granville* (2000) that "so long as a parent adequately cares for his or her children..., there will normally be no reason for the State to inject into the private realm of the family to further question the ability of that parent to make the best decisions concerning the rearing of that parent's children."

However, parents' interests and the child's interests do not always align. Their interests may occasionally conflict, such as when parents seek to involuntarily hospitalize their child for mental health reasons. Parents, even those not suffering from mental illness or substance abuse issues themselves, may have motives that run counter to the best interests of the child. Parents can be overly intrusive and micromanage their child's behavior to his or her detriment, or conversely may have exceptionally lax oversight—which is their right until the child or adolescent engages in behavior directly detrimental to himself or herself or others. Parents can also be punitive, in some instances want to get rid of a disruptive adolescent, or want to enforce their will on a rebellious adolescent. In some case they may just disapprove legitimately of a girlfriend or boyfriend, or the adolescent's experimenting with drugs, but the behavior might not warrant involuntary hospitalization. Adolescent development will be discussed further below, along with a brief discussion of emancipated and "mature" minors, two doctrines that carve out decision-making arenas in which adolescents may make decisions without the influence of their parents. Most of the time, however, in seeking involuntary hospitalization the parent is likely to be looking out for the welfare of the adolescent as opposed to the adolescent's immediate desires. Unless there is reason to think otherwise, the state should support the desires of the parent if such actions are consistent with state law.

Many states have given all adolescents the right to consent to things like abortion and mental health treatment without parental consent. California has such a provision, but parental consent is needed for psychotropic medication. It is thought the advantages of giving adolescents these rights outweigh the disadvantages, though every state handles it differently and may not give adolescents these rights. Adolescents may be immature in their thinking and behavior, but in some situations the advantage of giving them these rights might outweigh the disadvantage. It is important for clinicians to be aware of the laws in their jurisdiction.

Government intrusions into the lives of minors in the legal and criminal context can range from police stops of minors on the street to searches of the person, the home, computers, electronic documents, email communications, and social networking sites. Government also functions as a protector of children more broadly, with so-called *parens patriae* powers, as seen in legislation discussed below. With the advent of the Internet and advances in wireless technology, children and adolescents are accessing the Internet in greater numbers and with a variety of tools to do so, including smartphones, tablets, and laptops (Lenhart et al., 2010). This increased access to the Internet exposes children and adolescents to greater risks (inappropriate content, contacts, etc.). Initially, the federal government made moves to put limits on the material available on the Internet, but congressional attempts to regulate content were seen as overbroad infringements of constitutionally protected speech, in violation of the First Amendment (Communications Decency Act, 1996). Later efforts by Congress have prevented certain entities that receive federal funding (i.e., public libraries and public schools) from providing unfiltered Internet access through the Children's Internet Protection Act. A separate 1998 law, the Children's Online Privacy Protection Act, authorized the Federal Trade Commission (FTC) to prevent websites from obtaining information from minors without parental consent. Under the authority granted by this statute, the FTC recently issued a regulatory proposal seeking additional oversight in light of possible violations (Singer, 2012). Adolescents may thus be protected in ways that adults are not, to guard against their vulnerability due to greater impulsivity and frequent failure to consider all consequences.

Linking and often navigating between minors and parents are mental health professionals. Mental health professionals have no traditional governmental authority, but they are charged with the power to initiate involuntary commitments, a deprivation of liberty, and this power brings them into the court system. The role of mental health professionals as a neutral third party when making decisions positions them in an advisory role and is complicated by ethical, legal, and moral obligations to all participants in this increasingly complex arrangement.

Treating medically or psychiatrically ill children and adolescents is thus complicated by the unique relationship among parents, children, and physicians. When all parties agree to a specific treatment, the law and biomedical ethics are more straightforward—informed consent is obtained from the responsible parent, assent is obtained from the minor, and treatment proceeds. Assent is defined as consent by somebody legally incapable of giving consent. In cases where parents and physicians disagree, or where a minor and parents disagree, the law and concurrent ethical constructions can raise conundrums. At common law there were and continue to be exceptions to the necessity of parental consent for treatment, namely when a minor is "emancipated" or deemed to be sufficiently "mature" to proceed with a treatment or procedure without the consent of responsible parents. Examples of emancipation include minors who are self-supporting and/or not living at home, married, pregnant or a parent, in the military, or declared to be emancipated by a court (Commission on Bioethics, 1995). In *Bellotti v. Baird* (1979), the Supreme Court invalidated a Massachusetts statute requiring either the consent of both parents or a judicial order for a pregnant minor to obtain an abortion. In so doing, the Court argued that such a statute would subject a minor to an "absolute veto" of her decision, even in cases where the minor was "well enough informed to make her abortion decision in consultation with her physician independently of her parents' wishes."

The mature minor doctrine, adopted in various forms by most states, gives deference to judges to determine whether an individual minor is sufficiently mature to make his or her own medical decisions. However, some argue that a more sensible approach to the various legal tests of maturity would be to give deference to health professionals who have "researched and debated the issue of maturity" and who therefore have "all the necessary tools to determine the maturity of a minor" (Slonina, 2007, p. 209). A responding concern notes that not all practitioners have such training and knowledge or such interest. West Virginia took this approach via the West Virginia Health Care Decisions Act of 2000, which statutorily defines a mature minor as "a person less than eighteen years of age who has been determined by a qualified physician, a qualified psychologist or an advanced nurse practitioner to have the capacity to make health care decisions" (West Virginia Health Care Decisions Act, 2002). This approach is consistent with the deference to health-care professionals to decide in cases where the parent seeks to involuntarily hospitalize a minor child. In *Parham v. JR* (1979), the Supreme Court upheld a Georgia statute allowing parents to institutionalize a child as long as an "independent third-party physician" evaluated the child initially and periodically for the appropriateness of institutionalization in a mental health facility. The holding in this case is frequently cited as the basis for similar state statutes throughout the United States (see Kentucky, Nevada, Louisiana legal codes).

■ SCIENTIFIC CONSIDERATIONS FOR CHILD AND ADOLESCENT RIGHTS

Special consideration is given to child and adolescent criminal culpability. The basis for this distinct consideration stems from common law and was observed as early as in Roman times. An 1845 criminal case, *The Queen v. Smith*, laid out the common law Rule of Sevens (Mlyniec, 1996). It provided bright-line, age-specific rules for criminal culpability of minors whereby, for instance, children younger than seven were immune to prosecution for criminality. Between the ages of seven and 14 there was a rebuttable presumption of no capacity, ages 14 to 21 had a rebuttable presumption of an "adult capability" to perform "evil acts," and by the age of 21, individuals were determined to have full capacity. In civil as compared to criminal courts, the age of adulthood was historically 21. These precise age distinctions have eroded over time, by statute, common law, and even a constitutional amendment reducing the voting age to 18, though "there remained the general rule that the law granted parents broad decision-making power over their children" (Slonina, 2007, p. 188).

The uniqueness of adolescent behavior (compared to that of both children and adults) has long been observed, as Aristotle mused that the young were "hot-tempered, and quick-tempered, and apt to give way to their anger" (Roberts, 1941). Child and adolescent development was first formally studied by prominent psychological thinkers in a theoretical and observational context, such as by Piaget and Kohlberg, in the mid-twentieth century. Advances in neuroimaging and behavioral studies over the past 20 years have formalized what is often presumed to be a self-evident truth, that adolescents think and act differently from both children and adults. The Centers for Disease Control and Prevention conducts the Youth Risk Behavior Surveillance System, a nationwide survey of high-school students around the country, which provides data about their risky behaviors. The data show a high prevalence of risky behaviors, including high-risk sexual behavior, texting while driving, binge drinking, drinking while driving, and physical altercations. These data confirm the general public perception that teenagers engage in risky behavior (Eaton et al., 2012).

Advances in neuroimaging techniques have allowed a much more detailed look at the structure and function of the brain. The frontal lobe of the brain is widely considered a command center that controls executive processing and is necessary for high-level decision making. Frontal lobe development, beginning with a gray matter surge during puberty and subsequent neural "pruning," continues from puberty until late adolescence, and likely into early adulthood (Kambam & Thompson, 2009). Gray matter density decreases as a result of pruning in the frontal lobe until the third decade of life, while white matter density and volume increase as a result of myelination, both of which occur in the maturing brain (Sowell et al., 1999). These anatomical changes likely underlie the development of more efficient communication between the frontal cortex and other parts of the brain.

Research using fMRI and diffusion tensor imaging has identified multiple areas of immaturity in the adolescent brain that may relate to adolescents' well-recognized behavioral limitations, including impulse control, reward motivation, and perception of self and others (Pope et al., 2012). Impulse control and response inhibition involve a wide circuitry believed to be mediated by the ventrolateral prefrontal cortex, the development of which may underlie an improvement in performance on inhibitory control tasks into early adulthood (Luna et al., 2010).

Several fMRI studies have been cited as evidence of the immaturity of adolescent reward motivation systems, specifically with regard to the underactivation of circuitry involved in assessing risk and overvaluation of circuitry involved in reward seeking when compared to mature brains (Geier & Luna, 2009). Furthermore, adolescents appear to be more susceptible to peer influence than their adult counterparts. Studies have identified increased activation of reward areas during risk taking in the presence of peers (Chein et al., 2011).

In an attempt to marry biological studies with behavioral studies of brain development, Steinberg (2010) proposes a dual systems model of adolescent risk taking. He proposes a "socioemotional" system, localized in limbic and paralimbic areas of the brain, and a "cognitive control" system, composed of the lateral prefrontal, parietal cortices, and connecting tracts. According to his work, self-report questionnaires and performance on the Tower of London study show a linear decrease in impulsivity from age 11 to 30, while self-report questionnaires and performance on the Iowa Gambling Task show a curvilinear pattern of reward seeking peaking in mid-adolescence. He hypothesizes that adolescent risk taking and reward seeking is stimulated by a rapid increase in dopaminergic activity within the socioemotional system around the age of puberty. He also hypothesizes that a temporal delay occurs as the cognitive control system matures more gradually, creating a heightened vulnerability to risk taking during middle adolescence (Steinberg, 2010).

Current research is limited by extrapolation of findings from theory-based and population-based studies to assumptions about individual children and adolescents. Studies do not yet definitively identify the causation between brain development and behavioral maturity in the individual adolescent. An additional difficulty with the formal study of adolescent behavior is its relevance to the "real world." In this realm, the theories of "hot cognition" and "cold cognition" are pertinent—they compare decision making while under the influence of peers and in high-arousal situations (hot) with decision making in low-arousal or even hypothetical situations (cold) (Kambam & Thompson, 2009). The consideration of different settings suggests that low-arousal decision making, for instance in study settings or the physician's office, may not reflect the realities of decision making in the emotion-filled environment of an adolescent's daily life, and this should in turn be taken into account when assessing the "maturity" of minors (Silber, 2011). As such, one should be cautious in interpreting present studies and making generalizations to clinical care.

The Supreme Court has waded into the issue of child and adolescent immaturity in criminal law. In *Thompson v. Oklahoma*, a 1988 case, a 15-year-old who committed a capital crime was sentenced to death. In barring the death penalty for crimes committed prior to age 16, the Court reasoned (*Thompson v. Oklahoma*, 1988):

> Thus, the Court has already endorsed the proposition that less culpability should attach to a crime committed by a juvenile than to a comparable crime committed by

an adult. The basis for this conclusion is too obvious to require extended explanation. Inexperience, less education, and less intelligence make the teenager less able to evaluate the consequences of his or her conduct while at the same time he or she is much more apt to be motivated by mere emotion or peer pressure than is an adult.

More recent decisions highlight the Supreme Court's willingness to consider adolescent immaturity to evaluate the degree of criminal culpability and sentencing of minors convicted of crimes. It has not removed responsibility, but rather limited the most extreme punishments. In *Roper v. Simmons* (2005), the Court held that imposition of the death penalty to a minor is unconstitutional, violating the Eighth Amendment as cruel and unusual punishment. It based its decision primarily on developments around the country and around the world, where virtually no other countries were executing adolescents. In 2010, in *Graham v. Florida*, the Court held that juveniles convicted of a non-homicidal crime could not be sentenced to life without the possibility of parole. They recognized the immaturity of adolescents in their decision. In 2012, in *Miller v. Alabama*, the Court used the precedents of *Roper v. Simmons* and *Graham v. Florida* to strike down sentences of life without the possibility of parole for two 14-year-olds convicted of murder, reasoning that the judiciary must take into account their adolescence as a mitigating circumstance. The Court argued that not doing so violated the Eighth Amendment right of proportionality. In *Miller v. Alabama* the Court cited the aforementioned cases' use of "science and social science," reasoning that adolescents are unique in three ways: (1) they lack maturity and are therefore "reckless, impulsive, and heedless risk takers," (2) they are more vulnerable to outside pressures from peers and family, and (3) their character is not "well-formed" and is not fixed, so their immaturity is potentially transient. However, *Miller v. Alabama* does not make such life sentences impermissible so long as mitigating factors have been considered and the sentence is not automatically imposed. It also mentions the fact that a significant transfer to adult court sometimes can be made solely by a prosecutor. States can have provisions to consider the mitigation of such a sentence at a later time, as was just adopted in California, but they are not required to do so and most currently do not.

■ SOCIAL NETWORKING SITES

Social networking sites have become a major part of our lives, providing an efficient medium for communication with relatives, friends, and coworkers (Ginory et al., 2012). Facebook, the most popular of these sites, enlists over 500 million users: as many as 51% of Americans over the age of 12 are reported to have a Facebook profile (Webster, 2011). The advent of mobile devices with Internet access facilitates the use of social network sites, and Facebook recently reported that over 200 million users may be accessing the site from a mobile device at any given time (Facebook, 2012a). Though Facebook is a leading social networking site, there are a number of other sites and applications that similarly allow for the formation of connections among users and a display of personal information. Twitter, for instance, is a service that allows users to follow postings made by other users. The posts can be made and read quite rapidly from a variety of mobile and stationary computer-based devices, and Twitter is becoming increasingly popular with many demographics, including adolescents, young adults, and celebrities such as actors, musicians, and professional athletes. In fact, news and journalism increasingly draws from services such as Twitter: in fact, previously well-established media sources such as television, radio, or print are reporting based on the Twitter feeds of people of interest.

For the purpose of this discussion we will focus on Facebook, which has received the most attention of the social network sites in the biomedical literature. Many of the insights to follow, however, will be generalizable to other social networking sites that share properties with Facebook and therefore raise similar ethical dilemmas for physicians.

Given Facebook's growing presence in our society, it is inevitable that both patients and physicians have become regular users of the site. A study from the University of Florida in 2008 found that 44.5 percent of medical trainees, students, and residents had Facebook profiles (Thompson et al., 2008). More recent foreign studies from France and New Zealand have identified higher figures of Facebook use among multispecialty residents, at 73 and 65 percent respectively (MacDonald et al., 2010; Moubarak et al., 2011). In a recent anonymous, voluntary survey of residents on the American Psychiatric Association email listserv (Ginory et al., 2012), 89 percent reported ever having Facebook profiles, 9.7 percent had received "friend" requests from patients, and 18.7 percent admitted to viewing patient profiles on the site. Although this survey is limited in scope, it clearly suggests that psychiatry residents are using Facebook at a similar rate as other specialties, if not more.

Recent data demonstrate that psychiatrists must assume that their adolescent patients are using the Internet and are also using Facebook. The Pew Internet & American Life Project reported that as of September 2009, 93 percent of Americans between the ages of 12 and 17 had used the Internet, with adolescents representing the age range with the highest rate of online use (Lenhart et al., 2010). Furthermore, they reported that 63 percent of teens go online every day. The Pew Project also reported that of online teens in September 2009, 73 percent had used a social networking site, increased from 65 percent in February 2008 and 55 percent in November 2006 (Lenhart et al., 2010). This 73 percent figure is slightly higher than the 72 percent of those 18 to 29 years old who go online and use social networking sites, and certainly higher than the 40 percent for adults age 30 and up.

The above statistics reflect the growing role of social networking sites in the lives of adolescents and young adults. For instance, it is not feasible or advisable for medical school deans or residency program directors to prohibit use of sites such as

Facebook, given the integral part this site plays in the social lives of medical trainees. Adolescents are displaying an even greater reliance on these social networking sites, reflected in the above figures and moreover in the qualitative importance of these sites to their social fabric. Sites such as Facebook are increasingly used for virtual social communication and coordination of real-life social events alike. An adolescent's Facebook profile is often an important aspect of his or her identity, and his or her Facebook behavior may in turn be followed by a number of peers. Teens often use Facebook as a forum to express themselves through statements, links, and photos posted on their own profiles or those of others. Sometimes these posts may communicate their distress, directly or indirectly, and this phenomenon may be of particular relevance to the field of psychiatry and mental health at large.

Physician Use of Social Networking Sites

A number of ethical issues arise in the use of social networking sites by both physicians and patients, beginning with those related to a physician's own use of such sites. An obvious example involves a clinician's posting material that either directly or indirectly identifies a particular patient, even if intended for a professional audience. It is at least as unethical, and likely more so, than writing a paper or giving a lecture without parental consent and adolescent assent, given the ability for unauthorized people to access this information. This also depends on the effectiveness of privacy protection. Posting identifiable information about a patient is a breach of confidentiality that violates the Health Insurance Portability and Accountability Act (HIPAA), as well as the ethical principle of patient autonomy. Such postings have the potential to harm the patient or his or her family, violating the principle of nonmaleficence. Even without mentioning the patient's name, sufficient identifying features may allow some readers to identify the individual being mentioned. A proposed standard holds that, in the absence of informed consent, the information should be sufficiently disguised that even the patient would not recognize it. Furthermore, the broad range of information that can be posted on social networking sites by a physician can lead to negative repercussions and cause others to question the professionalism of the physician. There have been numerous recent examples of physicians whose careers have been significantly compromised by the nature of their posts on the Internet. It is important for medical boards or professional organizations to determine whether they should consider such posts if they do not affect the physician's practice. However, rightly or wrongly, physicians can get into trouble for such posts. Given the high rates of Internet and social network site use by adolescents, psychiatrists who treat them should exercise particular vigilance regarding what they post on any publicly or even privately viewable site.

Psychiatrists should be particularly mindful of privacy settings that can be modified on social networking sites, owing to the uncertainty over how their information is managed. Sites such as Facebook can falsely feel like a private diary. Yet it has been widely noted that there is no single authority that oversees the collection of personal information on the Web by companies such as Facebook, Google, and Microsoft (Wyatt & Wingfield, 2012). Consider how Facebook, for instance, has made multiple changes to its privacy policies over the course of its existence, and not all users, including adolescents and psychiatrists, are aware of such changes and their implications. Facebook now allows users to choose between various levels of privacy that are applicable to the myriad of Facebook offerings. Yet the result is a 5,376-word privacy policy that few people read, and a maze of options and opportunities and potential errors (Facebook, 2012b). The privacy policy contains nebulous language providing Facebook surprisingly broad discretion. For instance, Facebook claims it may share information "when we believe the sharing is permitted by you, reasonably necessary to offer our services, or when legally required to do so" (Facebook, 2012b). Other companies such as Microsoft and Google, as will be relevant in the following section, have drawn particular criticism from privacy advocates for similarly vague and unsupervised privacy policies (Wyatt & Wingfield, 2012). Internet privacy is thus an area that saliently highlights the dilemma of a technological advance outpacing regulatory oversight, and the lack of appreciation by users and especially of adolescents of the risks of what they post.

Furthermore, data posted on the Internet may be used and accessed widely by companies and government alike. For instance, irrespective of chosen privacy settings, communications made on Facebook may not be protected by the Fourth Amendment from government intrusion. As the Supreme Court explained in *Katz v. United States* (1967) long before Facebook's emergence, "what a person knowingly exposes to the public, even in his own home or office, is not a subject of Fourth Amendment protection." That position has been translated to our current technological tools and practices, leading some to conclude that Internet communications on social networking sites are in the public domain and are not subject to Fourth Amendment limitations against unreasonable search and seizure (Semitsu, 2011). Physicians using Facebook should therefore assume a minimal degree of privacy with respect to the data they volunteer. As such, issues related to privacy can be added to concerns regarding biomedical ethics and professionalism, which combine to warrant heightened vigilance by the psychiatrist who uses social networking sites.

Physicians, Patients, and Social Networking Sites

Much discussion on ethical dilemmas related to physicians and patients on social network sites has been devoted to the possibility of the physician and patient becoming virtual "friends," adding each other to their respective social networks on websites such as Facebook. The instantiation of such a relationship thereby grants the patient increased access to the physician's profile on the site, and vice versa. Most commonly, it has been posited that the patient is the one "requesting" this virtual relationship. Applied to our discussion, an adolescent patient would in such a case seek the psychiatrist on a social networking site such as Facebook and request to add the psychiatrist to his or her own social network.

The majority of the literature has interpreted the acceptance of a patient's "friend request" to compromise the boundaries of the doctor–patient relationship, and as such has cautioned against establishing these dual relationships. Specifically, it has been argued that befriending a patient on a social networking site may violate the principle of nonmaleficence by harming the therapeutic relationship. It is often considered that psychiatrists optimize the treatment setting by making it clear they will only assume a treating role to the patient. In the absence of any further relationship with the clinician, the patient is not burdened by social consequences outside of the psychiatrist's office; nothing he or she says will spill over to the outside world. According to this line of thinking, the patient will therefore be more likely to reveal potentially shameful, painful, or socially undesirable information. Such an optimized degree of openness is thought, in turn, to be essential to developing a therapeutic relationship with the psychiatrist. In addition, it has been suggested that dual relationships may affect the process of transference in psychotherapy. Transference, often described as the redirection of a patient's feelings for a person toward the therapist, is considered an essential component of psychotherapy, particularly in psychoanalytic or psychodynamic schools of thought. Another consideration concerning physicians who add patients to their online social network is that they may draw negative attention from other friends in the network, or that knowledge of this may spread to others who pass judgment on this practice. Finally, it has been noted that becoming an online "friend" of a patient may generate confusion as to the nature of the established relationship— this may be interpreted to mean that the patient and physician are then friends in the literal sense of the word, and might lead to boundary violations.

Given the study by Ginory and colleagues cited previously, where 9.7 percent of responding psychiatry residents reported receiving "friend" requests from patients, it is likely that many psychiatrists will and currently do face the challenge of responding to such a request. In the study by Ginory and colleagues, a hypothetical was posed regarding such a patient "friend" request: 85.7 percent said they would ignore the request, 14.2 percent said they would discuss it with the patient first before declining, and none said they would accept it. Differing approaches to this may yield varying results in preserving the therapeutic relationship, but this has not been studied formally, nor have official recommendations been made beyond not befriending patients on social networking sites.

The adolescent patient may merit particular caution from the treating psychiatrist when it comes to interactions on social networking sites. Adolescents' developmental immaturity, as discussed previously, may lead them to request online friendship with a psychiatrist with greater frequency than adult patients. This may result from a lack of understanding of physician–patient boundaries, which may be more commonly recognized by adult patients. Furthermore, they might think such a request is not appropriate but be unable to control their impulse, owing to the developmental immaturity discussed previously. For these reasons, it may be particularly wise to discuss the "friend" request with an adolescent in the clinical setting prior to declining the request. This situation has been likened to that of a patient presenting a gift to the clinician, where it has been recommended that the conscious and unconscious motivations and expectations associated with the patient's actions be explored (Brendel et al., 2007). Consider the following scenario:

> A 14-year-old presents to his psychiatrist for his tenth treatment session. Historically the patient had suffered significant abandonment at the age of nine by his father, who had struggled with alcoholism for many years and was physically abusive. He was referred to a school counselor by one of his teachers, who noted that he appeared depressed in the classroom and was prone to profane, disruptive outbursts. Given concerns regarding these incidents, the patient's association with students known to abuse alcohol and illicit drugs, and a marked decline in academic performance, he was referred to the psychiatrist. In this session, the patient continues to build on a previously growing sense of trust for the psychiatrist, identifying the psychiatrist as a stable source of support in the face of his struggles. As an avid user of Facebook, he returns home that evening, searches for his psychiatrist, and asks to add him to his social network. The psychiatrist does not check his Facebook profile for several days. He sees his patient's request but declines it based on his concern for a violation of professional boundaries. Meanwhile the patient suffers from a growing sense of rejection that is channeled into recklessness and culminates in escalating alcohol use. Two scheduled sessions pass but the patient does not show up, and the psychiatrist contacts the school counselor only to learn that he was involved in a severe incident of vandalism at a nearby liquor store. The patient had been apprehended by police and held in a juvenile detention center.

Such a vignette highlights the importance of proceeding delicately with an adolescent for whom social networking comes naturally but whose sensitivity to rejection is particularly problematic. In such a case, it may have been advisable for the clinician to delay in denying the request until they could discuss the incident with the adolescent. The psychiatrist may also have attempted to contact the adolescent upon seeing the request, either to expedite their next session or to discuss the incident.

Befriending the adolescent patient online may also complicate the relationship between the psychiatrist, the adolescent, and the parents. As discussed previously, this triad can be fraught with legal and ethical complexity, and introducing dual relationships may add further complication. The parent may be particularly protective of the child and as such may be quite put off by any interaction via the

Internet that may be interpreted as inappropriate or a boundary violation, even if it is at most a boundary crossing.

Despite valid concerns regarding interactions between physicians and patients on social networking sites, there may be contextually driven exceptions where minimal dual relationships may be ethically justifiable. One might also consider that not every request to be a Facebook "friend" by a patient carries the implications of a real friend. Older psychiatric practitioners unfamiliar with this difference may in particular misinterpret the request. The adolescent most likely understands the limitations of a Facebook "friend" more than an older psychiatrist less familiar with Facebook and sees it as no more than making a casual connection with the therapist. It also is not uncommon in treating adolescents to make small boundary crossings to establish a therapeutic alliance. Furthermore, most treatment these days is not classically psychoanalytic, and thus does not require the therapist to be a blank screen. Similar to a patient offering a gift, the meaning should be discussed, but if the gift is modest and even symbolic it should not necessarily be rejected. Doing so may carry a loss of therapeutic alliance that will come across as cold and rejecting, and that should at least be considered. Allowing the adolescent to be a Facebook "friend" may help the therapeutic alliance in some unique cases especially of adolescents, where some boundary crossings of a limited nature might be appropriate. If there are very strict privacy limitations on the clinician's Facebook page, and responsibly monitored content, it is less likely that information to be shared would lead to legal liability or upset parents, and it might even facilitate and not complicate treatment in some instances. However, accepting a "friend" request should be the rare exception and only done for a good therapeutic reason.

Consider the adolescent patient who suffers from an autism spectrum disorder, crippling social anxiety, or schizophrenia. These patients all often share a common difficulty in communicating socially, and in such a subset of patients it is conceivable that communication via Facebook or other computer/Internet-based platforms affords a degree of comfort that is otherwise not achieved in face-to-face interaction. For such a patient one may conceivably maximize the principle of beneficence by establishing a relationship on a social networking site. Thus one may perform minimal boundary crossings that allow the patient to build a therapeutic alliance, and lead in therapy to an ability to communicate basic facts about his or her emotional state. Here one sees the relevance of the care ethics approach where the context of the clinical scenario, along with an emphasis on the relationship established with a particularly vulnerable patient, might combine to make a less traditional plan of action the most ethical and beneficial one for patient care.

Again, entering into dual relationships with adolescents on social networking sites will only rarely be ethically justifiable, but nevertheless might merit evaluation on a case-by-case basis. In a subset of patients like the one described previously, one might achieve great therapeutic benefit in using a tool such as Facebook, though it may feel ethically uncertain and unconventional. In most cases, however, such action is not justified. In particular, a request by a patient clearly pushing the boundaries of treatment and desiring a boundary violation should unequivocally be rejected. If the psychiatrist has no privacy settings on the Facebook page, he or she would be well advised to reject all "friend" requests until he or she sets up privacy restrictions that would preclude a patient from having access to any private information. This should be a prerequisite to any psychiatrist even beginning to consider befriending a patient on a social networking site. Furthermore, clinicians may want to consider the use of a formal disclaimer regarding appropriate Internet use, as we will discuss in an upcoming section on email communication.

While caution is always advised in online interactions with patients on social networking sites, it is important to note the growing and valuable role that these sites play in informing a psychiatrist in today's day and age. Given the established adolescent use of social networking sites, it is no surprise that adolescents often post quite intimate and psychiatrically relevant information, as discussed previously. When their posts begin to raise concern for an acute safety risk, such as an adolescent becoming psychotic or suicidal, the benefit of accessing this information and acting on it may begin to outweigh concerns regarding privacy and the principle of autonomy. This is analogous to standard psychiatric practice, where one must break confidentiality in the case of a patient endorsing suicidality or homicidality in the office. Certainly, posts on sites such as Facebook may be used as collateral when a parent, teacher, or friend of the adolescent reports a concerning incident. It may behoove the clinician, however, to go a step further and search for the patient's profile in very limited instances where the patient's safety is clearly at risk. Obtaining information in such instances may hinge on whether the patient has modified his or her own privacy settings—if the teen has not, his or her posts may be available to be seen publicly, including by the physician. This is an ethically delicate scenario related to the dilemmas associated with search engines and will be discussed further in the following section.

In evaluating scenarios related to social networking sites, as in any ethical challenge, it may be useful to reference a set of recommendations when evaluating the relevant contextual details of the scenario. The following guidelines have been proposed, in the study by Ginory and colleagues regarding psychiatric residents (2012, p. 47), with regard to maintaining professionalism in social media:

1. Physicians should regularly update their privacy settings.
2. Physicians should remain aware of guidelines regarding patient confidentiality and refrain from posting identifying information about patients, including photographs.
3. When interacting with patients online, all boundaries should be maintained based on previously set forth guidelines.
4. Entering into dual relationships with patients should be avoided.
5. Physicians should maintain adequate separation of personal and professional information, and on their personal profiles, they should be wary of

the pictures and information available, as even with privacy settings items may be visible publicly.

6. Inappropriate behavior online should be discussed with the individual, and if it remains uncorrected, it should be reported to the proper authorities.

7. Physicians should regularly monitor their Internet presence by conducting regular Web inquiries to search for information that may be publicly available.

8. Training programs should develop policies for professional use of social media and educate residents on possible boundary crossings and violations of professionalism.

9. Physicians should be aware that there might be negative repercussions for content posted.

These guidelines are appropriately cautious given the potential problems raised by social networking sites and are particularly relevant when treating adolescents. However, a consideration of contextual factors should always accompany an acknowledgment of commonly espoused norms, in the event that the most ethical course of action does not align with these principles. In the case of certain psychopathologies, this may be particularly relevant. Also, inappropriate postings would need to be extreme, such as indicating suicidal or homicidal plans, before requiring reports to authorities, similar to behavior in other traditional settings.

In summary, the ethical dilemmas associated with physicians' and patients' use of social networking sites are significantly complex. Psychiatrists should always consider the effects their actions may have on the therapeutic relationship with an adolescent, and understand that these effects may vary depending on the patient and situation. When boundaries are crossed there need to be good therapeutic reasons, and the meaning to the adolescent must be explored.

■ SEARCH ENGINES

Another powerful tool associated with the Internet and technology is the search engine, which can amass significant data on a subject with a simple prompt. As mentioned above, there may be scenarios where seeking information about a patient can be of important clinical use and ethically justifiable. Search engines may be used within social network sites, for instance searching for a person on Facebook, or in global contexts, such as using sites like Google. A growing literature is emerging that addresses the topic of "patient-targeted Googling" and patients' own use of search engines and sites designed to provide information about providers. Psychiatrists were formerly able to exist outside of the clinical world with great anonymity. Search engines like Google, or websites where physicians may be rated, afford patients greatly expanded opportunities to find out more about a provider's social affiliations, professional engagements, and reputation in the community. Some websites accumulate information on everybody without permission, and include information about psychiatrists. Although psychiatrists may now be tempted to request that patients not search for them on the Internet, patients do not themselves follow a professional code of ethics. It might be very legitimate for a patient to check out a psychiatrist's education, publications, and reputation. As such, the ethical principle of respect for autonomy would indicate that psychiatrists should not place constraints on a patient's freedom to pursue public information (Gabbard et al., 2011). In fact, doing so might stimulate the curiosity of some patients to find out more information. Of course this would be superseded by legitimate danger to self or others—for instance, a patient searching for a physician who has intent to harm this physician.

Clinical information was formally obtained exclusively via in-person patient observation and clinical assessment, examination of records, and collateral information. The Internet can provide a form of observation that is not in person but can be quite powerful. Perhaps more than any other field, psychiatrists can glean clinically relevant data on the Internet about a patient's personal, professional, or website affiliations. In some instances, such as the evaluation of grandiosity that may be prevalent in pathologies such as bipolar disorder or narcissistic personality disorder, practices such as patient-targeted Googling can be a form of "fact-checking" that influences diagnostic formulation. There have also been case reports of searching on forums such as Facebook as invaluable contributions to clinical decision making if the patient cannot provide a coherent history or reliable collateral contacts (Ben-Yakov & Snider, 2011). Finally, as mentioned above, this practice can also be a vital modern component of evaluating for suicidality or homicidality in cases where safety is called into question.

While satisfactory reasons often exist to perform patient-targeted Internet searches, the practice should be done only with the aim of furthering patient care. The American Psychiatric Association Ethics Committee (2009) has offered guidelines regarding such information searches about patients:

> Googling a patient is not necessarily unethical. However, it should be done only in the interests of promoting the patient's care and well-being and never to satisfy the curiosity or other needs of the psychiatrist. Also important to consider is how such information will influence treatment and how the clinician will ultimately use this information.

This statement provides useful guidance for the psychiatrist who is considering using a search engine to obtain information about a patient. Translating such considerations into normative ethical decisions will of course depend on a physician's consideration of contextual factors and on his or her ability to reason flexibly. Informing such a process is a pragmatic framework such as the one offered by Clinton and colleagues (2010, pp. 105–107), who suggest considering six questions before searching:

1. Why do I want to conduct this search?
2. Would my search advance or compromise the treatment?

3. Should I obtain informed consent from the patient prior to searching?
4. Should I share the results of the search with the patient?
5. Should I document the findings of the search in the medical record?
6. How do I monitor my motivations and the ongoing risk-benefit profile of searching?

Given the rate of Internet use among adolescents highlighted above, it may be particularly tempting to search for an adolescent patient on the Internet. Owing to developmental immaturity, adolescents may be more likely to make postings or affiliate themselves with sites in a way that does not consider their behavior's implications. Adolescents may thus convey more information regarding their mental states than adults would, in a raw and possibly impulsive manner, making their Internet behavior particularly clinically relevant. They may post sexually explicit, defamatory, or otherwise offensive material. Given these possibilities, psychiatrists may be well served to exercise more careful checks on their own behavior, and as such the above frameworks may be of added relevance to the psychiatrist treating adolescents. The psychiatrist also should exercise fiduciary responsibilities to assist the adolescent to be cautious in postings if he or she becomes aware of such risky behavior. Questionable postings could cause later problems if patients pursue a position with social responsibility like a professional or a politician. Internet postings can remain forever. In some jurisdictions, patients who share nude pictures of themselves with other adolescents could be charged with child abuse; the adolescent may even be required to register as a sex offender. So if a psychiatrist becomes aware of these things, it would be important to educate the adolescent about such problems, since he or she may incorrectly see the behavior as harmless. That does not, however, justify intrusion by the therapist without a good reason.

■ EMAIL COMMUNICATION

Email communication has emerged, like social network sites and search engines, as a relevant topic in biomedical ethics owing to its increased popularity as a communication method between patients and physicians (Baker et al., 2003). Often email communication is improved by protected portals and encryption systems that safeguard confidentiality for all patients. But even if encrypted by the therapist, the communications from the adolescent are likely not so protected. As leading users of the Internet and electronic forms of communication, adolescents may exhibit a penchant for email communication that may be both clinically useful and deserving of increased caution by the psychiatrist. Though it is an efficient form of communication, email poses clinical challenges such as the loss of nonverbal cues and the risk of misconstrued meanings. Potential liability issues are associated with email communication as well, such as whether there should be a requisite standard for response time. How rapidly are physicians required to respond to email? Another issue relates to documentation and whether emails should be saved into the official medical record.

It is clear that physicians should take certain precautions when communicating via email with patients. For instance, it may be advisable to use separate email addresses for their personal and professional communication, given that email addresses are often associated with website affiliations and can be plugged into search engines to discover these affiliations. Email systems used should always have a robust mechanism for data encryption to ensure patient privacy. Furthermore, as DeJong and colleagues pointed out in a recent article regarding professionalism and the Internet in psychiatry, it may be increasingly advised for psychiatrists to sign a consent form for email communication that addresses these and other issues (DeJong et al., 2012):

- Turnaround time for messages
- Restriction on non-urgent use
- Appropriate message headers
- Privacy and confidential issues
- Permissible content

The potential for confusion in email message interpretation, or for inappropriate use and content, is only magnified when adolescents are involved. Complexities related to patients and their parents will also be amplified by email communication. All of the above are cause for increased vigilance on behalf of the treating psychiatrist, who should consider the above measures along with having frequent and explicit discussions with patients and families about the appropriateness of email use. With adolescent patients as with adults, as DeJong and colleagues point out, email like any technology "should be used in a boundaried, confidential fashion, with the patient's (and/or parent's) written consent or assent, to support, rather than to establish or maintain, the doctor-patient relationship" (DeJong et al., 2012, p. 357).

However, there may be very specific clinical scenarios where email communication is the most effective method of maintaining this relationship, where the adolescent's pathology limits the use of face-to-face interaction. These patients will be similar to those identified in the section on social networking sites, those for whom virtual communication via the Internet can markedly improve their ability to form social connections and express themselves. Unique, contextual factors may thus play a role in determining a physician's use of email communication. For most patients it will be advisable to limit the use of email, as DeJong and colleagues pointed out, but in a few select patients it may be ethically advisable to use email as a primary form of therapeutic intervention. It would be advised, in any case, to alert the adolescent to the fact that confidentiality of email communications cannot be totally assured, since adolescents may not consider this. When feasible, encrypted email should be used. Some emails may be for simple matters like setting up or canceling an appointment or changing a time. In many cases it might not be the place for the patient to share sensitive personal information, particularly that which merits emergent attention, and this issue should be addressed frequently.

Similar considerations should apply for texting, another widespread means of adolescent communication. In fact, texting seems generally the more common form of electronic communication among adolescents. Although emails can be encrypted, texts in most instances are not. So email is likely preferable to the use of texting, which is best avoided for sensitive information.

■ CONCLUSION

Perhaps the most pragmatic recommendation for psychiatric practice in the adolescent population relates less to the dilemmas of direct physician–patient interactions via the Internet and more to the content a psychiatrist seeks to explore with the adolescent patient. In this chapter we have described the high prevalence of technology use in the adolescent population. Moreover, in this and previous chapters, there are enough data to suggest that the Internet and such forms of communication as social networking sites and email are integral to the social fabric of the lives of most teens. To maximize the principle of beneficence, psychiatrists may be best served to regularly check in with their adolescent patients regarding their technology use. They may ask how often they use their computers and smartphones, how often they use social networking sites, whether they engage in problematic Internet behaviors such as excessive pornography use or gambling, and whether they have experienced any cyber-bullying. Psychiatrists may seek to understand how technology fits in the adolescent's life, and as such gain invaluable data about the adolescent's thought process, emotions, and relationships that affect clinical care. They may also be justified in exploring the adolescent's opinions regarding the privacy of the information he or she posts on the Internet, given the concerns about the use of data that have been cited. Given that adolescents are less likely to consider privacy on the Internet, the psychiatrist may have a unique opportunity to raise this as an issue with their adolescent patients. Finally, frequently checking in with their patient about Internet use may help prevent undesirable situations of significant ethical and legal conflict.

As we have seen, there are many ethical dilemmas associated with treating an adolescent in a world of technological advances. The psychiatrist who faces challenging ethical dilemmas will be enriched by an understanding of the history of biomedical ethics, along with contemporary approaches to ethical decision making in a clinical setting. Those who treat adolescents will gain from knowledge of case law and from exposure to the scientific research that informs our view of adolescent development. In this chapter we have begun to explore these topics and have touched on the ethical considerations associated with social networking sites, search engines, and email communication. In so doing, we have attempted to identify common themes in the biomedical ethics of psychiatry as applied to technology use.

As technology advances, psychiatrists treating adolescents will continue to face challenges that require them to become familiar with the parameters and uses of any new form of communication. They should continue to draw on established ethical frameworks and on keen observation of contextual clinical factors. Guidelines for Internet and technology use will develop and will be useful in directing physicians' behavior but should not always be used as rigid rules. Such rigidity may misinterpret valid reasons for using these new types of communication, based on limited understanding or inappropriate application of guidelines from other settings. However, any new type of communication should always be used with caution and only for good clinical reasons. It should involve consideration and exploration with the adolescent patient and possibly the family to get consent and explore the meaning of such communication. The psychiatrist who is discerning, flexible, and very explicit about risks and benefits will thus be the best equipped to face the new challenges posed by adolescents and technology use. Ariel Seroussi has no conflicts to disclose. He is a third-year resident physician in the UCLA Department of Psychiatry & Biobehavioral Sciences.

■ DISCLOSURES

Ariel Seroussi has no conflicts of interest to disclose.

Daniel Bonnici has no conflicts of interest to disclose.

Gregory B. Leong has no conflicts to disclose. His only income derives from his employment with the University of Southern California and the state of California.

Robert Weinstock has no conflicts of interest to disclose.

■ REFERENCES

American Academy of Child & Adolescent Psychiatry (2009, Jan. 30). *Code of Ethics.* Accessed September 30, 2012. http://www.aacap.org/App_Themes/AACAP/docs/about_us/transparency_portal/aacap_code_of_ethics_2012.pdf.

American Medical Association (1994). *Code of Medical Ethics. Opinion 1.02: The Relation of Law and Ethics.* Accessed November 13, 2013. http://www.ama-assn.org/ama/pub/physician-resources/medical-ethics/code-medical-ethics/opinion102.page?.

American Psychiatric Association (2009). *The principles of medical ethics (with annotations especially applicable to psychiatry).*

American Psychiatric Association Ethics Committee (2009). Is it ethical to Google patients? *Psychiatric News, 44*(11).

Baker, L., Wagner, T. H., & Singer, S. (2003). Use of the Internet and e-mail for healthcare information: results from a national survey. *Journal of the American Medical Association, 289,* 2400–2406.

Beauchamp, T. L. (2009). The philosophical basis of psychiatric ethics. In S. Bloch & S. A. Green (Eds.), *Psychiatric ethics*. (pp. 25–48). New York: Oxford University Press.

Beauchamp, T. L., & Childress, J. F. (1979). *Principles of biomedical ethics*, 1st ed. New York, Oxford: Oxford University Press.

Beauchamp, T. L., & Childress, J. F. (2001). *Principles of biomedical ethics*, 5th ed. New York, Oxford: Oxford University Press.

Bellotti v. Baird, 443 U.S. 622 (1979).

Ben-Yakov, M., & Snider, C. (2011). How Facebook saved our day! *Academic Emergency Medicine, 18*, 1217–1219.

Brendel, D. H., Chu, J., Radden, J., Leeper, H., Pope, H. G., & Samson, J. (2007). The price of a gift: An approach to receiving gifts from patients in psychiatric practice. *Harvard Review of Psychiatry, 15*(2), 43–51.

Candilis, P.J.,& Layde, J.B. "Professional Development in Forensic Psychiatry: The Role of the American Academy of Psychiatry and the Law." *Academic Psychiatry, 31*, 110–111.

Chein, J., Albert, D., O'Brien, L., Uckert, K., & Steinberg, L. (2011). Peers increase adolescent risk taking by enhancing activity in the brain's reward circuitry. *Developmental Science, 14*(2), F1–F10.

Children's Internet Protection Act, 47 C.F.R. §54.520.

Children's Online Privacy Protection Act, 16 C.F.R. §312.3.

Children's Online Protection Act, 47 U.S.C.A. §231.

Clinton, B. K., Silverman, B. C., & Brendel, D. H. (2010). Patient-targeted Googling: the ethics of searching online for patient information. *Harvard Review of Psychiatry, 18*, 103–112.

Clouser, K. D. (1993). Bioethics and philosophy. *Hastings Center Report, 23*(6 Suppl.), S10–S11.

Communications Decency Act, 47 U.S.C.A. §230.

Commission on Bioethics. American Academy of Pediatrics. (1995). Informed consent, parental permission, and assent in pediatric practice. *Pediatrics, 95*, 314.

DeJong, S. M., Benjamin, S., Meyer Anzia, J., John, N., Boland, R., Lomax, J., & Leon Rostain, A. (2012). Professionalism and the Internet in psychiatry: What to teach and how to teach it. *Academic Psychiatry, 36*, 356–362.

Eaton, D. K., Kann, L., Kinchen, S., Shanklin, S., Flint, K. H., Hawkins, J., Harris, W. A., Lowry, R., McManus, T., Chyen, D, Whittle, L., Lim, C., Wechsler, H., and Centers for Disease Control. (2012). Youth Risk Behavior Surveillance—United States 2011. *Morbidity and Mortality Weekly Report, Surveillance Summaries, 61*(4). Accessed November 15, 2012. http://www.cdc.gov/mmwr/pdf/ss/ss6104.pdf.

Edelstein L. (1006). *The Hippocratic oath: text, translation and interpretation*. Baltimore, MD: The Johns Hopkins University Press.

Endacott, R., Wood, A., Judd, F., Hulbert, C., Thomas, B., & Grigg, M. (2006). Impact and management of dual relationships in metropolitan, regional, and rural mental health practice. *Australia and New Zealand Journal of Psychiatry, 40*, 987–994.

Facebook Press Room (2012a). Accessed November 3, 2012. http://facebook.com/press/#!/press/info.php?statistics.

Facebook Privacy Policy (2012b). Accessed November 12, 2012b. http://www.facebook.com/note.php?note_id=%20322194465300.

Fieser, J. (2009). Ethics. *Internet Encyclopedia of Philosophy: A Peer-Reviewed Academic Resource*. Updated May 10, 2009. Accessed November 3, 2012. http://www.iep.utm.edu/ethics/#SH3b. ISSN 2161-0002.

Foot, P. (1990). Ethics and the death penalty: Participation by forensic psychiatrists in capital trials. In R. Rosner & R. Weinstock (Eds.), *Ethical practice in psychiatry and the law* (pp. 207–217). New York: Springer.

Gabbard, G. O., Kassaw, K. A., & Perez-Garcia, G. (2011). Professional boundaries in the era of the Internet. *Academic Psychiatry, 35*(3), 168–174.

Geier, C., & Luna, B. (2009). The maturation of incentive processing and cognitive control. *Pharmacology, Biochemistry and Behavior, 93*(3), 212–221.

Ginory, A., Sabatier, L. M., & Eth, S. (2012). Addressing therapeutic boundaries in social networking. *Psychiatry, 75*, 40–48.

Gordon, J. S. (2012). Bioethics. *Internet Encyclopedia of Philosophy: A Peer-Reviewed Academic Resource.* Updated November 3, 2012. Accessed November 5, 2012. http://www.iep.utm.edu/bioethic/#H2. ISSN 2161-0002.

Graham v. Florida, 130 S. Ct. 2011 (2010).

Gutheil, T. C. (2005). Boundary issues and personality disorders. *Journal of Psychiatric Practice, 11*, 88–96.

Herissone-Kelly, P. (2011). Determining the common morality's norms in the sixth edition of *Principles of Biomedical Ethics. Journal of Medical Ethics, 37*, 584–587.

Hundert, E. M. (1990). Competing medical, legal, and ethical values: Balancing problems of the forensic psychiatrist. In R. Rosner & R. Weinstock (Eds.), *Ethical practice in psychiatry and the law* (pp. 53–72). New York: Springer.

Kambam, P., & Thompson, C. (2009). The development of decision-making capacities in children and adolescents: psychological and neurological perspectives and their implications for juvenile defendants. *Behavioral Sciences and the Law, 27*, 173–190.

Katz v. United States, 389 U.S. 347, 351 (1967).

Ky. Rev. Stat. Ann. §202A.021 (1982).

La. Child. Code Ann. art. 1463 (1992).

Lenhart, A., Purcell, K., Smith, A., & Zickuhr, K. (2010). *Social media & mobile Internet use among teens and young adults.* Pew Internet & American Life Project. Accessed November 17, 2012. http://pewInternet.org/Reports/2010/Social-Media-and-Young-Adults.aspx.

Luna, B., Padmanabhan, A., & O'Hearn, K. (2010). What has fMRI told us about the development of cognitive control through adolescence? *Brain and Cognition, 72*(1), 101.

MacDonald, J., Sonh, S., & Ellis, P. (2010). Privacy, professionalism, and Facebook: a dilemma for young doctors. *Medical Education, 44*, 805–813.

Meyer v. Nebraska, 262 U.S. 390 (1923).

Miller v. Alabama, 132 S.Ct. 2455 (2012).

Mlyniec, W. J. (1006). A judge's ethical dilemma: assessing a child's capacity to choose. *Fordham Law Review, 64*, 1873, 1877.

Moubarak, G., Guiot, A., & Benhamou, Y. (2011). Facebook activity of residents and fellows and its impact on the doctor-patient relationship. *Journal of Medical Ethics,37*, 101–104.

Nev. Rev. Stat. § 433.471 (2012).

Parham v. JR, 442 U.S. 584 (1979).

Pew Internet & American Life Project. Accessed October 20, 2012. http://www.pewInternet.org.

Pope, K., Luna, B., & Thomas, C. (2012). Developmental neuroscience and the courts: How science is influencing the disposition of juvenile offenders. *Journal of the American Academy of Child and Adolescent Psychiatry, 51*(4), 341–342.

Rauprich, O. (2011). Specification and other methods for determining morally relevant facts. *Journal of Medical Ethics, 37*, 592–596.

Rauprich, O., & Vollmann, J. (2011). 30 years Principles of Biomedical Ethics: introduction to a symposium on the 6th edition of Tom L. Beauchamp and James F. Childress' seminal work. *Journal of Medical Ethics, 37*(8). 454–455.

Richardson, H. S. (1990). Specifying norms as a way to resolve concrete ethical problems. *Philosophy and Public Affairs, 19*, 279–310.

Roberts, W. R., Translation; cited from *Aristotle's Rhetoric,* Book II, Chapter 12. Accessed November 19, 2012. http://rhetoric.eserver.org/aristotle/rhet2-12.html.

Roper v. Simmons, 543 U.S. 551 (2005).

Sander-Staudt, M. (2011). Care ethics." *Internet Encyclopedia of Philosophy: A Peer-Reviewed Academic Resource.* Updated March 19, 2011. Accessed November 3, 2012. http://www.iep.utm.edu/care-eth/#H2. ISSN 2161-0002.

Semitsu, J. P. (2011). From Facebook to mug shot: How the dearth of social networking privacy rights revolutionized online government surveillance. *Pace Law Review, 31*(291), 296.

Silber, T. J. (2011). Adolescent brain development and the mature minor doctrine. *Adolescent Medicine, 22*, 207–212.

Singer, N. (2012, Sept. 27). U.S. is tightening web privacy rule to shield young. *New York Times.* Accessed November 4, 2012. http://www.nytimes.com/2012/09/28/technology/ftc-moves-to-tighten-online-privacy-protections-for-children.html?emc=eta1&_r=0.

Slonina, M. I. (2007). State v. Physicians et al.: Legal standards guiding the mature minor doctrine and the bioethical judgment of pediatricians in life-sustaining medical treatment." *Health Matrix, 17*(181), 188.

Sowell, E. R., Thompson, P. M., Holmes, C. J., Batth, R., Jernigan, T. L., & Toga, A. W. (1999). Localizing age-related changes in brain structure between childhood and adolescence using statistical parametric mapping. *Neuroimage, 9*(6), 587–597.

Steinberg, L. (2010). A dual systems model of adolescent risk-taking. *Developmental Psychobiology, 52*, 216–224.

The Queen v. Smith, 1 Cox C.C. 260 (Crim.) (1845).

Thompson, L. A., Dawson, K., Ferdig, R., Black, E. W., Boyer, J., & Coutts, J. (2008). The intersection of online social networking with medical professionalism. *Journal of General Internal Medicine, 23*, 954–957.

Thompson v. Oklahoma, 487 U.S. 815 (1988).

Troxel v. Granville, 530 U.S. 57, 60 (2000).

W. Va. Code §16-30-3 (2002).

Weinstock, R., Leong, G. B., & Silva, J. A. (1990). The role of traditional medical ethics in forensic psychiatry. In R. Rosner & R. Weinstock (Eds.), *Ethical practice in psychiatry and the law* (pp. 31–51). New York: Springer.

Webster, T. (2011, March 24). Facebook achieves majority. Accessed November 4, 2012. http://www.edisonresearch.com/home/archives/2011/03/facebook_achieves_majority.php.

Wyatt, E., & Wingfield, N. (2012, Oct. 19). As Microsoft shifts its privacy rules, an uproar is absent. *New York Times.* Accessed October 22, 2012. http://www.nytimes.com/2012/10/20/technology/microsoft-expands-gathering-and-use-of-data-from-web-products.html?emc=eta1.

15 Conclusion: Understanding Adolescent Sexual Development and the Law in the Digital Era

■ CHRISTOPHER W. RACINE AND
STEPHEN BATES BILLICK

The objective of this book has been to review our current understanding of adolescent sexual development in a world where emerging electronic technologies are ever-expanding. In addition, this book has sought to highlight the areas in which the changing landscape of sexual expression and behavior among minors affects and is affected by the law. As novel technologies emerge, so too does the potential for these technologies to influence sexual development. While there are many potential benefits of electronic technologies, increased access to social communication through cellphones, the Internet, and other forms of social media also creates opportunities for abuse and exploitation of adolescents in various forms. By thoroughly understanding these developments and their effects on adolescent behavior, we can harness technology both to facilitate teens' development and to create strategies to punish clearly dangerous and threatening activities. We will of course still need to provide understanding and tolerance for normal sexual development in the digital age.

While the current state of the literature has been discussed in this book, one theme of this volume is the relative lack of longitudinal data on these effects. Clearly the rapid growth of the technology has made it difficult to follow adolescents longitudinally. Adolescents have progressed from dominating their family's home landline telephone to cellphone use to texting and social networking. Their behaviors change before longitudinal studies can even be designed. This new technological age will require a more complete appreciation of both normative and pathologic adolescent sexual development in a world where youth have ubiquitous access to technology. With this knowledge, legislative and clinical strategies can be designed to keep pace with new technology.

■ HUMAN SEXUALITY—LIFELONG

Humans are clearly sexual beings from birth until death. The American Association of Retired Persons (Leshnoff, 2009) encouraged seniors to sext, stating, "sexting is not just for kids." Regarding the beginning of life, one has only to take a preschooler or early elementary-school child to an art museum to suddenly be presented with a sexually stimulated child. Not yet having gained the self-control and impulse control of later elementary-school children, the younger child may begin to shout and point quite excitedly when confronted with some of the very realistic portrayals of nudity and sexuality in great art. There is abundant nudity and many sexual themes, including even surprising ones such as trans-generational sexual activities, sadomasochism, and even rape. Friedrich and col-leagues (1998) studied the sexual behaviors of children and found that in two- to five-year-olds, 26.5 percent of boys and 15.1 percent of girls touch their genitalia when in public places and 60.2 percent of boys and 43.8 percent of girls touch their genitalia at home. In this age group, 42.4 percent of boys and 43.7 per-cent of girls try to touch their mother's breasts. Both the boys (26.8 percent) and the girls (26.9 percent) try to look at people when they are nude or undressing. Fewer six- to nine-year-olds touch their genitalia when at home (boys: 39.8 per-cent, girls: 20.7 percent). In these older children, fewer try to look at people when they are nude or undressing (boys: 20.2 percent, girls: 20.5 percent). These older children have begun to incorporate some of the norms of the society they live in. In 10- to 12-year-olds, 24.1 percent of the boys and 28.7 percent of the girls had become very interested in the opposite sex.

Friedrich and colleagues (1991) also found that children sometimes drew sex parts in pictures of people. In two- to six-year-olds, 7.7 percent of boys and 6.3 per-cent of girls had done it at least once. In seven- to 12-year-olds, 17.5 percent of boys and 16.7 percent of girls had at some point also drawn sex parts in their pictures of people. Using the Child Sexual Behavior Inventory, Friedrich and colleagues stud-ied normative behavior in children aged two to 12 years and found that they were in fact sexually interested and somewhat active at all of these age groups. Lamb and Coakley (1993) found that children had sexual themes in narratives such as kissing games (6.1 percent), experimental stimulation (14.3 percent), genital expo-sure (15.3 percent), and playing doctor (18.4 percent) and in fantasy play including themes of imitation of adult sexual acts, love scenes, and coercive scenes. Actual physical sexual play in games included kissing (14 percent), exposure (26 percent), clothed genital touching (15 percent), unclothed genital touching (17 percent), inserting objects into genitals (6 percent), and oral–genital contact (4 percent). Only 17 percent of the children surveyed had no sexual content in their games.

There are great concerns that children, and in this book adolescents, are not ready for sexuality, sexual acts, and human sexual interactions. Clearly, sexuality is an innate part of being human; as the U.S. Supreme Court stated in *Bragdon v. Abbott* (1998), "reproduction and the sexual dynamics surrounding it are cen-tral to the life process itself." Discussions of competency to have sexual play and sexual activities are fraught with difficulties and complexities. In studies of compe-tency to give consent to pediatric health care and pediatric psychiatric treatment, Billick and colleagues (1998, 2001) found that children had a developing capacity to understand and participate. By age 12, with a fifth-grade reading level, children had reached the minimal cognitive level expected of a "competent adult." This finding is consistent with Piaget's (Piaget & Inhelder, 1973) developmental stages of cognition and Dulit's (1972) finding on adult levels of cognitive abilities. During adolescence, one adds experience and judgment to the cognitive abilities. Even here, the U.S. Supreme Court, in *Roper v. Simmons* (2005), opined that the human brain is not fully mature until around age 25, and thus no minor under the age of 18 was competent to be executed for horrid crimes of any severity. They clearly did not require full maturation and development to be equated with achieving a competent state.

Regarding competency to have sexual play and interaction, how should children and adolescents be evaluated? There is a difficult balance between permitting developmental independence and still providing parental protection and guidance. The new technology creates further complexities and also adds some urgency to finding a proper approach to childhood sexuality. This book will serve to encourage much-needed scientific research and understanding of this subject.

▪ ADOLESCENT SEXUAL DEVELOPMENT IN THE INTERNET AGE

Even prior to the Internet age, empirical knowledge about "normal" sexual behavior in adolescents was still evolving. Studying sexology in adolescents is risky and difficult, largely due to sociocultural influences that make research on this topic difficult to generalize from and also somewhat culturally taboo. Therefore, what is known about adolescent sexual development and normal behavior is somewhat limited. Adolescence is an important developmental transition period for sexuality because of the natural and dramatic increase in adolescents' desires and urges that emerge during puberty. For today's adolescents, the Internet has become an important context in which these changes are occurring. Peer communication is one of the most popular uses of technology by modern youth. Within just a few years, online communication modalities have become normative outlets for adolescents as they adjust to their developing sexuality online and offline.

The Internet is becoming one of the key conduits through which adolescents explore their emerging sexuality. Developmental psychologists Smahel and Subrahmanyam have proposed a co-construction model in this volume and their earlier work (Subrahmanyam & Smahel, 2011) to integrate adolescents' digital worlds with their offline lives, as these environments are interactive and bidirectionally influential. As Cooper (1998) proposed more than a decade ago, the "Triple A Engine" of the Internet (i.e., accessibility, affordability, anonymity) creates a forum in which sexuality is pervasive. In 2006, it was estimated that there were over 400 million pornography sites (FamilySafeMedia, 2006). Thus, adolescents can and do use the Internet to explore their emerging sexuality with ease.

Internet-based activities include searching for information about sexuality and sexual health, creating and presenting oneself as a sexual person, accessing sexually explicit content, and engaging in sexual activities online (i.e., cybersex). As access to sexually explicit online material becomes increasingly easy, it clearly influences adolescents' perceptions of normal sexual development and behavior.

■ STRIKING THE BALANCE IN THE DIGITAL AGE

As described in this book, adolescents increasingly interact in an online world that represents another context for development, similarly to traditional ones such as family, school, and neighborhoods (Subrahmanyam & Smahel, 2011). Communication forms such as Internet chat rooms, text messaging, image sharing, and social networking provide young people with an opportunity to explore their world in a way that has never been available. Young people today can create social connections on a scale that is exponentially larger than that of previous generations. Online interactions allow teens to make more friends but also can expose them to new dangers. The breadth and depth of information that is now available via digital technology has never been seen in the history of the world. The Internet can provide young people with increased opportunities to develop healthy social outlets, explore educational programs, and stay in tune with cultural developments. From a sociological perspective, the Internet creates opportunities for young people to develop more completely than ever before.

However, as seen in the preceding chapters, there is a dark side to adolescents' use of technology. Digital images and text can be easily communicated electronically to large numbers of people for whom they were not necessarily initially intended. Technology allows for the posting of pictures, videos, and messages with sexualized images and content documenting or seemingly promoting social interaction with other adolescents. Unlike the nude or seminude Polaroid photos taken by adolescents in the past, these digital images can be sent to an enormous population nearly instantly. And once an image is on the Internet, it becomes virtually impossible to remove. These seemingly innocent and casual digital image transmissions can become a permanent reminder of an adolescent indiscretion and can have significantly worse consequences than before the digital age.

Also with this new technology, youth may develop sexually compulsive online behavior and sexual addictions. Sexual invitations, wanted and unwanted, are common and present adolescents with opportunities for risky behavior. Limited longitudinal data suggest that increased exposure to online sexual content is associated with more casual sexual exploration in offline settings (Lo & Wei, 2005). Chat rooms and social networking sites can also be used by adult predators seeking to exploit youths via pornographic images and child prostitution. In Wisconsin in 2009, an adolescent homosexual male was accused and convicted of posting a nude image of an adolescent female online (Walker, 2009). He requested that male adolescents interested in a real relationship connect with the female by sending nude photos of themselves to her. When he received these nude digital photos of other male adolescents, he then blackmailed these young men into having sex with him, threatening otherwise to post their photos online. He was convicted of a felony and imprisoned. However, for his victims, their photos would have endured forever in cyberspace if posted. These dangers are real and are not yet fully appreciated by the adolescents of today.

As the risks increase for adolescent users of technology, there is debate over where and when regulatory agencies and government could and should intervene to prevent negative outcomes. Thus, policymakers, legislators, clinicians, and parents are left to strike a difficult balance between preserving the important opportunities for exploration provided by digital technologies while maintaining appropriate safeguards to prevent dangerous outcomes for adolescents. Legislative initiatives have been the primary strategy used thus far in an attempt to maintain this balance. Laws have been passed at both the state and federal levels that limit known sexual offenders from accessing chat rooms and social networking sites, theoretically creating a space where adolescent exploration of such sites is protected. For example, the Keeping the Internet Devoid of Sexual Predators Act (KIDS Act) of 2008 requires that sexual offenders provide all of their Internet identifiers to a central sex offender registry and that the these identifiers be stored and monitored by the U.S. Attorney General. Moreover, as seen in Chapter 5, several state legislatures have passed sexting laws, although these statutes are not uniform and vary in scope and punishment. While many of these laws are innovative, it is yet to be seen which, if any, of these legislative strategies are effective at protecting adolescents as they mature sexually.

As noted in the preceding chapters, there is limited evidence regarding the complex interactions between adolescents, the Internet, social networking, and sexuality. Many of the potential dangers of adolescents' use of electronic technologies have been noted. However, educational initiatives that focus on sexuality and technology are as of yet underused as a means of promoting healthy adolescent sexual exploration on the Internet. Large-scale, evidence-based efforts at promoting Internet safety with a specific focus on sexuality are lacking. Young people, their parents, their teachers, and their clinicians would all be important targets for such educational programs. Creating widespread educational programs to help adolescents comprehend the potentially drastic consequences of their behavior on social networking sites and the Internet could help deter abuse and misuse of such technologies. Ideally, these programs would be based on knowledge from existing research and designed to appeal to adolescents. Perhaps young people could be educated using the very social networking sites, chat rooms, and websites they frequent. Formal investigation into how to reduce the traditional gap between sexually related material that is educational and entertaining may help in developing programs that support healthy sexual development among adolescents.

New strategies aimed at maximizing the benefit of digital technology while minimizing harm should be rigorously evaluated. The balance alluded to above will be difficult to achieve and will be constantly shifting with developments in digital technology. Strategies aimed at promoting responsible use of such technology by adolescents should involve multidisciplinary efforts by key stakeholders; lawmakers, law enforcement agencies, clinicians, parents, and developers of electronic technology all have a place in this discussion. In addition, including adolescents themselves as the primary and most knowledgeable stakeholders will be important in developing strategies to understand shifting sociocultural norms about sexuality and technology. Flexible, informed, and innovative approaches to facilitate normative sexual development in the face of emerging technologies will require collaborative development and consistent reassessment of shifting needs.

■ SEXUAL DEVELOPMENT, TECHNOLOGY, RESEARCH, AND MOVING FORWARD

What effects do these new technologies have on adolescent sexual development? As elucidated in the chapters of this book, the new technology has serious social, psychological, and legal implications for adolescent sexual development. The effect of new technologies and forms of communication should be considered, studied, and thoroughly evaluated because new and increasingly complex questions abound. Research initiatives on important topics such as adolescent pornography addiction, cyber-bullying, social networking, and sexting have begun, but researchers are only just beginning to explore the complex interaction between technology, sexuality, and development. Research into these areas will be important in creating a framework from which to make informed policy decisions and treatment recommendations. Without such information, it will be difficult if not impossible to understand normal sexual development as influenced by modern communication modalities and the Internet.

Beyond research into topics of sexuality and technology, however, it will also be important to study the impact of attempts to promote safe adolescent sexual development. Research on the impact of the laws being put into place will help to tease out which approaches are most useful and which are not. In some instances, differing local statutes will offer opportunities for naturalistic study of different interventions. Individual treatment approaches that take into account the impact of digital technology on adolescent behavior should be tracked, evaluated, and considered. These data can then be used to help create evidence-based legislation and treatment approaches for future adolescent cohorts. The importance of a strong knowledge base will become even more important as today's computer-literate, social-networking youth go on have children themselves. As alluded to above, accurate and quantifiable longitudinal data will be important in influencing future directions as we strive to balance the potential benefits versus the pitfalls of digital technology.

As investigators move into the next phase of research, we will need to reconsider the current paradigm of study into how adolescent sexuality adapts to new technology. Technologies will likely continue to advance at an increasingly rapid pace. If we continue to focus our research interest in response to new technologies, we will fall farther and farther behind. Already, research initiatives about the influence of relatively old phenomena such as social networking sites and chat rooms are becoming outdated. Thus, moving forward, the "gold standard" for research will involve anticipating the effects that new technologies may have on adolescent sexuality. These types of forward-looking studies will involve recognizing patterns that electronic technologies have on adolescent development and anticipating effects even while specific new technologies are still in development. To do this, researchers will increasingly have to partner with those on the cutting edge of developing new technologies. This type of anticipatory research is not yet possible, but these types of projects will be essential if scholars hope to keep pace with technology.

■ PRACTICE IMPLICATIONS

As scholarly interest into adolescent development expands, it will be important for clinicians who interact with adolescents to consider the impact that emerging technologies have on the world these youths live in. Current treatment approaches and techniques will have to be considered in the context of the digital age. As technology continues to advance, a flexible approach to treating adolescents will be especially important. Sex educators and therapists who treat adolescents and young adults should consider how Internet use shapes teens' understanding of sexuality, sexual identity, and the ability to develop and maintain intimate relationships. Integrating the most recent research approaches will also allow for greatest sensitivity to an ever-changing world. To care for adolescents and young adults in today's world and in the future, clinicians must stay abreast of the latest developments in digital communication modalities and the key issues that arise from them. Increasingly, as communication technologies break down traditional barriers between clinician and client, ethical considerations will be of utmost importance. Finally, clinicians who treat adolescents will need to consider the recovery of children who are exposed to harm from the Internet and to stay abreast of available treatments.

Even more important than treating adolescents affected by Internet sexual technology is preventing these difficulties in the first place. Educational programs for children and adolescents should provide them with the skills they need to cope with technology as they develop sexually. Educational programs already exist to teach driving skills, computer skills, social skills, and pro-social values. The Perry School Project programs that teach pro-social skills beginning in three-year-olds have been shown to lead to drastically reduced rates of antisocial behaviors, juvenile delinquency, and adult criminality compared to a matched control group with a 40-year follow-up study (Schweinhart et al., 2005). Similar programs should be developed to help children and adolescents deal safely and appropriately with rapidly advancing technology.

■ **SUMMARY**

Technology has irreversibly altered the world of adolescents. Today's teen-agers must learn to navigate the delicate balance between online and offline forms of communication. Technology will continue to advance at an incredible rate, making it difficult to study sociocultural effects at a single point in time. Parents, educators, mental health professionals, lawyers, and law enforcement agencies have all been left to contend with the positive and negative effects of new technology on adolescents. Protecting the liberties of adolescents as they explore their sexuality in the digital age will need to be balanced against providing appropriate protections from the new dangers of the digital age. A multidisciplinary approach, as demonstrated in this book, will be helpful in confronting this ever-shifting balance as technologies continue to evolve. Innovative and flexible research initiatives, legislative strategies, preventive educational programs, and treatment approaches will all be important in helping youths in achieving normative sexual development in the twenty-first century.

■ **DISCLOSURES**

Christopher W. Racine and Stephen B. Billick have no conflicts of interest to disclose.

■ **REFERENCES**

Billick, S. B., Burgert, W., Friberg,, G., et al. (2001). A clinical study of competency to consent to treatment in pediatrics. *Journal of the American Academy of Psychiatry and the Law, 29*, 298–302.

Billick, S. B., Edwards, J. L., Burgert, W., et al. (1998). A clinical study of competency in child psychiatric inpatients. *Journal of the American Academy of Psychiatry and the Law, 26*, 587–594.

Bragdon v. Abbott, 524 U.S. 624 (1998).

Cooper, A. (1998). Sexuality and the Internet: surfing into the new millennium. *CyberPsychology and Behavior, 1*, 181–187.

Dulit, E. (1972). Adolescent thinking a la Piaget: the formal stage. *Journal of Youth and Adolescence, 1*, 281–301.

FamilySafeMedia (2006). Pornography statistics. Retrieved March 19, 2013, from http://www.familysafemedia.com/pornography_statistics.html

Friedrich, W. N., Fischer, J., Broughton, D., et al. (1998). Normative sexual behavior in children: a contemporary sample. *Pediatrics, 101*, e9.

Friedrich, W. N., Grambsch, P., Broughton, D., et al. (1991). Normative sexual behavior in children. *Pediatrics, 88*, 456–464.

Lamb, S., & Coakley, M. (1993). "Normal" childhood sexual play and games: differentiating play from Abuse. *Child Abuse & Neglect, 17*, 515–526.

Leshnoff, J. (2009). Sexting not just for kids. Retrieved April 13, 2013, from http://www.aarp.org/family/love/articles/sexting_not_just_for_kids.html

Lo, V., & Wei, R. (2005). Exposure to internet pornography and Taiwanese adolescents' sexual attitudes and behavior. *Journal of Broadcasting & Electronic Media*, 49, 221–237.

Piaget, J., & Inhelder, B. (1973). *Memory and intelligence*. London: Routledge and Kegan Paul.

Roper v. Simmons, 543 U.S. 551 (2005).

Schweinhart, L. J., Jeanne, M., et al. (2005). *The High/Scope Perry Preschool Study through age 40: Summary, conclusions, and frequently asked questions*. Monographs of the High/Scope Education Research Foundation 14. Ypsilanti, MI: High/Scope Press, 2005.

Subrahmanyam, K., & Smahel, D. (2011). *Digital youth: The role of media in development*. New York: Springer Publishing.

Walker, L. (2009). Stancl gets 15 years in prison in Facebook coercion case. *Milwaukee Journal and Sentinel*. Retrieved April 14, 2013, from http://www.jsonline.com/news/waukesha/85252392.html

■ INDEX